Indiana Through Tradition and Change 1920-1945

THE HISTORY OF INDIANA

VOL. V

INDIANA
THROUGH
TRADITION
AND CHANGE

A HISTORY OF THE
HOOSIER STATE
AND ITS PEOPLE
1920-1945

by James H. Madison

Indianapolis
INDIANA HISTORICAL SOCIETY
1982

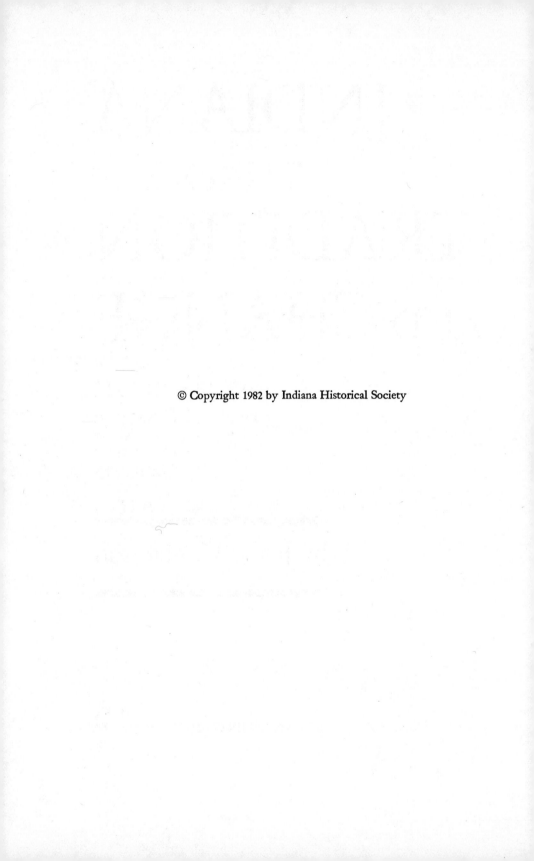

PREFACE

This is Volume V of a history of Indiana, three volumes of which (Volumes I, III, and IV) have been published jointly by the Indiana Historical Bureau and the Indiana Historical Society. This volume, published solely by the Indiana Historical Society, like the other volumes follows a generally topical organization, with initial chapters devoted to politics and later chapters to social, economic, and cultural questions. The last chapter provides an overview of the home front during World War II. Each chapter is intended to stand alone, but a fuller understanding of subjects and themes treated in any one chapter will result from a reading of the whole book. Readers interested in a specific subject will wish to consult the index as well as the occasional cross-reference in the text.

This book does not presume to be an account of everything that happened in Indiana from the end of World War I to the end of World War II. The choice of topics and the manner in which they are explored were dictated by several considerations. Where good scholarly research was available, I have followed gratefully in the paths of others. At many other times, however, I have had to rely on my own basic research in primary sources. And on occasion, I fear, significant topics have gone largely unexamined due to limitations of secondary or primary sources and to limitations of my own abilities. I must confess also to leaning toward fuller exploration of questions that I consider most important and most interesting.

Choice of topics also depended on my attempt to keep the focus as fully as possible on the state as the unit of analysis. Historical problems and issues that were statewide in scope generally receive the largest attention. State politics is the most important example, as Chapters II through V indicate. But I have tried also to give much attention to social, economic, and cultural issues, especially those that had important state dimensions, such as public education and public health.

While the approach is essentially that of state history, I have often found it necessary also to shift to the level of local or community history in order to illustrate major themes. I have in no sense treated any Indiana community thoroughly, however, leaving that task to others and hoping that this book will provide some of the general background and context for those wishing to understand a single community or a problem within communities. Indeed, the most important next step necessary to understand the history of Indiana in these years is for more and better studies of how institutions, groups, and individuals functioned and behaved within local communities and how they were affected by forces from without.

With the state as the first focus of attention and the local community as the second, the regional and national arenas provide the third. Much of what happened in Indiana in these years was similar to events and issues in other states. While wishing that more scholarly studies of other states had been available as guides, I have profited greatly from those that exist, and from time to time I have made explicit comparisons to other states, especially those in the Midwest. I hope that this history of Indiana illuminates regional and national themes and issues, but such has not been my primary purpose. I have dealt with national issues only where necessary to explain what happened in Indiana, as, for example, the treatment of New Deal era unemployment relief. Some readers may regard this state focus as stubborn provincialism. I prefer to see it as an assertion that many, though not all, of the most important issues and questions in American history can be understood as well and sometimes better by a focus on the state. The people of Indiana in the years 1920-1945 certainly thought of themselves as Americans (indeed, often as the most typical Americans), but they also thought of themselves as Hoosiers, as citizens and residents of a state as well as a nation and a local community.

This study of twentieth-century Indiana presents no single thesis or theme to encompass the many and varied issues Hoosiers faced. Several themes weave through the chapters that follow and, I hope, provide a context for a fuller understanding of specific problems. Most interesting to me is the contrast and sometimes conflict between traditional ideas, values, and beliefs, formed in the small towns and farms of the nineteenth century, and the more modern concerns of urban, industrial, technological, and professional America. Some Hoosiers resisted the changes of the twentieth century, especially those that seemed to emanate from outside their local communities and institutions. Whether Hoosiers approved or not, change was the order of the day, and often they had no choice but to adjust, to accommodate, to accept new institutions and ways, though the process of accommodation was often bumpy and incomplete. Janus-like, many Indianans looked back, often through rose-colored glasses, to the comforting nineteenth century while they looked forward with anxiety to the mid- and late-twentieth century. Americans in the late-twentieth century might sympathize with the traditional attachments of an earlier generation, recognizing that the quest for progress and modernization has been an expensive one. Some will conclude that the benefits of change have far exceeded the costs and will regard those who earlier resisted change as unimaginative traditionalists stuck in ruts on roads no longer traveled. Such judgments are personal ones for each reader. The chapters that follow attempt more modestly to show the dimensions of change, to explain the sources of change, and to represent fairly the processes of rejection, adjustment, accommodation, or acceptance. The purpose is neither to condemn nor praise Hoosiers for attachments to or rejections of past traditions, nor is it to represent the changes of the twentieth century as arguments for unilinear progress or decline. The purpose simply is to understand better a people and their state as they moved through tradition and change in the years 1920 to 1945.

ACKNOWLEDGMENTS

Many people and institutions contributed to the preparation of this book. Indiana University, Bloomington, provided an ideal environment in which to work. Most of the research and writing was done in the university library. There and in the Lilly Library I received excellent help from many librarians, and I became more aware of debts owed earlier generations of scholars and librarians who carefully collected and preserved the sources necessary to study Indiana history. In the university history department many colleagues provided intellectual support and stimulus. Several Bloomington colleagues read parts or all of the manuscript and provided useful suggestions. I am especially grateful to Ann Carmichael, who made important suggestions for my treatment of public health, and to Lorna Lutes Sylvester, my colleague at the *Indiana Magazine of History*, who taught me much about Indiana's past. Lori Bell and Debra Chase of the history department staff provided prompt and efficient typing. The Indiana University Oral History Research Project, with support from the National Endowment for the Humanities and the Indiana Historical Society, produced important interviews, and I am grateful to Project Director Richard Kirkendall and Oral Historian R. T. King. Finally, a university faculty fellowship freed me from responsibilities other than research and writing in the summer of 1979.

Outside Bloomington several scholars generously shared their insights and learning. Martin Ridge and Richard Jensen read a very early draft of one chapter and helped shape my ideas about the general scope and direction of the book. Ronald D. Cohen and James B. Lane helped me to understand better the special place of Gary in Indiana's history. Many librarians and archivists beyond my home base provided capable service. In Indianapolis, the staffs of the Indiana Historical Society Library, the Indiana Division, Indiana State Library, and the Archives Division, Indiana Commission on Public Records, helped me to use their essential collections. I wish to thank also the staffs of the National Archives, Washington, D.C.; the Franklin D. Roosevelt Library, Hyde Park, New York; and the Newberry Library, Chicago. The Newberry Library not only allowed me to use its outstanding collection of midwestern history but also, through its Family and Community History Center, awarded me a fellowship that made possible an extended stay in Chicago during 1978.

Few authors are as well served by their publishers as I have been. The Indiana Historical Society provided financial support for my research travel and for a preliminary bibliography, ably prepared by Stephen Vaughn. The Society's Executive Secretary, Gayle Thornbrough, has been most encouraging and helpful, and the editorial staff, including Douglas Clanin, Paula Corpuz, Dorothy Riker, Lana Ruegamer, and Amy Schutt, have done a superb job in preparing the manuscript for publication.

Thanks are due also to Lawrence Connor of the Indianapolis *Star*, Wendall Phillipi of the Indianapolis *News*, Paul Gass of Washington High School, Washington, Indiana, Duncan Schiedt and Vane Jones both of Indianapolis, Gregg Buttermore of the Auburn-Cord-Duesenberg Museum, Richard Cochran of the Notre Dame Archives, and James Lane of the Calumet Regional Archives for permission to use illustrative material. Mrs. Sandra Fitzgerald of the *Star-News* library was also very helpful. John McCord drew the map found on page 379.

I am most appreciative of all this help, but I alone am responsible for any errors and shortcomings in this book. I encourage readers to point them out, especially by writing new books and articles that further our understanding of Indiana's history in these years.

Finally, my largest debts are to the non-historians in my life: to my children, Julia and John, and, above all, to Jeanne, who did not type, edit, or read the manuscript but who helped in ways more important.

January, 1981   James H. Madison

CONTENTS

ILLUSTRATIONS

Page

MAPS AND CHARTS

INDIANA
THROUGH
TRADITION AND CHANGE

CHAPTER I

THE STATE AND THE PEOPLE:
AN INTRODUCTION

THE GENERATION of Hoosiers born at the end of the nineteenth century faced a range of challenges and opportunities unknown to their nineteenth-century forebears. To Indiana author Booth Tarkington, writing in 1928, the years since 1900 were "an overturning thorough enough to bear the aspect of revolution to middle aged and elderly people." He was living, Tarkington concluded, through the "swiftest moving and most restless time the world has known . . . ."[1] The modern America that was rapidly developing in the twentieth century included new technologies and economic organizations, expanded governmental responsibilities, changing social relationships and institutions, and new attitudes and beliefs. Many Hoosiers participated fully in these economic, social, and political transformations, very aware that they were living in an age of rapid change. Indiana author George Ade wrote in 1929 that "the miracle of our times has been the transformation in living conditions, in aspirations and in the habits of thought of the people of the Commonwealth." As with others, however, Ade's exultation was tempered by uncertainty about the extent and speed of change: "the question is," he wrote, "how far do we go before we slow up?"[2]

Although the American proclivity to regard change as synonymous with progress received strong expression in Indiana, the

---

[1] Newton Booth Tarkington, *The World Does Move* (New York, 1928), p. 290. This sense of rapid change is found in much of Tarkington's fiction. See especially *The Magnificent Ambersons* (New York, 1918), pp. 386-391.

[2] George Ade, "A Few Paragraphs Relating to Indiana," in Kin Hubbard (ed.), *A Book of Indiana: The Story of What Has Been Described as the Most Typically American State . . . Told in Terms of Biography* (n.p., 1929), p. 26. For an argument that the rate of social change had indeed slowed by the mid-twentieth century see Theodore Caplow, "The Measurement of Social Change in Middletown," *Indiana Magazine of History*, LXXV (1979), 344-357.

years from 1920 to 1945 also dealt severe blows to this ideal. By the mid-1940s Indianapolis newspaper reporter John Bartlow Martin looked back on the tribulations experienced by his fellow Hoosiers since World War I: "If they came through farm depression and the Klan unscathed—and who did, wholly?—they found themselves in an industrial Indiana full of long lines of unemployed at factory gates. And soon another war began."[3] Martin's laconic listing of the "great events" in these years captured some of the most obvious and disruptive forces affecting Indianans. Often, as Martin's prose implied, these forces were beyond the influence and control of individual Hoosiers, with causes or remedies, if any, far removed from their immediate lives and local institutions. That indeed was one of the major lessons to be learned in modern America. And yet, contrary to Martin's implications, not all Hoosiers simply waited passively for distant events and forces to shape their lives, nor did they all respond in similar ways to these events and forces. Much of the history of Indiana in the years from 1920 to 1945 includes the different and often conflicting ways in which people and groups reacted to and sometimes initiated change that would move the state and its people far from their nineteenth-century origins.

§ §

The economic, political, and social changes of the period 1920-1945 often brought conflict and turmoil to Indiana. In the face of new challenges or opportunities some Hoosiers stuck closely to more traditional ways of the nineteenth century: to one-room schools when education reformers called for consolidation; to their horses and mules when Purdue University experts told them of the efficiencies of tractors and cornpickers; to their local governments when state and federal officials argued for progress and equality through centralization in Indianapolis or Washington; to patent medicines when trained medical doctors offered new forms of treatment; to patronage politics when professional social workers and civil service reformers called for efficiency and

[3] John Bartlow Martin, *Indiana: An Interpretation* (New York, 1947), p. 270.

honesty; to small, craft-oriented woodworking enterprises when large-scale metal working factories began to appear; to the poetry of James Whitcomb Riley, "whose lyrics had in them the click of the mowing-machine in the wheat . . . ,"[4] when the sounds more familiar to most Hoosiers were those of automobiles, trucks, and trains. In these and many other areas the degree and duration of attachment to traditional forms and attitudes varied. Most Indianans probably gave up their horses more quickly than they abandoned Riley's poetry, for example. Nor did people up and down the state march in unison to a single drumbeat of change or modernization. Farmers in southern Indiana adopted tractors less rapidly than their counterparts in the central and northern sections of the state. Pasteurized milk appeared in larger cities years earlier than in smaller towns and villages. Automobile manufacturers developed more complex organizations than did limestone producers or furniture makers.

Indeed, to understand the history of Indiana in these years requires an appreciation of the contrasting strands of homogeneity and heterogeneity that characterized the state and its people. To many who observed it, Indiana did cast a bright and single-colored light. The large majority of the people were native-born, white Protestants who lived on farms and in small towns. In 1920, 95 percent of the population was native-born, and 97 percent was white, giving Indiana the largest proportion of white, native-born population in the nation. Approximately 75 percent of Hoosier church members were Protestants. Thirty-one percent of all Indianans lived on farms, another 19 percent in rural nonfarm homes, and another 21 percent in small towns with between 25,000 and 2,500 residents.[5]

When Hoosiers and others referred favorably to these homogeneous social and demographic features, they often commented on less quantifiable characteristics of the state, on features that Indianapolis newspaperman Martin labeled "the Indiana idea,"

[4] Irvin S. Cobb, *Indiana* (New York, 1924), p. 47.
[5] United States Bureau of the Census, *Sixteenth Census* (1940), II, *Population*, Pt. 2, p. 675; United States Bureau of the Census, *Religious Bodies*, 1926 (2 volumes, Washington, D.C., 1930), I, 172-174.

which he described as the "conception of Indiana as a pleasant, rather rural place inhabited by people who are confident, prosperous, neighborly, easygoing, tolerant, shrewd."[6] It was this "Indiana idea" that led to assertions that the state was "the most typically American State in the American democracy," as writer Irvin S. Cobb argued in 1924, or that, as Heath Bowman concluded nearly two decades later, Indiana "is still accepted as best typifying America, and American citizens."[7] To Cobb the Hoosier character was to be found in the large degree to which "Indiana holds by the pioneering culture and its offshoots— old-fashioned cookery, old-fashioned decencies, old-fashioned virtues, old-fashioned vices, old-fashioned bigotries, old-fashioned philosophies springing out of the soil and smelling of the pennyrile and the sassafrack."[8] Similar sentiments were reflected in the activities of such organizations as the Society of Indiana Pioneers, the Indiana Society of Chicago, and the Indiana Club of New York. The latter group of Hoosier expatriates received wide publicity in 1931 when they refused to eat the *chicken à la Maryland* served at their dinner—insisting on waiting while the dish was returned to the kitchen, the batter removed, and the chicken fried with plain flour in grease, just as it was back home in Indiana.[9]

[6] Martin, *Indiana*, p. viii. See also Theodore Dreiser, "Indiana: Her Soil and Light," in Ernest Gruening (ed.), *These United States: A Symposium* (2 volumes, New York, 1924), II, 264-276.

[7] Cobb, *Indiana*, p. 14; Heath Bowman, *Hoosier* (Indianapolis, 1941), p. 13. It is likely that Indiana was typical in many ways among the forty-eight states. But such a question is of limited historical utility when considered only in a general way and especially when the primary goal is to understand a single state. In the chapters that follow, specific Indiana attributes or characteristics are compared with other states largely to help place Indiana's experience in context. For an effort at general comparisons of states see Charles Angoff and H. L. Mencken, "The Worst American State," *American Mercury*, XXIV (1931), 1-16, 175-188, 355-367, where Indiana's average rank among the states for dozens of social and economic indicators was twenty-fourth. For evidence of typicalness prior to 1920 see Clifton J. Phillips, *Indiana in Transition: The Emergence of an Industrial Commonwealth, 1880-1920* (*The History of Indiana*, Vol. IV, Indianapolis, 1968), pp. 361-363.

[8] Cobb, *Indiana*, p. 49.

[9] Martha Tucker Morris, "The Society of Indiana Pioneers," *Indiana Magazine of History*, XXXV (1939), 400-402; *Eighteenth Annual Dinner of the Indiana*

Perhaps the Indiana idea received its widest and simplest expression in William Herschell's poem, written in 1919, "Ain't God Good to Indiana?" The last verse read:

Ain't God good to Indiana?
Other spots may look as fair,
But they lack th' soothin' somethin'
In th' Hoosier sky an' air.
They don't have that snug-up feelin'
Like a mother gives a child;
They don't soothe you, soul an' body,
With their breezes soft an' mild.
They don't know th' Joys o' Heaven
Have their birthplace here below;
Ain't God good to Indiana?
Ain't He, fellers? Ain't He, though?[10]

The state's towns and cities also reflected this Indiana idea, so commentators argued. Sociologists Robert Lynd and Helen Merrell Lynd brought lasting and national fame to Muncie when they chose it for their studies of a typical American community, published in 1929 and 1937.[11] *Life* magazine shared this view, noting that Muncie "is every small U.S. city from Maine to California," where "year in and year out, these earnest midland folk still steer their customary middle course, still cling to their old American dream."[12] Even Indianapolis, despite its large population of more than 300,000 people in 1920,[13] was not an urban alien set uncomfortably in rural and small-town Indiana. Rather, according to

---

Society of Chicago (n.p., 1922); New York *Times,* March 4, 1931. For a more recent statement of the Indiana idea see Howard H. Peckham, *Indiana: A Bicentennial History* (New York, 1978), pp. 187-195.

[10] William Herschell, "Ain't God Good to Indiana?" in *The Smile-Bringer and Other Bits of Cheer* (Indianapolis, 1919), pp. 69-70.

[11] Robert S. Lynd and Helen Merrell Lynd, *Middletown: A Study in Contemporary American Culture* (New York, 1929); Robert S. Lynd and Helen Merrell Lynd, *Middletown in Transition: A Study in Cultural Conflicts* (New York, 1937). For a suggestion that some features of Muncie's population were not so typical see Richard Jensen, "The Lynds Revisited," *Indiana Magazine of History,* LXXV (1979), 303-319.

[12] "Muncie, Ind. Is the Great U.S. 'Middletown,'" *Life,* May 10, 1937, pp. 16, 24.

[13] United States Bureau of the Census, *Sixteenth Census* (1940), *Indiana,* p. 3.

a writer in the *New Republic*, "the two are inseparable. Indianapolis is in everything simply Indiana."[14] Instead of dominating or existing apart from the rest of the state, as was the case with Chicago and Illinois, for example, Indianapolis was viewed as "a somewhat blurry but nevertheless authentic mirror of Hoosierdom at large."[15] And as with the state, claims also were made for the typicalness of the capital city. In 1931 *American Magazine* chose Indianapolis as the typical city in which to find the typical American family.[16] The Indianapolis *News* could only agree, pointing to the large native-born population, central location, high proportion of home ownership, and, above all, "certain intangible qualities that so many American cities once boasted and then lost."[17] A similar sentiment was expressed from a business perspective in 1921 by the general secretary of the Indianapolis Chamber of Commerce: "We see the evils that have come to Cleveland and Detroit from too quick expansion. We want to encourage a balanced development."[18] Or, as another commentator wrote about this "average or a little better than average American community," "being no mean city, after all, may be better than being an extreme city, whether best or worst."[19]

The belief that Hoosiers were generally alike, that they avoided extremes, that they held on to past traditions, that they represented what was typical and perhaps even best about America— all this provided a leitmotif running through the history of the state in the period 1920-1945. Impossible to quantify, often impossible to see clearly in the records that remain, this Indiana idea affected nearly every feature of public life in the state even while the sentiments and realities on which it was based were challenged

[14] Jonathan Brooks, "Indianapolis: A City of the Middle of the Road," *New Republic*, November 14, 1928, p. 347.

[15] Cobb, *Indiana*, p. 34.

[16] M. K. Wisehart, "Is This Your Family Too?" *American Magazine*, CXI (June, 1931), 54-56. This article is an excellent illustration of popular perceptions of a "typical" middle-class family. The family was that of Merrill J. Brown.

[17] Indianapolis *News*, May 20, 1931.

[18] "Chamber Helps Manufacturers Enter Foreign Markets," Indianapolis Chamber of Commerce, *Activities*, IV (November, 1921), 21.

[19] Brooks, "Indianapolis: A City of the Middle of the Road," *New Republic*, November 14, 1928, p. 348.

and changed. The rise to power of the Ku Klux Klan in the 1920s, the changing technology of agriculture, the devastation of the Depression, the social upheaval of World War II at home, these and other more subtle influences and events brought considerable shock to the Indiana idea. Events from the end of World War I to the end of World War II, John Bartlow Martin concluded, showed that "this Indiana idea, this conception of the state as a bucolic place inhabited by pleasant, simple, neighborly folk, contains a good deal of mythology." Yet Martin noted, "Hoosiers today try to conform to the myth."[20] It is possible that, even with the conflicts and changes of these years, many continued not only to conform to but also to believe in the Indiana idea. And it is possible that there continued to be enough truth in the idea to make it credible. It is even likely that this Indiana idea, rooted firmly in the nineteenth century, became more important to some Hoosiers as it seemed more threatened by the modern environment of twentieth-century America.

§ § §

The significance and influence of the Indiana idea should not obscure important characteristics of the population that did not entirely fit this belief or myth. Hoosiers were not all alike: age, sex, race, religion, place of birth, and place of residence differentiated them in ways that significantly affected the state's history in the years 1920-1945.

Blacks were the most obvious segment of the population whose experiences called for a modification of the Indiana idea, especially its assumption of homogeneity and tolerance. Blacks accounted for only 2.8 percent of the state's population in 1920, 3.5 percent by 1930, and 3.6 percent by 1940. But these small percentages obscured important shifts, particularly during the 1920s, when the state's black population increased by 39 percent, compared to a 9 percent increase in white population. During the early twen-

[20] Martin, *Indiana*, p. 277. Martin's book is a strong indictment of Indiana, suggesting a golden age of great promise in 1900 and a precipitous decline in that promise after 1920. Though Martin's work is of great value and interest, there is considerable room for disagreement about his conclusions.

tieth century, Indiana received large portions of the massive migrations of blacks from the rural, agricultural South to the urban, industrial North. By 1930, when less than a fourth of white Hoosiers had been born outside Indiana, two thirds of black Indianans had been born outside the state, principally in Kentucky, Tennessee, Alabama, and Mississippi. Indianapolis and the Lake County industrial cities of Gary and East Chicago became the new homes of most of these rural migrants and accounted for almost 60 percent of the state's black population by 1930. By that year blacks constituted about 18 percent of the population in Gary, 10 percent in East Chicago, and more than 12 percent in Indianapolis. Jobs in growing industrial cities such as South Bend, Fort Wayne, Anderson, Kokomo, and Muncie also began to attract black newcomers. Towns in southern Indiana generally were much less enticing: the black populations in Evansville, Jeffersonville, New Albany, and Madison remained stable or decreased during the 1920s. Rural Indiana continued to lose black residents after World War I. The Great Depression slowed the growth of black population, as it did white population, but the return of prosperity with World War II brought a new wave of black migration from the South, nearly all to industrial cities.[21]

Indiana's reputation for friendliness, neighborliness, and tolerance often did not extend to blacks. Racism and segregation were common experiences for most blacks in Indiana. These and other themes important to black Hoosiers are treated in the chapters that follow, but it is useful by way of introduction to note the pervasiveness of discrimination and segregation. It was nearly impossible to find in Indiana a public place, institution, or group where whites accorded blacks an equal and open reception. Indeed, in many ways segregation intensified in Indiana after World War I, partly a reaction by white Hoosiers to the growth

[21] United States Bureau of the Census, *Sixteenth Census* (1940), II, *Population*, Pt. 2, p. 676; United States Bureau of the Census, *Negroes in the United States, 1920-1932* (Washington, D.C., 1935), pp. 7, 24, 30-31, 53, 58; Emma Lou Thornbrough, *Since Emancipation: A Short History of Indiana Negroes, 1863-1963* ([Indianapolis], 1963), pp. 17-20. Indiana's increase in black population during the 1920s was far below the average 95 percent overall increase for the east-north-central states of Michigan, Illinois, Ohio, Wisconsin, and Indiana.

of black population. The most illustrative case of this trend toward more segregation was the construction of new, all-black high schools in Indianapolis and Gary, discussed in Chapter IX. But the evidences of prejudice and discrimination were everywhere. Theaters, public parks, cemeteries, restaurants, hotels, beaches, swimming pools, orphans' homes, hospitals, newspaper society columns, the state militia, and other places and institutions in many Indiana towns and cities excluded blacks or assigned them a separate place, such as the balcony in a theater. In many small towns where no blacks resided there were often informal "Sundown Laws"—social pressures that discouraged black workers or travelers from tarrying beyond dusk. Such social barriers existed not only in southern Indiana towns but also in such newer industrial cities as Hammond and Whiting in Lake County. In larger cities, often out of necessity, blacks created their own social institutions, sometimes assisted by whites: black churches, lodges, and clubs; black American Legion posts; black settlement houses, YWCAs, and YMCAs, such as Flanner House and the important Senate Avenue YMCA in Indianapolis.[22]

As in most of America prior to 1945, employment and educational opportunities also were severely limited for blacks. The large majority of employed blacks worked in menial jobs, the men as general laborers, the women as domestics. Opportunities to move up the occupational or economic ladder were much fewer

[22] Thornbrough, *Since Emancipation*, pp. 21, 84-89; Crawfordsville *Journal*, January 19, 1925; Richard M. Clutter, The Indiana American Legion, 1919-1960 (Ph.D. dissertation, Indiana University, Bloomington, 1974), p. 196; Charles Kettleborough, *Constitution Making in Indiana, a Source Book* . . . , III, *1916–1930* (Indianapolis, 1930, reprint, 1977), p. xviii; Report of the Commission to Consider the Question of Establishing a State Home for Colored Orphan Children in Indiana [1930], Box A, Drawer 46, Harry G. Leslie Papers, Archives Division, Indiana Commission on Public Records, Indiana State Library and Historical Building; Hurley Goodall and J. Paul Mitchell, *A History of Negroes in Muncie* (Muncie, Ind., 1976), pp. 16-28; Lynd and Lynd, *Middletown*, p. 479; James B. Lane, *"City of the Century": A History of Gary, Indiana* (Bloomington, Ind., 1978), p. 233; Elizabeth Balanoff, A History of the Black Community of Gary, Indiana: 1906-1940 (Ph.D. dissertation, University of Chicago, 1974), pp. 452-453; Work Projects Administration, *The Calumet Region Historical Guide* . . . (n.p., 1939), pp. 51-54, 233; *The Leisure of a People: Report of a Recreation Survey of Indianapolis* (n.p., 1929), pp. 215, 335, 389.

for blacks than whites.[23] Classified newspaper advertisements for domestics indicated the primacy of race: "Colored Girl—Neat, wants care of a small apartment," "Neat White Woman—Desires cleaning," or "Wanted Girl—White, cooking and general housework."[24]

One of the most significant features of black experience in the post-World War I era was the hardening pattern of residential segregation. In small towns and large cities blacks had often clustered in neighborhoods distinct from the white population. As black population and demands for housing increased in the 1920s, white pressure to raise higher barriers of residential segregation intensified. Indianapolis provided the clearest example of this phenomenon. Black movement northward from the tight enclave on the near northwest of Indianapolis led the White Citizens Protective League and other civic and neighborhood associations to urge that the city council enact a new residential zoning ordinance. Passed in March, 1926, the ordinance prohibited blacks from moving into white neighborhoods without the written consent of a majority of the neighborhood residents. The National Association for the Advancement of Colored People (NAACP) fought a hard legal battle against the segregation ordinance, winning a victory in November, 1926, when the Marion County Superior Court declared the ordinance unconstitutional. It was, however, as historian Emma Lou Thornbrough has written, "the only significant legal victory in the fight in Indiana against segregation during the 1920s."[25] And the single legal victory did little to reverse the pattern of residential segregation. White home-

[23] United States Bureau of the Census, *Negroes in the United States, 1920-1932*, p. 305; Natalie Rogoff, *Recent Trends in Occupational Mobility* (Glencoe, Ill., 1953), pp. 64-74; Max Parvin Cavnes, *The Hoosier Community at War* (Bloomington, Ind., 1961), p. 110.

[24] Indianapolis *News*, September 20, 1928.

[25] Emma Lou Thornbrough, "Segregation in Indiana during the Klan Era of the 1920's," *Mississippi Valley Historical Review*, XLVII (1960-1961), 597-601. Thornbrough concludes that the Ku Klux Klan was not a prime mover in intensifying segregation in Indianapolis in the 1920s but rather that the pressure came from many whites who never joined the Klan. Klan membership was largest in the white neighborhoods immediately adjacent to black neighborhoods. Kenneth T. Jackson, *The Ku Klux Klan in the City, 1915-1930* (New York, 1967), p. 153.

owners and real estate brokers continued to co-operate to restrict black home buying or renting. Real estate advertisements separately and specifically indicated rental and sale properties for "Colored."[26] The federal government continued the pattern of residential segregation, while providing better housing for some 748 black Indianapolis families during the Depression. In 1937 the Public Works Administration constructed one of the first public housing projects for blacks in the nation on Indiana Avenue in the center of the city's major black neighborhood. Ironically, opposition from white building trade unions kept blacks from obtaining all but unskilled jobs on this New Deal construction project. Two federal housing projects in Gary in the late 1930s also improved housing for blacks but perpetuated patterns of racial segregation that had also intensified there after World War I.[27]

Despite the large degree of discrimination and prejudice and the use of intimidation and threats against blacks, there was little violence. There was none of the serious rioting of whites against blacks that occurred in some northern cities in the early twentieth century, nor was there the degree of vigilante violence that had been directed toward blacks in the state during the late nineteenth century. Even the Ku Klux Klan generally used emotional rather than physical weapons. The major exception to this pattern of nonviolence was the lynching of two blacks in Marion in 1930, a tragedy that was significant not only as an expression of intense racism but also in its uniqueness. Two Marion blacks, aged eighteen and nineteen, were jailed on charges of assaulting a white girl and murdering her boyfriend. On a hot August night an armed mob of local citizens, encountering little resistance from the county sheriff, removed the two youths from the Grant County jail. With thousands of citizens watching, the mob beat the two blacks and then lynched them from a tree on the courthouse square. No whites were punished or arrested, but strong

[26] Indianapolis *News*, September 20, 1928.

[27] Thornbrough, *Since Emancipation*, pp. 22-24, 76; Powell A. Moore, *The Calumet Region: Indiana's Last Frontier* (Indianapolis, 1959), pp. 390-391; Work Projects Administration, *Indiana: A Guide to the Hoosier State* (New York, 1941), p. 218; Cavnes, *The Hoosier Community at War*, pp. 165-166.

condemnation came not only from the NAACP but also from many state leaders, including Governor Harry G. Leslie, and from many Indiana newspapers, including the two in Marion. The state legislature passed a law requiring the dismissal of the sheriff in any county where a lynching had occurred. A testimonial to the extremes of racial prejudice, the Marion lynching has been the only such recorded event in Indiana since 1902.[28]

Indiana blacks did not accept discrimination and segregation without protest. As noted earlier they formed their own institutions, often extolling them as expressions of racial pride. A black consumers' co-operative in Gary achieved considerable success in the 1930s. Some blacks joined separatist causes, most notably Marcus Garvey's Universal Negro Improvement Association, which achieved a large following in Gary in the 1920s. Some black community leaders, particularly teachers, lawyers, doctors, and ministers, frequently spoke out against unequal treatment, sometimes through the NAACP, while others counseled patience and forbearance.[29] Perhaps most important in the interwar years was the political movement of black leaders and black voters from the Republican to the Democratic party, where in the 1930s they helped form a liberal coalition that later would begin a serious offensive against discrimination.[30] (See Chapter V.) The war years also provided some new opportunities for blacks, especially in employment, and led to further efforts to open doors. Yet

[28] Walter White to James M. Ogden, August 22, 1930, Box 1, Drawer 45, Leslie Papers; Thornbrough, *Since Emancipation*, p. 38; Indianapolis *News*, August 8, 9, 11, 1930.

[29] Balanoff, Black Community of Gary, pp. 200-211, 495-501; Lane, "*City of the Century*," pp. 185–187; "Consumers' Cooperation among Negroes in Gary, Ind.," *Monthly Labor Review*, XLII (1936), 369-371. One scholar has concluded that Indianapolis blacks, despite their opposition to neighborhood and school segregation, were generally conservative, adopting a policy of "pragmatic passiveness" in the face of white discrimination. Judy Jolley Mohraz, *The Separate Problem: Case Studies of Black Education in the North, 1900-1930* (Westport, Conn., 1979), p. 123.

[30] See, for example, the political pressure employed by Indianapolis black businessman and community leader F. B. Ransom in his letters to Pleas Greenlee, Governor McNutt's patronage director, March 29, April 20, November 8, 1935, Box A, Drawer 86, Paul V. McNutt Papers, Archives Division, Indiana Commission on Public Records, Indiana State Library and Historical Building.

Survey Graphic

1945 teen canteen at Flanner House, an
Indianapolis community service organization
for blacks

Indianapolis **News**

Indianapolis study class in Americanization for foreign-born, 1922

Ku Klux Klan newspaper's victory edition in 1924

Albert J. Beveridge

James A. Watson

actual progress in the period from 1920 to 1945 was slight. During the 1920s the movement had been backward, toward more segregation, and throughout the period calls for equality between whites and blacks were too few and too weak to be heeded. The problem, left to later generations, constituted the most difficult and disheartening heritage from the past and the most visible contradiction of the assumption of neighborliness among Hoosiers.

§ § § §

Although blacks were the largest and most visible group separated from the mainstream of Hoosier life, those of foreign birth also provided a rejoinder to observers who saw the state as entirely homogeneous. Indiana's foreign-born white population was very small, however, and, unlike the black population, was declining. The twentieth-century peak in the percentage of foreign-born was reached in 1910 with 5.9 percent, declining to 5.1 percent in 1920, 4.4 percent in 1930, and 3.2 percent in 1940. State-level data on the foreign-born population are of limited value, however, since only a few Indiana cities and counties were the homes of most foreign-born Hoosiers. Only 2.2 percent of the state's rural population was foreign-born in 1920, while 8.0 percent of the urban population was born outside the United States. Indianapolis had the largest foreign population in 1920 (16,968 persons), followed closely by Gary, East Chicago, and South Bend, and then by Hammond and Fort Wayne. Together these six large cities accounted for more than half the state's foreign-born population of 150,868 in 1920. Smaller towns with sizable numbers of foreign-born residents included Clinton, Michigan City, Mishawaka, and Whiting, all with 15 percent or more of their residents foreign-born in 1920.[31]

There was, of course, little homogeneity among foreign-born residents of Indiana, most obviously because they came from different parts of the world. Countries which accounted for more than 5 percent of Indiana's foreign-born population in 1920 were

[31] United States Bureau of the Census, *Fourteenth Census* (1920), III, *Population*, pp. 282, 297-302.

Percent of Foreign-born White
in Total Population by Counties, 1920

Germany (24.8 percent), Poland (11.8 percent), Hungary (6.2 percent), Austria (6.0 percent), England (5.6 percent), and Russia (5.1 percent). In Indianapolis nearly one third of the foreign-born residents in 1920 were from Germany, followed by large numbers of immigrants born in Ireland, Russia, and England. The capital city received only small numbers of immigrants from southern and eastern Europe. In South Bend more than half the foreign-born were from Poland and Hungary. In Fort Wayne nearly half were from Germany, while in Gary the principal sources of foreign-born were Austria, Greece, Yugoslavia, Poland, and Russia. In East Chicago immigrants from Poland and Hungary dominated.[32] After World War I both Gary and East Chicago began to attract large numbers of Mexicans as well. Differences of language, religion, and culture, and of the size and timing of migrations produced variety in the ways in which foreign-born peoples lived in Indiana and the rate at which they and their children were assimilated into the general population. Each group maintained or developed important ethnic institutions, such as clubs and churches, and each group tended initially to cluster in ethnic neighborhoods, though often without the degree of restriction placed on blacks. Signs of ethnicity were especially visible in Gary and East Chicago, where approximately half the population was foreign-born and where most were recent arrivals, but they were to be seen also in German Catholic and Lutheran parochial schools in Fort Wayne; in the educational, relief, and recreational work of the Jewish Federation in Indianapolis; in classified advertisements in Indianapolis newspapers where, for example, a woman seeking employment described herself as "Experienced—Second maid. Irish"; and in 1931 in the opening of a Greek afternoon school in Anderson. Such ethnic institutions and evidences persisted beyond the first generation, even in some places beyond the second and third generations. The people of rural Dubois County in southern Indiana held strongly to their mid-nineteenth-century German heritage, even

[32] *Ibid.*, p. 304; United States Bureau of the Census, *Sixteenth Census* (1940), II, *Population*, Pt. 2, p. 693.

though by 1920 less than 2 percent of the population had been born outside the United States.[33]

While ethnic groups clung to much of their European heritage, there was significant modification and abandonment of those ties after World War I. The Great War nearly shut off European migration to America and gave impetus to a movement to restrict immigration that bore fruit in federal legislation passed in 1924. The new federal quota system severely curtailed immigration from southern and eastern Europe especially. The end of unrestricted immigration meant an end to the constant renewal of ethnic ties brought by newcomers. World War I also stimulated a strong movement to encourage assimilation, a movement which continued through the postwar decade. This "Americanization" movement enjoyed hearty support in Indiana from native-born Hoosiers and sometimes from many born outside the United States. The intense patriotism generated during the war produced a sentiment that equated "foreign" with "unpatriotic." Such sentiment was directed especially toward signs of German culture, and it produced in Indiana, as elsewhere, legislation prohibiting German language instruction in public schools, pressure on German language newspapers to stop publication, a cessation of public performances of German music, and changing of German street names.[34] Although the war with Germany ended in 1918, the emotional opposition to German culture continued. An effort to repeal the 1919 law prohibiting the teaching of German language in schools failed in 1921 but finally passed in 1923, though few schools took advantage of the opportunity. Many Hoosiers doubtless agreed with the president pro tem of the state senate, James

[33] Moore, *The Calumet Region*, pp. 342-366, 394-398; Francisco A. Rosales, Mexican Immigration to the Urban Midwest during the 1920s (Ph.D. dissertation, Indiana University, Bloomington, 1978), *passim*; Myra Auerbach, A Study of the Jewish Settlement in Indianapolis (M.A. thesis, Indiana University, Bloomington, 1933), pp. 110-121; Indianapolis *News*, September 20, 1928; Evangelos C. Vlachos, The Assimilation of Greeks in the United States with Special Reference to the Greek Community in Anderson, Indiana (Ph.D. dissertation, Indiana University, Bloomington, 1964), pp. 158-162.

[34] Phillips, *Indiana in Transition*, pp. 600-604; Darrel E. Bigham, "Charles Leich and Company of Evansville: A Note on the Dilemma of German Americans during World War I," *Indiana Magazine of History*, LXX (1974), 95-121.

Nejdl, a Lake County Republican. Nejdl conceded in the 1923 senate language debate that the schools should be free to teach German if they wished, but he boasted: "Though I am a foreign-born citizen, a Bohemian, and my wife is an American-born citizen of Bohemian parents, I am proud to say that neither of my children can speak a word of any language except English."[35]

The Americanization movement developed not only out of the wartime hatred of Germany but also from a fear of radicalism, which many assumed was spread by foreign-born agitators in the labor movement and in the Socialist and Communist parties, influenced by the Russian Revolution of 1917. Cited as evidence were the 1919 labor strikes in Indiana and elsewhere. In response to fears of radical agitation, the 1919 session of the General Assembly passed a state sedition law that outlawed advocating the overthrow of the government of Indiana or the United States. With the newly formed American Legion in the vanguard and many newspaper editors and community leaders close behind, anti-radical sentiments and campaigns flourished in 1919 and for several years after.[36] The objective was not only to stifle socialists, labor organizers, and other presumed radicals but was also to encourage a hearty patriotism that would enable other Americans to resist such pied pipers of the left. Parades and meetings showed the nation's colors. In the spring of 1921, with "a mass of flags and bunting," the Marion County Council of the American Legion attracted an estimated nine thousand people to "the greatest Americanism meeting that has been held in the middle west . . . ."[37] The state political parties called for "absolute devotion to Americanism and all steps necessary thereto," while the German-born

[35] Indianapolis *News*, March 1, 1923. See also *ibid.*, February 3, 1921; David Brody, *Labor in Crisis: The Steel Strike of 1919* (Philadelphia, 1965), pp. 134-136, 158-159; *Laws of Indiana*, 1919, p. 823; 1923, p. 262; Lesta Marie Berry, A Survey of Foreign Language Teaching in the Schools of Indiana in 1935-1936 (M.A. thesis, Indiana University, Bloomington, 1936), p. 49.

[36] Errol W. Stevens, Heartland Socialism: The Socialist Party of America in Four Midwestern Communities, 1898-1920 (Ph.D. dissertation, Indiana University, Bloomington, 1978), pp. 92-99, 213-231; Phillips, *Indiana in Transition*, pp. 612-613.

[37] Indianapolis *News*, April 4, 1921.

Hoosier conservationist, Richard Lieber, advanced his program of new state parks and monuments as "the finest sermon in true Americanism."[38]

Schools also played a large role as inculcators of patriotism and as cultural homogenizers. The State Board of Education joined the movement in 1920, adopting a resolution presented by the Rotary Clubs of Indiana which called for "systematic education in Americanism" as a necessary response to "the social and industrial unrest now spreading . . . and constituting a serious menace to our institutions."[39] Local schools took up the cause, expanding prewar Americanism programs and beginning new ones, including more emphasis on American history and citizenship training. Religious and reform groups also participated in efforts to teach patriotism and to "melt" all in an American mold. Settlement houses in Gary generally encouraged the erasure of ethnic heritages. Only the International Institute of Gary, established by the YWCA in 1919, made a serious effort to retain the community's diverse cultural heritage in its general program of Americanization.[40] In addition to these external pressures, the drive for peer conformity helped modify or eradicate Old World ideas and habits. The Work Projects Administration's guide to the Calumet region, published in 1939, noted that although many foreign-born adults, especially women, still "adhere to the customs of their native lands," their children were "quick to adopt the speech, especially slang phrases, dress, and mannerisms of

[38] Party platforms, 1920, in Indiana State Platforms, 1902 1938 (Scrapbooks, 2 volumes, Indiana Division, Indiana State Library), I; Indiana Year Book, 1925, p. 322. See also Robert Allen Frederick, Colonel Richard Lieber, Conservationist and Park Builder: The Indiana Years (Ph.D. dissertation, Indiana University, Bloomington, 1960), p. 373.

[39] Indiana State Board of Education, Minutes, March 19, 1920, p. 226, Archives Division, Indiana Commission on Public Records, Indiana State Library and Historical Building.

[40] Raymond A. Mohl and Neil Betten, "Paternalism and Pluralism: Immigrants and Social Welfare in Gary, Indiana, 1906-1940," American Studies, XV (Spring, 1974), 12-15; Moore, The Calumet Region, pp. 375-378; Raymond A. Mohl and Neil Betten, "Ethnic Adjustment in the Industrial City: The International Institute of Gary, 1919-1940," International Migration Review, VI (1972), 361-376.

their schoolmates, [so that] these children, by the time they are ready to enter high school, are Americanized."[41]

§ § § § §

That Hoosiers were not all alike was demonstrated by the experience of racial and ethnic groups in the years 1920-1945. Yet there were other important ways in which the people of Indiana differed. Slightly over 49 percent of the state's population in 1920 was female.[42] While the differences among women were great, there were important features of women's lives that were unlike the lives of men. Young people also experienced life differently from the rest of the population. The "roaring" twenties, the Depression decade, and the World War II home front—as well as more subtle changes—all provided youth and women of all ages with new challenges, sometimes different from those of adults or men, as the chapters that follow indicate.

Hoosiers also could be divided into urban and rural categories. Granting some validity to the common assumption that Indiana towns and cities, even Indianapolis, were still closely bound to rural and small-town ways, it is important to appreciate rural-urban differences and sometimes conflicts. Basic to such differences were the growth of urban population and the decline of rural population. The federal census of 1910 was the first to reveal a decline rather than increase in the number of rural Hoosiers, as shown in Table I. Only the Depression reversed the downward trend, as rural population increased slightly rather than continuing to decline during the 1930s. Urban population grew rapidly in the first three decades of the century and then dropped off in the 1930s. Just as general population growth changed, so, too, did it vary among Indiana cities. Smaller towns and cities between twenty-five hundred and twenty-five thousand residents declined

[41] Work Projects Administration, *The Calumet Region Historical Guide*, p. 171. For a sophisticated analysis of Americanization in the Gary schools see Ronald D. Cohen and Raymond A. Mohl, *The Paradox of Progressive Education: The Gary Plan and Urban Schooling* (Port Washington, N.Y., 1979), pp. 84-109.

[42] United States Bureau of the Census, *Sixteenth Census* (1940), II, *Population*, Pt. 2, p. 683.

TABLE I[43]
Urban and Rural Population, Indiana, 1900-1940

Census Year	The State		Urban Places			Rural Territory		Percent of Total	
	Population	Percent Increase Over Preceding Census	Number of Places	Population	Percent Increase Over Preceding Census	Population	Percent Increase Over Preceding Census	Urban	Rural
1940	3,427,796	5.8	98	1,887,712	5.1	1,540,084	6.8	55.1	44.9
1930	3,238,503	10.5	95	1,795,892	21.1	1,442,611	−0.3	55.5	44.5
1920	2,930,390	8.5	93	1,482,855	29.6	1,447,535	−7.0	50.6	49.4
1910	2,700,876	7.3	88	1,143,835	32.6	1,557,041	−5.8	42.4	57.6
1900	2,516,462	14.8	80	862,689	46.2	1,653,773	3.2	34.3	65.7

[43] *Ibid.*, p. 675.

from 21 percent of the state's total population in 1920 to 16 percent in 1940, while medium-sized cities of between twenty-five thousand and one hundred thousand people remained nearly stable at 19 percent of the population in 1920 and 18 percent in 1940. The largest change was in cities of over one hundred thousand population, which in 1920 included only Indianapolis, with 11 percent of the total state population. By 1940, South Bend, Gary, and Fort Wayne joined Indianapolis in this large-city category, comprising 21 percent of the state's population. Nearly all this growth occurred in the prosperous 1920s, when the state's total population increased by 10.5 percent. These four largest cities added between twenty-eight thousand (Fort Wayne) and fifty thousand (Indianapolis) new residents, increasing their populations from 16 percent (Indianapolis) to 81 percent (Gary). During the 1930s South Bend's population declined by three thousand residents, while the other three largest cities grew only slightly, as did the state as a whole. It increased in total population by only 5.8 percent as economic hardship led to postponed marriage and childbearing.[44]

Much of the growth in Indiana's cities came from in-migration during the 1920s, particularly of younger people. Because agriculture offered fewer opportunities after World War I, young men and women left family farms for jobs in towns and cities. By 1930 only 24 percent of Indiana's farm population was between the ages of twenty and thirty-nine, while 34 percent of the urban population was in this young adult category.[45] Youths left small towns as well as farms. Of the 132 graduates of Brookston High School in the period 1920-1928, 80 were living elsewhere by 1938, mostly in Lafayette, South Bend, Kokomo, and Gary.[46] Even

[44] Ibid. The state's fifth largest city, Evansville, grew to 102,249 people by 1930 but dropped to 97,062 in 1940. Ibid., Indiana, pp. 2-3. See also Thomas F. Barton, "Notes on the Size, Distribution, and Growth of Indiana Cities," Indiana Academy of Science Proceedings, LVIII (1948), 222-224.

[45] United States Bureau of the Census, Sixteenth Census (1940), II, Population, Pt. 2, pp. 680, 682. See also Lynn Robertson et al., Rural Youth in Indiana (Purdue University Agricultural Experiment Station Bulletin, No. 467, Lafayette, Ind., 1942), pp. 9-11.

[46] Grover L. Hartman, Brookston: A Study of the Cultural Evolution of an Indiana Agricultural Community, 1829-1940 (Ph.D. dissertation, American University, Washington, D.C., 1946), pp. 118-119.

larger towns lost their educated young people. A 1930 study of the migratory trends of graduates of thirty-six representative high schools concluded that "it is not until a community has passed the 10,000 mark in population that it can expect to receive a number of graduates from other high schools equal to the number it loses by migration."[47] The Lynds observed this phenomenon in Muncie in "the constant process whereby Middletown tends to recruit its population from the outlying smaller communities about it and itself in turn to lose certain of its young potential leaders to larger cities."[48] Young women left farms and small towns in even larger numbers than their male counterparts, preferring jobs in cities as teachers, nurses, and office workers.[49]

The growing urban and declining rural populations and the sometimes different interests they represented were often important factors in the tensions and conflicts of the period. Rural-urban differences and antagonisms were a noticeable feature in education, religion, public health, highway construction, taxation, and politics in general, as the chapters that follow suggest. In such conflicts, however, two mitigating considerations were especially important: no large metropolis ruled the state, and rural and small-town Indiana continued to exert a strong, perhaps dominant influence on many aspects of the state's development in the years 1920-1945. There was change, to be sure, but change that was far from revolutionary and change that nearly always involved significant concessions to the rural and agrarian traditions of Hoosiers and to the Indiana idea.

§ § § § § §

The people of Indiana could also be divided along sectional lines, as the geographic regions of the state were not homogeneous. The major difference was between southern Indiana and the rest

---

[47] Otis E. Young, Migratory Trends of Graduates of Indiana High Schools, 1900-1930 (Ph.D. dissertation, Indiana University, Bloomington, 1930), p. 69.

[48] Lynd and Lynd, *Middletown*, p. 37. Some black as well as white youths of ambition and talent also left Muncie. Goodall and Mitchell, *A History of Negroes in Muncie*, p. 29.

[49] Young, Migratory Trends, pp. 128-130; Robertson et al., *Rural Youth in Indiana*, pp. 9-10, 14-15.

of the state. The rolling and hilly terrain of the southern third of the state contrasted with the flatter and generally more fertile land of central and northern Indiana. Settled first and largely by people from Virginia, the Carolinas, Tennessee, and Kentucky, southern Indiana remained in the twentieth century more rural, more isolated, and more attached to the traditions and ways of life of the mid-nineteenth century than northern Indiana. Southern Indiana was the most distinctive large section within the state, but any manager, director, or official with statewide responsibilities knew or soon learned of the different and special concerns of other geographical areas: the coal region in western Indiana; the old Quaker stronghold on the eastern border; the corn belt in the west-north-central section; the depleted natural gas belt in the east-north-central region; the special industrial and ethnic qualities in the "state of Lake";[50] Vanderburgh County's lonely position as the only large urban county on the southern border; and on and on. Political parties and politicians running for statewide office were especially sensitive to these variations and took considerable pains to balance tickets and campaigns between south and north and in other ways as well.[51]

Politics was, in fact, the feature of Indiana that most united the state—even granting the acrimony and conflict that often marked political wars. State government and politics provided the arenas in which various differences separating Hoosiers were fought and sometimes compromised and adjusted. Indiana had a long tradition of strong two-party politics, formed during the Civil War era and matured in the late nineteenth century when the state's swing vote

[50] In response to strong beliefs in Lake County that the rest of the state did not pay sufficient attention to the county's special needs, Lake County legislators sponsored a bill in 1935 to permit the county to secede from Indiana and form the forty-ninth state. The Indiana House approved a first reading of the bill, presumably in jest. News-Week, March 2, 1935, p. 10; Indiana House Journal, 1935, pp. 596, 604, 644.

[51] Frank Munger, Two-Party Politics in the State of Indiana (Ph.D. dissertation, Harvard University, 1955), pp. 225, 234-235; George W. Rauch to Martin H. Spangler, March 12, 1926, George W. Rauch Papers, Lilly Library, Indiana University, Bloomington; James E. Watson to Warren C. Fairbanks, January 19, 1928, Warren C. Fairbanks Papers, Lilly Library, Indiana University, Bloomington.

was often a major consideration in presidential politics. The tradition of intensive two-party politics and popular involvement continued into the post-World War I era, best illustrated by the large turnout of eligible voters in Indiana elections. Although the percentage turnout in general elections was not as high after 1920 as it had been in the 1880s and 1890s, it ranged from 67.6 percent in 1924 to 80.1 percent in 1940, ranking Indiana no lower than third nationally in turnout throughout these years.[52] The two major parties were highly organized with county, district, and state chairmen and committees, with substantial if not overflowing campaign treasuries, and with an assemblage of political workers, skills, and ambitions that likely were second to none in the forty-eight states.[53] Politics continued to be a major part of the spectacle, the entertainment, and leisure-time activity of Hoosiers, just as it had been since the early nineteenth century. Critics could charge, with some truth, that Indiana was "full of people who never see the economic or social ends of politics but are fascinated merely by the day-to-day business of vote getting, buttonholing, horse trading, drink buying . . . ."[54] The success of the Ku Klux Klan in disrupting the two parties in the 1920s is partly indicative of the propensity of politicians to ignore divisive social and cultural issues. And yet the parties were not without meaningful issues or differences, as the 1930s would show most clearly. Indeed, the interparty and intraparty battles and the activities of politicians and government officials at state and local levels represented important guides to the kinds of public issues and problems that Indianans considered most important. The years from the end of World War I to the end of World

[52] Charles S. Hyneman, C. Richard Hofstetter, and Patrick F. O'Connor, *Voting in Indiana: A Century of Persistence and Change* (Bloomington, Ind., 1979), pp. 18-28. Hyneman, Hofstetter, and O'Connor attribute the percentage drop in turnout after 1920 to the Indiana voter registration law, first effective in 1912, and the vote for women, first occurring in 1920. *Ibid.*, p. 27.

[53] For an example of this party intensity and professionalism see the very detailed Report on Senator Beveridge's Meeting at DeLuxe Theater, Hammond, Thursday Evening, April 20, 1922, Will Hays Papers, Indiana Division, Indiana State Library. See also Munger, Two-Party Politics in the State of Indiana, pp. 5-6.

[54] Martin, *Indiana*, p. 273.

War II were marked by the significant extension of the federal government's power, but state and local government and politics remained an essential and, in many instances, the primary means of responding to public problems in Indiana. Politics was the best place to begin to understand the state and its people: in their similarities and differences, in their attachments to past traditions, and in their successes and failures in responding to the challenges of life in modern America.

CHAPTER II

THE POLITICS OF THE 1920s:
REPUBLICANS, DEMOCRATS, AND DISRUPTERS

WHEN PRESIDENT WARREN G. HARDING promised Americans
a return to "normalcy," Hoosiers understood. They had heard
enough of great issues, of crusades for domestic reform and international peace. Although the great issue of whether the United
States should join the League of Nations was debated in Indiana
in the summer and fall campaigns of 1920, the state's major parties
followed national party leadership unenthusiastically. The Indiana
Democratic party platform of 1920 favored membership in the
League of Nations and ratification of the Treaty of Versailles but
did not get around to mentioning these issues until near the end of
its list of planks. The state's Republican party opposed membership in the League.[1]

Paralleling lukewarm interest in national and international concerns was a desire to restrict the role of state government. The pre-
1920s gubernatorial administrations of J. Frank Hanly, Thomas
Marshall, Samuel M. Ralston, and James P. Goodrich had achieved
a moderate degree of progressive reform, including legislation
dealing with corrupt political practices, protection of labor, voter
registration, and regulation of railroads.[2] Republican Governor
Goodrich had urged especially the need for reorganization and
centralization of state government to meet more efficiently the increasing demands placed on it. In his valedictory address to the
legislature in January, 1921, Goodrich referred to the "multitude
of important business questions" facing state government; yet, he
warned, "the structure of our state government, the organization
of the executive and administrative machinery upon which econ-

---

[1] Democratic and Republican state platforms, 1920, in Indiana State Platforms,
I; Raymond L. Shoemaker, "Henry Lane Wilson and Republican Policy toward
Mexico, 1913-1920," *Indiana Magazine of History*, LXXVI (1980), 117-120.

[2] Phillips, *Indiana in Transition*, pp. 108-131, 611-612.

omy, efficiency and service to the public depend, is outgrown and obsolete."[3] Goodrich's Republican successors in the governor's office failed to heed his call. Although sixteen states enacted reorganization plans between 1917 and 1930, Indiana was not among them.[4] Not until 1933 did the Depression and the political strength of Democratic Governor Paul V. McNutt combine to effect long-overdue government reorganization.

It was not only Governor Goodrich's call for reorganization but also his general model of a moderately progressive and active governorship that was rejected by his successors of the 1920s. His immediate successor was Warren T. McCray, in many ways a Hoosier version of Warren G. Harding. Born near Kentland in 1865, McCray assumed the presidency of his father's bank in 1913 and also invested in a livestock farm on which he raised prize cattle. Basing his gubernatorial campaign largely on his experience and success as a farmer-businessman, McCray was elected in 1920 with 55 percent of the vote.[5]

McCray followed outgoing Governor Goodrich's call to the 1921 legislature for government reorganization with a very general and brief message that ignored the issue of reorganization and advised instead a simple reduction of state government activity and expenditures.[6] To the 1923 session of the General Assembly McCray called for even less vigorous government: "What the people of Indiana want is a season of government economy and a period of legislative inaction and rest. They demand a closed season on new legislation. They would like to see you come together, pass a few important and constructive laws, repeal many that now cumber the statute books and then adjourn."[7]

[3] Indiana *Senate Journal*, 1921, p. 28.
[4] Midwestern states that reorganized their governments in the postwar decade were Illinois, Ohio, Michigan, and Minnesota. A. E. Buck, *The Reorganization of State Governments in the United States* (New York, 1938), pp. 8-9, 93-94.
[5] Indianapolis *News*, November 2, 1920; Robert J. Pitchell (comp.), *Indiana Votes: Election Returns for Governor, 1852-1956, and Senator, 1914-1958* (Bloomington, Ind., 1960), p. 43. Good short sketches and portraits of Indiana governors are available in Wilbur D. Peat, Diane Gail Lazarus, and Lana Ruegamer, *Portraits and Painters of the Governors of Indiana, 1800–1978* (Indianapolis, 1978).
[6] Indiana *House Journal*, 1921, p. 150.
[7] Indiana *Senate Journal*, 1923, p. 6.

McCray's call for limited government was echoed even more loudly by Hoosier Democrats in the 1920s. No doubt influenced by the fact that Republicans controlled the statehouse, Democrats professed as their cardinal principle a strong allegiance to local government and a distrust of centralization and power at the state capital. The party's 1920 platform charged that "the administration of Governor Goodrich has done more to centralize the government in Indianapolis and to destroy local self-government, than that of all other state administrations since the adoption of the present constitution." Moreover, "powers rightfully belonging to the people have been taken away from them and wrongfully centralized in highly paid boards located in Indianapolis."[8] A 1922 Democratic pamphlet continued the attack on the powers assumed by state government, with particular scorn for the moderately progressive legislation passed in the first two decades of the century. The seeds of this reform legislation had originated in Wisconsin, the anonymous pamphleteer charged, "the original hot-bed for fads and issues in government." "Now that all the 'Wisconsin ideas' have been tried out in Indiana to the detriment of every taxpayer and we have none successful, it is time to clean house, repeal every law which carries the Wisconsin twaddle, and a few others, and return to local government."[9]

Despite the political rhetoric, the differences between Democrats and Republicans over the proper role of state government were minor, with Republicans only slightly more willing to act at the state level, though always under the banner of businesslike efficiency. It was in this vein, for example, that Republicans in the early 1920s claimed as achievements improved public schools, a growing highway construction program, and a new prison at Pendleton.[10] Democrats tended to oppose even these modest efforts, ever returning to their themes of big government in Indianapolis and waste of taxpayers' money.

[8] Democratic state platform, 1920, in Indiana State Platforms, I. See also Committee to Make a Survey of Boards and Commissions of Indiana, *Report* (Indianapolis, 1925), pp. 2-3.
[9] *Back to Real Democracy in Indiana: Platform Ideas for 1922* (n.p., [1922?]), pp. 1, 2.
[10] Republican state platform, 1922, in Indiana State Platforms, I.

In light of the conservative stance of the two major parties it is not surprising that the most discussed political issue of the early 1920s was taxation. Indiana depended on property taxes for the bulk of tax revenue, with assessment the responsibility of locally elected township and county assessors. Such a system was designed to meet the needs of mid-nineteenth-century Indiana, when much of the wealth was in the form of tangible property, particularly land and improvements on land, and when local government units, particularly the townships, met the simpler needs of a rural, agrarian economy. By 1920 the locally administered property tax seemed outdated in an urbanizing, industrializing society.[11] One kind of opposition to the property tax came from property owners, especially farmers, who charged that reliance on property tax placed an unfair burden on them and benefited those who had increasingly large amounts of intangible property that was not taxed. One proposed remedy was an income tax, but legal experts advised in the 1920s that such a change could be accomplished only by an amendment to the state constitution, and Indiana voters had long been reluctant to approve constitutional amendments of any sort. The legislature approved an income tax amendment in 1919 and 1921, but the electorate voted against the measure in special elections held in September, 1921, and again in the general elections of 1926. There was also some demand to relieve property owners by means of a sales tax, but it also seemed to require a constitutional amendment, which neither the legislature nor voters approved during the 1920s.[12]

Another response to the taxation issue was the effort to reform the administration and operation of the property tax itself. Critics charged that Indiana's decentralized, locally administered tax system, controlled by the township assessor, led to abuses, inequities, and inefficiencies. A comparison of assessed valuations with actual real estate transfers made in 1916 showed not only

[11] Frank G. Bates, "State Control of Local Finance in Indiana," *American Political Science Review*, XX (1926), 352-353.

[12] Kettleborough, *Constitution Making in Indiana*, III, xvi; Charles F. Remy, "Governor Goodrich and Indiana Tax Legislation," *Indiana Magazine of History*, XLIII (1947), 41-56; Harold C. Feightner, *Our State Government* (Indianapolis, 1930), p. 70.

that property was greatly underassessed but that there was considerable variation from county to county in the degree of underassessment, from a low assessment of 23 percent of true value in Starke County to a high of 73 percent of true value in Floyd. Little could be done to correct such variation prior to 1919 because there was no central supervisory power over the local township assessor.[13]

Both parties recognized shortcomings in property tax assessment and administration, but it was the Republicans, and especially Governor Goodrich, who were responsible for a new tax law in 1919, designed to improve and standardize methods of tax assessment and to limit the power of local governments to set tax levies and borrow money by control of a new state tax commission. The new tax law quickly became a major issue in the political campaigns of the early 1920s. Republicans claimed that the 1919 tax law resulted in a fairer, more efficient, and uniform system of taxation, that it prevented extravagant spending by local governments, and that it was "the greatest achievement of the Republican party in Indiana since the Civil War."[14] Yet less than two years after they passed the tax legislation, Republicans called a special session of the legislature to meet in July, 1920, during which they passed legislation that greatly reduced the authority of the state tax commission, only to restore some of it in the 1923 legislative session.[15]

This Republican vacillation in support of a state-supervised tax system was doubtless due in part to the Democratic party's effective opposition. Democrats asserted that granting supervisory authority to the state tax commission had dangerously centralized power in Indianapolis and denied Hoosiers "the right of local self-government."[16] They argued also that the new law resulted in higher taxes and larger state government expenditures. Demo-

---

[13] John B. Phillips, *Problems of Taxation in Indiana* (n.p., 1919), pp. 7-11.

[14] Indiana Republican State Committee, *The Operation of the 1919 Tax Law* (Indianapolis, [1919]), p. 31.

[15] Bates, "State Control of Local Finance in Indiana," *American Political Science Review*, XX, 354-355.

[16] Democratic state platform, 1920, in Indiana State Platforms, I.

crats especially singled out as unnecessary expenditures for public education and for "the boards and commissions," such as the conservation commission, board of health, and public service commission. And to the list of extravagances, Democrats added new furnishings for the governor's mansion, including "a grand piano, Oriental rugs and a gravey boat, costing $5,005.22."[17]

Democrats thus charged Republicans with freedom-denying centralization and extravagance, charges Republicans responded to by boasting of the efficiency and savings resulting from their changes in the tax law.[18] Despite the large amounts of campaign rhetoric devoted to the tax issue, neither party exhibited either the will or the ability to effect significant changes in the tax system. The subject was too daring and too controversial for the political leadership of the 1920s.

§ §

The generally conservative nature of Indiana politics in the 1920s as well as some of its other features was well illustrated in the senatorial campaign of 1922. The campaign was especially difficult for the Republican party because of the development of bitter factions within the party—factions that tended to focus on rival ambitions of Republican leaders rather than on differences of principle. One of the candidates for the senatorial nomination was Harry S. New, the incumbent, who had been first elected in 1916. New was a very conservative Republican, colorless and uninspiring on the campaign stump, but he had the advantage not only of incumbency but of the strong backing of the regular Republican organization in Indiana and in the nation. He was also a close political friend of President Harding, having pushed hard for Harding's nomination in 1920.[19]

Opposing New for the Republican nomination was Albert J. Beveridge. First elected to the Senate in 1899, Beveridge soon

---

[17] Indiana Democratic State Committee, *Tales of Two Tax Laws* (n.p., [1923?]).

[18] Indiana Republican State Committee, *Tax Facts* (n.p., [1922]).

[19] John Braeman, *Albert J. Beveridge: American Nationalist* (Chicago, 1971), pp. 279, 282.

made a national reputation as a spokesman for American expansion overseas and then as a progressive reformer, especially in his advocacy of child labor laws and pure food laws. He was a superb political orator with a strong popular following in Indiana, but his desertion of the party in 1912 to follow Theodore Roosevelt's Bull Moose Progressive party forever left the taste of wormwood and gall in the mouths of regular Hoosier Republicans. Although Beveridge had commenced a successful literary career with his multivolume biography of John Marshall, published between 1916 and 1919, and although he was spending much of his time outside Indiana, his political ambitions caught fire again in the early 1920s. In 1922 he entered the Republican primary against Senator New.[20]

The bitter primary race between New and Beveridge had little to do with issues or ideology. There was no mistaking New's standpat Republican conservatism. What may have been surprising for an observer in 1922 who knew only the pre-World War I Beveridge was the degree to which the former progressive now supported the staples of 1920s Indiana conservatism. Influenced by the economic difficulties and political radicalism of the immediate postwar years, Beveridge vehemently asserted the necessity of reducing government regulation of business, lowering the federal income tax, curbing labor union power, and lowering wages for workers. His campaign motto, rather than calling for "a new armageddon" or even moderate reform, was a Harding-like "Normal Times and Sound Government."[21]

The campaign thus came down to one of personalities, in which the fiery Beveridge was the popular choice of many Hoosiers over the lackluster New. But Beveridge had one further and crucial advantage—the cunning and ambition of James E. Watson, Indiana's other incumbent senator. Elected in 1916 to fill the vacancy caused by the death of Democrat Benjamin F. Shively, Watson represented the state in Washington until 1933, standing tall as a leading proponent of conservative, old-guard Republicanism. In

[20] *Ibid.*, especially Chapters 3, 4, 8, 9, 16, 19, 20.
[21] *Ibid.*, pp. 273-275, 280-284.

early 1922 Watson stepped forward in a bid to take over the Republican State Committee, which was controlled by New and former Governor Goodrich, setting off "a nasty fight" which Watson finally won in early May, 1922.[22] Watson dominated the Republican organization for the remainder of the decade, though not without opposition from the New–Goodrich faction and others. In 1922 Watson publicly supported New, but he did not campaign for his colleague. Indeed, it is possible that a deal was made whereby some of Watson's supporters backed Beveridge against New in return for the aid of the Beveridge faction in their struggle for the state chairmanship.[23] Thus, although Beveridge was regarded as "an apostate of the first order" by many regular Republicans, as Indianapolis newspaperman Harold C. Feightner later recalled,[24] there were some regular Republicans whose political ambitions allowed even apostates as bedfellows.

The Republican bed was never very comfortable in 1922, however. Beveridge defeated New in the primary by more than 20,000 votes, but the bitterness of the spring campaign was not forgotten in the fall. Party leaders assured the membership that Beveridge was preferable to a Democrat and that even the defeated New was supporting him, although the senator in fact gave only one campaign speech and did not mention Beveridge in it.[25] Democrats could not miss such an opportunity. Fresh from victories in the local elections of 1921[26] and hoping to capitalize on economic discontent, they united behind Samuel M. Ralston, who had been

[22] Hilton U. Brown to Delavan Smith, May 10, 1922, Fairbanks Papers.

[23] Braeman, *Beveridge*, pp. 283-284. This alleged "double-cross" of Harry S. New by James E. Watson's supporters continued as a sore spot in Republican politics long after the 1922 campaign. New York *Times*, November 29, 1925.

[24] Harold Feightner interview by Thomas Krasean and Richard Gemmecke, February 28, October 24, 1968, transcript, p. 29, Indiana Division, Indiana State Library. Feightner recalled that regular Republicans "turned his [Albert J. Beveridge's] picture to the wall down at the old Columbia Club."

[25] Warren McCray to Joseph D. Oliver, October 12, 1922, Warren McCray Papers, Archives Division, Indiana Commission on Public Records, Indiana State Library and Historical Building; Braeman, *Beveridge*, p. 286.

[26] Indiana Democrats elected forty-five mayors compared to twenty-seven for Republicans in 1921. Fort Wayne *Journal-Gazette*, November 13, 1921.

a popular and moderately progressive governor from 1913 to 1917.[27] In 1922 Ralston's positions on issues differed only slightly from Beveridge's, notably in that the Democratic candidate advocated an eight-hour day for railroad workers and denounced Beveridge's proposed nationwide sales tax as discriminatory against poorer Americans. But Ralston's principal theme was his gubernatorial record of low taxes and government economy in comparison to the increased spending and higher taxes under Republican Governors Goodrich and McCray.[28] Ralston was especially successful in keeping potentially divisive issues out of his campaign, above all prohibition. His method was simply to deny prohibition the status of an issue. In response to one request for his views on the federal prohibition law, for example, Ralston wrote: "I am not discussing the Volstead Act, in this campaign."[29] This conspiracy of silence extended to both parties: neither discussed this controversial issue in 1922.[30]

Ralston won the Indiana senatorial election of 1922, but his victory did not indicate a repudiation of either conservatism or the Republican party. With the exceptions noted, Ralston made nearly as conservative an appeal to the voters as Beveridge. Indeed, an Indiana vote for the popular Ralston was as much a vote for "normalcy" as was a vote for Beveridge.

Nor did the election of 1922 represent a major shift to the Democratic party. Republicans continued to control both houses of the state legislature until 1931, and Republicans would continue their hold on the governor's office until 1933. At the local level also the majority of elected officials in the 1920s were Republican. Yet their success in the postwar decade did not mean an absolute

---

[27] Suellen M. Hoy, Samuel M. Ralston: Progressive Governor, 1913-1917 (Ph.D. dissertation, Indiana University, Bloomington, 1975).

[28] Braeman, Beveridge, pp. 285-286.

[29] Samuel M. Ralston to B. A. Worthington, October 20, 1922, Samuel M. Ralston Papers, Lilly Library, Indiana University, Bloomington.

[30] Ralston to William J. Bryan, September 19, 1922, Ralston Papers. In fact, Ralston favored prohibition. He assured Bryan, the most widely known spokesman for prohibition, that his coming to Indiana to speak for the Democratic candidates would not "cause any discord between 'wet' candidates and myself," so effectively had the issue been covered over.

Republican domination of the state. On the contrary, despite the tendency of the Republican party to win most of the elections most of the time, the Democratic party remained strong; it was able to put up a good fight in statewide contests, and it sometimes won and almost always received a large share of the vote.[31]

§ § §

The relatively even balance between the major parties made them very sensitive to issues, organizations, groups, and events that could alter the voting habits of Hoosiers. Such disruptive forces appeared in abundance in the 1920s. With origins in economic, cultural, and moral concerns of Hoosiers these disruptions introduced unpredictable elements into the campaigns by threatening to mobilize new voters or push old voters into different patterns. Beveridge lamented, for example, that the 1924 campaign "showed a swirl of cross-currents beneath the surface which I could not and cannot make heads or tails of."[32] The "swirl of cross-currents" in the 1920s was generated by the direct primary; the voting interests of women, veterans, farmers, and labor; and the pressure group politics of the Anti-Saloon League and the Ku Klux Klan. Political leaders tended to respond to these disruptive forces cautiously, even timidly, attempting to ignore or suppress divisive issues and thereby avoid alienating potential voters. By this cautious response many politicians survived during the 1920s; few demonstrated energetic or positive leadership in their parties, the legislature, or the governor's office.

One source of difficulty for politicians in the 1920s was the state's direct primary law. This measure had been passed in 1915 to increase popular control of government. The law provided for nominating candidates for governor and United States senator by voters in statewide party primaries. Other candidates were nominated by the party's state convention, which also nominated candidates for governor and senator if no candidate received a majority in the primary. Although the direct primary failed to

31 Hyneman, Hofstetter, and O'Connor, *Voting in Indiana*, pp. 42-61.

32 Albert J. Beveridge to William E. Borah, November 13, 1924, quoted in Claude G. Bowers, *Beveridge and the Progressive Era* (New York, 1932), p. 540.

produce the degree of popular control progressive reformers had hoped, it did reduce the control party leaders had over the nomination process, as exemplified in Beveridge's successful appeal to the voters in the 1922 Republican primary. As long as the direct primary functioned, there was always the possibility that fickle voters would ignore party direction and discipline in response to new leaders, issues, or causes outside the major party organizations. And the primary added to campaign expenses and internal party disharmony. Professional politicians thus had good reasons for strongly opposing the direct primary, as they generally did throughout the decade. At the 1929 session of the General Assembly they at last succeeded in repealing the odious law that had made political life unpredictable and more subject to disruptive issues and leaders.[33]

Another source of potential disruption to the discipline and organization of the two major parties in the 1920s was the enfranchisement of new voters by the nineteenth amendment. The Indiana legislature ratified the federal women's suffrage amendment at a special session in January, 1920. In a special election held in September, 1921, Hoosier voters also ratified an amendment to the state constitution granting women the vote.[34] This doubling of the eligible electorate produced new strategies from the two parties to welcome and attract women voters. At their state conventions in the spring of 1920 both parties advocated the entry of more women into political life, and both sent women delegates to the national party conventions. The Democrats nominated a woman for state office (Adelaide Steele Baylor, for superintendent of public instruction), and in the fall, voters in Delaware

[33] Frederic H. Guild, "The Operation of the Direct Primary in Indiana," American Academy of Political and Social Science *Annals*, CVI (1923), 172-180; Democratic and Republican state platforms, 1920, in Indiana State Platforms, I; Indianapolis *News*, January 9, 1923, January 5, 1925, March 12, 1929. It is likely that the repeal of the direct primary was partly a reaction against the Ku Klux Klan, which had made effective use of the primary.

[34] Kettleborough, *Constitution Making in Indiana*, III, xiv-xv. This special election also amended the constitution to deny the vote to aliens. Previously they had only to state their intent to become citizens in order to vote.

County elected the first woman to the state legislature, Republican Julia D. Nelson of Muncie.[35]

The possibility that women voters or officeholders would significantly disrupt traditional politics seemed less likely as the 1920s progressed. Of the total of 500 seats in the Indiana House of Representatives from 1921 through 1929, women held only 9. No woman was elected to the Indiana Senate until 1943.[36] Women generally showed less interest in politics than men, or at least they voted less frequently. Even the vote on the suffrage amendment to the state constitution in 1921 attracted a smaller number of female voters than observers had expected.[37] Perhaps most important, women played only limited roles in the political organizations. Although women served in both parties as vice-chairmen at the county and state level, the position in most instances was little more than honorary. As Emma M. May, Democratic vice-chairman for Vigo County, complained in 1929: "Why are women not asked to help raise finances, help select party tickets and do all the things that [the] organization requires of men?"[38] Women also chose—or were influenced by men—to restrict their active political involvements to limited and often traditionally feminine concerns. In almost exactly the same language both state platforms in 1920 called for the appointment of women to "the various boards of the state dealing with the employment of women and children, public health, morals and education."[39] The interests of the nonpartisan Indiana League of Women Voters were simi-

[35] Democratic and Republican state platforms, 1920, in Indiana State Platforms, I; Indianapolis News, May 21, November 3, 1920.

[36] Indiana Legislative Bureau, Indiana General Assembly (Typescript, Indiana Division, Indiana State Library, 1954), pp. 37, 39. Of the total of 500 house seats filled in the sessions from 1931 through 1939, women held only 5 seats, 3 by the same person, Bess Robbins, of Marion County.

[37] Hyneman, Hofstetter, and O'Connor, Voting in Indiana, p. 27; Indianapolis Star, September 7, 1921.

[38] Emma M. May to Franklin D. Roosevelt, December 5, 1929, Box 193, Democratic National Committee Papers, Franklin D. Roosevelt Library, Hyde Park, New York.

[39] Democratic state platform, 1920, in Indiana State Platforms, I. See also Republican state platform, 1920, in ibid.

larly limited, as evidenced by the organization's standing committees: child welfare, education, efficiency in government, living
costs, social hygiene, uniform laws, and women in industry.[40]
Although the League made some important contributions in
these areas, it was often difficult to stimulate interest in such
issues. After the victory in the suffrage struggle, one League
president wrote, many women "felt unequal to the challenge of
a new demanding task."[41] Given these restrictions on their interests and the prevailing notions of women's place in general, it is
likely that women did not significantly alter the traditional
political environment in the 1920s.

Perhaps more distinctive as a new political force than women
was a group of men—veterans of the World War. In the immediate postwar years politicians and the general public sincerely
wished to provide special honors and benefits to those who had
served in the Great War. Politicians were particularly sensitive to
the voting strength of Hoosier veterans, especially on issues that
affected them. Most significant as a potential force in Indiana politics was the American Legion, organized after the war and by 1920
claiming twenty-eight thousand members and nearly three hundred posts in the state.[42] In 1919 Indiana Legionnaires had succeeded in locating the national as well as the state headquarters in
Indianapolis, thereby assuring a high degree of visibility in the
state.[43] The Legion devoted major attention to promoting Americanism, especially among young people, but its primary political
activity was its effort to gain the support of state and local governments for construction of a war memorial plaza and buildings in
Indianapolis. Strong Legion pressure led the General Assembly in
July, 1920, to authorize two million dollars to construct a war
memorial. Similar pressure on Marion County and Indianapolis
governments also led them to approve the project by passing

[40] Indiana League of Women Voters, *Convention* (Indianapolis, 1923).

[41] Katherine Croan Greenough, *A History of the League of Women Voters
of Indiana, 1920-1952* (n.p., n.d.), p. 3. See also Indiana League of Women Voters,
Year Book, 1927 (Shelbyville, Ind., 1927), p. 20.

[42] Clutter, The Indiana American Legion, pp. 36-37, 93. Membership declined
to fourteen thousand in 1925, but increased to twenty-nine thousand by 1929.

[43] *Ibid.*, pp. 24-29, 67-79.

bond issues to finance purchase of land and construction of the buildings. The first structure was completed in 1925 and housed the Legion's state and national offices. In 1927 General John J. Pershing presided at the cornerstone laying of the most visible portion of the plaza, the Indiana World War Memorial, an immense square and pyramidal limestone structure. There was some criticism of the war memorial project. Some veterans preferred instead a state bonus for each veteran as a more practical indication of appreciation for war service. And some citizens argued that tax dollars would be better spent to alleviate crowded conditions at the county poor farm and insane asylum. But the Legion successfully overcame these objections.[44]

Although the Legion represented a large and potentially strong political force, its major achievements were limited to the memorial plaza and the Americanism program, projects on which there was considerable agreement within and without the organization. Neither on these issues nor others in the 1920s did the Legion as an organization prove to be a large political threat or disruptive force for the two major parties.

Another potentially disruptive force in Hoosier politics in the 1920s came from economic groups who felt most severely the depression of 1921-1922 and who continued to constitute economic "sore spots" in the prosperity boom of the mid-1920s. Many labor groups had economic grievances, but their unions were generally weak and could often be ignored by political leaders. Farmers were more active. They began organized political effort through the Indiana Farm Bureau and played a significant role in tax policy. But farm group political concerns were generally limited and focused increasingly on the federal rather than state government. Still, the unpredictable farm vote was a source of some anxiety for Hoosier politicians.[45]

[44] *Ibid.*, pp. 111-119. In 1923 the state legislature passed a bill authorizing a popular referendum on a state bonus for Hoosier veterans, but Governor McCray vetoed it on the grounds that a bonus was too costly, unconstitutional, and the responsibility of the federal government.

[45] See, for example, Thomas Duncan to Ralston, May 20, 1924, Ralston Papers. Farm and labor issues are discussed more fully in later chapters, especially Chapters VI and VIII.

Groups tied by common economic concerns, such as agriculture and labor, and groups bound by presumably shared experiences, such as womanhood or service in wartime, had important but limited political effects during the 1920s. Although state and local government and the two major parties acknowledged their special concerns and interests and sometimes responded to their requests, these groups did not disrupt or significantly alter traditional political life in the state. Another kind of group was based on long-standing, deep cultural and moral values and provided a much more powerful voice in Hoosier politics. During the 1920s Indiana politicians were forced to listen to two such groups in particular: the Anti-Saloon League and the Ku Klux Klan.

§ § § §

The Indiana Anti-Saloon League was the dominant voice supporting prohibition in the 1920s and represented a long tradition of Hoosier support for this moral reform. During the 1850s and again beginning in the late nineteenth century various temperance groups had advocated legislation to prohibit the manufacture and sale of alcohol, at times suggesting in their zeal that this one evil was the basis for much if not all that was undesirable and immoral. Prior to World War I, temperance advocates had succeeded in pushing through the state legislature several local option laws, which allowed a township or county to go "dry" if it wished. Greater success came with the statewide prohibition law passed in 1917 and the federal prohibition amendment, ratified by Indiana in 1919 and declared effective in January, 1920. Both these measures benefited from the moral and emotional responses to the war, in particular from the anti-German sentiment fostered by the war and from the linking of alcohol manufacture and consumption with German-Americans.[46]

Although the 1920s began with victory for the prohibitionists, the battles were far from over. Two threats dominated: that the prohibition law would be laxly enforced and that the federal amendment itself would be repealed. Standing as a bulwark against

[46] Phillips, *Indiana in Transition*, pp. 494-498.

these threats was the Indiana Anti-Saloon League, a branch of the national organization that was formed in the state in 1898. The League, the organized prohibition army of the Protestant churches, worked through local, especially Methodist, congregations to educate the public and convince politicians of the need for prohibition. Unlike the much less powerful Indiana Prohibition party, the league did not function like a traditional third political party.[47] Rather, the League offered either support or opposition to major party candidates, depending solely on their stand on prohibition. In close contests particularly this method had a significant effect on parties and candidates and made the League an important force in Indiana politics.

The superintendent of the Indiana Anti-Saloon League was Edward S. Shumaker, a DePauw University graduate and a Methodist minister who worked tirelessly to further the League's goals, relying strongly on political action.[48] In the early 1920s Shumaker's chief concern was inadequate enforcement of the prohibition law, especially in the cities where it was relatively easy to purchase bootleg alcohol. The Calumet region, close to the center of bootlegging in Chicago, was notably wet throughout the decade. But some rural areas were also far from dry, as in predominantly German-American Dubois County, where a local moonshine, known as Dubois County Dew, gained a wide reputation. And many Legion posts throughout the state, despite their professed attachment to law and patriotism, often sold beer and liquor without restraint.[49]

To counter these violations of the prohibition law in Indiana,

[47] The Indiana Prohibition party focused on one issue, but it also advocated a variety of moral reforms, including compulsory Bible reading in the schools, strict observance of the Sabbath, and censorship of movies. The party never played a large role in Indiana politics. See Indiana Prohibition Party platforms, 1920, 1924, 1930, 1932, in Indiana State Platforms, I; Hyneman, Hofstetter, and O'Connor, *Voting in Indiana*, pp. 78-79.

[48] Ernest H. Cherrington (ed.), *Standard Encyclopedia of the Alcohol Problem* (6 volumes, Westerville, Ohio, 1925-1930), III, 1309-1310, V, 2436; Clarence E. Flynn (ed.), *The Indianapolis Area of the Methodist Episcopal Church 1924-1928: A Record and History* (Indianapolis, n.d.), pp. 88, 111-112.

[49] Munger, Two-Party Politics in the State of Indiana, p. 65n; Clutter, The Indiana American Legion, pp. 34-35; Moore, *The Calumet Region*, pp. 548-551.

Shumaker drafted and pushed through the 1925 legislature a bill designed to strengthen and codify state prohibition legislation in one all-encompassing law. Known popularly as the bone-dry law, the 1925 act not only prohibited the manufacture and sale of alcoholic beverages but also provided severe penalties for possession of alcohol, including a minimum fine of $100 and thirty days in the county jail for the first offense. The bone-dry law defined possession broadly, stipulating that "the possession of empty bottles, kegs, cases or vessels that have contained intoxicating liquor, shall be admitted as evidence of the illegal possession of such liquor."[50] The law did not make Indiana bone-dry, but it was regarded as a step in that direction, and as such it very much pleased Shumaker and the League.[51]

Shumaker's efforts to press enforcement of the prohibition laws led him into battle with politicians and particularly with the Indiana Supreme Court. Shumaker singled out Supreme Court Judge Benjamin F. Willoughby for attack, and charged that he was "bitterly hostile to prohibition." Actively seeking Willoughby's electoral defeat, Shumaker urged voters to "give us a Supreme Court that will be dry not wet."[52] For his criticism of Willoughby and the court, the court found Shumaker guilty of contempt and sentenced him to sixty days at the state farm. Governor Jackson pardoned Shumaker in October, 1928, but the supreme court rejected the pardon and upheld the sentence. On February 11, 1929, Shumaker became a hero to his cause as he began serving his time at the state farm.[53]

Through much of the 1920s, Shumaker was a potent force in

[50] *Laws of Indiana*, 1925, pp. 145, 159-160; Indianapolis *News*, January 14, February 28, 1925.

[51] Edward S. Shumaker, *Indiana Wet and Dry* (Indianapolis, [1925]), p. 5; Harold C. Feightner, 150 Years of Brewing in Indiana: The Story of Politics, Prohibition, and Patronage (Typescript, Indiana Division, Indiana State Library, n.d.), Chapter 14, p. 1. The *Indiana Catholic and Record*, March 6, 1925, called the bone-dry law "the production of the mentality of fanatics. . . ."

[52] Indiana Anti-Saloon League, *Annual Report*, January 19, 1926 (Indianapolis, 1926), pp. 8, 13.

[53] Indianapolis *News*, February 11, 1929; Feightner, 150 Years of Brewing in Indiana, Chapter 13, p. 4, Chapter 15, p. 1; Cherrington (ed.), *Standard Encyclopedia of the Alcohol Problem*, V, 2436.

Indiana politics and was occasionally allied with the Ku Klux Klan in support of dry candidates.[54] Although the Indianapolis *News* exaggerated his strength when it editorialized in 1927 that "if there is one man in this state whose word is law it is Doctor Shumaker . . . ,"[55] doubtless he was among the half dozen most politically powerful men in Indiana. Through League publications, movies, meetings, and, above all, through his efforts to identify and oppose those political candidates not fully supportive of prohibition, Shumaker acted as a disruptive force in Hoosier politics.

The cause of prohibition suffered severe blows at the end of the decade. The first was the death of Shumaker, as no one appeared to take his place as an energetic and widely known spokesman for the cause.[56] The second and more significant blow was the Depression, which made other problems seem more important than consumption of alcohol and which provided the primary issue for the return to state and national offices of the party less committed to the cause. In 1932 the Hoosier Democratic party came out foursquare in favor of repeal of the eighteenth amendment.[57] Republicans found it more difficult to abandon the prohibition ship and split bitterly over the issue at their 1932 state convention, which a reporter described as "one of the wildest scenes witnessed at a state convention in years . . . ."[58] With many delegates from the urban counties, especially Lake, pushing strongly for a wet plank and with rural delegates split or dry, the Republican convention voted 823 to 620 in favor of repeal of the bone-dry law and in favor of the resubmission of the eighteenth amendment to the people for a vote. To ease the sting of repeal, the convention called for state supervision and taxation of liquor manufactures and sales, with the revenue to be used to relieve Depression-

[54] Testimony of Hugh Emmons, South Bend Klan leader, February 20, 1928, *State of Indiana* v. *The Knights of the Ku Klux Klan*, Marion Circuit Court Attorney General, Ku Klux Klan, Reel 200, Archives Division, Indiana Commission on Public Records, Indiana State Library and Historical Building.

[55] Indianapolis *News*, June 1, 1927.

[56] New York *Times*, December 8, 1929, May 18, 1930.

[57] Democratic state platform, 1932, in Indiana State Platforms, I.

[58] Indianapolis *News*, June 9, 1932.

burdened taxpayers. Nonetheless, as the New York *Times* noted, the Republican abandonment of prohibition left "the whole State gasping."[59] The Democratic landslide victories in the fall elections assured an end to the noble experiment. In June, 1933, a special election resulted in a 64 percent vote in Indiana favoring repeal of national prohibition.[60] Soon Hoosiers could again legally purchase and consume alcoholic beverages, and many politicians could breathe easier, with the troublesome issue greatly diminished if not extinguished.

§ § § § §

The Indiana Anti-Saloon League focused on one target. The other major organization in the 1920s that was based on moral appeal was more wide-ranging, sweeping across the political landscape in search of enemies of all sorts, real and imagined.

The first signs of Ku Klux Klan activity in Indiana appeared in Evansville in 1920. The organization grew slowly at first, but by 1923 its presence was evident throughout most of the state, in nearly all the cities and towns, and in many rural areas. In the spring of 1923 large Klan rallies and parades were held in Hammond, Shelbyville, Valparaiso, and South Bend. In white robes and masks, marching silently through the streets in torchlight procession, the Klan presented an awesome spectacle, one that usually culminated with a cross-burning ritual.[61] The organization's largest exhibition in Indiana in 1923 occurred at Melfalfa

[59] New York *Times*, June 12, 1932; Indianapolis *News*, June 3, 9, 1932; Republican state platform, 1932, in Indiana State Platforms, I. The intensity of the issue is apparent in the flood of letters to Governor Harry G. Leslie arguing against repeal. See Prohibition File, Box C, Drawer 45, Leslie Papers.

[60] David E. Kyvig, *Repealing National Prohibition* (Chicago, 1979), p. 178. In the thirty-seven states that held elections on repeal the wet vote averaged nearly 73 percent compared to Indiana's 64 percent.

[61] Norman F. Weaver, The Knights of the Ku Klux Klan in Wisconsin, Indiana, Ohio and Michigan (Ph.D. dissertation, University of Wisconsin, Madison, 1954), pp. 146-147; Neil Betten and James B. Lane, "Nativism and the Klan in Town and City: Valparaiso and Gary, Indiana," *Studies in History and Society*, IV (Spring, 1973), 6; Jill Suzanne Nevel, Fiery Crosses and Tempers: The Ku Klux K'an in South Bend, Indiana, 1923-1926 (Senior thesis, Princeton University, 1977), pp. 56-57; Marian McFadden, *Biography of a Town: Shelbyville, Indiana, 1822-1962* (Shelbyville, Ind., 1968), p. 292.

Indianapolis women waiting to vote for the first time, November, 1920

Governor Warren T. McCray in custody of
United States Marshall, 1924

Indiana's Democratic leaders, November, 1932: (l. to r.) R. Earl Peters, Paul V. McNutt, Frederick Van Nuys, Thomas Taggart, Jr., Pleas Greenlee

Officers of Indiana County and Township Officials Association, 1936

Park in Kokomo where on a hot Fourth of July a crowd estimated at a hundred thousand people gathered for a picnic and speeches. They heard patriotic oratory by the Klan's national leader, Imperial Wizard Hiram W. Evans, and by the newly installed Indiana chief, Grand Dragon David C. (D. C.) Stephenson, who awed the crowd by arriving via airplane. The holiday ended with an evening parade, the burning of a cross, and singing of "The Old Rugged Cross."[62]

By the summer of 1923 the Klan claimed four hundred thousand Hoosier members. Opponents of the Klan set the figure considerably lower, at less than three hundred thousand.[63] Whatever the exact size, there can be no doubt that a large number of Hoosiers joined the Klan in 1923 and 1924. Some Indianans doubtless wanted to believe, as Elmer Davis reported in 1926, that the Klan membership was "almost exclusively composed of the hill-billies, the Great Unteachables." The Klan did enjoy support among farmers in rural Indiana, including "hill-billies," but Klan membership came from all walks of urban and rural life and often included some of a community's "better" citizens. Not only farmers and factory workers but also some merchants, small businessmen, and Protestant ministers donned the white robe and hood in small towns and villages and in larger cities.[64]

The appeal of the Klan to Hoosiers varied from individual to individual and from place to place. For some, the Klan performed social and emotional functions similar to many fraternal organiza-

[62] Robert Coughlan, "Konklave in Kokomo," in Isabel Leighton (ed.), *The Aspirin Age, 1919-1941* (New York, 1949), pp. 105-108; New York *Times*, July 6, 1923. Later estimates of attendance at the Kokomo meeting are as low as eight to ten thousand. See Bradford W. Scharlott, The Hoosier Newsman and the Hooded Order: Indiana Press Reaction to the Ku Klux Klan in the 1920s (M.A. thesis, Indiana University, Bloomington, 1978), p. 35.

[63] John A. Davis, The Ku Klux Klan in Indiana, 1920-1930: An Historical Study (Ph.D. dissertation, Northwestern University, Evanston, Ill., 1966), p. 61.

[64] Elmer Davis, "Have Faith in Indiana," *Harpers Magazine*, CLIII (1926), 621; Jackson, *The Ku Klux Klan in the City, 1915-1930*, pp. 153-154; Nevel, Fiery Crosses and Tempers, pp. 63-66. See also a typed list, Local Officers of the Ku Klux Klan in Indiana, 1925, in Indiana Historical Society Library. For each county the list includes membership figures, names of officers, and indications of the stand of local police and government officials on the Klan.

tions. It provided a sense of group solidarity, of belonging, high-lighted by extensive ritual and mystery. For many Hoosiers it was a social organization—a part of their entertainment and leisure-time activity. But the Klan's appeal rested also on its success in touching basic attitudes and beliefs.[65] At the core of the Klan's success were two of the simplest and most fundamental truths for most Hoosiers—patriotism and Protestant religion. When, for example, ten thousand Klansmen swarmed across the race grounds at the Indiana State Fair on Klan Day in 1923, they did two simple but most symbolic things: they sang "America," and they recited the Lord's Prayer.[66]

The Klan's appeal, however, was to a narrow and anxious patriotism and religion, often defined by reference to the ideas and peoples meant to be excluded, opposed, and hated. The constant Klan refrain of "100 percent Americanism" assumed a cultural, moral, and political superiority and exclusiveness that not only denied the Klan seal of approval to those defined as less than 100 percent American but also required a stance of opposition. In short, the Klan defined itself and its ideals primarily in the identification of its enemies.

First on the list of Klan enemies were Roman Catholics. The intense Protestantism of the Klan burned with the centuries-old anti-Catholicism that had burst forth at various times in American history. Lurid tales of Catholic immorality and of Catholic political subversion were whispered and, in closed Klan meetings, shouted. There was special attention to the church's hierarchical and authoritarian structure, which allegedly denied democracy and individual freedom, and to its foreign leadership, particularly the pope, who was supposedly intent on the overthrow of American government and American democracy.[67] And, of course, Klan

[65] Davis, The Ku Klux Klan in Indiana, pp. 308-317. For a good general discussion of the Klan see Robert M. Miller, "The Ku Klux Klan," in John Braeman, Robert H. Bremner, and David Brody (eds.), Change and Continuity in Twentieth-Century America: The 1920's (Columbus, Ohio, 1968), pp. 215-255.
[66] Indianapolis News, September 7, 1923.
[67] Weaver, The Knights of the Ku Klux Klan, pp. 159-161, 303; Davis, The Ku Klux Klan in Indiana, pp. 34, 48, 281-282; Davis, "Have Faith in Indiana," Harpers Magazine, CLIII, 617. The Indianapolis Fiery Cross, the voice of the

leaders noted, the church's membership contained so many foreigners, who were accused of being led like sheep and unable to appreciate the liberty and freedom of America. In its support of restrictions on immigration the Klan sounded a widely popular note in post-World War I Indiana.[68]

The Hoosier Klan also identified blacks as among the enemy and beyond the realm of 100 percent Americanism, though blacks generally received less attention than Catholics. Here, too, long-held prejudices were voiced, sometimes in a vague general way in those many parts of Indiana where there were no blacks and sometimes more directly in reaction to a specific event, as when a Lake County Klavern protested a scheduled boxing match because it featured "Jack Johnson, famous Negro white slaver . . . who's [sic] open boast . . . is that he can get any white woman he wants. . . ."[69] The Klan's strongest opposition to blacks came in the larger cities, where black populations were growing rapidly and where black workers and expanding black neighborhoods were perceived by white Hoosiers as social and economic threats. This was the case in Indianapolis, where the Klan attracted strong support from the white, middle- and working-class neighborhoods near expanding black neighborhoods, particularly the northwestern area between Twenty-seventh Street and Crown Hill Cemetery.[70]

The Klan also used traditional anti-Jewish propaganda to convince Hoosiers of the virtues of 100 percent Americanism. But there were fewer than twenty-five thousand Jews in Indiana, so this feature never became a dominant part of the Klan's appeal.

Much of the Klan's 100-percent-Americanism campaign

Indiana Klan, is filled with attacks on the Roman Catholic Church in 1923 and 1924.

[68] The Indiana Republican party in 1920 called for federal restriction on the number of immigrants entering the United States, a call that was answered in federal legislation enacted in 1922 and 1924. Republican state platform, 1920, in Indiana State Platforms, I.

[69] K.K.K. to Emmett F. Branch, August 8, 1924, Emmett F. Branch Papers, Archives Division, Indiana Commission on Public Records, Indiana State Library and Historical Building. See also Davis, The Ku Klux Klan in Indiana, pp. 266-269.

[70] Jackson, The Ku Klux Klan in the City, pp. 153-154.

against Catholics, blacks, and Jews was vented in words rather than deeds—in speeches at Klan rallies, in whispers and jokes, and in the pages of the *Fiery Cross* and dozens of Klan pamphlets. There is little evidence of the use of violence in Indiana. Rather, the Klan's most effective weapon was its immense power of intimidation. By giving organized form and expression to traditional religious and racial prejudices it made them more focused and threatening. And the Klan acted on these prejudices just enough to give their threats meaning and force. Anonymous telephone calls, the initials "KKK" soaped on window screens, a burning cross, or a parade of masked marchers through the streets to the town square served as intimidating evidence of the Klan's presence. The Klan's ability to induce such fear and anxiety was exacerbated by the element of secrecy. Because many Hoosiers were never certain who belonged to the Klan and who did not, they feared talking openly with neighbors or even family members about the Klan and the issues it raised. In this atmosphere of uncertainty, wild rumors spread through Hoosier communities: the Klan was going to burn the Catholic church or lynch an individual Catholic or black. Physical violence was almost never used, although in a few instances at least Klan intimidation caused Catholics to flee from their hometowns—a veterinarian in Brookston, a schoolteacher in Delphi, for examples—but in many more instances Klan intimidation caused anxiety and fear that many Hoosiers would remember vividly for the rest of their lives.[71]

The Klan also made use of economic weapons to further its cause. Some merchants were persuaded to join the organization under threat of boycott by Klansmen. The *Fiery Cross* carried advertisements of retail stores from across the state, urging their

[71] William E. Wilson, "Long, Hot Summer in Indiana," *American Heritage*, XVI (August, 1965), 62–63; John Lewis Niblack, *The Life and Times of a Hoosier Judge* (n.p., [1973]), pp. 193–194; Coughlan, "Konklave in Kokomo," in Leighton (ed.), *The Aspirin Age*, pp. 110–114; Josephine Cartwright Ives to William A. Wirt, May 19, 1923, William A. Wirt Papers, Lilly Library, Indiana University, Bloomington; Hartman, Brookston, p. 178; Claude R. Wickard interview by Dean Albertson, 1952–1953, No. 7, pp. 314–325, Claude R. Wickard Papers, Franklin D. Roosevelt Library, Hyde Park, New York.

patronage as 100 percent American businesses. Jewish-owned businesses were sometimes threatened with boycott, and, most intimidatingly, in 1923 the *Fiery Cross* published a list of Roman Catholic businessmen in Indianapolis, all presumably unworthy of Klan patronage.[72]

Klan attacks on Catholics, Jews, and blacks were united with campaigns against those Hoosiers who violated traditional moral standards. The Klan opposed violation of the prohibition laws, prostitution, premarital sex, and adultery. In the changing moral climate of the 1920s the Klan found more than sufficient evidence of sin to justify its mission of upholding traditional religious and patriotic virtues. Klan efforts to encourage morality and law and order sometimes took the form of vigilante activity, stopping cars in search of alcohol, intimidating amorous couples parked along country roads, or raiding gambling houses. Much of this vigilante effort was conducted under the auspices of Horse Thief Detective Association, authorized by a law of 1852 to use voluntary, amateur constables to apprehend horse thieves and other criminals. Revived in the early 1920s, the Horse Thief Detective Association was closely tied to the Klan and often functioned as its law enforcement arm.[73] This sort of vigilante activity was not new to Indiana. Indeed, vigilante violations of established legal procedures were more serious in nineteenth-century Indiana than in the 1920s, especially in terms of the large number of lynchings in the earlier period compared to the absence of such extreme, extralegal actions in the 1920s. Yet the size of the Horse Thief Detective Association, estimated at between fifteen and twenty-

[72] Davis, The Ku Klux Klan in Indiana, pp. 317-323; Feightner interview, February 28, October 24, 1968, pp. 12-13, Indiana Division; Jackson, *The Ku Klux Klan in the City*, p. 148.

[73] Williamsport [Ind.] *Pioneer*, September 7, 1923; Hartman, Brookston, p. 178; Davis, The Ku Klux Klan in Indiana, pp. 119-125. The former head of the South Bend Klan, Hugh Emmons, testified in 1928 that all members of the Horse Thief Detective Association in South Bend were Klansmen. Emmons described the activities of the association, after which the transcript reads: "Q. Did you ever look for horse thieves? A. Why, no—there weren't no horses, that I know of." Testimony of Hugh Emmons, February 20, 1928, *State of Indiana* v. *The Knights of the Ku Klux Klan*, Reel 200.

two thousand members, and its ties to the Klan made for a potentially more disciplined and rigorous vigilante activity than the
more sporadic actions of the late nineteenth century.[74]

The Klan also presented itself as a force for clean government.
In several communities, including Muncie and Gary, the Klan
initially appealed to some residents as a means of combating local
political corruption.[75] Dismay over corruption at the state level
also may have aided the Klan. In particular, Hoosiers were shocked
when Governor McCray was indicted in late 1923 and convicted
in April, 1924, on charges of using the mails to defraud his credi-
tors. Like many other farmers and businessmen, McCray suffered
severe economic losses in the early 1920s. Taking advantage of
his position as governor, McCray borrowed more than one million
dollars from Indiana banks that were depositories of state funds
and used fraudulent collateral to secure the loans. He also borrowed money for his personal use from the state agricultural
board. On April 30, 1924, McCray resigned the governorship and
Lieutenant Governor Emmett F. Branch[76] assumed the office. On
the same day McCray boarded a train for the Atlanta federal
penitentiary, where he served three years and four months of his
ten-year sentence. He was pardoned by President Hoover in 1930.
McCray's conviction seemed to be strong evidence for the need of
the Klan's call for honesty in government and may have served
to switch the loyalties of some disenchanted Hoosiers from the
established party system to the Klan. The McCray scandal also
made Republicans especially fearful for their party's success in
the coming 1924 elections and may have thus added to the party's
propensity to ally with the Klan in order to avoid defeat by Democrats shouting charges of corruption.[77]

[74] Phillips, *Indiana in Transition,* pp. 371-378; Davis, The Ku Klux Klan in
Indiana, p. 124. See above, Chapter I, for a discussion of the Marion lynchings of
1930.

[75] Betten and Lane, "Nativism and the Klan," *Studies in History and Society,*
IV, 7; Lynd and Lynd, *Middletown,* pp. 481-482.

[76] Branch, a Martinsville lawyer and businessman, was known, at least among
politicians, to have a weakness for alcohol. See James P. Goodrich to Will Hays,
May [?], 1924, Hays Papers.

[77] Niblack, *The Life and Times of a Hoosier Judge,* pp. 163-186; Indianapolis
News, October 2, November 30, 1923, April 29, 30, 1924; New York *Times,* April

In its support of clean government and traditional morality and in its self-professed embodiment of 100 percent Americanism, patriotism, and Protestant religion, the Klan struck at themes basic to the beliefs and concerns of most Hoosiers. Klan emphasis on one or another specific aspect of these many themes varied from place to place, as did the degree to which the Klan publicly appealed to the baser emotions of prejudice and hate. Sensitive to their actual and potential membership, Klan leaders were careful, as the head of the South Bend Klan later noted, to "sell them the thing they want."[78]

This flexibility of specific appeals, yet firm attachment to traditional religion and patriotism, helped account for the small and often ineffective opposition to the Klan, especially in the years prior to 1925. Much of the initial opposition came from groups identified by the Klan as its enemies. None was well organized or prepared to combat this growing organization effectively. Roman Catholics were perhaps most energetic. The *Indiana Catholic and Record*, published in Indianapolis, was a vigorous critic of the Klan and of political leaders who failed to condemn the organization. The newspaper gave wide publicity to the Catholic Information Bureau, which was established in Indianapolis in the summer of 1924 to counter Klan propaganda for the fall elections.[79] Opposition also came from the American Unity League, which had its main office in Chicago and was led by Catholic clergymen. The Unity League was very active in Indiana in 1922 and 1923, sponsoring local chapters and distributing its weekly newspaper, *Tolerance*, which published refutations of Klan propaganda and lists of Klan members. In May, 1923, for example,

30, May 1, June 7, 1924, August 31, 1927; Meredith Nicholson to J. O'H. Cosgrave, September 4, 1923, and Gertrude F. McHugh to Ralston, September 26, 1923, Ralston Papers. There is considerable irony in the fact that soon after his release from prison McCray testified as a prosecution witness at the trial of Governor Ed Jackson. Jackson was accused of attempting to bribe McCray with Klan money late in 1923. See below, this chapter.

[78] Testimony of Hugh Emmons, February 20, 1928, *State of Indiana v. The Knights of the Ku Klux Klan*, Reel 200.

[79] See, for example, *Indiana Catholic and Record*, November 3, 1922, October 3, 17, 1924.

Tolerance listed the names of more than twelve thousand alleged Klansmen living in Indianapolis.[80]

Black and Jewish opposition to the Klan also developed in the early 1920s in the form of reports and editorials in the *Indiana Jewish Chronicle*, an independent Jewish newspaper in Indianapolis, and the Indianapolis *Freeman*, one of the state's leading black newspapers. Both publications encouraged their readers to vote against Klan-supported political candidates. The National Association for the Advancement of Colored People made similar appeals in Indianapolis.[81]

The state's general press was much less forceful in its opposition to the Klan, especially in the early years when most newspapers either ignored the organization or gave it generally favorable coverage. The Indianapolis *News* at first condemned the Klan, editorializing in early 1922 that it was composed of "adult boys in grotesque masks who seek to exploit a primitive fear of ghosts."[82] But *News* editorials in 1923 and 1924 showed much less hostility.[83] The South Bend *Tribune*, Vincennes *Sun-Times*, Indianapolis *Times*, and Muncie *Post-Democrat* were notable for their criticism of the organization. Editor George Dale of the Muncie paper engaged in a vitriolic attack on the Klan, leading to his conviction for contempt of court by Delaware County Circuit Court Judge Clarence W. Dearth, a Klan sympathizer.[84] Only after the Klan began its decline in 1925 did many other newspapers begin to comment negatively on the organization.[85]

[80] Jackson, *The Ku Klux Klan in the City*, pp. 102-104, 148; Davis, The Ku Klux Klan in Indiana, pp. 51-55; Nevel, Fiery Crosses and Tempers, p. 60. The list of Klan members was stolen from the organization's Indianapolis headquarters on April 1.

[81] Davis, The Ku Klux Klan in Indiana, pp. 181, 198-199; New York *Times*, May 13, 1924.

[82] Indianapolis *News*, April 26, 1922. See also Scharlott, The Hoosier Newsman and the Hooded Order, pp. 51-57.

[83] See, for example, Indianapolis *News*, July 6, 1923.

[84] Scharlott, The Hoosier Newsman and the Hooded Order, pp. 64-67, 72-75; Nevel, Fiery Crosses and Tempers, pp. 61-63; Carrolyle M. Frank, Politics in Middletown: A Reconsideration of Municipal Government and Community Power in Muncie, Indiana, 1925-35 (Ph.D. dissertation, Ball State University, Muncie, Ind., 1974), pp. 54-55.

[85] Scharlott, The Hoosier Newsman and the Hooded Order, pp. 57-60;

Even then there was no rush to condemn. As Meredith Nicholson lamented in 1926: "Our newspapers have been markedly timid about denouncing it. There's a fear upon the state."[86]

The Klan proved to be an especially difficult issue for many Protestant churches, often bitterly dividing congregations and denominational leaders. Some ministers took courageous stands in opposition, sometimes in the face of harsh criticism from their congregations. In Indianapolis the Reverend Frank E. Davison of Englewood Christian Church and the Reverend Clay Trusty, Sr., of the Seventh Christian Church were forced to resign by their congregations, which were generally sympathetic to the Klan. (Trusty was replaced by Gerald L. K. Smith, later a nationally prominent anti-Semitic propagandist.) Many ministers tolerated and some encouraged the Klan by participation in Klan affairs because of the organization's appeals to Protestant religion and morality. Klan leaders were very sensitive to the benefits of church co-operation, and they actively sought this support through financial donations as well as persuasion. A common tactic was for a group of Klansmen to appear in the middle of a worship service and march in full regalia to the front of the church to present the minister with a cash donation, occasionally to the accompaniment of cheers from the congregation. Above the local level, few of the major Protestant denominational organizations went on record in opposition to the Klan. The Indianapolis Diocese of the Protestant Episcopal Church adopted a resolution of strong condemnation, and the Christian Ministers Association of Indianapolis publicly stated its opposition to Klan interference in church matters, but the denominational meetings of Baptists, Methodists, and Disciples of Christ generally ignored the issues raised by the Ku Klux Klan.[87]

George E. Stevens, "Winning the Pulitzer Prize: The Indianapolis *Times* Battles Political Corruption, 1926-27," *Journalism History*, II (Autumn, 1975), 80-83.

[86] Nicholson to Claude G. Bowers, March 9, 1926, Claude G. Bowers Papers, II, Lilly Library, Indiana University, Bloomington. There are three separate collections of Bowers Papers at Lilly Library.

[87] Davis, The Ku Klux Klan in Indiana, pp. 278-307; Jackson, *The Ku Klux Klan in the City*, p. 150; Indianapolis *News*, May 12, 1924; Frank Elon Davison, *Thru the Rear-view Mirror* (St. Louis, 1955), pp. 75-78; *Indiana Catholic and*

Other groups and organizations also divided over the question of the Klan and in some cases took stands in opposition. In 1923 the Indianapolis Central Labor Union passed by a narrow margin a resolution condemning the Klan as "un-American and unconstitutional," but at least three local unions withdrew from the body to protest consideration of an issue not directly related to labor.[88] The American Legion also divided over the Klan, although it shared much of the Klan's patriotic fervor. Some Hoosier Legion leaders publicly repudiated the Klan's racial and religious prejudices, but a resolution of condemnation presented at the state convention in 1924 did not pass. Indiana fraternal organizations also provided some opposition: not only the Knights of Columbus and Ancient Order of Hibernians, but also some local Masonic, Kiwanis, and Elks groups condemned the Klan.[89] And in the summer of 1923 the Indiana Bar Association vigorously condemned any organization "which would substitute for the open and orderly proceedings of the courts the decrees of secret tribunals the members of which conceal their identity behind robes and masks."[90]

An example of the most direct form of opposition to the Klan came in South Bend, where in mid-May, 1924, several thousand Klansmen gathered for a picnic and parade. Robed Klansmen in the city's streets were soon joined by University of Notre Dame students and others. Several verbal and physical altercations resulted. The Klan retreated from the downtown and, dampened also by spring rain, eventually canceled the scheduled parade. The violence of the South Bend "riot" was minimal, and it proved

Record, June 15, 1923; Henry K. Shaw, Hoosier Disciples: A Comprehensive History of the Christian Churches (Disciples of Christ) in Indiana (St. Louis, 1966), p. 332; John F. Cady, The Origin and Development of the Missionary Baptist Church in Indiana (Berne, Ind., 1942), pp. 295, 305-306.

[88] Indianapolis News, August 8, 1923; Indiana Catholic and Record, August 10, 1923.

[89] Clutter, The Indiana American Legion, pp. 83-93; Davis, The Ku Klux Klan in Indiana, pp. 56-61.

[90] Indianapolis News, July 6, 1923. See also Lex J. Kirkpatrick, Address to the Bar Association of the Ninth Congressional District at Annual Meeting, June 30, 1923 (Frankfort, Ind., n.d.).

to be one of the few examples of this kind of direct opposition
to the Klan.[91]

§ § § § § §

The Ku Klux Klan raised intense moral and cultural issues that
attracted many Hoosiers but also divided them, sometimes bitterly. It proved a troublesome problem for many social and religious organizations. And, ultimately, the Klan became, above all
else, a political issue: one that disturbed and disrupted Hoosier
politics in a way no other question did during the 1920s. By 1924
politics was the dominant activity of the Indiana Klan, and the
Klan was the dominant issue in politics. As one Republican
lamented: "Times have changed in Indiana. Ideas of race and
religion now dominate political thought. Agencies and influences
that were once powerful now are without influence . . . ."[92]

The politicization of the Klan was due in considerable part to
its leadership, particularly to D. C. Stephenson. A shrewd and
immensely capable leader, Stephenson had power in the Klan and
in Indiana politics that by 1924 was probably unmatched.[93] Born in
Texas in 1891, he served in the World War and in 1920 settled in
Evansville, where he operated a retail coal business and ran for
political office as a Democrat opposing prohibition. By 1921 he
had switched to dry and Republican politics and had begun his
association with the Klan, first in Evansville and then in organizing
Klaverns throughout Indiana and Ohio. He was a superb orator

[91] Nevel, Fiery Crosses and Tempers, pp. 68-74, 89. Opposition to the Klan
in South Bend was generally stronger than elsewhere, coming from a chapter of
the American Unity League, leaders of the local American Legion and Masons,
and the South Bend *Tribune*. The large Roman Catholic population and presence
of the University of Notre Dame doubtless accounted for some of this opposition.
Ibid., pp. 60-61.

[92] Bert Morgan to Will Hays, May 29, 1924, Hays Papers.

[93] As powerful as D. C. Stephenson was there was a tendency for commentators to exaggerate that power and to see the Klan solely as reflected in Stephenson. See, for example, Morton Harrison, "Gentlemen from Indiana," *Atlantic
Monthly*, CXLI (1928), 676-686; Merritt Dixon, "Klan and Anti-Klan in Indiana,"
Outlook, December 8, 1926, pp. 465-469. For an example of a scholarly account
that ascribes more power to Stephenson than seems warranted see David M.
Chalmers, *Hooded Americanism: The First Century of the Ku Klux Klan, 1865-
1965* (New York, 1965), p. 163.

who gloried in public attention, yet he also could exude charm and intelligence in conversation, always carefully learning first names and insisting on being called "Steve" or, while still in his thirties, "the Old Man." In 1923, at the Klan's July Fourth rally in Kokomo, Stephenson became Grand Dragon of the Indiana Realm, a reflection of his popular standing in Indiana and his leadership abilities as perceived by the Klan's national officers.[94]

Operating from an eight-room suite of offices in Indianapolis, Grand Dragon Stephenson built his political organization, often referred to as the "military machine." Selected Klan members in each community were responsible for screening candidates for office, recommending slates of approved candidates, circulating the slates, and getting out the vote on election day. Functioning much like political machines elsewhere, the "military machine" was co-ordinated and controlled from Indianapolis by Stephenson. The Klan slates and information sheets were crucial to its operation. Sometimes simply a list of approved candidates, they later consisted of descriptive information on each candidate.[95] The Klan information sheet for the 1926 primary election described two of the candidates for the United States Senate thusly:[96]

Republican: James E. Watson, Rushville. Age, 61 years. Has served in Congress and in the United States Senate. Has otherwise been actively and definitely associated in State, National, civic and political life for a number of years. His record and capabilities as a public official is [sic] easily ascertainable on account of his years of public service and conduct. He and his family are Protestant. He is a 32° Mason, also a member of other fraternal organizations. He has at all times assisted and otherwise manifested a willingness and readiness to

[94] Weaver, The Knights of the Ku Klux Klan, pp. 147-150.

[95] Ibid., pp. 201-218; Davis, The Ku Klux Klan in Indiana, pp. 125-130; Deposition of D. C. Stephenson, October 15, 1928, State of Indiana v. The Knights of the Ku Klux Klan, Reel 199, pp. 97-98. The Klan leader in South Bend testified that Klansmen often distributed slates by inserting them in Sunday School papers. "We had a wonderful machine in 1924," he noted. Testimony of Hugh Emmons, February 20, 1928, ibid., Reel 200. The New York Times later reported that Stephenson "had a machine which made [New York's] Tammany seem amateurish," doubtless an overstatement. New York Times, October 2, 1927.

[96] Quoted in U. S. Senate, Senatorial Campaign Expenditures, Hearings before a Special Committee Investigating Expenditures in Primary and General Elections, Part 3 (69th Congress, 1st Session, 1926), pp. 2033-2034.

assist in all Americanization measures. He is dry. His services have been entirely satisfactory. He is favorable.

Democrat: William A. Cullop, Vincennes. Age, about 70 years. He has been a practicing attorney in Vincennes for a number of years. Has enjoyed a fair practice and bears a fair reputation. Has been in political life for a number of years. He was elected to Congress for one term and made a fair record. He and his family are Protestant but do not take a very active interest in church work. He does not belong to any fraternal organization. His political affiliations have been in the main Catholic; his personal friends and associates are such. He is considered fairly capable. He is wet. He is liberal in his views. He is unfavorable.

The key information was the candidate's religion, stand on prohibition, and, above all, his approval or disapproval of the Klan. The closing notation was always "favorable," "neutral," or "unfavorable" and referred to the candidate's attitude toward the Klan. Political party identification counted much less than these considerations, as the Klan supported both Democrats and Republicans in primary and general elections, although the latter more so than the former.

By raising the issues it did and crossing back and forth over party lines, the Klan became a deeply troubling force in Indiana politics. There were signs of Klan activity in the 1922 campaign, especially in Klan support of Ralston over Beveridge in the Senate election and in the opposition to Eleventh District Republican Congressman Milton Kraus, a Jew.[97] But the real turbulence began in 1924, with the spring primary and state party conventions. The Republican primary set the tone. The campaigning began as early as the fall of 1923, when popular Indianapolis Mayor Lew Shank announced his candidacy for the gubernatorial nomination. Among the handful of local officials who had spoken publicly against the Klan, Shank was perhaps its most vigorous opponent.[98] He and his police chief, Herman Rickhoff,

[97] Indianapolis *News*, November 1, 1922; *Indiana Catholic and Record*, November 3, 1922. Neither Beveridge nor Ralston spoke out on the Klan in the 1922 campaign. Braeman, *Beveridge*, pp. 287-288. Kraus was defeated in his bid for re-election by Samuel E. Cook.

[98] In addition to Lew Shank, his predecessor, Charles Jewett, Gary Mayor R. O. Johnson, Terre Haute Mayor Ora Davis, Lafayette Mayor George R. Durgan, and Evansville Mayor Benjamin Bosse had spoken out against Klan

had prohibited burning crosses in the city limits and had denied
parade permits to masked marchers, which earned them the
enmity of the Klan.[99] Five other candidates eventually entered the
Republican gubernatorial race, but the struggle was between
Shank and Ed Jackson, who had very enthusiastic and effective
support from Stephenson's organization. Jackson, a lawyer and
politician from Henry County and a veteran of the World War,
had been elected secretary of state in 1920 and 1922. With the
Klan military machine finely tuned, Stephenson sent out more
than 225,000 letters urging Jackson's nomination, while Klansmen distributed slates and literature and held rallies. To Stephenson, the effort to nominate Jackson was a test of his organization's
strength. Other observers agreed: Jackson was everywhere identified as the Klan candidate, and it was "an out-and-out Klan and
anti-Klan fight."[100]

There was no doubt as to the victor in the May primary. Ed
Jackson polled 227,785 votes, carrying all but three of the state's
ninety-two counties, compared to 95,494 votes for Shank, who
carried only Bartholomew County. The other four candidates
split a total of 89,943 votes. While some Hoosiers doubtless voted
for Jackson in spite of his Klan support, the primary was widely
interpreted as a landslide victory for the Klan. The Republican
primary demonstrated Klan strength at the local level also, notably in the Seventh District, where the Marion County Klan
pushed Ralph Updike to an upset victory over five-term Congressman Merrill Moores.[101]

The Republican state convention met in late May, 1924, and
certified Klan influence in the party. Indianapolis *News* general

activities prior to 1925. Davis, The Ku Klux Klan in Indiana, pp. 28, 30, 179;
Lane, "*City of the Century*," p. 94; *Indiana Catholic and Record*, November 2,
1923.

[99] Indianapolis *News*, August 8, 1923; New York *Times*, June 27, November
7, 1923; Indianapolis *Fiery Cross*, July 6, 1923.

[100] Indianapolis *News*, May 6, 1924. See also *ibid.*, April 15,1924; Carl S. Wise
to Will Hays, July 20, 1923, Hays Papers.

[101] Indiana *Year Book*, 1924, pp. 15-16; Indianapolis *News*, May 6, 8, 9, 1924;
New York *Times*, May 7, 1924.

manager Hilton U. Brown noted privately that the convention was "acting as if under restraint, and certainly operating by unseen wires. There was not much of a whoop-em-up spirit . . . ."[102] Stephenson and his lieutenants and bodyguards worked the floor of the Tomlinson Hall meeting, successfully urging the delegates to nominate, among others, F. Harold Van Orman for lieutenant governor and Bernhardt H. Urbahns for state treasurer. Stephenson failed to get all he wanted, however, as the delegates chose Arthur L. Gilliom for attorney general despite strong Klan opposition.[103]

Though Stephenson's presence and power were apparent to all, in fact he shared his influence in the Republican convention and in the party with Senator James Watson. In 1924 the two men—each beset with factional political squabbles—apparently entered into a limited marriage of convenience. Stephenson broke with the national Klan organization and resigned his office as Grand Dragon in late 1923. He was eventually succeeded by Walter Bossert, of Liberty, Indiana, who had the support of the national Klan. Stephenson, nonetheless, remained the most visible and powerful Klan leader in Indiana, as he and Bossert constantly challenged each other in a bitter internal struggle. The Republican party was also split by factions. The dominant group in 1924 was Watson's, but the old Goodrich-New group continued to challenge them, though its power had declined after New's defeat in 1922 and especially after the death of New's political friend, President Harding, in 1923. The Goodrich-New faction endeavored to keep the party free of Klan influence, but by 1924 neither of the Republican factions felt they could afford to alienate the Klan. The Goodrich-New faction formed an alliance with the

---

[102] Brown to Warren Fairbanks, May 22, 1924, Fairbanks Papers. Stephenson claimed that 811 of the approximately 1,300 delegates were loyal to him. Stephenson to Roy V. West, August 9, 1924, David C. Stephenson Collection, Indiana Historical Society Library, Indianapolis.

[103] Davis, The Ku Klux Klan in Indiana, p. 187; Feightner interview, February 28, October 24, 1968, p. 97, Indiana Division; Indianapolis *Star*, May 23, 1924. It was Attorney General Arthur L. Gilliom who conducted the state's investigation of the Klan in 1928.

Bossert Klan group, while the more powerful Watson-Stephenson alliance dominated the party in 1924.[104]

The Democratic party also was deeply troubled by the Klan issue in 1924 but ultimately took a stand in opposition to the Klan. As in the Republican party, Democratic attention focused on the gubernatorial primary, where eight candidates entered the campaign. Mayor George R. Durgan of Lafayette played the role in his party that Shank played in the Republican party, strongly denouncing the Klan. The Klan's candidate was Olin R. Holt of Kokomo, although it did not campaign as strongly for him as for Jackson. None of the eight candidates obtained a majority of the primary votes, so that the decision had to be made at the party convention. In the primary, anti-Klan candidate Durgan ran second and Klan-slated Holt fifth. The front-runner was Carleton B. McCulloch, who received 33 percent of the total vote. McCulloch was an Indianapolis physician who had been the party's gubernatorial candidate in 1920 and who had not taken a public stand on the Klan issue in the 1924 primary. But McCulloch changed his strategy after the primary. In response to the Jackson-Klan victory in the Republican party and in an effort to undercut Durgan, his leading Democratic rival, McCulloch in mid-May took a position opposing the Klan. The issue was now squarely before the Democratic convention, scheduled to meet in early June. Seldom had Hoosier Democrats been in such turmoil.[105]

Tied to Washington by senatorial obligations, Democratic party leader Samuel Ralston sent out dozens of letters in early and mid-May asking party leaders over the state for reports on political conditions. The responses all focused on one issue, the Klan, but varied considerably in their assessment of the party's proper strategy, particularly in regard to the choice of a gubernatorial

[104] Indianapolis *Star*, May 12, 15, 24, 1924; Hilton U. Brown to Warren Fairbanks, May 22, 1924, Fairbanks Papers; Davis, The Ku Klux Klan in Indiana, pp. 76-87, 177, 185; U.S. Senate, *Senatorial Campaign Expenditures*, p. 2134. Grand Dragon Walter Bossert had supported Edward Toner of Anderson, rather than Jackson, in the gubernatorial primary. Indianapolis *Star*, May 8, 1924.

[105] Indiana *Year Book*, 1924, pp. 17-18; Indianapolis *Star*, May 10, 12, 1924; Indianapolis *News*, May 8, 13, 1924; Thomas Duncan to Ralston, May 20, 1924, Ralston Papers.

candidate and in the wisdom of a platform plank that specifically condemned the Klan.

Some of Ralston's correspondents believed that the party's best course was to ignore the issue, that to do otherwise would alienate party supporters. One Democrat informed Ralston that the Klan "is in control of a very large majority of the Democratic organizations throughout the State and you know from the history of 'Know Nothingism' and the 'A.P.A.' movement, that it will fizzle out in a very short time . . . ."[106] Another writer asserted: "I am not a Catholic nor Kluxer, and why should I be drawn into their fight. The whole thing is a Bogy . . . and there is no political question involved." Moreover, he added, an anti-Klan stand will "drive shoals of Democrats away from us . . . and where will we get the votes to take their places?"[107] Several Democrats suggested that the effort to have the party take a stand on the Klan was a trap set by the Republicans to lure Democrats' attention away from the real issues of high taxes and Republican scandals in the statehouse and White House.[108]

But other Democratic leaders advised Ralston of the need to take a stand against the Klan, though few wished to mount a vigorous crusade. A Lafayette correspondent regretted the issue had been brought forward, but he concluded "that there is no escaping it and . . . sooner or later the citizens of Indiana must toe the mark and fight the question out to its last analysis." He warned that if the party does not "squarely go on record against the domination of the Klan . . . we shall lose the coming election."[109] A Boonville Democrat also advised an anti-Klan strategy as the best route to victory over Jackson: it would attract Catholic and

[106] William A. Pickens to Ralston, May 19, 1924, Ralston Papers. The Know Nothing party was a nativist and anti-Catholic movement in the 1850s. The American Protective Association was a similar movement during the late nineteenth century. Other Democrats also referred to these earlier examples, suggesting part of the 1856 Democratic platform as a guide. See, for example, Thomas Taggart to Ralston, April 7, 1924, Ralston Papers.

[107] John T. Barnett to Ralston, May 26, 1924, Ralston Papers.

[108] Ibid.; Leroy Sanders to Ralston, May 24, 1924, and L. G. Ellingham to Ralston, May 20, 1924, ibid.

[109] Dan W. Simms to Ralston, May 22, 1924, ibid.

black votes, "a large percent of the protestant vote who are at heart against the principles of the klan," and "the vote that is always against a radical proposition like the klan."[110]

The contradictory advice Ralston received from the Democratic grass roots did not alter his own mind. As in the 1922 campaign, when he had refused to grant prohibition the status of an issue, so now too Ralston believed that the Klan should not be a political issue. He worked hard in May to convince others. He lamented McCulloch's decision to stand against the Klan, but he especially tried to stop those Democrats who were pushing the party convention in a similar direction. When he learned that his Indianapolis law partner, Frederick Van Nuys, was preparing a strong anti-Klan keynote speech for the state convention, Ralston warned him that he would "magnify the controversy that is now on in our party . . . ."[111] And he cautioned Van Nuys and others of the dangers of "going to extremes in our platform declaration on any subject," but especially the Klan, which he urged should not be mentioned in the platform. Rather, he felt Democrats must focus on Republican failures.[112]

Only one other man stood as high in the Democratic party in Indiana as Ralston, and that was Thomas Taggart, an Irish immigrant (not Catholic, but Episcopalian), who entered politics in the 1880s, served three terms as mayor of Indianapolis, and functioned as the acknowledged leader of the party in Indiana for the first two and a half decades of the twentieth century. Immensely popular, Taggart was charming and always hospitable, not only as manager of his popular French Lick Springs Hotel but also in the heat of political strife. Like most skillful politicians who survived for decades, Taggart was usually eager to make the compromises necessary to ensure Democratic victory. Although Taggart and Ralston were longtime and close political and personal friends, in 1924 Taggart's position was at odds with Ralston's.[113] Ralston assumed,

[110] W. B. Carleton to Ralston, May 19, 1924, *ibid*.

[111] Ralston to Frederick Van Nuys, May 21, 1924, *ibid*. See also William A. Pickens to Ralston, May 19, 1924, and Ralston to Pickens, May 21, 1924, *ibid*.

[112] Ralston to Van Nuys, May 21, 1924, and Ralston to Pickens, May 21, 1924, *ibid*.

[113] Meredith Nicholson to author and editor Norman Hapgood, September [?], 1923, *ibid*.

probably correctly, that Taggart had advised McCulloch to take an anti-Klan position after the May primary. And Taggart appears to have felt more keenly than Ralston the pressure from other Democrats for an anti-Klan plank in the party platform. Though Ralston urged him to resist, pleading that "conservative and level headed men may be chosen as members of the Resolution Committee," by late May Taggart was supporting a moderate anti-Klan plank.[114]

The issue was fought out first in the Democratic State Committee, which, the state vice-chairman wrote, was "torn between the desire to protect our Catholic friends and to treat fairly the Democratic Klan vote."[115] A delegation of Catholic Democrats presented the committee with a so-called radical plank, specifically naming and strongly criticizing the Klan. Support for such a strong anti-Klan plank came from Democratic leaders in the state's three northernmost congressional districts (the twelfth, thirteenth, and tenth) and in the southwestern district (first). A majority of the state committee opposed any extreme position, however. Bitter division persisted, so much, lamented one Democrat, that "party lines and party affiliations are being lost sight of. . . ."[116]

Yet by the time the Democratic state convention met in early June, under Taggart's influence the party leadership had effected an acceptable compromise. Although many Klan delegates were in attendance and Klan slates circulated at the convention, party leaders united strongly behind McCulloch and a ticket distributed geographically across the state. Most important, they led the convention to adopt a compromise anti-Klan plank without a floor fight.[117] Nowhere did the platform mention the Klan, intending

[114] Taggart to Ralston, April 7, 1924, Ralston to Pickens, May 15, 1924, Ralston to Taggart, May 20, 1924, and Leroy Sanders to Ralston, May 24, 1924, all *ibid*.

[115] Mrs. Adelbert P. Flynn to Ralston, May 16, 1924, *ibid*.

[116] Charles A. Greathouse to Ralston, May 22, 1924, *ibid*. See also Flynn to Ralston, May 16, 1924, *ibid*.; Indianapolis *Star*, May 23, 1924.

[117] Indianapolis *News*, June 2, 5, 6, 1924; Indianapolis *Star*, June 4, 1924. In mid-May Van Nuys estimated that 400 of the 1,293 delegates and 40 of the 92 county chairmen at the Democratic state convention would be Klansmen. Van Nuys to Ralston, May 17, 1924, Ralston Papers. Later the New York *Times* estimated the number of Klan delegates at 240. New York *Times*, October 16, 1924.

thereby not to alienate committed Klan Democrats. Yet the meaning was unmistakable for those who wished to see it: "No organization has the right to set itself above the law and the courts." "We
condemn the efforts of our opponents to make religion, race, color
or accidental place of birth a political issue . . . ." And, the platform
charged, "the Republican party of our state has, for the time
being, retired from the political arena, having been delivered into
the hands of an organization which has no place in politics and
which promulgates doctrines . . . repugnant to the principles of
government advocated by Lincoln and Morton."[118]

The issue was thus squarely drawn for the November elections,
yet each party worked to keep the Klan question from offending
its traditional supporters. Indeed, both gubernatorial candidates
emphasized other issues. Jackson promised efficiency and economy and identified himself with Republican prosperity and stability, while McCulloch attacked Republicans for high taxes and
large state government. Despite his party's anti-Klan plank,
McCulloch did not mention the Klan in the fall campaign—an
obvious effort to hold Klan Democrats to the party. And Republican candidate Jackson carefully promised full civil and religious
liberty for Jews, Catholics, and blacks. Republicans made a special
effort to hold black voters (who since the Civil War had traditionally voted Republican), charging that the Democratic party
was racist, as evidenced by its support of Jim Crow segregation
in the South.[119] And some Republicans feared that quiet anti-Klan
sentiment among middle- and upper-class urban voters would
hurt the ticket. One party worker reported in late October that
"polls taken in every city of the state indicate a loss to Jackson
among the better class of people . . . due to the anti-Klan movement. . . ."[120]

Each party was also aware of the Klan's potentially beneficial

[118] Democratic state platform, 1924, in Indiana State Platforms, I.

[119] Weaver, The Knights of the Ku Klux Klan, p. 162; Washington [Ind.]
Democrat, November 1, 1924; Indianapolis News, October 24, 29, 1924; Indianapolis Star, November 2, 1924.

[120] Robert G. Tucker to Will Hays, October 24, 1924, Hays Papers. See also
Bert Morgan to Hays, October 24, 1924, ibid.

disruption of Hoosier voters. Democrats were confident of the support of Catholic voters. With the exception of the earlier opposition of German-American Catholics to President Woodrow Wilson's foreign policy, Catholics had generally supported the party before the Klan came to prominence and were working hard for McCulloch in 1924. Democrats made an effort to attract traditionally Republican black voters by equating the Republican party with the Klan. The Democrats received help from the National Association for the Advancement of Colored People, which urged blacks to vote against Jackson and sponsored a large rally for Indianapolis blacks. The Indianapolis black newspaper, the *Freeman*, also urged blacks to abandon the party of Lincoln. Jewish voters received similar advice from the normally nonpartisan *Indiana Jewish Chronicle*.[121] Republicans, of course, hoped to benefit from the votes of white Protestant Democrats who would follow Stephenson and the Klan to the Republican column on the ballot. One Republican reported that in Indianapolis "when you go into the factories and mills they are all for him [Jackson]. I was out in West Indianapolis recently, the Democratic stronghold, and it looked as though there was a Jackson picture in nearly every window."[122]

The outcome was decisive. Jackson defeated McCulloch by a vote of 654,784 to 572,303, carrying sixty of the ninety-two counties. He was particularly popular in the large urban counties and carried five of the six counties that had more than thirty thousand total votes: Lake, Marion, Vanderburgh, Vigo, and St. Joseph. McCulloch's strength was in the smaller rural counties: the only large urban county he won was Allen.[123]

121 New York *Times*, May 13, October 16, 1924; *Indiana Catholic and Record*, October 3, 17, 1924; Davis, The Ku Klux Klan in Indiana, pp. 181, 196-199; Ralston to Burt New, October 25, 1924, Ralston Papers; John K. Jennings to Carleton B. McCulloch, August 20, 23, 1924, John K. Jennings Papers, Lilly Library, Indiana University, Bloomington; Thornbrough, "Segregation in Indiana during the Klan Era of the 1920's," *Mississippi Valley Historical Review*, XLVII, 611-615. Indianapolis black wards, normally Republican, voted Democratic in 1924.

122 Bert Morgan to Will Hays, October 24, 1924, Hays Papers. See also Tucker to Hays, October 24, 1924, *ibid.*

123 Indiana *Year Book*, 1924, pp. 50-51.

Stephenson and the Klan claimed credit for Jackson's victory. Yet the election was far from a landslide success for the Klan, and Jackson's victory may have resulted more from general Republican strength in the 1920s than from the appeal of the Klan. In fact, though Jackson was clearly the most prominent Klan-supported candidate, he did not lead the Republican state ticket. That honor went to Republican secretary of state candidate Frederick E. Shortemeier, who polled 681,948 votes to his opponent's 527,695. Jackson also lagged far behind Republican presidential candidate Calvin Coolidge, who polled 703,042 votes in Indiana, even though 31,800 more votes were cast in the gubernatorial than in the presidential race. National Republican leaders had decided to protect Coolidge from possible negative effects of the Klan and ran his Indiana campaign separate from the state campaign. In addition, Hoosier voters elected at least three candidates who were strongly opposed by the Klan: Attorney General Arthur L. Gilliom, Supreme Court Judge Benjamin F. Willoughby, and Auditor Lewis S. Bowman.[124] It would appear then that Klan success with Hoosier voters was limited. Voters had neither repudiated nor endorsed the Order.

Yet Indiana now had a governor tied to the Ku Klux Klan. Jackson was inaugurated in January, 1925. At the reception following the ceremony D. C. Stephenson stood next to Jackson, greeting well-wishers and symbolizing his presumed influence with the governor.[125] Doubtless they believed it was the beginning of a glorious reign for the Klan and Republicans. The legislature that assembled that January was overwhelmingly Republican. While the number of Klan legislators is not known, it was generally assumed that the majority were either Klansmen or very sympathetic to the organization and that the legislature would do the Klan's bidding.[126] "This legislature," one Republican la-

---

[124] Ibid., pp. 52-55; Davis, The Ku Klux Klan in Indiana, pp. 200-201; New York Times, October 19, 1924.

[125] Feightner interview, February 28, October 24, 1968, pp. 34-35, Indiana Division; Niblack, The Life and Times of a Hoosier Judge, p. 200.

[126] Weaver, The Knights of the Ku Klux Klan, pp. 163-165; Feightner interview, February 28, October 24, 1968, p. 23, Indiana Division.

mented, "will not be responsive to party advice or control."[127]

The Klan focused its 1925 legislative program on proposals for Americanization and education, most of which were directed against parochial schools or against alleged Roman Catholic influence in the public schools. Among several measures sponsored by the Klan were bills to make mandatory in public schools the daily reading of the King James version of the Bible; to establish a state textbook commission to insure uniform selection of books, both for public and parochial schools; to require that only graduates of public schools could qualify for a teacher's license; and to prevent the wearing of "religious garb" in public schools. In votes that seldom followed party lines each of these measures was defeated. The religious garb bill generated the most controversy. Directed against Catholic nuns who taught in public schools, particularly in rural areas and small towns in southern Indiana, the bill passed the house by a large majority (sixty-six to twenty-two) but was narrowly defeated in the senate. Opponents argued that the issue properly rested with the local communities, not the state. This argument was used against many of the other Klan-backed bills, sometimes along with a defense of individual freedom or of separation of church and state.[128]

The fears some Hoosiers had of the presumably Klan-dominated legislature of 1925 were not realized: the Klan's effort ended in nearly total failure.[129] At the session's close the *Indiana*

---

[127] Morgan to Hays, May 29, 1924, Hays Papers. Morgan reported that he and Goodrich feared that the "Ku Klux legislature" would enact legislation harmful to big business, especially "a reckless change in our tax laws [that] might mean . . . increased taxes to such institutions as the Standard Oil, the steel corporations, the railroads and other large interests." No evidence of such efforts has been found for the 1925 legislature, but the investigation by Thomas H. Adams, Republican editor of the Vincennes *Sun-Times*, in 1926 accused Stephenson of attempted misuse of government power against business. New York *Times*, December 11, 1926.

[128] Indianapolis *News*, January 21, 23, February 5, 17, 26, March 9, 1925; Weaver, The Knights of the Ku Klux Klan, pp. 165-166.

[129] Stephenson later claimed Klan credit for passage of the bone-dry law, but it is likely that the Indiana Anti-Saloon League was just as important a factor and probably more so in the success of this measure. See Deposition of Stephenson, October 15, 1928, *State of Indiana* v. *The Knights of the Ku Klux Klan*, Reel 199, p. 73.

Catholic and Record noted thankfully that "the honor of Indiana, as a home of religious liberty has been redeemed by the Legislature of 1925."[130] Attachment to religious liberty doubtless influenced many legislative opponents of the Klan's Americanization-education measures, but the Klan's failure also came from the continuation of its own internal struggles. Klan lobbyists combed the halls but often worked at cross-purposes, with one faction loyal to Stephenson and his independent Indiana Klan, the other to Grand Dragon Bossert and the national organization. In their struggle to dominate the legislature each faction appears to have canceled much of the power of the other.[131]

Doubtless many Klansmen left the 1925 General Assembly confident that this was but the first faltering step toward enacting a Klan program. In fact, it was the last hurrah for major statewide Klan influence. Less than three months after the legislature adjourned, D. C. Stephenson was in jail.

Stephenson was not an ascetic leader. "The Old Man" enjoyed not only power but also a mansion in Irvington, a yacht, good gin, and the companionship of women. One of these women was Madge Oberholtzer, an attractive, twenty-eight-year-old employee of state government. Oberholtzer testified that Stephenson forced her to board a northbound train on the evening of March 15, 1925, and then assaulted and raped her in a sleeping car. The distraught Oberholtzer took poison, suffering without medical treatment for two days before Stephenson returned her to her Indianapolis home. On April 15, Oberholtzer died, but not before giving testimony that served on November 14, 1925, to convict Stephenson of second-degree murder and earn him a life sentence.[132]

130 *Indiana Catholic and Record,* March 13, 1925.
131 Weaver, The Knights of the Ku Klux Klan, pp. 163-168; Davis, The Ku Klux Klan in Indiana, pp. 208-209, 257-262; Indianapolis *News,* February 6, 28, 1925.
132 Weaver, The Knights of the Ku Klux Klan, pp. 169-172; Indianapolis *News,* November 16, 1925; Indianapolis *Star,* November 16, 1925. Transcripts and much other information regarding Madge Oberholtzer's death and Stephenson's trial are in the Stephenson Collection, Indiana Historical Society Library. Stephenson filed more than forty court actions arguing that he did not have a fair trial. He was not paroled until 1950, and then on the condition that he leave Indiana.

The sordid details revealed in Stephenson's trial and his conviction doubtless caused many Hoosiers to abandon the Ku Klux Klan. Stephenson's fall also opened the way for special investigations into the Klan and for damning charges and counter-charges by Klansmen and former Klansmen. The first major investigation began in the spring of 1926, when fifteen editors belonging to the Indiana Republican Editorial Association met to assess rumors of corruption and Klan influence in state government. Their concern led to an investigation headed by Thomas H. Adams, Republican editor of the Vincennes *Sun-Times*. Adams raked up such muck that many of his fellow Republicans disavowed him.[133] In a four-page letter to party stalwarts, state Republican chairman Clyde A. Walb attempted to discredit Adams as a disappointed office seeker and called the "Adams fiasco" "the greatest hoax in political history."[134] But Adams persisted, claiming that his investigation had "showed that Stephenson dictated legislation, controlled Governor Jackson and harrassed [sic] industry by threats to exercise his power in councils of the State."[135] Adams's calls for indictments from the Marion County Grand Jury and for investigations by the state legislature were not answered, leading the Indianapolis *News* to editorialize in early 1927 that "not often has there been a more successful case of suppression or covering up."[136] Even Democrats, who might have hoped to gain from exposés of Klan influence in Republican-controlled government, were generally silent and did not press for action in the 1927 legislature, perhaps fearing that the scandal might soil them also. That the Democrats failed to counter effectively the Klan-Republican alliance is indicative of the party's general lack of leadership and cohesiveness, espe-

---

He violated the parole agreement and was again imprisoned until 1956. Stephenson died in 1966. Weaver, The Knights of the Ku Klux Klan, p. 187; Indianapolis *Star*, September 18, 1978.

[133] Thomas H. Adams to Ed Jackson, May 11, 1926, Harold C. Feightner Papers, Indiana Division, Indiana State Library; Scharlott, The Hoosier Newsman and the Hooded Order, pp. 80-82; New York *Times*, September 29, October 3, 14, 1926.

[134] Clyde A. Walb to "Dear Friend," October 14, 1926, Feightner Papers.

[135] New York *Times*, December 11, 1926.

[136] Indianapolis *News*, February 26, 1927. See also *ibid.*, March 5, 1927.

cially in the late 1920s when both Ralston and Taggart were gone.[137]

But there was too much to cover up, as others joined Adams to publicize allegations of Klan influence in politics. In the fall of 1926 a national investigation of electoral corruption, chaired by Democratic Senator James A. Reed of Missouri, produced testimony by Klansmen and former Klansmen regarding the organization's activities in Indiana, particularly its support of Republican senators Watson and Arthur Robinson. Both senators vehemently denied any Klan affiliations or sympathy.[138] The Reed investigation sparked a bitter exchange between Robinson and Reed on the Senate floor in early 1927, with Robinson charging that Reed's investigation "had degenerated into a garbage wagon," which was "political, purely political."[139]

Closer to home, some Indiana newspapers also began to investigate Klan influence. In addition to Adams's Vincennes *Sun-Times*, the Indianapolis *Times* was especially vigorous after 1925 in publishing evidence of Klan involvement in politics and in calling for an official investigation. The Indianapolis *Times*'s anti-Klan crusade won the newspaper the Pulitzer Prize for most outstanding public service in 1928.[140]

The major boost to the anti-Klan efforts came from D. C. Stephenson, who had gone to jail in 1925 mistakenly convinced that his friend Governor Jackson would pardon him. When no pardon came, Stephenson started talking, giving bits and pieces of information and evidence regarding his role in Indiana politics. As Stephenson released the contents of his little black boxes to the Marion County prosecutor, the New York *Times* noted in July, 1927, "you can hear a pin drop in Indiana these days, and

---

[137] *Ibid.*, February 26, 1927. By 1924 both Ralston and Taggart were in ill health. Ralston died in 1925, Taggart in 1929. An analysis of roll call votes for the period from 1923 to 1963 shows that the 1920s stand out as the low point of Democratic party cohesiveness and discipline in the legislature. William E. Bicker, The Assembly Party: Change and Consistency in Legislative Voting Behavior in the Indiana House, 1923-1963 (Ph.D. dissertation, Indiana University, Bloomington, 1969).

[138] U.S. Senate, *Senatorial Campaign Expenditures*.

[139] *Congressional Record*, 69th Congress, 2nd Session, February 24, 1927, LXVIII, Pt. 5, p. 4645.

[140] Stevens, "Winning the Pulitzer Prize," *Journalism History*, II, 80–83.

politicians are walking about on tiptoe."[141] The crash came in September, 1927. As a result of Stephenson's testimony the Marion County Grand Jury indicted Governor Jackson on charges of bribery. "Indiana bows its head in shame," the Indianapolis *Star* lamented.[142] Stephenson testified that he had contributed large amounts of Klan money to win Jackson's nomination and election in 1924, money that Jackson did not report among his campaign contributions and even had denied receiving. As evidence, Stephenson produced a canceled check for $2,500 made out to Jackson. Jackson responded that the check was payment for a horse that he now did not have because it choked to death on a corncob —a story that inspired considerable amusement and disbelief among many. But the most damning charge against Jackson was that in September, 1923, he and Stephenson had offered a bribe to then Governor McCray to appoint their Klan candidate as Marion County prosecutor. At Jackson's trial in early 1928, witnesses, including former Governor McCray, recently released from the federal penitentiary, testified that Jackson and his Klan associates promised McCray immunity from the charges then pending against the governor and offered him $10,000 in cash, which McCray refused. The evidence against Jackson was very strong, and nearly all observers at the trial, including Judge Charles M. McCabe, had little doubt that Jackson was guilty. But Judge McCabe regretfully concluded that because charges were not filed within two years after the act and because active efforts to conceal the bribe were not shown, state law required the verdict be not guilty. Acquitted on this legal technicality, Jackson served out the remainder of his term, despite calls for his resignation. At the Republican state convention in May, 1928, party leaders adjourned the proceedings early in order to prevent the governor from delivering his planned address.[143]

By 1928 Hoosier Republicans had snubbed not only Jackson but the Klan. The revelations made since Stephenson's fall in

---

[141] New York *Times*, July 7, 1927.

[142] Indianapolis *Star*, September 10, 1927.

[143] *Ibid.*, September 10, 1927, February 17, May 24, 1928; Indianapolis *News*, February 17, 1928; Niblack, *The Life and Times of a Hoosier Judge*, pp. 219-225, 249-258.

1925 and the precipitous decline in Klan strength made the organization a political liability, and the party endeavored to dissociate itself from the Klan, particularly at its spring convention in 1928.[144] The Democrats appealed to growing anti-Klan sentiment by charging that the secret order had "taken possession of the Republican organization" and that only Democrats could "purge the state government of the slime and corruption that has caused self-respecting Hoosiers to hang their heads in shame."[145] They could joke that the word *Hoosier* derived from *hoosegow* and that all prisons would soon have a separate Indiana room.[146] But the voters did not respond to the Democratic calls for a clean sweep, as incumbent Republican Senator Arthur R. Robinson won re-election by more than 150,000 votes over his opponent Albert Stump, despite Robinson's earlier taint of Klan support. Republicans also elected ten of thirteen congressmen and gubernatorial candidate Harry G. Leslie, who was opposed by Democrat Frank C. Daily, although Leslie trailed behind other Republican candidates.[147] The party's most impressive showing in Indiana was in the presidential contest, where Republican Herbert Hoover defeated Alfred E. Smith by approximately 283,000 votes. Smith's overwhelming defeat in Indiana was due in part to opposition to him because he was a Catholic from New York City and a wet; even though many Hoosiers had deserted the Klan, they continued to hold some of the convictions on which the organization had been built.[148]

[144] Davis, The Ku Klux Klan in Indiana, pp. 234-237; James E. Watson to Fairbanks, May 10, 1928, Fairbanks Papers.

[145] Democratic state platform, 1928, in Indiana State Platforms, I.

[146] Louis Ludlow, "What's the Matter with Indiana?" speech given at the Indiana Democratic Editorial Association, February 16, 1928, copy in George W. Rauch Papers.

[147] Robinson had been appointed to succeed Ralston, who died in October, 1925. Reporter Feightner later remembered that Leslie was "not one of the most brilliant [men] in the world but he was honest." Feightner interview, February 28, October 24, 1968, p. 48, Indiana Division. Leslie had served as speaker of the Indiana House in the 1927 session. Major issues in his administration are considered in the chapters that follow, especially Chapters II and IV.

[148] Wayne L. Francis and Sharron E. Doerner (comps.), *Indiana Votes: Election Returns for United States Representative, Election Returns for State General Assembly, 1922-1958* (Bloomington, Ind., 1962), pp. 16-17; Pitchell,

The 1928 elections were neither a wholesale repudiation of the Klan nor a dramatic call for reform in Indiana politics. The Republican party had dissociated itself from the Klan, but the old-guard leadership of Watson and Robinson continued in power. The real shock to Republicans came the following year, in 1929, when in local elections across the state voters turned out candidates tainted by earlier Klan support and generally replaced Republicans with Democrats. Evansville, Terre Haute, Fort Wayne, Muncie, Anderson, Lafayette, Elkhart, and Indianapolis all replaced Republican mayors with Democrats, marking, the New York *Times* hoped, "the dawning of a more liberal and cleaner political day in Indiana . . . ."[149]

Perhaps the most significant Democratic victory in 1929 was in Indianapolis, where there had been strong Klan influence in local government. The city's Republican mayor, John L. Duvall, was elected in 1925 with large Klan support, and the Marion County Republican organization, headed by George V. Coffin, was also closely tied to the Klan. The city council and school board were also composed of men elected with Klan support. By 1927 opposition to Duvall and Coffin and to corruption and Klan influence in local government coalesced in the Indianapolis City Manager League. The League mounted a campaign to replace the elected politician-mayor with an appointed city manager who, the League argued, would introduce more efficiency and business-like administration and less politics and corruption to the city. In special elections in June, 1927, Indianapolis voters endorsed a city manager plan by a margin of more than five to one, despite strong opposition from Duvall and Coffin. Before the plan went into effect, however, an adverse court decision held it unconstitutional.[150] By that time Mayor Duvall had other problems: in the

Indiana Votes, pp. 47, 80-81; Davis, The Ku Klux Klan in Indiana, pp. 237-241; Robert Lee Gildea, The "Religious Issue" in the 1928 and 1960 Presidential Elections: A Study of Six Indiana Newspapers (M.A. thesis, Indiana University, Bloomington, 1963), pp. 13, 23-27.

149 New York *Times*, November 8, 1929. See also *ibid.*, November 10, 1929; Indianapolis *News*, November 6, 1929; Davis, The Ku Klux Klan in Indiana, pp. 242-243; Frank, Politics in Middletown, pp. 220, 257-258.

150 Indianapolis *News*, May 6, November 2, 4, 1925, April 11, May 18, June 1, 22, 1927, November 4, 1929; New York *Times*, November 8, 1929; John Paul

fall of 1927, he was convicted of violating the Corrupt Practices
Act, sentenced to thirty days in jail, fined $1,000, and prohibited
from holding public office. Several members of the city council
were also convicted on various charges of political corruption.[151]
The landslide victory of Democratic mayoral candidate Reginald
H. Sullivan in 1929 was a strong repudiation of both Duvall and
Coffin, who had maintained control of the local Republican organization. It marked the end of the last significant remnant of Klan
influence in the city's politics.[152]

By late 1929 the New York *Times*'s Indiana correspondent,
Harold C. Feightner, could note that the "Klan is virtually dead
as a political element . . . ."[153] Feightner was correct, but it had
been a slow and agonizing death, one in which there were few
heroes. Only after Stephenson's conviction in 1925 and really not
until he began to release the contents of his little black boxes did
efforts to repudiate the Knights of the Ku Klux Klan make strong
headway in Indiana, and then often as measures of political self-
preservation or ambition. Certainly the Klan's rapid rise to power
and its slow death resulted from the broad appeal it made to large
numbers of Hoosier citizens, reflecting basic beliefs and attitudes
strongly held in the 1920s. But the Klan's success also reflected the
nature of the decade's politics. Both major parties—each, especially the Republican party, troubled by factional disputes and
each intent, above all else, on winning elections—wished to avoid
or repress issues that might adversely alter traditional voting
patterns. The Klan raised cultural, moral, and economic as well
as political issues and threatened to attract voters in ways that
cut across traditional party loyalties and voting patterns, thereby

---

Duncan, Control of the City Government in Indianapolis, Evidenced by the
Forces Determining Its Ordinances, 1925-1941 (Ph.D. dissertation, Indiana University, Bloomington, 1943), pp. 416-428; J. W. Esterline, "The Indianapolis City
Manager Campaign," Indiana League of Women Voters, *Year Book*, 1928 (n.p.,
1928), pp. 41-42.

[151] New York *Times*, October 13, November 2, 1927; Niblack, *The Life and
Times of a Hoosier Judge*, pp. 241-245.

[152] Indianapolis *News*, May 8, November 4, 6, 1929; New York *Times*,
November 10, 1929.

[153] New York *Times*, December 8, 1929. See also *ibid.*, May 18, 1930.

injecting a strongly unpredictable element into the politics of the 1920s. Most Hoosier politicians responded by adopting a "safe," conservative approach. And in that stance they revealed their lack of courage and their mediocrity as leaders. Meredith Nicholson might have included Republicans with his own party leadership when he wrote fellow Democrat Claude Bowers in 1926, "Our party is in sore need of men—never so badly off in my time."[154] Later that same year, Nicholson again lamented the lack of leadership: "We are governed by swine," and "No young men of conspicuous promise are coming on."[155] In fact, the leadership of the 1920s represented the end of a political generation, one that had grown to maturity in the nineteenth century and was rapidly replaced by a new generation of leaders in the early 1930s.

The politics of the 1920s was thus a conservative politics that was in tune with the nationwide emphasis on "normalcy" and material prosperity. Both parties appealed to voters' interest in low taxes and limited governmental services. Both attempted to avoid divisive issues, whether they were raised by women, veterans, labor, farmers, Anti-Saloon Leaguers, or Klansmen. For charismatic political leadership Hoosiers looked to Shumaker or Stephenson rather than Watson, New, or McCulloch. Indeed, the heroes of the decade were not political leaders but authors, movie stars, baseball players, and members of high school basketball teams.[156] Most Hoosiers, like most Americans elsewhere, did not expect much from their politicians or their governments, whether local, state, or federal. In this, as in other major ways, the politics of the next decade would be different.

154 Nicholson to Bowers, February 20, 1926, Bowers Papers, II. For other adverse comments on the political leadership of the 1920s see Nicholson to J. O'H. Cosgrave, September 4, 1923, Ralston Papers; Indianapolis *News*, June 4, 1926, March 8, 1927; New York *Times*, November 7, 1923.

155 Nicholson to Bowers, March 9, 1926, Bowers Papers, II.

156 In 1922 the Indianapolis *News* asked its readers to submit a list of their choice of the ten greatest living Indianans. The *News* received 802 lists. The top ten vote getters included only two politicians: Thomas R. Marshall, former governor and Woodrow Wilson's vice-president, and Albert J. Beveridge, whom many voters classified as historian rather than politician. In addition to Beveridge, five of the ten were professional writers. Indianapolis *News*, August 19, 1922.

CHAPTER III
THE POLITICS OF THE 1930s:
PAUL V. McNUTT AND POLITICAL POWER

SELDOM HAVE THE POLITICS of two decades been so different as those of the 1920s and 1930s. The Depression that began in 1929 and continued through the 1930s upset political patterns of the 1920s and, in some cases, patterns that had persisted for decades before World War I. In a process of partisan realignment the Democrats became the majority party, as large numbers of voters entered the polls for the first time and as others cast their first non-Republican ballots. New issues, especially ones relating to social welfare, echoed in election campaigns, legislative debates, and statehouse meetings. Politics became more important, more exciting, and government became more powerful, more influential in effecting social and economic change. The focal points of government shifted: state government challenged and sometimes won from local governments new responsibilities and powers, countering strong home-rule sentiment in Indiana and expanding significantly the process of political centralization in Indianapolis. Also during the 1930s Franklin D. Roosevelt's New Deal brought to the federal government a much enlarged role, though many New Deal programs depended heavily on state and local administration and co-operation. Finally, the 1930s differed from the 1920s in Indiana because of the presence of a different kind of governor, a man whose political power reached proportions unparalleled in twentieth-century Indiana politics.

Paul Vories McNutt was born July 19, 1891, in Franklin, Indiana. His family soon moved to Indianapolis and, when Paul was seven, to Martinsville, where he grew up in a staunch Methodist and Democratic home. A good student, young McNutt was also president of his junior and senior high school classes and editor of the school yearbook. At Indiana University he achieved distinction as editor of the school newspaper and as a campus politician, culminating in his election as president of the senior class in 1912. Like some other ambitious Hoosiers, McNutt then went east, to Harvard, where in 1916 he received his law degree. He returned to Indiana and practiced law in Martinsville until March, 1917, when he joined the faculty of the Indiana University Law School, only to leave the following August to enlist in the Great War against Germany. In 1919 he returned to the faculty of the Bloomington law school, where in 1925 he became the youngest dean in the school's history.[1]

McNutt's position in the university law school provided him with experiences and acquaintances that would prove useful in politics, but at least as important was his participation during the 1920s in the American Legion, the veterans group organized in the state and nation after World War I. Chosen as commander of the Bloomington Legion post in 1921, McNutt was elected state commander in 1926 and national commander in 1928. Each of these Legion campaigns was carefully planned and vigorously fought. The 1928 national campaign was especially important as a publicity vehicle and political training ground for McNutt. The Legion campaigns of the 1920s also provided the primary means of recruiting McNutt's closest political advisers. With the exceptions of Wayne Coy and Virgil Simmons, nearly all the major figures in McNutt's gubernatorial administration were Legionnaires. Most important was Frank McHale, a Logansport native who practiced law in Indianapolis after serving in the war. McHale was also a Roman Catholic and a former football star at the University of Michigan. From the Legion campaign of 1928 through the years in the governor's office and McNutt's presidential bid of 1940, McHale worked tirelessly to promote McNutt's political career. Though he never held a major office himself, McHale did serve as Democratic national committeeman from 1937 to 1952. Other McNutt men who learned their political ABC's in the Legion included Bowman Elder, who served as treasurer of the Hoosier Democratic Club; Pleas Greenlee, a newspaperman from Shelbyville who became McNutt's executive

[1] Robert R. Neff, The Early Career and Governorship of Paul V. McNutt (Ph.D. dissertation, Indiana University, Bloomington, 1963), pp. 1-33.

secretary and chief patronage director; Clarence Jackson and Paul Fry, who served in several important administrative posts; and Sherman Minton, whom McNutt pushed into the United States Senate in 1934. All these men learned about politics and about McNutt through the American Legion. Young, ambitious, and energetic, they were soon a powerful force in Indiana politics.[2]

Because of his achievements in the Legion and his deanship at Indiana University, McNutt was widely known by the time he made his first significant foray into state politics in 1930. His keynote address at the Democratic state convention that year was a rousing piece of oratory, blaming Republicans for the economic crisis. In the campaign that followed, McNutt traveled the state, not as a candidate but as a party booster, speaking every day during the closing weeks. The election was a major Democratic victory, as the party took control of the Indiana House of Representatives for the first time since the 1914 elections and elected the secretary of state, the only state office up for election.[3] The Democratic victory was doubtless primarily the consequence of voter discontent caused by growing unemployment and the Depression generally, but McNutt also received great credit. Letters of congratulation poured in. A Logansport attorney exulted: "Everyone feels that you are entitled to anything you want within the gift of the Democrats of Indiana . . . ."[4]

McNutt already knew what he wanted. He would settle for

[2] *Ibid.*, pp. 36, 75; I. George Blake, *Paul V. McNutt: Portrait of a Hoosier Statesman* (Indianapolis, 1966), p. 107; Clutter, The Indiana American Legion, pp. 171-176. For indications of the intensity and skill with which McNutt sought Legion offices see Paul V. McNutt to Robert R. Batton, August 16, 1926, and McNutt to Frank McHale, September 20, 1928, Paul V. McNutt Papers, Lilly Library, Indiana University, Bloomington. Legion politics, of course, was an example of ways in which women were informally denied full access to political participation.

[3] Indianapolis *News*, June 10, November 1, 5, 1930; Steven M. Buck, The Public Speaking of Paul V. McNutt (Ph.D. dissertation, Purdue University, West Lafayette, Ind., 1960), pp. 33-35; James Stevens, "Indiana's Magnificent McNutt," *American Mercury*, XLI (1937), 434; McNutt to William C. Rose, October 1, 1930, McNutt Papers, Lilly Library.

[4] Michael L. Fansler to McNutt, November 6, 1930, McNutt Papers, Lilly Library. See also McHale to McNutt, November 5, 1930, *ibid.*; Neff, Paul V. McNutt, pp. 66-80.

nothing less than the governor's office, and in late 1930 he and his Legion associates began the campaign that would last until November, 1932. By January, 1931, when he declared his candidacy, he was the front-runner and remained so until his nomination by acclamation at the 1932 convention.[5] However, this victory was not achieved without engendering bitterness that would remain with the party throughout the decade.

McNutt's most specific opposition within the party came from a group of South Bend Democrats, led by Frank Mayr, Jr., who was elected secretary of state in 1930. Mayr was an obvious candidate for the gubernatorial nomination. In early 1931 McNutt expressed his concern about "the political activities of the members of the South Bend group, who expect to build an organization for themselves through patronage distributed by the Secretary of State's office." "I," McNutt added, "do not fit in their picture. . . ."[6] The South Bend faction failed in their bid for the governor's office, but the effort caused considerable intraparty bitterness.[7]

A less direct but more important intraparty tension was the division between the McNutt forces and the older regular party leadership. Through the party's difficult years of the 1920s, when Republicans controlled most state and national offices and the patronage that accompanied office, Democrats worked with little reward. Now, in the early 1930s, with the electoral wind clearly changing, these older party workers anticipated at last the bounties of success. The regular party workers had a significant liability, however, for none of them had emerged as a capable leader. Indeed, part of the Democratic party's difficulties in the 1920s had been due to the declining power and physical health of its longtime boss, Thomas Taggart. After his death in 1929 his son, Thomas Taggart, Jr., continued to entertain state and national party workers at the family's French Lick Springs Hotel, and the

[5] McNutt to Carl B. Wolflin, July 9, 1930, McNutt Papers, Lilly Library; Neff, Paul V. McNutt, pp. 84-120.

[6] McNutt to Hermann A. Wenige, January 21, 1931, McNutt Papers, Lilly Library.

[7] Donald F. Stiver to Pleas Greenlee, March 22, 1932, Box A, Drawer 82, McNutt Papers, Archives Division; Greenlee to Hallie L. Myers, June 7, 1932, *ibid.*

younger Taggart was made a member of the Democratic National Committee in 1931, but he never wielded the influence of his father. Another potential leader was R. Earl Peters, the state party chairman who had been elected in 1926. But Peters's hold on the job was tenuous, so much so that in 1931 he joined the McNutt bandwagon to support his own position.[8]

The Democratic party organization in 1930 was thus without a strong leader yet was composed of older party workers anticipating victory. Into this party jumped McNutt and his young Legion crowd—outsiders who, no doubt, were welcome to many Democrats as engines of party victory but were also threatening to upset the party's established order. The McNutt newcomers did just that, most notably in building a strong, independent organization in the form of McNutt for governor clubs, appealing to independents and Republicans as well as Democrats, and making use of American Legion ties throughout the state. Indianapolis newspaper reporter Harold C. Feightner later recalled that prior to 1932 many young, politically ambitious veterans felt blocked by older politicians in both parties. To them "McNutt was spectacular all right and they began to say: We got a cause, we got something to fight for. . . . It wasn't the things he exactly stood for. There were no great issues."[9]

For the Indiana Democratic party McNutt's nomination in 1932 was the beginning of new leadership. As the New York *Times* noted, "the young men took over control of the party." McNutt "dominated the convention . . . ," and "names familiar in Hoosier politics for a quarter of a century were scarcely heard . . . ."[10] But McNutt's victory did prompt some concessions, both

---

[8] Charles A. Greathouse to Samuel M. Ralston, March 26, 1924, Ralston Papers; New York *Times*, June 4, 1926; Indianapolis *News*, November 24, 1931; Feightner interview, February 28, October 24, 1968, p. 83, Indiana Division.

[9] Feightner interview, February 28, October 24, 1968, p. 84, Indiana Division. For an example of one local legionnaire's work for McNutt see Ray O. Williams to McNutt, October 7, 1931, McNutt Papers, Lilly Library.

[10] New York *Times*, June 26, 1932. See also Wickard interview, 1952-1953, No. 13, pp. 530-531, Wickard Papers. In Michigan the old-line Democrats elected one of their own, William A. Comstock, in 1932, producing an administration very different from McNutt's in Indiana. See Sidney Fine, *Frank Murphy: The New Deal Years* (Chicago, 1979), pp. 205-209.

symbolic and real, to the older organization Democrats. Indeed McNutt and his advisers were very much aware of the dangers of needlessly alienating "the old timers." In recommending one of them, Joseph Cravens, a veteran of twelve sessions of the General Assembly, to head the Indianapolis campaign headquarters, Greenlee advised McNutt: "He will keep the old timers sweetened, and that is all we have to worry about, as the young crowd and the women will be with us." And, Greenlee added, "There is a feeling amongst the old timers, as you are aware, that if you would be elected, that all appointments would go to Legionnaires."[11] Other concessions were more substantial. At the state convention, McNutt bid for party and intergenerational harmony by supporting Frederick Van Nuys, an old-line Taggart Democrat who had been state chairman in 1918, for the United States Senate nomination and even backed Mayr for secretary of state. Although McNutt probably could have won the nomination and election without these concessions, they undoubtedly broadened his base of support in the 1932 campaign and in 1933 when he assumed the duties of governor.[12]

Indiana Democrats campaigned in the fall of 1932 against Republicans and the Depression, arguing that only by throwing out those in office and electing a Democratic majority could the Depression and its associated ills be conquered. The state party platform declared that "the paramount issue in this campaign is the lowering of taxes, and economy in government." McNutt and other candidates hit hard on this theme, promising a more economical and efficient government and a more equitable adjustment of the tax burden, although avoiding commitments to specific tax proposals. The state platform did promise "a just and equitable old age pension system . . . ," but made few other references to social reforms. Rather than promising an active, energetic state government, the platform committed the party to

[11] Greenlee to McNutt, October 10, 1931, McNutt Papers, Lilly Library. See also Eugene B. Crowe to Greenlee, August 9, 1932, *ibid.*

[12] Neff, Paul V. McNutt, pp. 118-119; Feightner interview, February 28, October 24, 1968, p. 83, Indiana Division; New York *Times*, June 26, 1932; Indianapolis *News*, June 21, 1932.

seeking "economics [sic] in decentralization rather than further centralization of governmental power."[13]

The Republicans were caught in a nearly hopeless campaign, saddled tightly if unfairly with blame for economic ills afflicting the state and nation. For the United States Senate they again nominated James E. Watson, the state's Republican leader who had served in the Senate since 1916. The gubernatorial nomination went to Raymond S. Springer of Connersville, a colorless campaigner whose main credentials appeared to be his election as the first state Legion commander. Republicans promised to reduce government expenses and lift the burden of property taxes. On the bitterly fought issue of prohibition, they favored repeal of the bone-dry law and submission of the eighteenth amendment to state conventions. Above all, they warned, "this is no time to experiment with radical doctrines of government." They presented Herbert Hoover, Watson, and Springer as bulwarks against those unnamed opponents who "would overthrow our cherished institutions. . . ."[14]

With millions of Americans unemployed in 1932, the Republican warning not to change leadership in a crisis, one Democratic orator suggested, was like a plea to "not change barrels while walking the street."[15] Hoosier voters agreed: seldom had they voted so overwhelmingly to change their political leadership. The Democratic vote for secretary of state (a good indicator of general party strength) in the elections of 1920, 1924, and 1928 averaged only 43.5 percent of the two-party vote in Indiana. In 1932 the Democratic vote was 56.3 percent. Not since 1916 had Hoosiers turned out to vote in such force, with 77.9 percent of the eligible electorate voting in 1932. Throughout the 1920s Republicans had occupied the governor's office and a majority of seats in the General Assembly. In 1930 Democrats had gained control of the house, but after the 1932 elections they held every

13 Democratic state platform, 1932, in Indiana State Platforms, I; Neff, Paul V. McNutt, pp. 107-108.

14 Republican state platform, 1932, in Indiana State Platforms, I. See also Indianapolis News, June 10, November 4, 1932.

15 Indiana Democratic Handbook: Campaign of 1932 (n.p., 1932), p. 14.

state office except one holdover judgeship and had 91 of 100 seats in the house and 43 of 50 seats in the senate. All twelve federal congressmen were Democrats. Indiana also cast its presidential vote for Franklin D. Roosevelt by a margin of 184,870 over Hoover. But FDR ran behind McNutt, who defeated Springer by 192,330 votes (55.0 percent of the total vote), and Frederick Van Nuys, an Indianapolis lawyer, who beat old-guard Republican Watson by 208,303 votes. In a crisis year, when Hoosiers might have been expected to abandon the two traditional major parties in favor of a more radical third party, they in fact cast only 2.2 percent of the total vote for all five third-party gubernatorial candidates, with more than half the third-party ballots (18,735 votes) going to Socialist party candidate Powers Hapgood.[16]

§ §

Democratic dominance of state government in 1933 was most forcefully displayed in the state legislature that sat from early January to March 6 of that Depression year, adjourning two days after Roosevelt took office. At the center of the legislative stage was Governor McNutt, with supporting roles played by his advisers Pleas Greenlee and Frank McHale. The legislators themselves seemed often to be playing bit parts in the drama and at times even to be members of the audience. Seldom had an Indiana governor so dominated a legislature.

McNutt's Republican predecessors of the 1920s, as well as most Indiana governors in the late nineteenth century, had generally acted according to the traditional separation of powers doctrine. While they made occasional general proposals for legislative attention, they seldom actively initiated specific legislation or forcefully encouraged its passage. The model Hoosier governor was a caretaker executive who ran the day-to-day business of government but played only a minimal role in initiating significant policy changes in that government. This generally weak executive governed with a legislature that sat in biennial sessions of only

[16] Pitchell (comp.), *Indiana Votes*, pp. 48-49; Hyneman, Hofstetter, and O'Connor, *Voting in Indiana*, pp. 27, 40, 54, 104.

sixty-one days. The citizen legislators were low-paid, often inexperienced, and usually leaderless.[17] A weak governor and legislature represented the political wishes of many Hoosiers: they did not expect or want an active, energetic state government. Like Thomas Jefferson, they tended to favor the government that governed least, and they tended to distrust power at a distance, whether in Indianapolis or Washington. Such ideas were especially important to Indiana Democrats with party and ideological roots deep in the nineteenth century, but Republicans also tended to have limited expectations of state government. During the decade and a half prior to World War I, there had been a slight tendency toward increased state power through progressive reform legislation, but Indiana experienced considerably less progressive reform than Wisconsin, Minnesota, and other midwestern states.[18]

McNutt and the Great Depression changed the central wisdom of the Democratic party and the practice of state government in Indiana—not radically and not in all cases permanently—but in major ways and with far-reaching consequences. McNutt presented the 1933 legislature with a large program that included specifically drawn bills, and he aggressively forced those bills through the legislature. By mid-1933 he was the most powerful governor Indiana had yet produced, with the possible exception of Civil War Governor Oliver P. Morton. In 1933 McNutt stood out also in comparison to other state governors. In the words of one historian, "Most governors were nobodies—moderate, undramatic, yawn-inspiring men with legislative programs as pedestrian as they were unsuccessful."[19] No one ever accused Paul McNutt of being a nobody.

[17] Political scientist Charles S. Hyneman's study of Indiana legislative sessions between 1925 and 1935 shows that in each session at least 50 percent of the house was composed of freshmen legislators. More than half the committee chairmen in both houses in these years were first-time chairmen. This inexperience, Hyneman concluded, made the General Assembly "utterly inadequate for the service which modern life demands of a legislative body." Charles S. Hyneman, "Tenure and Turnover of the Indiana General Assembly," *American Political Science Review*, XXXII (1938), 328.

[18] Phillips, *Indiana in Transition*, pp. 85-131.

[19] James T. Patterson, *The New Deal and the States: Federalism in Transition* (Princeton, N.J., 1969), p. 153.

McNutt's inaugural was a portent of his administration. The elaborate and colorful ceremony began and ended with uniformed trumpeters playing flourishes and included an all-state American Legion band performing while Legion, state, and national flags waved in the chilly January wind. McNutt appeared, as always, handsome and precisely groomed, his clothing well tailored to his tall and lean frame and his silver-gray hair adding a touch of maturity to his otherwise youthful appearance.[20] He was always, as one commentator later noted, "physically magnificent." Seldom was he the folksy, backslapping politician, but rather he was more aloof, always dignified, and a man who "parades even when he is sitting down."[21] His inaugural address adopted a tone of strength with forcefully stated themes of 1930s liberalism—themes that had not appeared in the election campaign. The change in party control, he stated, "offers an opportunity to prove that government may be a great instrument of human progress." McNutt laid out "the immediate tasks." The first was to provide food, clothing, and shelter for the destitute, followed by the necessity of lowering the cost of government, reducing and redistributing the burden of taxation, and maintaining an adequate system of public education.[22] In his message to the General Assembly the following day he reiterated these tasks in slightly more detail.[23]

The first and hardest problem for McNutt was relief—a problem his predecessor had largely ignored. A fuller examination of this complex issue as it affected local, state, and federal government is presented in Chapter IV. Here it is important simply to note McNutt's genuine sensitivity to the dimensions of the problem and his serious attempts to deal with it, as indicated by his efforts to establish the Governor's Commission on Unemployment Relief in March, 1933, and especially by his very positive cooperation with federal New Deal relief agencies.

[20] Indianapolis *Times*, January 9, 1933; Neff, Paul V. McNutt, pp. 131-132.

[21] Stevens, "Indiana's Magnificent McNutt," *American Mercury*, XLI, 434. Harold Ickes noted in his diary that "McNutt is one of the handsomest men I have ever seen . . . ." Harold L. Ickes, *The Secret Diary of Harold L. Ickes* (3 volumes, New York, 1953-1954), II, 679.

[22] *Inaugural Address of Governor Paul V. McNutt of Indiana* (Indianapolis, 1933). See also Indianapolis *Times*, January 10, 1933.

[23] Indiana *House Journal*, 1933, pp. 102-106.

The issue that probably was most discussed in the election campaign and in the 1933 legislature was not relief, however, but taxation—a hardy perennial in the garden of Indiana politics which took on new growth as the Depression continued. There were two major complaints: local taxes were too high and must be reduced, and the state's tax system placed an unfair burden on property holders. Leaders of both parties had long voiced these concerns, as did a special legislative tax survey committee in 1931.[24] State legislators were deluged with complaints from angry citizens.[25] A special session of the legislature met in the summer of 1932 specifically to consider taxation. The session passed a property tax limitation law that set a maximum rate of $1.50 on each $100 of taxable property. The 1932 tax limitation law was a major effort by state government to control local taxing power—an effort initiated by Governor James P. Goodrich in 1919 and often referred to as the "Indiana plan." But the actual results disappointed the plan's supporters. A provision in the 1932 law allowed for higher rates in emergency situations as decided by the county tax adjustment board, with possibility of review by the state tax board. In 1931 only 49 of 1,591 tax units in the state had rates of $1.50 or less. In 1934, after the limitation law was in effect, the number of units with rates of $1.50 or less had increased to only 135 and most of them were rural township governments. The 1932 legislation thus had little effect in reducing the local tax rate.[26]

A more significant proposed change in the taxation system was

[24] Indianapolis *News*, June 5, 1930, March 11, 1931; Indianapolis *Star*, July 6, 1932; Indiana Tax Survey Committee, *Report to the Seventy-seventh General Assembly* . . . (Indianapolis, 1931).

[25] One constituent wrote legislator Claude Wickard, warning him and his colleagues: "If the Sons-O-bitches increase our taxes they can show us how to pay them and we'll show em in 1934." W. Van Garrott to Wickard, January 24, 1933, Box 5, Wickard Papers.

[26] *Laws of Indiana*, 1932, pp. 17-18; Carl R. Dortch, "The 'Indiana Plan' in Action," *National Municipal Review*, XXVII (1938), 525-528; Indiana *House Journal*, 1932, pp. 6-8. The 1932 tax limit was modified in 1933. The maximum rate was lowered to $1.00 on each $100 of taxable property outside incorporated cities and towns. The maximum rate in incorporated cities and towns remained at $1.50. *Laws of Indiana*, 1933, p. 1085.

to shift the burden away from the property tax, which in the years 1926 to 1932 accounted for 81 percent of total state and local tax revenues in Indiana.[27] The problem, as the 1931 legislative tax committee noted, was "apparent to everyone . . . . a large amount of intangible wealth in the state escapes taxation, and, as a result, tangible property, including real estate, pays more than its fair share . . . ."[28] The solution was less apparent. Both parties supported more equitable taxation, but efforts to achieve such results failed in 1931 and 1932. A proposed amendment to the state constitution to provide for a state income tax did not pass in 1932. The amendment was approved by a majority of voters who bothered to vote on the amendment, but not, as was assumed necessary at the time, by a majority of the total electorate who voted in the 1932 elections.[29] Though McNutt was among the leaders of both parties who called for tax changes, like the others he made only vague proposals prior to taking office.[30]

To the legislative session of 1933, however, the new governor presented a specific tax program—the first such program proposed since Governor Goodrich's efforts in 1919.[31] McNutt called for a gross income tax levied on receipts of manufacturers, retailers, and wholesalers and on personal income (with a $1,000 personal exemption)—in effect combining an income tax and a sales tax.[32] The proposal generated strong opposition from several business groups, particularly the Retail Merchants of Indi-

[27] Indiana Gross Income Tax Division, *Tax Facts Review: A Study of Recent Tax Trends in Indiana* (n.p., 1940), pp. 6-7.

[28] Indiana Tax Survey Committee, *Report to the Seventy-seventh General Assembly . . .*, p. 4.

[29] In 1935 the Indiana State Supreme Court held in the case *In re Todd* that a proposed amendment was approved if a majority of votes cast on only the amendment were favorable, which made constitutional amending easier. John A. Bremer (ed.), *Constitution Making in Indiana: A Source Book . . .*, IV, *1930-1960* (Indianapolis, 1978), pp. 22-64, 301-303.

[30] Indianapolis *News*, June 5, 1930, March 10, 1931; Indianapolis *Star*, August 16, November 11, 1932; Indiana *House Journal*, 1931, pp. 6, 15.

[31] Indianapolis *Star*, March 5, 1933.

[32] Students of state government have generally included Indiana's gross income tax in tabulations of state sales taxes. James A. Maxwell and J. Richard Aronson, *Financing State and Local Governments* (3d ed., Washington, D.C., 1977), p. 102.

ana, who argued that the sales tax feature would add to the cost of their businesses, reduce sales, and make it more difficult for border city merchants to compete with out-of-state retailers.[33] Some Indiana manufacturers also objected, as one wrote, to taxing "receipts that have no profit."[34] There was also some opposition from organized labor: the South Bend Central Labor Union passed a resolution opposing the tax because it was a regressive sales tax, penalizing "those who are least able to pay. . . ."[35] But the tax plan received strong support from property owners and especially from farmers, who came to Indianapolis by the thousands to show the legislature their support. The Indiana Farm Bureau also gave vigorous backing to the proposal.[36] The most important proponent of the bill, however, was McNutt himself. With Frank McHale, Bowman Elder, and Virgil Simmons working the heavily Democratic legislature, "the McNutt steamroller," as the press labeled the effort, succeeded in suspending the rules and pushing his tax bill through with almost no legislative debate.[37]

The result was a significant readjustment in the state's tax system—notably in reducing the property tax burden. Largely because of this new source of revenue, the percentage share of total revenue from property taxes declined from 81 percent in the period 1926-1932 to 60 percent in the period 1933-1939. The

[33] Retail Merchants of Indiana to McNutt, February 1, 1933, Congressmen-Executive Orders File, 1933, McNutt Papers, Archives Division. State legislator Wickard received many letters from Indiana merchants that made these arguments against the sales tax. See, for example, Warren M. Knapp to Wickard, February 4, 1933, Box 5, Wickard Papers.

[34] E. B. Baltzly to Wickard, February 22, 1933, Box 5, Wickard Papers.

[35] M. L. Garner to McNutt, January 25, 1933, Indiana Reformatory-Liquor Bill File, 1933, McNutt Papers, Archives Division. See also Neff, Paul V. McNutt, pp. 172-175.

[36] Indianapolis Times, February 16, 1933; Wickard interview, 1952-1953, No. 13, pp. 536-537, Wickard Papers; Lewis Taylor, "Smoke Screen," Hoosier Farmer, February 1, 1933, p. 3; Lewis Taylor, "Tax Facts," ibid., April 1, 1933, p. 12; Indiana Farmer's Guide, March 15, 1933, pp. 1, 3.

[37] Indianapolis Times, February 22, 23, 1933; Neff, Paul V. McNutt, pp. 175-176. The law taxed gross personal income and income to retailers at the rate of 1 percent. Gross income to manufacturers, wholesalers, and farmers was taxed at the rate of ¼ percent. All received a $1,000 exemption. Laws of Indiana, 1933, pp. 388-407. Earlier doubts about the constitutionality of such a law faded in the face of the need for new revenue. See Neff, Paul V. McNutt, pp. 186-189.

gross income tax not only shifted the burden of taxation away from the property tax but also enabled the state to stay close to its pre-Depression level of total revenue. Total tax revenue in the state declined only slightly, from $1,016,646,696 in the period 1926-1932, to $962,965,232 during the years 1933-1939.[38] McNutt and his fellow Democrats claimed that the new tax allowed the state to balance its budget, to continue to provide necessary social services, and especially to keep the schools open by means of increased state aid.[39] They were less ready to acknowledge that the new tax also resulted in a significant step toward further centralization of power in state as opposed to local government. The property tax was a local tax and accounted for about 97 percent of total local taxes throughout the 1930s. Because of the 1933 legislation, state taxes increased and local taxes decreased. As a state tax study reported in 1940, "The gross income tax and distribution plan is based on the proven concept that education and welfare problems go beyond the local units and are state-wide in scope."[40] McNutt's tax program not only shifted the burden away from the property tax but increased the power of state government at the expense of local government, because a larger proportion of taxes was collected and distributed by the state according to local needs as defined in Indianapolis.[41]

§ § §

Just as Indiana political candidates and leaders had long promised to make the state's tax system more equitable, so too had they called for more efficiency in government. After World War I, Governor Goodrich had urged government reorganization as the means to achieve this efficiency, but his Republican successors

[38] Indiana Gross Income Tax Division, *Tax Facts Review*, pp. 6-7; Indiana Tax Study Commission, *Report* (n.p., 1939), p. 26.

[39] Indiana Democratic State Central Committee, *Facts! Gross Income Tax, Sales Tax or What?* (Indianapolis, 1936), pp. 4, 8-9, 13.

[40] Indiana Gross Income Tax Division, *Tax Facts Review*, p. 18.

[41] Indiana Inter-Organization Council, *Eleven-Year Trend in Indiana State Government Payments and Receipts, 1928-1938* (Indianapolis, 1938), pp. 3, 15. This shift was especially important in public education, as explained in Chapter IX.

paid little more than lip service to this advice. In 1925 Governor Ed Jackson appointed a committee to survey the various state boards and commissions to determine "which of them from the standpoint of economy or efficiency could be abolished or consolidated." The committee's bland report made no recommendations for significant change, however, and neither Jackson nor his successor, Harry G. Leslie, pushed the issue.[42] In many states, one scholar has written, the 1920s were years "of increasing influence on the part of administrators, planners, and rationalizers . . . and of a developing organizational base upon which the bureaucracies of the next decade would rise."[43] Such was not the case in Indiana: the 1920s produced few innovations, so that McNutt inherited a state administrative structure in 1933 that had changed little in response to twentieth-century demands placed on it.

Indiana's administrative system in 1933 consisted of more than one hundred distinct and largely independent departments and agencies. Since the turn of the century, boards, commissions, and bureaus had proliferated—tacked on as demands for new government services arose, with little attention given to integration or co-ordination of the total system. In this decentralized and patchwork structure, functions overlapped, and authority, control, and responsibility were often uncertain. By 1933 Indiana government had achieved twentieth-century proportions in bureaucratic size, but it remained at nineteenth-century levels in its degree of centralization and integration.[44]

In January, 1933, McNutt presented the General Assembly with a plan for reorganizing state government—a plan which greatly centralized power in the hands of the governor. The

[42] Committee to Make a Survey of Boards and Commissions of Indiana, *Report,* p. 1. See also Buck, *The Reorganization of State Governments in the United States,* pp. 93-94.

[43] Ellis W. Hawley, *The Great War and the Search for a Modern Order: A History of the American People and Their Institutions, 1917-1933* (New York, 1979), p. 70.

[44] Frank G. Bates, "Indiana Puts Its Faith in Governor," *National Municipal Review,* XXII (1933), 137; Indiana State Committee on Governmental Economy, *Report* (Indianapolis, 1935), pp. 43-45.

Democratic legislature approved the plan by large majorities with almost no debate. The Executive Reorganization Act of 1933 placed all state agencies and commissions in eight departments: executive, state, audit and control, treasury, law, education, public works, and commerce and industry. The governor was the head of the new executive department, but the other seven departments were each headed by a board, which on the surface might seem a continuation of the plural and decentralized administrative structure. But, in addition to the governor, the state constitution required the election of five officers[45]—each a potentially independent state official. McNutt's reorganization plan placed the relevant constitutional officer with the relevant department, making that person the chief administrator in the department: the secretary of state in the state department; auditor in audit and control; treasurer in treasury; superintendent of public instruction in education; and lieutenant governor with special but not statutory responsibility for commerce and industry. The potential of these popularly elected officials to direct independent departments was severely limited by the Reorganization Act's requirement that they work through their department's board, the majority of which always consisted of the governor and members appointed by and removable by him. In other words, the plural leadership represented by department boards was intended in reality to make the departments and the popularly elected officials heading them responsible to the governor. This purpose was further secured by the act's provision that all department employees except the constitutional officer and one deputy for each be appointed by the governor and serve at the will of the governor.[46]

[45] The attorney general was a statutory not a constitutional officer, elected by popular vote. McNutt's reorganization act made this an appointive position that was filled by the governor. The 1933 act also reduced the power of the attorney general, especially by taking control of the auto license bureau from this office and placing it in the treasury department. Neff, *Paul V. McNutt,* pp. 231-232.

[46] *Laws of Indiana,* 1933, pp. 7-17; Bates, "Indiana Puts Its Faith in Governor," *National Municipal Review,* XXII, 137-139; Buck, *The Reorganization of State Governments,* pp. 94-100.

The Executive Reorganization Act of 1933 attracted national interest. In Indiana and elsewhere attention focused on the central feature: the immense power granted to the governor. *Literary Digest*'s editors concluded that as a consequence of this legislation McNutt had become the nation's "first state dictator," though they conceded that it was "a constitutional dictatorship."[47] Other observers agreed: McNutt was the nation's most powerful governor. Observations on this new power were sometimes critical, especially when they came from Republicans, who were quick to charge that reorganization was a threat to the system of checks and balances that had traditionally prevailed in state government. But initial reaction in Indiana was generally favorable and included support from the Indiana Chamber of Commerce, the Indiana Federation of Labor, and the Indiana Farm Bureau.[48] This support was doubtless based in part on the high degree to which McNutt's reorganization adhered to basic and widely accepted principles of administrative organization in the 1930s. Reorganization was generally advanced as the solution to inefficient government. And, as one authority noted in 1939, "The major premise of the whole [reorganization] movement was: strengthen the governor, put your trust in the governor."[49] Even the Indianapolis *Star*, often a vigorous critic of McNutt, noted that his reorganization was "in line with modern ideas of business efficiency in public service."[50]

McNutt's reorganization moved state government toward a more centralized and integrated system—one in which responsibility was more hierarchically arranged and more clearly defined. Of course, the 1933 act did not revolutionize the practice of state

[47] *Literary Digest*, March 4, 1933, p. 12.

[48] Walter Davenport, "Indiana Gets a New Brew," *Collier's*, November 18, 1933, pp. 45-46; Bates, "Indiana Puts Its Faith in Governor," *National Municipal Review*, XXII, 137; Buck, *The Reorganization of State Governments*, p. 94; Indianapolis *Times*, February 21, 1933; Legislation Folder, Indiana Reformatory-Liquor Bill File, 1933, McNutt Papers, Archives Division.

[49] Leslie Lipson, *The American Governor from Figurehead to Leader* (Chicago, 1939), p. 268. See also Council of State Governments, *The Administrative Organization of State Government* (Chicago, 1950), pp. 4-7; Indiana State Committee on Governmental Economy, *Report*, pp. 42-45.

[50] Indianapolis *Star*, April 14, 1933. See also Indianapolis *Times*, November 11, 1933; Neff, Paul V. McNutt, pp. 233-240.

government. The Indiana State Committee on Governmental Economy, authorized by the 1933 legislature and appointed by McNutt, reported in 1934 that despite the reorganization act "many of the old separate departments have continued to operate as distinct units with little or no real supervision from the new department heads."[51] The committee recommended further tinkering and adjustment, and, most significantly, it advised giving more authority to elected officers as department heads, but concluded that the 1933 plan was a great step forward in achieving administrative efficiency and economy in state government.[52]

There was one aspect of McNutt's reorganization that especially troubled the Committee on Governmental Economy and many others as well. It was not so much the new structure of state government they feared as it was the application of the old system of political patronage to the new structure. Here was the Achilles' heel—the potential to centralize not only administrative power but political power for partisan and individual gain. The McNutt administration made the most of the potential.

§ § § §

Political patronage has a long history in Indiana, where it has been the stomach if not the heart or soul of the body politic. In the late nineteenth century the strength of the two major parties derived partly from their ability to appoint party workers to jobs in federal, state, and local government. After World War I, patronage continued as a major force in politics and government. The rapidly growing State Highway Commission offered especially lucrative opportunities. On taking office in 1921, Governor

[51] Indiana State Committee on Governmental Economy, *Report*, p. 45. The Committee on Governmental Economy was chaired by Bernard C. Gavit, of the Indiana University Law School. Other faculty members, especially from Indiana University, played major roles in preparing the report, notably R. Clyde White, who served as the committee's executive secretary; Frank G. Bates, who wrote the section on state administrative organization; and Clyde F. Snider, who prepared the report on local government. The lengthy report is a most significant document for understanding many aspects of government in the 1930s.

[52] *Ibid.*, pp. 46-49. The 1933 reorganization was partially overturned by the 1941 General Assembly. See Chapter XII.

Warren McCray replaced two Democrats on the Highway Commission with Republicans and appointed his own man, Lawrence Lyons, later Republican state chairman, as Highway Commission director. By the mid-1920s critics were charging that the Highway Commission was inefficient and poorly managed because of partisan influence in hiring both professional and unskilled workers, in purchasing materials, and in locating new road construction and improvements.[53] Patronage extended far beyond the state executive branch. Each house of the General Assembly had a committee—known as the plunder committee—to select doorkeepers, reading clerks, secretaries, and other service personnel, all on the basis of political considerations.[54] Township, county, and city governments also responded to the siren calls of partisanship. In Indianapolis the spoils system reached deep into city government: even the supervisors and instructors for the city's parks and playgrounds were chosen largely on the basis of political considerations.[55] Patronage at the state and local as well as national level led longtime Indiana civil service reformer William Dudley Foulke to warn in 1923 that the situation had become "pretty bad." "We have got to be at work again," Foulke advised, "and I am hoping some new steps may be taken by our people to stay the encroachments of the spoils system."[56]

Despite the hopes of Foulke and other patronage foes, the McNutt administration took office in a political environment that tolerated considerable patronage influence. McNutt's own desire for political power, the depth of the Depression which created

[53] F. E. Shortemeier to Frank Singleton, May 1, 1924, Branch Papers; Warren T. McCray, Memoirs (Typescript, Indiana Division, Indiana State Library), pp. 347-348; Indianapolis News, April 19, 1922, January 24, 1925; J. M. Henry, A Short History of the Indiana State Highway Commission (Indianapolis, 1926), passim. For an example of political pressure to locate a state road see James Dunbar to Harry G. Leslie, March 19, 1929, Leslie Papers.

[54] Indianapolis News, January 9, 1923; Feightner, Our State Government, p. 13.

[55] The Leisure of a People, pp. 230-232; Indianapolis Star, March 7, 1939; Lucius B. Swift, "Civil Service in Indianapolis," Good Government, XLI (1924), 113-116.

[56] William Dudley Foulke to Theodore Stempfel, October 2, 1923, Indiana History Manuscripts, Lilly Library, Indiana University, Bloomington.

thousands of political job seekers, and the return of Democrats to the statehouse after long years out of power—all combined to cause wide expansion of the patronage system.

There was no doubt that McNutt was the ultimate authority in questions relating to patronage, but the burden of administering it and taking much of the criticism from patronage opponents and disappointed job seekers fell on Pleas Greenlee. Greenlee's patronage correspondence was of alpine proportions. From a single county chairman in the period from June through September, 1933, Greenlee received at least twenty-six letters, all recommending deserving local Democrats for state jobs or complaining of Greenlee's failure to reward rank-and-file party workers adequately.[57] Greenlee's files bulged with lists, recommendations, and endorsements by county and district chairmen, often including information on party service, job experience, nationality, marital status, and age.[58] Perhaps to screen out Johnny-come-latelies—of whom there were many in 1933—many letters commented on the applicant's party lineage, including such recommendations as "He comes from one of the old line Democratic families of the county."[59] It was an impossible situation, as Greenlee lamented to one correspondent: "Nothing would give me greater happiness than to take care of my friends, but I am no miracle man. Because of the many people out of work as a result of the depression, I find myself unable to take care of 50,000 applicants with 3,000 jobs."[60]

Greenlee and McNutt could not turn stones into bread, but they could and did replace many Republicans with Democrats, a process made easier by the provision in the Reorganization Act of 1933 that required resignations of all executive branch employees on or before June 30, 1933, and allowed for reappointment or replacement by the governor. During 1933, for example, Rich-

57 See J. C. Whitesell File, June-December, 1933, Box 34, McNutt Papers, Archives Division. Whitesell was Democratic chairman in Marshall County.
58 See, for example, the eight-page annotated list of deserving East Chicago Democrats in Luther M. Swiggert to McNutt [1933], Box A, Drawer 88, ibid.
59 Henry S. Murray to McNutt, February 24, 1933, Box A, Drawer 88, ibid.
60 Greenlee to Clarence L. Martin, June 19, 1934, Box A, Drawer 82, ibid.

mond State Hospital hired 71 new employees, all but two of whom were Democrats. By the end of 1933 all but 34 of the institution's 181 employees were Democrats.[61] Most appointments went through the governor's office—usually across Greenlee's desk—and they included not only top-level policy makers and low-level unskilled workers, but professional and skilled employees as well. Thus the medical superintendent at Madison State Hospital wrote Greenlee, "If you can find two good registered nurses for us, we could use them to good advantage."[62] The Department of Conservation, headed by Richard Lieber, was affected from top to bottom. Clerks, park custodians, and wardens were appointed primarily on the basis of party loyalty. And at the top, Lieber, who had won national recognition for his progressive parks and conservation achievements, was demoted to director of the Division of State Parks and Lands and Waters, while McNutt's political and personal friend Virgil M. Simmons became not only commissioner of the Department of Conservation but also head of the Department of Public Works, into which the conservation agency was incorporated in the 1933 reorganization. In early July, 1933, Lieber resigned—driven out, his friends charged, by divided authority and patronage. It is important to note, however, that Lieber himself had charged that through the 1920s Republicans had attempted to force patronage appointments on him. Also, Lieber's enemies by 1933 included conservationists as well as Democratic politicians: the Indiana Izaak Walton League had passed a resolution condemning him in 1930. Nonetheless, it does seem that Lieber and his parks were indeed victims of a more intense and successful application of the spoils system in 1933 and after.[63]

The state police also felt the Greenlee-McNutt patronage power. Greenlee had approximately two dozen state policemen removed, and he required that new applications first be approved

[61] Neff, Paul V. McNutt, p. 295.

[62] James W. Milligan to Greenlee, August 29, 1934, Box A, Drawer 82, McNutt Papers, Archives Division.

[63] Frederick, Colonel Richard Lieber, pp. 333-340; H. H. Evans to Leslie, December 31, 1930, January 1, 1931, Leslie Papers.

by the applicant's Democratic precinct and county chairmen and then be sent to him. Greenlee also used state police personnel for political errands, often without the knowledge of the police superintendent, Al Feeney, who resisted this political interference until his dismissal in June, 1935. Librarians at the Indiana State Library also fell under the patronage umbrella in 1933. According to the Indiana Library Association the governor's office dismissed six qualified library employees in 1933 and in their place appointed Democrats, some of whom were not qualified by training or experience. The blow to professional morale was especially harsh for librarians, because, unlike police, hospital, park, and other state employees, they had been relatively immune from partisanship prior to the McNutt administration.[64]

Perhaps the boldest effort of the McNutt administration to reward loyal Democrats was through control of alcoholic beverages. The 1933 legislature repealed the bone-dry law and allowed the sale of beer and wine in Indiana but only under strict state supervision. Beer manufactured out of state had to be "imported" through one of ten licensed state importers—all appointed by a new state excise director. The 1933 legislature also required licenses for in-state manufacturers and for retailers and wholesalers, with no more than one wholesaler in each county for every twenty thousand people. The new liquor control system had several purposes: to prevent the return of the open saloon—a concession to temperance forces; to keep liquor racketeers out of the state; and to raise and collect efficiently revenue from fees charged for licenses and permits and from a new state excise tax on alcohol. By 1937 Indiana ranked sixth in state taxes and fees collected from the manufacture and sale of beer. But the liquor control system was also a part of McNutt's political organization. The excise director, Paul Fry, and Frank McHale, who played an even greater role, decided who would get the beer and liquor permits primarily on the basis of political loyalty. The list of importers and wholesalers, the Indianapolis *Times* noted, "reads

[64] Neff, Paul V. McNutt, pp. 317-319, 332-338; Walter Rader to Greenlee, April 24, 1935, Box A, Drawer 86, McNutt Papers, Archives Division; Indianapolis *News,* March 4, 1935.

like a 'who's who' of the McNutt faction of the Democratic Party. . . ."[65] These lucrative appointments provided large financial returns not only as a consequence of the system's monopolistic features, which allowed for higher prices charged from importer to wholesaler to retailer to consumer, but also because of the possibility, as was commonly believed at least, that importers assessed extra under-the-table fees to manufacturers and wholesalers for simply allowing them to do business.[66]

The appointment of loyal McNutt Democrats to the beer and liquor administration and to the state police, hospitals, parks, library, and other agencies and institutions of state government was only one step in building a patronage machine. Not only did the tenure of these appointees depend on their loyalty and service to the party, but it also came to depend on their financial contributions. Such contributions were a common and long-standing feature of Indiana politics, but, as in many other areas, the McNutt administration made even more thorough and more systematic the collection of state employee financial contributions. The vehicle designed to accomplish this was the Hoosier Democratic Club, established in mid-1933 with Simmons, Greenlee, and Elder as officers and composed primarily of state employees. Known more commonly as the "2 percent club," the organization collected 2 percent of each member's paycheck. Although club membership and contributions were voluntary in principle, it was commonly and often correctly assumed that no job was secure if the 2 percent assessment was not paid. Most departments and agencies had specially designated employees responsible for ensuring payment from coworkers. By late 1933 the club's income was approxi-

[65] Indianapolis *Times*, March 31, 1933; Indianapolis *News*, April 6, 1933; Feightner, 150 Years of Brewing in Indiana, Chapters 18-22; Neff, Paul V. McNutt, pp. 349-375; Warren Milton Persons, *Beer and Brewing in America: An Economic Study* (n.p., 1938), pp. 22-23; George L. Willis, The Administration of Alcoholic Beverage Control in Indiana (Ph.D. dissertation, Indiana University, Bloomington, 1953), pp. 65-76.

[66] Davenport, "Indiana Gets a New Brew," *Collier's*, November 18, 1933, p. 11. The 1935 legislation modified the liquor control system only slightly. In 1939, however, the legislature placed beer distribution on a more competitive basis, but the 1945 General Assembly, dominated by Republicans, reintroduced partisanship into the system. Feightner, 150 Years of Brewing in Indiana, Chapters 24-25.

mately $10,000 a month, income that was collected and controlled
not by the state Democratic organization but by McNutt loyalists,
who used it to support McNutt Democrats and later for the
governor's presidential bid.[67]

The expansion of patronage under the McNutt administration
did not go unchallenged. Republicans were loud in their charges
that state institutions had been "demoralized to a disgraceful point
by the injection of the 'spoils system' into their administration."
Democrats piously responded that they were only making state
employment bipartisan after so many years of Republican patronage appointments.[68] Less obviously partisan interest in patronage
came from the Indiana Committee on Governmental Economy,
which reported in late 1934. The section of the committee's report
on state government was written by Indiana University Professor
Frank G. Bates. As early as 1933, Bates, while strongly supporting
McNutt's government reorganization, had expressed fears that
"this power in the hands of a governor so disposed might become
a mighty engine of spoils and political plunder."[69] Such proved to
be the case, to the regret of Bates and apparently the majority of
the committee, who concluded that a formal merit system was
highly desirable. But such a direct attack on the patronage system
was foolhardy, the committee report stated, for it could be "effective only when there is an active general public sentiment to
uphold such a [merit] law. . . ." This sentiment did not exist in
Indiana, the report concluded. As a beginning and "until public
opinion demands and will support a further advance," the report
recommended designation of "certain state services as technical
and professional," with "suitable provision by law to 'take them

[67] Neff, Paul V. McNutt, pp. 304-315; Carleton B. McCulloch to Meredith
Nicholson, April 20, 1934, Box 2, Carleton B. McCulloch Papers, Indiana Historical Society Library. The 2 percent levy was continued by Republicans when they
returned to power. Its extent and duration in Indiana is the best known among
such efforts in several states. See Robert J. Huckshorn, Party Leadership in the
States (Amherst, Mass., 1976), p. 148.

[68] Republican and Democratic state platforms, 1934, in Indiana State Platforms, I.

[69] Bates, "Indiana Puts Its Faith in Governor," National Municipal Review,
XXII, 139.

out of politics' . . . ." The report included under this rubric positions in agencies and departments responsible for education, the state library, hospitals, prisons, public relief administration, police, highways, and conservation. To protect professional and technical positions in these areas, the committee recommended creation of a state personnel bureau which would hire and fire solely on the basis of merit.[70]

In 1935 this proposal for a limited merit system and a state personnel bureau reached the state senate, where it had strong backing by the Indiana League of Women Voters, probably the group most active in pushing for a state merit system throughout the 1930s.[71] But the senate bill encountered strong opposition and eventual defeat from the supporters of traditional patronage. Senator Claude McBride, a Democrat from Jeffersonville, said what many others doubtless thought: "All appointive offices should go to the victors. This bill is one of the dreams of theorists, the Crazy Janes, the Silly Sallies and the long-haired theorists who put over the Wright bone-dry law. They want to reform us by bringing in some college fellow who dreams of high things and let him set up a committee to select appointees. What incentive would the two political parties have to work at the polls?"[72] In the view of McBride and many other Democrats and Republicans patronage was the fuel that fired the engine of party. Their commitment to their own party and to the two-party system, as well as to their own individual place in the system, made movement away from patronage abhorrent.

And yet such movement did occur in the last half of the decade, if only in limited areas of government. In late 1936 the newly

[70] Indiana State Committee on Governmental Economy, *Report*, pp. 10, 53-54, 454.

[71] Indianapolis *News*, March 8, 1935; Pressly S. Sikes, *Indiana State and Local Government* (Bloomington, Ind., 1940), p. 168. For an example of the work of the League of Women Voters see Convention Patronage Survey [1938] State Conventions, 1929-1948, Indiana League of Women Voters Papers, Indiana Division, Indiana State Library. See also Greenough, *A History of the League of Women Voters of Indiana*, pp. 43-45, 47-48.

[72] Indianapolis *News*, March 8, 1935. See also Indiana *Senate Journal*, 1935, pp. 585, 1027.

created Department of Public Welfare and the Division of Unemployment Compensation co-operated to establish a joint Bureau
of Personnel. The new bureau had responsibility for recruiting
employees and for pay and promotion on the basis of merit
according to a detailed system of job classification. The new
personnel regulations also prohibited soliciting employees for
contributions to parties or candidates and prohibited employees
from participating in political work. By 1938 the bureau was
responsible for more than two thousand state employees. These
new regulations were the result in part of a detailed study supervised by the Public Administration Service of Chicago and conducted by professional, out-of-state experts in civil service, public
administration, and public welfare—the sort of people Senator
McBride would doubtless have included among his Silly Sallies
and long-haired theorists. The new personnel system adopted
jointly by the Department of Public Welfare and the Division of
Unemployment Compensation attracted nationwide interest, leading the Public Administration Service to publish a report on Indiana's program as a guide for other states interested in "the modern
concept of a personnel unit . . . ."[73] And the system apparently
met its major objectives, at least as far as patronage was concerned.
The League of Women Voters expressed their approval, and one
expert on Indiana's government noted in 1940 that as a consequence of the personnel bureau's work with the Department of
Public Welfare and the Division of Unemployment Compensation, "to a very great extent politics has been eliminated as a
factor in securing or holding positions in these units . . . ."[74]

There are several possible reasons why the McNutt administration allowed a limited merit system and why Governor M.
Clifford Townsend continued this system. First of all, it was very
limited, applying only to a portion of state government. There was

[73] Public Administration Service, *Personnel Administration and Procedure as
Installed in the Indiana Department of Public Welfare and Unemployment
Compensation Division* (Chicago, 1938), p. [iii] and *passim*.

[74] Sikes, *Indiana State and Local Government*, p. 169. See also Indiana Department of Public Welfare, *Four Years of Public Welfare in Indiana* (Indianapolis,
1940), pp. 239-257; *Public Welfare in Indiana*, XLVIII (September, 1938), 3.

also some movement away from patronage in the state police, the board of accounts, and the Division of Financial Institutions, but patronage and the 2 percent club continued to flourish elsewhere throughout the 1930s.[75] In addition, the application of the merit system came in a relatively new and special area of state government—public welfare. In the mid- and late 1930s many states adopted merit systems, resuming a civil service movement that had languished since World War I, and many of these state merit programs were instituted in departments and agencies responsible for rapidly expanding public welfare services—agencies that administered federal money. As noted in the following chapter, the federal social security program enacted in 1935 encouraged state agencies that administered social security benefits to develop progressive and professional personnel programs.[76] Indiana's limited merit system was part of this trend and was also a continuation of McNutt's generally co-operative response to federal welfare money and direction, as noted below. The McNutt administration may also have been influenced by other considerations. By waiting until late 1936 to initiate a limited merit system, the administration had sufficient time through the patronage process to remove most Republicans and put Democrats in their places. Thus, a merit system that protected incumbents as of 1936 would, in fact, protect McNutt's Democratic appointees. Also, the system became operative after the landslide Democratic victories of 1936, which ensured that Democrats would preside over its installation. And, while no direct evidence has been found, it is possible that McNutt's presidential ambition also pushed him toward support of the system. The McNutt machine and the 2 percent club, as much as they enhanced his power in the state, were likely to be political

[75] Sikes, *Indiana State and Local Government*, p. 168; Greenough, *A History of the League of Women Voters of Indiana*, pp. 47-48. In late 1936 McNutt transferred the state's benevolent and penal institutions from the Executive Department to the Department of Public Welfare, but these institutions do not seem to have been significantly affected by the merit system. Indianapolis *News*, January 1, 1937.

[76] G. Lyle Belsley, "The Advance of the Merit System," *State Government*, XII (January, 1939), 7-8, 18-19; Patterson, *The New Deal and the States*, pp. 195-196.

liabilities in the national arena. By the steps taken in late 1936, McNutt could leave office claiming credit for at least beginning a movement against patronage. Finally, it is possible that McNutt also acted because of a genuine belief in the efficiency and economy that the civil service experts promised would result from a merit system.

The limited merit system inaugurated in 1936 thus looked to the future. For the period of McNutt's governorship, patronage—applied systematically and sometimes ruthlessly—was the rule. Patronage was an integral part of McNutt's circle of political power. Patronage gave him power, and McNutt used that power to effect measures that extended his power. Government reorganization was the most notable example; it was McNutt's political strength that helped bring about reorganization, and the measure itself added greatly to that power in administering the affairs of government and in making patronage appointments. The gross income tax also resulted from McNutt's power, and the tax added to it by making more revenue available to state government. These measures and practices—patronage, reorganization, and the gross income tax—are prime examples of McNutt's exercise of power—of the way in which he used and expanded the power of the governor's office. They illustrate also his concern for efficiency, for, whatever one's opinions of his methods or objectives, under McNutt taxation, governmental administration, and patronage appointments were conducted more systematically and more efficiently than ever before in twentieth-century Indiana. The question remains whether this new power and efficiency were used to make government "a great instrument of human progress," as McNutt promised in his inaugural address.

CHAPTER IV

THE POLITICS OF THE 1930s:
RELIEF AND REFORM

PAUL McNUTT's attention to power and efficiency did not exclude the possibility of liberal social welfare policies and legislation in Indiana during the 1930s. A liberal or pro-McNutt view might argue that in order to achieve social reform McNutt first had to take care of the immediate political problems of taxation, administration, and patronage. The liberal achievements of some state governors in the 1930s were in part the consequences of their ability to draw on a tradition of progressive reform or agrarian radicalism in their states, sometimes from third parties. This was the case, for example, in Minnesota and Wisconsin.[1] Indiana did not have such a progressive tradition to any large degree, so that any Indiana governor hoping to pass liberal legislation needed first to have a strong political base within one of the two major parties. In short, partisan politics would be at least as important as ideology in any Hoosier New Deal. A less sympathetic view might emphasize that McNutt's limited social welfare reforms were designed to extend his power in the state and in the nation by attracting and holding new voters to the Democratic party.

Of all the problems Governor McNutt and most public officials faced in the 1930s, relief was the most important. McNutt acknowledged as much in his inaugural message in 1933. With tens of thousands of Hoosiers unemployed, relief agencies and public officials were beset with unprecedented demands for food, clothing, medical care, and jobs.[2] Bread lines and soup kitchens pro-

---

[1] Patterson, *The New Deal and the States*, pp. 130-133.

[2] Depression-era unemployment figures for Indiana exist only for the census count of 1930, when 86,379 of 1,251,177 gainful workers were unemployed—a rate of 6.9 percent. Unemployment increased rapidly thereafter and reached a high point in early 1933. Governor's Commission on Unemployment Relief, *Year Book*, 1933-1935, pp. 19-21.

liferated. So serious was the crisis that some warned of revolution. McNutt reminded his inaugural audience that "through the ages, hungry people have been in the vanguard of every revolt against the established order." And an Allen County attorney noted that more than five thousand families were on poor relief in the county and predicted that "the time is not far distant when we are going to be confronted with riots and violence in Fort Wayne."[3]

Society's desire for order, as well as a prevalent humanitarian attitude, called for response. But what kind of response and from where? The many and diverse efforts to relieve the suffering of the Great Depression showed local, state, and federal governments searching, vacillating, and experimenting with new forms of public relief and welfare. In the process there was significant adjustment in the relationships between various units of government and between government aid and private aid for needy Hoosiers. The result was a new degree of governmental responsibility for dependent citizens and a shift toward larger state and federal government.

§ §

Prior to 1933 local communities had full responsibility for relief. During the relatively prosperous 1920s, local voluntary charities had assisted some needy residents but had concentrated on broader philanthropic endeavors—particularly on such character-building organizations as the Boy Scouts and the YMCA. By 1930, as unemployment increased, local charity efforts began to focus on relief work. In many towns and cities community chests or federated charitable organizations, founded in the 1920s to co-ordinate all local charitable work, now devoted resources exclusively to relief. These local voluntary agencies made important contributions, but by 1932 the enormity of the relief problem had overwhelmed many of them. In early 1932, for example, Muncie's Community Chest failed for the first time to meet its relatively

---

[3] McNutt, *Inaugural Address*; Samuel C. Cleland to Earl Crawford, February 6, 1933, Unemployment (I) File, 1933, McNutt Papers, Archives Division.

modest budget, and Shelbyville's Federated Charities organization exhausted its funds and closed its doors.[4]

Like voluntary relief efforts, public relief was also locally financed and administered prior to the early 1930s. County governments appropriated relief funds from local taxes, and elected township trustees administered the money. The most obvious difficulty with the system after 1930 was insufficient local financing to meet the legitimate relief needs of Hoosiers, especially in urban areas. Conditions were probably worst in Lake County, where by 1932 officials were compelled to issue scrip for purchases of groceries and coal, and where the two urban townships of the county had overdrawn their relief funds by $2.4 million and had covered this deficit by tax-anticipation warrants on collections for 1933 and 1934. To reduce relief rolls, Lake County government and business leaders in 1932 organized a program to return immigrants who had come from Mexico during the prosperous 1920s. By the end of the year more than three thousand Mexicans had been repatriated, some voluntarily, others by force. Even in a small town like Shelbyville, requests for aid hopelessly exceeded the local financial resources.[5]

Governor Harry Leslie, like nearly all state and national leaders in the early years of the Depression, was reluctant to recognize the need for government action, though one scholar has characterized Leslie's attitude as "unusually reactionary."[6] In November, 1930, he called together an Indiana Advisory Committee for

[4] *Indianapolis Community Fund News*, October 29, 1925; McFadden, *Shelbyville*, pp. 304-305; Lynd and Lynd, *Middletown in Transition*, pp. 103-104, 113; Governor's Commission on Unemployment Relief, *Year Book*, 1933-1935, p. 20. For a detailed look at local relief efforts in Evansville see Activities of Unemployed Relief, 1931-1932, Notebook, Jennings Papers.

[5] Lake County Relief Committee, *The Story of Unemployment Relief Work in Lake County, Indiana* (East Chicago, Ind., 1932), pp. 2, 10-11; Oswald Garrison Villard, "Hammond and Gary Face the Disaster," *Nation*, March 29, 1933, pp. 343-344; Neil Betten and Raymond A. Mohl, "From Discrimination to Repatriation: Mexican Life in Gary, Indiana, during the Great Depression," *Pacific Historical Review*, XLII (1973), 370-388; Daniel T. Simon, "Mexican Repatriation in East Chicago, Indiana," *Journal of Ethnic Studies*, II (1974), 11-23; McFadden, *Shelbyville*, pp. 304-306; Governor's Commission on Unemployment Relief, *Year Book*, 1933-1935, p. 22.

[6] Patterson, *The New Deal and the States*, p. 34.

Relief of the Unemployed, composed mostly of Indiana businessmen. In his opening remarks to the committee, Leslie
commented on calls for government relief by cautioning that
"the greatest danger of a movement of this kind is pauperizing
people."[7] Committee members agreed, for they offered little
more than words of encouragement to the jobless and gave no
hint of state aid. A representative of labor, a member of the
Indianapolis printers' union, correctly summarized the committee's work: "We have talked and we have dealt in generalities.
No concrete proposition has been presented . . . ."[8] Governor
Leslie's message to the 1931 legislature did not mention issues
relating to unemployment or relief.[9] And the governor directed
the special legislative session called for July, 1932, to consider
only the question of taxation.[10] Leslie did request some aid from
the federal government's new Reconstruction Finance Corporation (RFC) but only reluctantly and only for a few cities. When
he advised that "we should care for our own," he meant a continuation of local aid without significant state or federal help.[11]

RFC loans for relief were the beginning. Much more important
stimuli to the shift from local to state and federal administration
and control of relief came with Franklin D. Roosevelt's New
Deal. With his election mandate of 1932 and with a multitude of
requests to respond to the worsening national disaster, Roosevelt
took office in March, 1933, and announced a series of relief measures and programs. The Public Works Administration (PWA),
established in June, 1933, provided federal support for large-scale
public construction projects such as water and sewage treatment

<hr/>

[7] Transcript of Unemployment Conference, November 6, 1930, p. 3, Governor's Commission on Unemployment Relief File, Box F, Drawer 45, Leslie
Papers.

[8] *Ibid.*, p. 51.

[9] Indiana *Senate Journal*, 1931, pp. 10-17.

[10] *Ibid.*, 1932, pp. 9-12.

[11] *Ibid.*, 1933, p. 10; Theodore Whiting (ed.), *Final Statistical Report of the
Federal Emergency Relief Administration* (Washington, D.C., 1942), pp. 2-4;
Indianapolis *Times*, October 31, 1932. Federal money from RFC went largely to
Indiana's urban counties. Marion County received more than 20 percent of the
state's total of $5,179,931. Governor's Commission on Unemployment Relief,
Year Book, 1933-1935, pp. 22-23.

facilities, highways, and public housing, but PWA did not spend money broadly or in sufficient amounts to provide significant relief.[12]

The most successful of the early federal programs was the Federal Emergency Relief Administration (FERA), established in May, 1933. FERA made grants-in-aid to states on approval of applications from the governors. State and local officials decided on eligibility for relief and amounts of relief aid for each individual. FERA provided Indiana with $71,189,631 in federal money—most of it from 1933 through 1935. During this period, FERA provided the great bulk of relief funds in the state, reaching a peak of 72 percent of total relief funds in the fiscal year ending June 30, 1935. During the same twelve months, local funds amounted to less than 28 percent of total relief and state funds were less than 1 percent.[13]

Because of popularly held beliefs in Indiana and the nation that a dole was demoralizing to the recipient and bad business for the government and taxpayer, there were several efforts made toward linking relief with work. The most important such program in the early years of the New Deal was the Civil Works Administration (CWA), established on November 9, 1933. Eight days later, Governor McNutt and federal representatives met in Indianapolis with two thousand county, city, and township officials to explain the program and encourage applications. Within a week more than twenty-six thousand Hoosiers were at work on CWA projects, one of the most rapidly instituted relief programs and one of the most successful. In its brief existence from November, 1933, through March, 1934, CWA paid out more than $22 million in wages to more than one hundred thousand needy Hoosier workers, which greatly assisted them through the difficult winter. Local governments provided the materials for the projects, which

[12] Indiana State Planning Board, *Preliminary Report on a State Plan for Indiana* (n.p., 1934), p. 134; Neff, Paul V. McNutt, p. 255. For a general summary of New Deal relief programs see James Leiby, *A History of Social Welfare and Social Work in the United States* (New York, 1978), pp. 217-244.

[13] Whiting (ed.), *Final Statistical Report of the Federal Emergency Relief Administration*, p. 145; Governor's Commission on Unemployment Relief, *Year Book*, 1933-1935, pp. 61, 113.

were mostly maintenance jobs on streets, highways, waterways, and public buildings.[14]

Local public relief, RFC loans, and later the federal relief agencies, particularly FERA and CWA, created a variety of often confusing and overlapping efforts during the years 1933 to 1935 to relieve the suffering caused by the Great Depression. To co-ordinate and centralize these efforts, McNutt, with the state legislature's approval, created in March, 1933, the Governor's Commission on Unemployment Relief (GCUR). GCUR membership included a relief chairman in each county and an executive committee of seven members. All served as volunteers. The director of the salaried staff was William H. Book, Jr., a former employee of the Indianapolis Chamber of Commerce, who also served as director of the Indiana Department of Public Welfare. GCUR began as a largely advisory body, but its power and authority increased greatly as federal money began to flow to Indiana in 1933 and 1934. In particular, the federal government made GCUR responsible for distributing funds from FERA and CWA and for insuring that minimum federal requirements and standards were met by local Indiana officials.[15]

§ § §

Federal relief money and GCUR's control and administration of it from Indianapolis were direct threats to the tradition of local autonomy for relief in Indiana. Until 1933 the township trustee decided who received relief aid and how much they received. The township trustee was generally a local politician, serving his community, his political party, and his personal friends—not

[14] Howard O. Hunter to Harry L. Hopkins, November 18, 1933, Field Reports, 406, Indiana, FERA State Files, 1933-1936, RG 69, National Archives, Washington, D.C.; Civil Works Administration, A History of Indiana State Civil Works Administration, November 15, 1933-March 31, 1934 (Typescript, National Archives, Washington, D.C.), pp. 17-19; Governor's Commission on Unemployment Relief, Year Book, 1933-1935, p. 246. For difficulties facing some local governments in financing and administering CWA and other federal projects see Carrolyle M. Frank, "Who Governed Middletown? Community Power in Muncie, Indiana, in the 1930s," Indiana Magazine of History, LXXV (1979), 329-341.

[15] Governor's Commission on Unemployment Relief, Year Book, 1933-1935, pp. 15-17, 84.

always in that order of priority. The township trustee could apply his own personal standards in granting or withholding relief and might do so on the basis of considerations other than need. He might provide groceries, fuel, or medical aid purchased only from his favored suppliers. In the more populous townships, where the trustee hired relief investigators, he had opportunities to make patronage appointments. Sometimes a trustee was guilty of corruption or excessive political partisanship. Often he simply lacked the time, capability, and/or training to deal adequately with relief problems as the number of unemployed increased.[16] With the formation of GCUR and the availability of federal money through GCUR, criticism of and challenges to this traditional, locally oriented relief system burst forth.

These challenges were part of a general struggle between people favoring home rule, as they often labeled their sentiments, and others arguing for more centralization and professionalization in government. Local township and county officials had traditionally been responsible for a variety of government functions—most notably education, relief, roads, and taxation. In each of these important areas there were major efforts after World War I to reduce or abolish this local control. In the field of education, there were attempts to organize and administer schools by a county rather than a township system and to increase state aid and control over local schools. The establishment of the State Highway Commission in 1919 was the beginning of an increasing trend toward state direction of highway construction and maintenance. State limitations on local taxation and McNutt's gross income tax were steps away from local autonomy in finance.[17] This general trend toward centralization received its most systematic expression in the report of the Committee on Governmental Economy, which

[16] *Ibid.*, pp. 10, 23-24; Indiana State Committee on Governmental Economy, *Report*, pp. 219-220; Indianapolis *News*, April 16, 1932. For a general description of Indiana's traditional relief system see Alice Shaffer, Mary Wysor Keefer, and Sophonisba P. Breckinridge, *The Indiana Poor Law* . . . (Chicago, 1936).

[17] E. B. McPheron, *A Summary of Indiana Centralization* (Bloomington, Ind., 1938), p. 2; Indiana Inter-Organization Council, *Eleven-Year Trend in Indiana State Government Payments and Receipts, 1928-1938*, pp. 3, 15; Feightner, *Our State Government*, pp. 9-10. See chapters that follow on education and transportation for elaboration of these changes in school and highway control.

had been appointed by McNutt. In 1934 the committee made two general recommendations for local governments: they needed more expert, professional personnel, and they needed structural reorganization. Both recommendations promised to produce greater economy and efficiency. The committee advised significant changes in the structure of county government, where, it concluded, power and responsibility had become so diffused that no official could be held responsible. As a remedy, the committee proposed a single county board to replace the county council and board of county commissioners. Most important, the committee recommended creation of a county executive—"a technically qualified administrator"—to manage county government but to serve at the pleasure of the county board.[18] The committee's recommendations for township government were more drastic: it advised abolition of township government and assumption of its functions in education and relief by county government. "Under modern transportation and communication systems a county unit of government is much more local, much closer to its constituency than was the township in 1850 . . . . It is therefore no violation of the principle of local self-government to change the local unit to conform to modern facts as to what constitutes a locality for governmental purposes."[19] There was even some sentiment outside the Committee on Governmental Economy to consolidate several county governments into one regional unit. In 1935 such a movement was under way in Vermillion, La Porte, Warren, and Fountain counties.[20]

Recommendations to reorganize township and county govern-

[18] Indiana State Committee on Governmental Economy, *Report*, pp. 149-150. See also pp. 160-163, 188.

[19] *Ibid.*, pp. 5-6. In his message to the General Assembly in 1931 Governor Harry G. Leslie, using similar arguments, had recommended combining township and county government: "In this modern age, when distances have ceased to be formidable and urban facilities have made all sections kin, the reasons for our numerous expensive political units have become obsolete. Mergers and consolidations in industry and business are the order of the new day." Indiana *House Journal*, 1931, p. 19. See also Indiana Tax Survey Committee, *Report to the Seventy-seventh General Assembly* . . . , pp. 5, 14.

[20] Conference on State Planning Administration, *Minutes . . . December 12 and 13, 1935* (Chicago, 1935), p. 66. The Indiana State Board of Health did develop regional, multi-county units in the late 1930s. See Chapter X.

ments and to place professional administrators as county managers unleashed a fiery opposition from local politicians, especially from the Indiana County Commissioners' Association and the Indiana State Association of Township Trustees. Their joint publication, the *Indiana County and Township Officer*, characterized the recommendations of the Committee on Governmental Economy as a "fantastic proposal [that] would remove the government entirely from the people . . . ."[21] Throughout the mid- and late 1930s these associations through their publications, annual conventions, and legislative lobbyists attacked the committee's recommendations and other similar proposals, and vigorously defended home rule. The argument was simple and always the same: "We believe in home rule because we can look the spender of our money in the eye."[22] Government at a distance could not be trusted. The county commissioners and township trustees associations also attacked efforts to introduce professional administrators and any form of merit system into local government, branding such proposals a racket propounded by colleges and universities which "would like to have a monopoly on all public offices . . . . to dictate the employment of every person in public life from the lowly janitor to the highest paid county director."[23]

The threats to home rule in the 1930s were perhaps made even more frustrating to supporters of local autonomy because they came when the Democratic party was in power. Indiana Democrats in the 1920s had strongly defended home rule, often against Republican-led attacks. As late as 1932 the Democratic state platform had declared that because "that government is best which is nearest those governed, we stand against consolidation of counties and the abolishment of township units . . . ."[24] The

21 "Trustees, Commissioners, and Others Affected," *Indiana County and Township Officer*, III (January, 1935), 4.

22 "An Open Letter to the Legislature," *ibid.*, [V] (February, 1937), 3.

23 Leo X. Smith, "The New Racket," *ibid.*, IV (November, 1936), 1. The *Indiana County and Township Officer* criticized college professors for supporting the merit system and local government reorganization, sometimes using pejoratively the label "brain trust." See "Another Professor Speaks," *ibid.*, V (April, 1937), 5.

24 Democratic state platform, 1932, in Indiana State Platforms, I. See also

Depression and the ambitions of Paul McNutt combined to help alter if not repeal this plank, especially in regard to local control of relief. McNutt's support of new directions in local government and particularly relief administration was critical.[25] Equally important was the impetus from the federal government and professional social workers.

§ § § §

The conflict over local government in general and the alleged shortcomings of local township trustee administration of relief in particular was well illustrated in a long letter written in early 1933 to Harry Hopkins, federal relief administrator. The Indiana correspondent was David Liggett, the professionally oriented manager of the Indianapolis Community Fund. Liggett warned Hopkins that "the expenditure of R.F.C. funds in Indiana has, up to date, only served to tighten a rotten political situation. . . . The township trustee state lobby makes any utility lobby look like a harmless collection of little Red Ridinghoods." Liggett was doubtful that the newly created Governor's Commission on Unemployment Relief would be of much help, since he had little confidence in GCUR Director Book: "Not by the slightest chance does he know a damn thing about relief administration," Liggett lamented. Above all, he pleaded to Hopkins, "if we don't have some help from the outside, the whole mess of greasy Hoosier politicians are going to be absolutely nowhere—and God help the semi-hopeless state after that." In short, Liggett feared that the parochialism and partisan politics of the township trustees would subvert efforts of professional social workers to provide efficient, rational, and fair delivery of relief in Indiana.[26]

Indianapolis *News*, June 3, 1926. By the late 1930s Republican party platforms were attacking Democratic infringement on home rule. See Indianapolis *News*, May 24, 1940.

[25] Paul McNutt publicly approved the recommendations of the Committee on Governmental Economy for restructuring local government. Neff, Paul V. McNutt, pp. 240-243.

[26] David Liggett to Hopkins, May 22, 1933, Indiana General, FERA State Files, RG 69. See also Liggett to Hopkins, May 26, 1933, *ibid.*

Hopkins forcefully answered Liggett's appeal for outside help: along with federal funds he sent FERA field representatives to Indiana to monitor relief policy and administration. Again and again the federal field agents reported difficulties growing out of the local power of township trustees. At the same time, however, their reports expressed positive evaluations of GCUR, contrary to Liggett's expectations. In particular, FERA field representatives and GCUR administrators agreed on the need to appoint trained and capable social workers to investigate relief cases. The director of GCUR's Social Service Department was Nadia Deem, a professional social worker who had served with the New York Charity Organization Society and with the Indianapolis Family Welfare Society. Deem faced at least two difficulties: an inadequate supply of trained caseworkers and the demand of township trustees and other local politicians to make their own appointments, not always with regard for the professional capabilities of the caseworker.[27] In October, 1933, FERA field representative Howard O. Hunter, who was responsible for reporting relief activities in several midwestern states, wrote from Indianapolis to Hopkins: "The situation in Indiana with regard to local political groups stampeding the relief organizations for jobs is the most violent I have seen yet." In a meeting with Hunter, Governor McNutt told him that there was strong criticism of Deem's professionally oriented personnel policy and that he was "under constant pressure from the township boys," especially in St. Joseph and Lake counties. Hunter insisted to McNutt that personnel selection and supervision "should be entirely in the hands of the State Commission [GCUR], subject to our [FERA's] approval." McNutt agreed to support Deem and her professional policy and to endeavor to resist the pressure from local politicians.[28]

Hunter's later reports from Indiana expressed high praise for

[27] Governor's Commission on Unemployment Relief, *Year Book*, 1933-1935, pp. 84-85.

[28] Hunter to Hopkins, October 17, 1933, Field Reports, 406, Indiana, FERA State Files, 1933-1936, RG 69. For the special difficulties in Lake County see Lee G. Lauck to Corrington Gill, September 7, 1933, Indiana, 406.2, *ibid*.

the co-operative efforts of McNutt and GCUR. In early 1934 Hunter reported that the GCUR staff and Director Book "are playing a strictly ethical game. . ." and that "Governor McNutt is backing them up." McNutt, Hunter concluded, "has done what we asked him to," even though political pressure on him was "very severe."[29] In late 1934 Hunter stated that "the Indiana Relief Commission [GCUR] continues to operate in an orderly manner and with about as little trouble to us as any State I know of."[30] McNutt, Hunter noted, "has certainly been as cooperative as we could possibly desire."[31]

Although it appears that McNutt and GCUR succeeded for a time in resisting local pressure for political appointments, home rule sentiment and township trustees proved constant stumbling blocks in efforts to develop a professional state relief structure. The solution, Hunter quickly concluded, was for Hoosiers to "get rid of their atrocious township system."[32] Professional social workers had long favored substituting a countywide system of relief administration for the township system.[33] By March, 1934, McNutt and GCUR leaders had agreed to "establish a county unit system of Relief Administration with County Commissions appointed by the State Commission."[34] In June, 1934, GCUR moved to a county relief system which centralized administration in Indianapolis. The new structure eliminated the township trustee, in Hunter's words, "from any active participation in the relief administration other than to furnish township money."

[29] Hunter to Hopkins, January 19, 1934, Field Reports, 406, Indiana, *ibid.*

[30] Hunter to Hopkins, September 19, 1934, *ibid.* See also William H. Book to Hopkins, January 31, 1934, Indiana Official Administrative Correspondence, CWA, RG 69, National Archives, Washington, D.C.

[31] Hunter to Hopkins, December 12, 1934, Group 24, Box 57, Harry Hopkins Papers, Franklin D. Roosevelt Library, Hyde Park, New York. For evidence of the lack of co-operation from many governors see Patterson, *The New Deal and the States*, pp. 57-63, and John Braeman, Robert H. Bremner, and David Brody, *The New Deal*. Vol. II: *The State and Local Levels* (Columbus, Ohio, 1975), pp. xiii and *passim*.

[32] Hunter to Hopkins, January 19, 1934, Field Reports, 406, Indiana, FERA State Files, 1933-1936, RG 69.

[33] Liggett to Hopkins, May 22, 1933, Indiana General, *ibid.*

[34] Hunter to Hopkins, March 20, 1934, Field Reports, 406, Indiana, *ibid.*

This change, Hunter reported, "was due to the fact that we could fix it by control of funds. . . ." The result, he concluded, was an "outstanding improvement of the personnel of local case workers and county directors." The more efficient and professional structure and administration resulting from the county relief unit was, Hunter predicted, to be a permanent part of Indiana's welfare system. McNutt recommended such a change in his message to the 1935 General Assembly.[35]

The high hopes of Hunter, Deem, Liggett, and other professional administrators and social workers and also of McNutt that they had created a centralized, professional relief system in 1934 and that the township trustee had been shut out of providing relief services were soon dashed. Instead, as Deem sadly noted, by late 1935 their "organization [was] crashing to bits. . ." and they were "about to enter a period of dark days. . . ."[36] Rather than the beginning of radical departures, the dramatic reduction of township trustee power in 1934 and 1935, the creation of the county unit system, and the power of GCUR were only temporary phenomena—consequences of the depths of the Great Depression, McNutt's political power, and the large amounts of federal money available through state agencies in Indianapolis. In 1935 federal relief policy shifted with the abolition of FERA and federal funding of direct relief. This shift left GCUR with little authority or money and returned to the township trustee the responsibility for aiding needy Hoosiers mentally or physically unable to provide for themselves. As in pre-FERA years, local taxes again provided all the direct relief (Indiana was one of only twelve states in which this was the case), and township trustees decided how that relief would be administered.[37]

Township trustees and others claimed that the partial resump-

---

[35] Hunter to Hopkins, August 13, 1934, *ibid.*; Indiana *House Journal*, 1935, p. 20.

[36] Nadia Deem to Gertrude Springer, September 14, 1935, Box 1, Projects, Correspondence, and Reports, Records of the Governor's Commission on Unemployment Relief, Archives Division, Indiana Commission on Public Records, Indiana State Library and Historical Building.

[37] Patterson, *The New Deal and the States*, pp. 74-75; State of Indiana, Governor's Commission on Unemployment Relief, *Year Book*, 1935-1936, pp. 4, 7-8.

tion of the traditional, locally funded and administered relief system was less costly and more democratic. Locally elected officials, familiar with local conditions, made the decisions—not an outsider with only a textbook knowledge of relief and no understanding of Center, Van Buren, or any of the approximately one thousand other townships in Indiana. A township trustee from Vanderburgh County doubtless voiced the sentiments of others when he wrote in 1936, after GCUR's professional social workers and their supporters had been routed: "I remember well the three years of trouble we had with Mr. Book and our college-bred supervisors and visitors. The trustees had to give them, besides road directions, the practical knowledge and the true history of the families."[38] Critics responded, of course, that after 1935 Indiana's direct relief system reverted to many of the old abuses, and that it was inefficient and costly, was subject to personal and partisan whims, and was often haphazard and chaotic in its delivery of aid to those who most needed it.[39]

But the shift in New Deal relief policy in 1935 enabled only a partial resumption of township trustee responsibility. Local authority was more limited and controlled than in the years prior to 1933. In place of FERA and GCUR, the state and federal governments created several new welfare agencies and programs in 1935 and 1936. Two in particular had critical effects on relief and on the relationship among local, state, and federal governments: the Works Progress Administration (WPA), which provided work relief (as distinct from direct relief) for employ-

[38] John Fridy to Wayne Coy, May 15, 1936, Correspondence, Union-Vigo, Records of the Governor's Commission on Unemployment Relief. See also Smith, "The New Racket," *Indiana County and Township Officer*, IV, 1; "Relief and Home Rule—Some Reasons against the County Unit System," *ibid.*, VI (March, 1938), 3-5.

[39] Donald S. Howard, *The WPA and Federal Relief Policy* (New York, 1943), pp. 54-56, 96-97, 371; Virginia S. Campbell to Gertrude Springer, February 6, 1936, Deem to Springer, September 14, 1935, Box 1, Projects, Correspondence, and Reports, Records of the Governor's Commission on Unemployment Relief. For evidence of some of the worst abuses see Governor's Commission on Unemployment Relief, Report on Poor Relief Administrative Policies and Procedures in Calumet, Hobart, and North Townships in Lake County, Indiana (Mimeographed, 1939, Indiana Division, Indiana State Library).

able Americans—the category in which the majority of relief cases in Indiana fell—and the Social Security Act, which brought federal and state money and administration to some dependent groups that were formerly the responsibility of local governments or of private benevolence.

§ § § § §

The Social Security Act of 1935 marked a new recognition by the federal government of public responsibility for aged and dependent Americans. But it was a responsibility the federal government insisted upon sharing with the states by requiring state administration and state financial support. McNutt eagerly cooperated. In 1936 he called a special session of the General Assembly to provide the legislation necessary for the state's participation in the several social security programs.[40] At the same time McNutt used the opportunity provided by federal legislation to make significant changes in the state's welfare system.

In 1934 the Committee on Governmental Economy had reported that Indiana was "far behind the more progressive states" in the organization and administration of public welfare work. To catch up, the committee recommended an integrated and centralized system of state control of public welfare activities.[41] Such a proposal received impetus from the changes in federal relief policy in 1935, which provided new programs and the bait of federal money to stimulate structural change in Indiana's welfare system.[42]

The special Indiana legislative session that met in March, 1936, provided the most significant changes in welfare in the history of the state. Three pieces of legislation were passed, all in response to the Social Security Act of 1935: the Public Health Act, which allowed the state to co-operate with federal health programs (see

[40] Indiana *House Journal*, 1936, pp. 9-13.

[41] Indiana State Committee on Governmental Economy, *Report*, pp. 198-283, quotation on page 276. FERA field agent Howard O. Hunter worked with the committee in preparing its report on public welfare. Hunter to Hopkins, September 19, 1934, Field Reports, 406, Indiana, FERA State Files, 1933-1936, RG 69.

[42] Martha A. Chickering, "States Look at Public Welfare," *Survey*, LXVIII (1937), 135-137.

Chapter X); the Unemployment Compensation Act, which provided for employer and employee contributions to a reserve fund
to be used for unemployment benefits; and the Public Welfare
Act. In the Public Welfare Act of 1936 the legislature established,
as the Committee on Governmental Economy had recommended,
a Department of Public Welfare with wide authority over a host
of state welfare areas, including state hospitals, correctional institutions, and child welfare services, and, most important, responsibility for implementing and administering the new federal social
security programs for dependent Americans.[43]

Perhaps the most important of these new social security programs was the provision for old-age assistance. The Depression
fell with special force on the elderly. Prior to 1933 the elderly
poor, like the poor of all ages, were the responsibility of local
government and sometimes of church and charitable organizations. They were eligible for township relief and, in many parts of
Indiana, for care in the county almshouse, commonly known as
the county poor farm or county home. The poor farm was a
nineteenth-century institution (with origins in Elizabethan England) that had once served the poor of all ages, but by 1930 it
functioned largely as a home for the aged and infirm. The physical
comforts and care provided by most county poor farms were
minimal at best.[44] One response to such conditions was the effort
to provide a state old-age pension—a proposal that raised strong
opposition. A Jasper lawyer summarized the opposing arguments

---

[43] *Laws of Indiana*, 1936, pp. 12-80. The Department of Public Welfare replaced the State Board of Charities and Corrections, established in 1889, which
had only very limited authority over state institutions, each of which was governed by a separate board of trustees (the so-called "Indiana Plan"). McNutt's
reorganization in 1933 changed the name of the board to the Department of
Public Welfare and placed it in the Executive Department, but this did not
change its functions. Not until 1936 did the department receive new functions
and become a separate state department. R. Clyde White, "Recent Public Welfare
and Social Legislation in Indiana," *Social Service Review*, X (1936), 206-226;
Indiana State Committee on Governmental Economy, *Report*, pp. 59, 277.

[44] Indiana State Committee on Governmental Economy, *Report*, pp. 220-225;
Lynn Robertson, J. B. Kohlmeyer, and J. E. Losey, *Indiana County Homes and
Their Adaptation to Present Conditions* (Purdue University Agricultural Ex-
periment Station *Bulletin, No. 525*, Lafayette, Ind., February, 1948), pp. 3-13.

when the state legislature considered a very limited pension plan in 1931: "It is socialism, pure and simple, bordering on communism and redism." More specifically, the lawyer asserted, the plan would penalize those who worked hard, particularly by increasing taxes, and would help the many undeserving poor, the "ex-saloon keepers, and old whiskey soaks and bloats, all of whom have fooled away their life and time. . . ."[45] But such traditional pocketbook and ideological objections receded as the Depression continued and as local relief money and county poor farms were unable to care for the aged. Labor unions and the Fraternal Order of Eagles were especially active in pushing for an old-age pension, aided by some social welfare experts.[46] In 1932 the Democratic platform called for an old-age pension, and in 1933 McNutt introduced and the legislature passed such a bill. However, the Indiana pension law was very limited and stringent. Only those over the age of seventy who had lived in the county for fifteen years and had no near relatives able to support them were eligible for the maximum of fifteen dollars a month, and pensions were deducted from the estate of the pensioner. By late 1934 about 16 percent of the state's population over seventy was receiving state pensions, and the mean amount received was less than eight dollars a month, considerably lower than the maximum allowed. Although the state paid half the pension and the counties the other half, the administration of the program was left entirely to the counties.[47]

[45] W. E. Cox to Leslie, February 12, 1931, Box D, Drawer 45, Leslie Papers.

[46] Indianapolis *Times,* February 22, 1933; R. Clyde White to McNutt, January 11, 1933, Box 16, January-May, 1933, McNutt Papers, Archives Division. White, who was director of the Bureau of Social Research at Indiana University, Indianapolis in 1933, played a leading role in drafting the section on public welfare in the Committee on Governmental Economy, *Report,* and he chaired the committee that drafted the welfare legislation passed in 1936. White, "Recent Public Welfare and Social Legislation in Indiana," *Social Service Review,* X, 206.

[47] Democratic state platform, 1932, in Indiana State Platforms, I; Neff, Paul V. McNutt, pp. 157-158; Indiana State Committee on Governmental Economy, *Report,* pp. 225-226; Indiana *Year Book,* 1940, p. 481. Approximately two dozen states passed old-age pension laws in the early 1930s, many of them with provisions similar to the Indiana law. James A. Maxwell, *The Fiscal Impact of Federalism in the United States* (Cambridge, Mass., 1946), pp. 114-115.

The 1933 pension law did accept a state obligation to the elderly poor, but the law failed to meet their needs. Elderly Hoosiers deluged McNutt with letters, often written with pencil held in shaky hand, pleading for expansion of the law.[48] The significant response came from the federal government in the old-age assistance provisions of the Social Security Act of 1935, which provided one federal dollar for every dollar the states contributed for assistance to the elderly, up to fifteen dollars per month. The federal act required a federally approved state agency to administer the assistance program. McNutt and the Democratic legislature co-operated: the Indiana Public Welfare Act of 1936 made the new Department of Public Welfare the agent of the federal program and established the administrative machinery necessary to carry out the provisions. The Department of Public Welfare also took similar steps to carry out portions of the federal Social Security Act that provided for shared federal-state assistance to the blind and to dependent children. By 1940 the Department of Public Welfare was responsible for more than twelve thousand children who were neglected, abused, or physically or mentally handicapped, and more than thirty-five thousand children who received financial aid as needy dependent children. McNutt designated the Public Welfare Act of 1936 as the most important legislation passed in Indiana in two decades.[49]

There was legislative opposition to the Public Welfare Act of 1936. Thirteen of the ninety-three votes cast in the house were negative—all from Republicans.[50] Their opposition was summarized by Henry County Representative Herbert H. Evans. The new laws, Evans asserted, would place "a premium on waste, and

[48] Many such letters are in Box A, Drawer 92, McNutt Papers, Archives Division.

[49] White, "Recent Public Welfare and Social Legislation in Indiana," *Social Service Review*, X, 207-219; Neff, Paul V. McNutt, p. 281; Indiana *Year Book*, 1940, pp. 454-459, 485. Perhaps indicative of the limited aid for elderly Hoosiers is the census report for 1940 that counted more than 50 percent of Indiana males between the ages of sixty-five and seventy-four still employed and 20 percent of those over the age of seventy-five still employed. United States Bureau of the Census, *Sixteenth Census* (1940), III, *Population*, Pt. 2, p. 965.

[50] Indiana *House Journal*, 1936, p. 56.

indolence . . ." and would make "the state automatically . . . a province of the National Government . . . ." It was "an invasion of state's rights and definitely destroys home rule."[51] Evans and other Republicans placed the blame for "bringing about a state of communistic or socialistic government . . ." squarely on Mc-Nutt, who, they charged, was a grossly ambitious dictator. The new welfare legislation was another example, one Republican asserted, of "the folly or the personal and political ambition of the Chief Executive alone . . ." which drove the bills through the legislature.[52]

The major feature of the federal and state welfare legislation of 1935 and 1936 was the considerable extent to which various levels of government had begun to assume responsibility for dependent Americans. The role of the federal government was most important in providing money and in laying out broad standards of eligibility and administration. State government in Indiana and most other states played a lesser but critical role in co-operating with the federal programs and contributing state money. The Indiana Department of Public Welfare represented a new recognition of the importance of systematic welfare administration at the state level and also established the administrative base onto which other programs could be built—not just for an emergency response to a temporary depression but for a continuing response to the always present dependent and needy individuals among the state's people.

But while federal and state money and administration were perhaps the most visible features of the new system, they did not remove local government from welfare responsibilities. Not only did township trustees maintain responsibility for direct relief to those unable to work, but home rule proponents forced those advocating a state-centralized welfare system to make major concessions to local control in the Public Welfare Act of 1936. The original draft of the bill contained provisions that transferred some of the responsibility for direct relief from the township trustees to the new state department. The original draft also pro-

[51] *Ibid.*, pp. 57, 58, 59.
[52] *Ibid.*, p. 101. See also pp. 105, 117-118.

vided for more state control over the county poor farms. Both of these provisions were deleted in the legislature, so that a major part of welfare activity in Indiana continued to be administered outside significant state or federal control. In another response to home rule concerns, the 1936 act established in each county departments of public welfare that were responsible to a nonsalaried county board of welfare appointed by the judge of the circuit court. The county board appointed the county welfare director. Efforts by professional social workers and others to allow the state Department of Public Welfare to nominate the candidates for the county board and for the director's position fell victim to home rule sentiment in the legislature. And similar attempts to bring the county welfare departments under the merit system initiated in the state Department of Public Welfare achieved only limited success in the late 1930s. Local control of county welfare departments was critical, for it was at this level that decisions regarding eligibility and assistance were made. And although that control was tempered by state and federal guidelines and by the right of appeal to the state welfare department by a discontented citizen, there was considerable freedom and considerable variation in the kind and quality of welfare assistance in Indiana.[53]

By late 1936, then, Indiana had experienced major changes in its welfare system, changes that made it more centralized, more progressive, more modern. Nevertheless, the large amount of local control that remained represented a continuing attachment to traditional attitudes toward relief and toward government. As of

[53] White, "Recent Public Welfare and Social Legislation in Indiana," *Social Service Review*, X, 209, 215-218; Virgil Sheppard, The Public Assistance Program in Indiana [address in a series of symposia relative to welfare and security in Indiana], pp. 5-10 (Mimeographed pamphlet [1936], Indiana Division, Indiana State Library); Public Administration Service, *Personnel Administration and Procedure as Installed in the Indiana Department of Public Welfare and Unemployment Compensation Division*, pp. 6, 15; Indiana Department of Public Welfare, *Four Years of Public Welfare in Indiana . . . 1936-1940*, pp. 6-8; Indianapolis *News*, March 2, 1937. For the year ending June 30, 1940, county welfare departments disbursed $22,893,063 and the state welfare department $1,222,590. The counties contributed $5,742,472, the state $8,280,441, and the federal government $10,092,739. Indiana *Year Book*, 1940, p. 468. Annual reports for the Department of Public Welfare are contained in the Indiana *Year Book*.

September, 1936, 42,000 Hoosiers depended on 92 county welfare departments for assistance; 6,000 depended on county commissioners that supported poor farms; and 112,000 looked to 1,016 township trustees for direct relief. In reporting these figures state welfare administrator Virgil Sheppard could well conclude that "we are far from an integrated and coordinated program of public assistance in the State of Indiana."[54] And there was little evidence of movement toward further integration or centralization during the remainder of the decade. Indeed, McNutt's successor, M. Clifford Townsend, seemed less willing than McNutt to rouse the anger of home rule advocates. During the late 1930s the *Indiana County and Township Officer* was lavish in its praise of the Townsend administration for "sincere and fair treatment of local units of government" and especially for its co-operation with local relief administrators.[55]

§ § § § § §

The other major federal welfare program established in 1935 in addition to Social Security was the Works Progress Administration. WPA's goal was to provide jobs for all unemployed workers capable of working—those who composed the great majority of relief cases. WPA was a more federally administered program than Social Security or FERA had been earlier. Although there was a state WPA office, staffed by many former GCUR employees, there was considerably more administrative centralization at the national level than under FERA. That Washington replaced Indianapolis as the focal point of work relief after 1935 is perhaps best illustrated by the fact that WPA employees with questions or complaints often wrote directly to Washington, bypassing state headquarters.[56] It is important to note, however, that although

[54] Sheppard, The Public Assistance Program in Indiana, p. 4. For a fuller description of the distribution of relief see Indiana Department of Public Welfare, *Quarterly Statistical Survey*, V (July, August, September, 1938), 3-15.

[55] "New Laws," *Indiana County and Township Officer*, V (March, 1937), 7; "Relief and Home Rule . . . ," *ibid.*, VI (March, 1938), 3-6.

[56] Governor's Commission on Unemployment Relief, *Year Book*, 1935-1936, pp. 4, 7-8; Work Projects Administration, Final Report of the Indiana Work Projects Administration, pp. 5, 8, 19, 34 (Typescript, 1943, Box 2, WPA, RG 69, National Archives); Howard, *The WPA and Federal Relief Policy*, pp. 54-56;

WPA reduced state responsibility for work relief, it did not eliminate the township trustee: throughout the late 1930s the trustees played a major role in certifying unemployed Hoosiers for WPA eligibility.[57]

WPA began to operate in Indiana in July, 1935. By October, 74,708 Hoosiers were on the rolls. In 1936, the monthly average of workers employed by WPA in Indiana was 73,273; in 1937, 52,507; in 1938, 88,463; in 1939, 70,008. Census figures for 1940 indicated that in March, 1940, 64,700 of Indiana's 172,000 unemployed workers were engaged in WPA projects. Throughout these years the percentage of Indiana residents on WPA rolls was considerably higher than the national average.[58]

Indiana men and women worked on a variety of WPA projects. The largest number of workers were employed on highway, road, and street projects, where they improved shoulders and ditches and built culverts, bridges, curbs, and walks. WPA workers also constructed sewers and waste treatment plants, water conservation and flood control projects, parks, swimming pools, baseball diamonds, airports, and a variety of public buildings. Nearly every Indiana community enjoyed some physical evidence of the program.[59] WPA and other federal aid to Indiana University's Bloomington campus resulted in new administration and classroom buildings, a large auditorium, sidewalks, and other improvements. The university comptroller estimated that by 1938 WPA had spent nearly two million dollars on the campus and "advanced our needed improvements at least ten years. . . ."[60]

Wayne Coy to Aubrey Williams, January 18, 1936, Indiana, 610, Special Litigation Folders, State Files, WPA, RG 69. Coy, who was Indiana administrator of WPA, resented this bypass because, he asserted, state administrators "have better knowledge of the various situations in their states and consequently are in a better position to make a direct answer."

[57] Governor's Commission on Unemployment Relief, *Year Book*, 1935-1936, pp. 4, 7-8; Howard, *The WPA and Federal Relief Policy*, pp. 54, 56.

[58] Howard, *The WPA and Federal Relief Policy*, pp. 538, 540, 556; National Emergency Council, *Report of Semi-Annual Meeting of Representatives of Federal Departments and Agencies Operating in Indiana* (n.p., [1935]), p. 74.

[59] Work Projects Administration, Final Report of the Indiana Work Projects Administration, pp. 58-60.

[60] W. G. Biddle to Dennis O'Harrow, March 8, 1938, Appraisal Report File, Box 188, WPA, RG 69. See also Thomas D. Clark, *Indiana University*,

WPA also offered employment that did not require sweat or a strong back. Perhaps most notable of the white collar programs was the Federal Writers' Project, which, after some delay and difficulty, eventually produced a very useful guide to Indiana history and to aspects of the state's contemporary life.[61] WPA men and women also indexed library collections, newspapers, and county histories.[62] They conducted surveys of real property and of traffic volume and flow in towns and cities.[63] Indiana artists found employment in producing public art, the most notable examples of which were the murals done in many post offices across the state. While some of these WPA projects were poorly done and never of much value beyond giving employment, others were exceedingly well done and continue to be of value today.

WPA made special efforts to provide help to certain groups of Hoosiers. Unemployed veterans received preference on WPA projects. There was also some attempt to go beyond the usual

---

Midwestern Pioneer. Vol. II: *In Mid-Passage* (Bloomington, Ind., 1973), pp. 251-264.

[61] Work Projects Administration of Indiana, *Indiana: A Guide to the Hoosier State*; Monty Noam Penkower, *The Federal Writers' Project: A Study in Government Patronage of the Arts* (Urbana, Ill., 1977), pp. 42-43, 91; Robert K. O'Neill, "The Federal Writers' Project Files for Indiana," *Indiana Magazine of History*, LXXVI (1980), 85-96; Errol Wayne Stevens, "The Federal Writers' Project Revisited: The Indiana Historical Society's New Guide to the State of Indiana," *Indiana Magazine of History*, LXXVI (1980), 97-102. The Federal Writers' Project files for Indiana are housed at Cunningham Memorial Library, Indiana State University, Terre Haute. WPA workers also made significant contributions to the archaeological investigations at Angel Site in southwestern Indiana. Glenn A. Black, *Angel Site: An Archaeological, Historical, and Ethnological Study* (2 volumes, Indianapolis, 1967), pp. 20-26.

[62] For example, the WPA indexed histories of counties alphabetically from Adams through Marion, a total of forty-nine counties. Bound, typed copies of the indexes are in the Indiana State Library, the Indiana Historical Society Library, and other libraries in the state. The project is now being completed. Three of the counties have been indexed locally. The remaining counties are being done by the Indiana Historical Society and the Allen County Public Library.

[63] The WPA Library Collection (National Archives, Washington, D.C.) contains many of these reports. See, for example, A Comprehensive Real Property Survey of South Bend, Indiana (Typescript, 1936, WPA, RG 69); Real Property Survey and Low Income Housing Survey of Indianapolis, Indiana (Mimeographed, 1941, *ibid.*); Report on City-Wide Traffic Survey: Anderson, Indiana, 1936-1937 (Mimeographed, 1937, *ibid.*).

meager effort to aid blacks, although on some Indiana projects it was deemed necessary to exclude blacks because of local sentiment.[64] Unemployed women were a special difficulty for WPA. In isolated rural areas and in large cities, there were many more unskilled women than there were productive or useful jobs. Needy black women in Gary and Indianapolis had the most difficulty obtaining WPA employment.[65] In Fort Wayne in 1936 WPA provided employment for thirty women who canned produce grown in relief gardens and another thirty-seven who collected and typed material relating to Johnny Appleseed.[66] Sewing projects were especially popular, employing as many as four thousand Hoosier women. WPA also employed women as housekeepers for the sick and elderly and as helpers in recreational and school lunch programs.[67]

WPA aroused criticism from various quarters. Some Indianans had little respect for projects they regarded as wasteful makework—leaf raking and shovel leaning. There was especially strong criticism against projects that did not produce immediately visible practical or physical results. Some labor unions also objected to WPA projects, many of which they argued should be PWA projects, which could use union labor at union wages.[68]

The most oft-repeated attacks on WPA centered on allegations of partisan politics. Such charges were neither new nor unique. All the New Deal projects were criticized for favoring Democrats in appointments and jobs and for coercing workers to vote for Democratic candidates. Certainly many local Democratic party officeholders and leaders put pressure on relief administrators to hire more Democrats and often charged that Republicans were

[64] Work Projects Administration, Final Report of the Indiana Work Projects Administration, p. 43.

[65] Beatrice Kasdin to Ellen S. Woodward, September 30, 1936, Professional and Service Division Narrative Reports, WPA, RG 69.

[66] Division of Women and Professional Projects, Indiana State Report, Allen County, p. 1, WPA, RG 69.

[67] Work Projects Administration, Final Report of the Work Projects Administration, pp. 22, 62-67.

[68] Brief of Indiana State Appraisal Committee Report [1938], p. 11, Appraisal Report File, Box 188, WPA, RG 69; Indiana State Federation of Labor, Proceedings (Indianapolis, 1937), p. 123.

overrepresented in relief jobs.[69] And there were doubtless many cases in which partisan politics affected decisions made in CWA, FERA, WPA, and other agencies. Yet Washington officials tried to minimize such partisanship, going so far as to enclose a note with paychecks sent to WPA workers prior to the 1938 election telling them to vote as they pleased.[70] In many instances it is likely that the charges of partisan politics served chiefly as weapons in party and intraparty battles.

FERA, CWA, and WPA were the largest and most important federal efforts to relieve the suffering brought on by the Great Depression. Lesser programs included the Civilian Conservation Corps (CCC), established in 1933 to provide employment for young men. By May, 1933, CCC had enrolled thirty-five hundred men in Indiana. They worked in state forests and parks on re-forestation and woodland improvement projects and construction of water supply systems, entrance gates, shelter houses, fire lanes, and picnic tables. In addition to providing employment for young men, the CCC made a significant contribution to conservation and recreation in Indiana.[71] Another New Deal effort to aid young Hoosiers was the National Youth Administration (NYA), which functioned from June, 1935, to July, 1943, providing employment for students attempting to complete high school or college.[72]

[69] William H. Larrabee to Harry L. Hopkins, January 23, 1934, Indiana Complaints, Administrative Correspondence (State), CWA, RG 69; Ernest B. Reeder to Pleas Greenlee, May 20, 1935, Box B, Drawer 86, McNutt Papers, Archives Division; Willis-Bobbitt Committee File, 1939, John K. Jennings Papers; Neff, Paul V. McNutt, pp. 267-268; Patterson, The New Deal and the States, pp. 82-83.

[70] Indiana Democratic county chairmen very much resented this federal effort at nonpartisanship. They deluged Democratic National Chairman James Farley with complaints. For examples see letters to Farley from Clarence A. Bertsch, December 22, 1938, C. W. East, December 19, 1938, and R. D. Faust, January 24, 1939, all in Box 95, OF 300, Democratic National Committee Papers.

[71] National Emergency Council, Report of Semi-Annual Meeting, pp. 65-66; Neff, Paul V. McNutt, pp. 250-251; Daniel DenUlyl, "History of the Civilian Conservation Corps," Indiana Academy of Science, Proceedings, LXVIII (1958), 308-310.

[72] National Youth Administration, Final Report of National Youth Administration for the State of Indiana (Typescript, 1943, Indiana University Library, Bloomington). For an example of NYA work see National Youth Administration, Survey of Recreational Facilities of South Bend, Indiana, July 1, 1936 (n.p., n.d.).

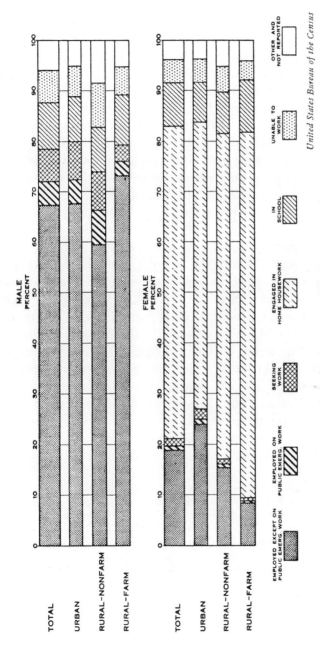

MALE
PERCENT

TOTAL

URBAN

RURAL–NONFARM

RURAL–FARM

FEMALE
PERCENT

TOTAL

URBAN

RURAL–NONFARM

RURAL–FARM

EMPLOYED EXCEPT ON
PUBLIC EMERG WORK

EMPLOYED ON
PUBLIC EMERG WORK

SEEKING
WORK

ENGAGED IN
HOME HOUSEWORK

IN
SCHOOL

UNABLE TO
WORK

OTHER AND
NOT REPORTED

United States Bureau of the Census

Employment Status of Persons in Indiana over Age 14, 1940

Federal and state relief agencies affected the lives of many Indianans, in thousands of cases greatly alleviating the hardships caused by the Depression. Yet for thousands of others the New Deal and its alphabet agencies had little direct effect. In some cases this was simply because relief failed to reach those who needed help. Hundreds of requests for aid from Hoosiers to FDR and Eleanor Roosevelt testify to that failure.[73] At the same time, some people were little affected by relief programs because they did not want help or because their local officials believed they did not need help. As late as March, 1934, some forty Indiana counties, most of them rural, had not applied for any federal aid.[74]

§ § § § § §

Although many Hoosiers who lived through the Depression were largely unaffected by the changes in public welfare and relief, these efforts permanently and significantly transformed not only the nature of welfare but also of government. From relying solely on local sources, both private and public, needy Hoosiers quickly came to depend on the state—first on the Governor's Commission on Unemployment Relief and later on the Department of Public Welfare—and on the national government—especially FERA, WPA, and the social security programs. Local aid continued after 1935—from county welfare departments and the township trustees and from private voluntary sources, such as community funds.[75] But never again did local government or voluntary social agencies have the near-complete

[73] Hundreds of letters from Hoosiers to FDR regarding the Depression and relief are in Box 95, FERA, RG 69. Eleanor Roosevelt was personally touched by one suffering Indiana correspondent: see Edward J. Ronsheim to Eleanor Roosevelt, December 6, 1933, and Eleanor Roosevelt to Harry L. Hopkins, director of FERA, January 5, 1934, Education, 430, Indiana, 1933-1936, FERA State Files, *ibid.*

[74] Hunter to Hopkins, March 20, 1934, Indiana General, FERA State Files, 1933-1936, *ibid.* See also editorial, *Hoosier Farmer*, March, 1939, p. 3.

[75] For efforts of the Indianapolis Community Fund to adjust to the changing governmental role in relief see *Indianapolis Community Fund News* (Fall, 1935); Indianapolis Community Fund, Report of Committee on Governmental Overlap (Mimeographed, 1937, Indiana Division, Indiana State Library); Thomas D. Sheerin, *To Community Fund Contributors* (n.p., 1938).

freedom and exclusive responsibility to grant or withhold support for the community's dependent citizens. In spite of home rule sentiment, more standardized, centralized, professional, and distant welfare agencies and personnel intruded into what had been almost entirely local decisions prior to 1933. The change was not revolutionary, especially because of continuing, if limited, local power, but the effects were substantial and lasting. For better or for worse, family and neighbors alone were no longer solely responsible for taking care of one another. In few other areas of life do the 1930s mark such a change as this from the decades that preceded.

CHAPTER V

THE POLITICS OF THE 1930s:
REPUBLICANS, DEMOCRATS, AND ELECTIONS

THE CHANGES in public welfare in Indiana in the 1930s were largely the consequences of the Great Depression, the New Deal response, and McNutt's and the Democratic party's control of government. McNutt's push for a state old-age pension in 1933 is indicative of an independent state-level battle, while his support of the Governor's Commission on Unemployment Relief and the Department of Public Welfare is an example of notable federal-state co-operation in Indiana. Doubtless McNutt was motivated by progressive sympathies and a desire for more energetic state government. Doubtless also he was influenced by his own political ambitions, seeking popularity at home and—especially through co-operation with the New Deal—in the nation. Like many other ambitious Democrats, he assumed that a strong, pro-New Deal governor had an excellent chance to succeed FDR in 1940. Mc-Nutt's moderate liberalism and intense political ambition thus combined to bring new power to Indiana government—not only in public welfare but also in government reorganization, taxation, and political patronage.

None of these measures was introduced or instituted without opposition. Republicans kept up a barrage of often vehement criticism that was directed almost exclusively at McNutt. This was the case in the 1934 elections, where the spotlight fell on the senatorial race between the Republican incumbent, Arthur R. Robinson, and the Democratic nominee, Sherman Minton. The latter was a relative newcomer to politics. A New Albany lawyer and an American Legionnaire, he was "a big, distinguished looking man with a flair for snappy clothes . . . ."[1] More important, he had McNutt's strongest support. Minton and the Democratic

---

[1] Indianapolis *Star*, June 14, 1934.

platform focused on McNutt's record of the previous two years—especially tax reform and the state old-age pension. Also Minton and his Democratic colleagues enjoyed ample campaign money from the 2 percent club, and they attached themselves firmly to FDR and the New Deal.[2]

In 1934 Republicans feared Roosevelt's popularity in Indiana and generally avoided references to him, concentrating instead on McNutt. Their campaign slogan was "Stop McNutt." Senator Robinson devoted large portions of nearly every speech to denouncing the governor. The party's state platform was a list of condemnations of McNutt legislation and programs, including the new tax system, government reorganization, and patronage.[3] According to one Republican pamphlet, the first task was "the eradication of one-man power in State Government . . . ."[4]

In the 1934 election voters spoke loudly and favorably for Democrats. They turned out to vote in large numbers (70.3 percent of the eligible electorate) in this off-year election. They chose Minton over Robinson by nearly 52 percent of the vote and elected Democrats to eleven of twelve seats in the United States House of Representatives. Though the size of their majority in the state legislature declined, Democrats after 1934 still held 65 out of 100 seats in the Indiana house and 38 out of 50 seats in the senate.[5] Hoosiers, it appeared, had given McNutt's administration and party a large stamp of approval. Among Democrats

[2] *Ibid.*, June 13, 1934; Indiana Democratic State Committee, *Sherman Minton for United States Senator* (Indianapolis, 1934); Carleton B. McCulloch to Meredith Nicholson, April 20, 1934, Box 2, McCulloch Papers. Sherman Minton became one of the most enthusiastic New Deal supporters in the Senate. James T. Patterson, *Congressional Conservatism and the New Deal: The Growth of the Conservative Coalition in Congress, 1933-1939* (Lexington, Ky., 1967), p. 204.

[3] Indianapolis *Star*, June 6, November 2, 1934; New York *Times*, October 21, 24, 1934; McCulloch to Nicholson, October 9, 1934, Box 1, McCulloch Papers.

[4] Indiana Republican State Committee, *Laugh This Off, Governor McNutt!* (Indianapolis, 1934).

[5] The lone Republican elected to Congress was Frederick Landis, from the second district in rural, northern Indiana. Landis died soon after the election, and in the special election to select a successor the second district chose Republican Charles A. Halleck, who began a long career in the House. Indiana *Year Book*, 1934, p. 140; Indiana Legislative Bureau, Indiana General Assembly, p. 56.

there was no doubt. As one noted after the election: "Paul is the absolute Boss of the Party."[6]

The 1936 election was similar to the 1934 contest in many ways. Indiana Democrats again ran on the record of the McNutt administration. The platform extolled the governor's achievements, and McNutt campaigned hard to elect as his successor M. Clifford Townsend, who had served loyally as his lieutenant governor.[7] Republicans again criticized reorganization, taxation, patronage, and relief efforts in campaign oratory that was often shrill and vehement in denouncing McNutt. William E. Jenner, a young state senator from Paoli, made one of the liveliest campaign speeches in twentieth-century Indiana politics: with humor, sarcasm, and biting criticism, Jenner lambasted "Paul the Fifth," "the flaxen-haired beauty of Bloomington."[8]

The attacks by Jenner and other Republicans were sufficiently effective to alarm some Democrats. In August, 1936, Democratic National Chairman James A. Farley sent letters to dozens of Indiana party leaders asking for predictions of the fall outcome. Nearly all who responded were optimistic about Roosevelt's prospects for re-election but were pessimistic about the state ticket. They feared opposition to the gross income tax, especially from small merchants, many of whom were attaching printed slips to customers' packages stating that the price of the goods purchased would have been less but for the governor's gross income tax. Some Democrats also feared that the new social security legislation and WPA relief might hurt them.[9] Such forebodings pushed Hoosier Democrats even more firmly into Roosevelt's arms. Eagerly, individual candidates sought his sup-

[6] McCulloch to Nicholson, November 13, 1934, McCulloch Papers.

[7] Indiana Democratic State Committee, *Sound Government in Indiana: A Democratic Achievement, 1932-1936* (n.p., 1936); Indianapolis *News*, June 16, 1936.

[8] Indianapolis *News*, June 3, 1936. See also Indianapolis *Times*, November 2, 1936.

[9] The responses from Indiana to James A. Farley's letter are in Box 86, OF 300, Democratic National Committee Papers. See especially the letters to Farley from Frank McHale, September 16, 1936, John W. Kern, September 9, 1936, and Wayne Coy, October 1, 1936. Also see R. Earl Peters to Farley, July 23, 1936, *ibid.*, and Louis Ludlow to Marvin H. McIntyre, October 10, 1936, Box 35, *ibid.*

port and begged him to visit Indiana, a trip the president finally made in September. McNutt himself participated in this endeavor to use the president's popularity to bolster the state ticket.[10]

The 1936 elections demonstrated either that Roosevelt's coat-tails were very long or that the pre-election fears of Indiana Democrats were exaggerated. Not only did Roosevelt carry Indiana by a large majority (57 percent of the two-party vote), so too did other Democrats. Townsend, though trailing the president, won more than 55 percent of the two-party vote, soundly defeating Raymond S. Springer in his second try for the governor's office. Democrats again captured all the congressional districts except the second, won twenty-three of twenty-six seats up for election in the state senate, and increased their numbers in the house from sixty-five to sixty-seven.[11] Again, as in 1934, the voters refused to repudiate the McNutt administration and the New Deal.

§ §

This large support for Democrats in 1934 and 1936 was part of an upsurge in voter interest and a partisan realignment that occurred both in Indiana and throughout the nation, upsetting decades-long patterns of voting behavior. The two major parties had been evenly balanced in the last decades of the nineteenth century, but Republicans tended to enjoy greater electoral success from the 1890s to 1930. During the first three decades of the twentieth century, voter turnout declined along with support for the Democratic party. But the Great Depression destroyed Republican prosperity and jolted many Hoosiers out of their political apathy and away from traditional party attachments, to the general benefit of the Democratic party. Comparison of elections in the first half of the 1920s and the first half of the 1930s illustrates the dimensions of the shift. In the elections of

[10] Virginia E. Jenckes to Franklin D. Roosevelt, August 28, 1935, Box 4, OF 175, Franklin D. Roosevelt Papers, Franklin D. Roosevelt Library, Hyde Park, N.Y.; Kern to Farley, September 9, 1936, Box 86, OF 300, Democratic National Committee Papers; Paul V. McNutt to McIntyre, February 22, 1936, Box 17, OF 268, Roosevelt Papers; McNutt to Farley, October 23, 1936, Box 35, OF 300, Democratic National Committee Papers.

[11] Indianapolis *News*, November 5, 1936.

1920, 1922, and 1924 Democrats won an average of only 45.1 percent of the two-party vote. The average Democratic share of the vote for the elections of 1932, 1934, and 1936 rose nearly 10 percent to 54.8 percent.[12] Accompanying the Democratic gains in the 1930s was a large increase in the percentage of eligible voters who turned out on election day. The increased turnout was evident not only in the presidential years of 1932 and 1936 (see Table I) but also in the off-year elections of 1934 and 1938.

TABLE I[13]
Estimated Voter Turnout for Presidential Election Years
in Indiana, 1920-1948

1920	73.4%	1936	76.7%
1924	67.6%	1940	80.1%
1928	74.0%	1944	70.6%
1932	77.9%	1948	65.9%

Off-year turnout in twentieth-century Indiana has generally been more than 10 percent below presidential year turnout. The average off-year turnout for 1922, 1926, and 1930 was 59.4 percent. In 1934, however, 70.3 percent of eligible voters went to the polling booth, and 72.6 percent turned out in 1938.[14]

The upsurge in voting in the 1930s was doubtless a response to the Depression, to the issues it raised, and to McNutt's and Roosevelt's efforts to lead the state and the nation. In the 1930s Democrats mobilized formerly apathetic or disaffected citizens in a way Republicans could not. While Democratic support was large and broad, there were certain groups of voters, defined by shared social or economic interests, who were especially important, either because they voted in large numbers for the first time or because they shifted their vote from the Republican to the Democratic column. One such group was urban voters. During the 1920s

[12] Hyneman, Hofstetter, and O'Connor, *Voting in Indiana*, p. 112. These are votes for secretary of state, usually the best indicator of voter support for a party.

[13] *Ibid.*, p. 40. The number of persons voting is based on the vote for secretary of state. For calculations of the number of eligible voters and other considerations in estimating turnout see *ibid.*, pp. 37-41.

[14] *Ibid.*, pp. 27-28, 34.

smaller percentages of voters in Indiana's urban counties tended to turn out than voters in rural counties, and the urban voters tended to vote Republican. However, the city elections of 1929 showed a new Democratic strength, which grew still more in the state elections of 1930 as overall urban turnout increased greatly. Moreover, the growing vote in more populous urban counties tended more strongly toward the Democratic party than did the vote in sparsely populated counties. Lake County provided the most striking example of this voter realignment. Strongly Republican in the 1920s, Lake County voters moved into the Democratic camp in 1930 and thereafter generally gave the party very large margins. Most other urban counties moved in the same direction, from Republican to Democratic, though usually with less intensity. Some, such as Marion County, slid back to the Republican column in 1940 and after. In general, although many farmers and other rural dwellers voted Democratic, particularly in southern Indiana, urban voters were a more critical part of the Democratic party's new strength in the 1930s. While Republicans continued to have strength in many cities, they became more dependent on rural and small town voters—especially in central and northern Indiana.[15]

Part of the Democratic party's support among urban voters derived from its new popularity among black, ethnic, and working-class voters. To these voters the Democratic party in Indiana and the nation seemed to be more liberal than the Republican party in support of relief and welfare for the poor and unemployed and in support of labor's effort to organize unions and bargain collectively (see Chapter VIII). In the 1930s blacks,

---

[15] *Ibid.*, pp. 34-35, 104-105, 112-119, 255-261; Munger, Two-Party Politics in the State of Indiana, pp. 57-69. The nature of realignment in Indiana, while generally sketched in these two studies, needs much further analysis to sharpen and clarify the changes in voting as they related to sectional and socio-economic variables. Readers seeking an introduction to the many problems and questions involved might start with Kristi Andersen, *The Creation of a Democratic Majority, 1928-1936* (Chicago, 1979); John M. Allswang, *The New Deal and American Politics: A Study in Political Change* (New York, 1978); and Paul Kleppner, "Searching for the Indiana Voter: A Review Essay," *Indiana Magazine of History*, LXXVI (1980), 346-366.

ethnics, and industrial workers flooded into the Democratic party. This is not to imply that native-born white businessmen, for example, did not vote for Democratic candidates; many did, but generally not in as large a proportion as other socioeconomic groups. In Muncie, for example, the Lynds estimated that in 1936 nearly 47 percent of the voters in business-class neighborhoods voted for Roosevelt, while in working-class neighborhoods the president's support exceeded 68 percent of the vote.[16]

A very important part of the shift in party allegiance in the 1930s occurred among Indiana blacks. Since the Civil War, they had traditionally voted Republican. The Ku Klux Klan spurred a movement toward the Democratic party in 1924, but the Republican party continued its hold on black voters until 1932. Suffering more than any other group from the Depression, large numbers of blacks voted for McNutt and Roosevelt in 1932, many casting their first Democratic ballot, though a majority in Indiana still remained tied to the party of Abraham Lincoln. By 1934 and 1936, however, black Indianans turned out in large numbers to abandon their traditional affiliation and gave wide majorities for Democratic candidates. This shift made both parties increasingly conscious of the importance of black voters. Republicans could no longer take black votes for granted, and Democrats began new efforts to attract and hold those votes, including the provision of some patronage for black party workers. Blacks showed up as delegates to the state party conventions and in the seats of the General Assembly. In 1932 both Marion and Lake counties sent blacks to the Indiana house, the first in the legislature since 1897. Thereafter, both these urban counties were usually represented by at least one black, and St. Joseph County joined them in 1939. These were important beginnings for effective black political participation in Indiana, but they were very limited in scope. In the five legislative sessions of the 1930s blacks held only 8 of a total of 500 house seats and none in the senate until 1941. Their patronage appointments in the Democratic party numbered only

[16] Lynd and Lynd, *Middletown in Transition*, pp. 359-360; Hyneman, Hofstetter, and O'Connor, *Voting in Indiana*, pp. 257-261.

a few, usually the most menial jobs, and, in the case of black clerical workers in the statehouse, jobs that were segregated from whites. The Democratic party and state legislature made no real effort to attack racial discrimination in Indiana. The 1933 and 1935 sessions did approve a proposal to delete the article in the state constitution that allowed only whites to serve in the state militia. Indiana voters ratified this proposal in 1936. There were other small concessions to the awakened political power of blacks but no major changes. Substantive responses to the new voting strength of black Hoosiers awaited a later period.[17]

The 1930s offered no radical political revolutions for blacks, ethnic groups, workers, or urban dwellers. Yet there occurred an immensely important shift in voting: an upsurge in voting and a realignment of those voting brought to the polling booths large numbers of voters who voted for Democratic candidates. The essential political changes of the 1930s derived not simply from the liberal sentiments of Democrats in Washington or Indiana but also from pragmatic (if often belated and limited) responses of Roosevelt, McNutt, Townsend, and others to the growing political power of new groups of voters. This liberal or New Deal coalition of voters was a major new ingredient in national and Indiana politics and government in the 1930s. It offered Hoosier Democrats the opportunity to build a firm majority that would last beyond the Depression of the 1930s—an opportunity McNutt and his fellow party leaders only partially realized.

[17] Thornbrough, *Since Emancipation*, pp. 33-37; Indiana Legislative Council, Indiana General Assembly, pp. 40-41; Hyneman, Hofstetter, and O'Connor, *Voting in Indiana*, p. 258; Richard J. Meister, A History of Gary, Indiana: 1930-1940 (Ph.D. dissertation, University of Notre Dame, Notre Dame, Ind., 1966), pp. 274-292; Bremer (ed.), *Constitution Making in Indiana*, IV, 60-64, 306-308. For Democratic party attention to blacks and for black discontent with that effort see Bob Skelton, Program for Colored Organization [1933], Racial Affairs File, Public Schools-Recommendations, 1933, McNutt Papers, Archives Division; F. B. Ransom to Pleas Greenlee, March 29, April 20, November 8, 1935, Box 8, Drawer 86, *ibid*. Ransom was a leading black Republican in Indianapolis who switched to the Democratic party in the 1930s and won election to the city council. An attorney, he was associated with the city's leading black business, the Madame C. J. Walker Manufacturing Company.

§ § §

Part of the Democratic party's failure to take full advantage of the upsurge in voter interest and the realignment of the 1930s was caused by intraparty conflicts. Indeed, it often seemed that McNutt's most dangerous opponents were fellow Democrats. This intraparty feuding was a constant feature of the party's history in the 1930s and grew as the decade progressed.[18] Usually it sprang less from differences over issues or ideology than from personal rivalries. As often, such rivalries flourished partly because the relative weakness of the opposition party did not force harmony among Democrats in order to win. But special features of the McNutt years also stimulated this intraparty warfare.

One cause of Democratic factionalism was generational. As noted in Chapter III, McNutt and his closest political advisers represented a new generation in Indiana politics. Trained in American Legion rather than governmental politics, they entered the Democratic party in the early 1930s as outsiders. And although they showed some tact in dealing with the older established party leaders, many of those leaders soon became disaffected and sometimes bitter about their loss of power. As Frank Brubeck of Terre Haute noted in late 1933: "The 'young democrat' is clearly in the saddle at the state house much to the disgust of many of the old liner."[19] About the same time Leonora Flynn of Logansport, Democratic state vice-chairman, lamented that "the utter disregard, in our state, by those elected to office, of the status of the organization women and men has crippled us for future victories."[20] The refrain continued through the decade, as, for example, in 1938 when former speaker of the house Walter Myers

[18] Referring to intraparty feuding, Louis Howe, Roosevelt's close political adviser, lamented in late 1933 that "the situation in Indiana is impossible. It gets more complicated every day." Howe to Joseph O'Mahoney, December 12, 1933, Box 35, OF 300, Democratic National Committee Papers. A few months later Howe wrote: "I don't pretend to keep track of what goes on about the Indiana mess." Howe to Farley, April 11, 1934, *ibid*.

[19] Frank Brubeck to Claude Bowers, September 14, 1933, Bowers Papers, I.

[20] Leonora Flynn to Mary Dewson, December 1, 1933, Box 66, Women's Division, Democratic National Committee Papers. See also Flynn to Dewson, April 5, May 1, 1934, *ibid*.

Lockefield Gardens, Indianapolis, public housing for blacks

Franklin and Eleanor Roosevelt and Paul McNutt in Indianapolis, 1936

Paul V. McNutt

Frederick Van Nuys

M. Clifford Townsend

Henry F. Schricker

complained that "for six years now we [Democratic leaders of the 1920s] have been ignored in state and nation."[21] If there was indeed a Hoosier New Deal, those holding the cards dealt out some of the old party players, creating sources of bitter factional dispute and ensuring that opposition to the "McNutt machine" would be bipartisan.

On several occasions some of the old leaders directly challenged the new, almost always hoping to unite those Democrats who were disaffected from the McNutt administration and sometimes hoping also for support from national party leaders, especially those in the White House. The first such challenge came in 1933 from R. Earl Peters of Fort Wayne, who had been state party chairman since 1926. Although Peters supported McNutt in his 1932 nomination bid, he was never a trusted member of the McNutt group. That fact became most obvious by late 1933 when McNutt and Peters feuded over control of the 2 percent contributions to the Hoosier Democratic Club. McNutt won and kept control of the 2 percent fund away from the state organization for the next several years.[22] Peters resigned the chairmanship in November, 1933, and made a bid for the senatorial nomination, setting off an angry contest with the McNutt people, who responded by vigorously pushing the candidacy of Sherman Minton. Minton's nomination in the party's 1934 convention was thus a grand victory for McNutt, certifying his dominance of the party.[23]

[21] Walter Myers to Stephen Early, December 26, 1938, Box 35, OF 300, Democratic National Committee Papers. Myers was intensely bitter and very much disliked McNutt. See his autobiography, presented in fictional form: Walter Myers, *The Guv: A Tale of Midwest Law and Politics* (New York, 1947), especially pp. 280-282, 285-288. See also Frank A. White to Walter E. Treanor, March 2, 1938, Walter E. Treanor Papers, Lilly Library, Indiana University, Bloomington.

[22] Indianapolis *Star*, October 10, 1933; Indianapolis *Times*, November 14, 1933; Feightner interview, February 28, October 24, 1968, p. 86, Indiana Division; Flynn to Mrs. James H. Wolfe, October 15, 1935, Box 66, Women's Division, Democratic National Committee Papers; George Ade to Will Hays, June 24, 1934, in Terence Tobin (ed.), *Letters of George Ade* (West Lafayette, Ind., 1973), pp. 184-185.

[23] Albert Stump, *R. Earl Peters: Logical Nominee of Indiana Democracy for*

Although McNutt dominated the party, Peters continued to be a source of irritation, partly because he was a rallying point for other disaffected older leaders, but also because he had support outside Indiana in the person of Democratic National Chairman James A. Farley. Peters had been an early Roosevelt supporter, before the Chicago national convention in 1932, while McNutt and his close adviser Frank McHale had waited until after the Roosevelt bandwagon was well under way to jump aboard. Farley and Roosevelt never forgot. Though McNutt was always treated in a friendly manner, he was never one of Roosevelt's trusted supporters. Peters, despite his antagonism to McNutt in Indiana, received special consideration from Farley. In 1934 Farley and Roosevelt let it be known that they privately supported Peters for the Senate nomination. When that bid failed, they appointed him head of the Federal Housing Administration in Indiana. There, where he had control of federal money and jobs, Peters remained throughout the decade, a constant irritant to McNutt.[24]

Another kind of intraparty feuding in the 1930s came from men who began as loyal McNutt supporters but eventually became disaffected. The most notable example of this sort of Democrat was Pleas Greenlee of Shelbyville, McNutt's executive secretary from 1933 to 1936.

As chief dispenser of patronage, Greenlee was one of the most powerful men in the McNutt administration. A backslapping, highly skilled politician, he was the primary architect of Minton's victory over Peters in 1934. By 1935 Greenlee concluded that it was his turn: he began his campaign for the 1936 gubernatorial nomination. Support for Greenlee was strong among the second level of party leaders—county chairmen and precinct committee-

---

United States Senator (n.p., 1934), pp. 9-12; Indianapolis Star, May 11, June 13, 14, 1934.

[24] Coy to Harry L. Hopkins, February 24, 1935, Indiana, FERA State Files, 1933-1936, RG 69; Sherman Minton to Farley, August 10, 1936, Box 86, OF 300, Democratic National Committee Papers; Neff, Paul V. McNutt, pp. 93, 311, 408-414; Peters to Roosevelt, July 23, 1940, PPF 6769, Roosevelt Papers; James A. Farley, Behind the Ballots: The Personal History of a Politician (New York, 1938), pp. 82, 110-111; Indianapolis News, June 27, 1940.

men who knew him well through their hunger for patronage. And Senator Minton also strongly supported Greenlee. But McNutt and most of his close advisers hesitated because they believed that Greenlee's talents did not qualify him for the governor's office. Failing to get McNutt's support, Greenlee resigned in early 1936 to seek the nomination on his own.[25]

Three major candidates sought the Democratic nomination: Greenlee; E. Kirk McKinney of Indianapolis, backed by Senator Frederick Van Nuys and Peters; and M. Clifford Townsend, supported by McNutt. It was an acrimonious spring, as one veteran Democrat noted: "This state is torn to pieces by the most vicious pre-primary and pre-convention fight I have ever known."[26] Greenlee joined the Van Nuys-McKinney faction in charging that the McNutt-Townsend campaign was unfairly influencing the vote of WPA workers[27]—a case if there ever was one of the pot calling the kettle black. Greenlee's campaign was a dismal failure. The man who had so successfully managed the patronage and the campaigns of others was no match for the McNutt group, who easily dominated the convention, even to the point of keeping the names of the state's two senators off the program in punishment for their failure to support Townsend.[28]

§ § § §

When McNutt left office in January, 1937, he was firmly in control of the Indiana Democratic party. Challenges from dissi-

[25] Indianapolis *Star*, April 7, 1935; Neff, Paul V. McNutt, pp. 287, 292, 420-423. McHale and Greenlee vehemently disliked one another.

[26] Flynn to Dewson, April 9, 1936, Box 66, Women's Division, Democratic National Committee Papers. See also Humphrey C. Harrington to Farley, April 25, 1935, Box 35, OF 300, Democratic National Committee Papers.

[27] Pierce Williams to Hopkins, May 20, 1936, Special Litigation Folders, 610 Indiana, State Files, WPA, RG 69; Hopkins to Frederick Van Nuys, May 20, 1936, *ibid.*; Coy to Hopkins, April 26, 1936, Box 18, Wayne Coy Papers, Franklin D. Roosevelt Library, Hyde Park, N.Y.; New York *Times*, May 22, June 16, 1936.

[28] Indianapolis *News*, June 17, 1936; New York *Times*, June 17, 19, 1936. Minton remained loyal to Greenlee and got into difficulties with the White House in 1939 when he pushed Greenlee for a federal appointment. Minton to Roosevelt, June 9, 1939, Box 15, OF 400, Appointments, Roosevelt Papers; Presidential Memorandum for the Secretary of the Treasury, July 24, 1939, PPF 2235, *ibid.*

dent Democrats such as Peters and Greenlee and from Republicans had been overwhelmingly repulsed, and McNutt's lieutenant governor and handpicked successor took his place in the governor's chair. In a farewell message to the legislature, McNutt summed up the achievements of his administration, focusing on the transition from 1933, when "we were on the brink of a major catastrophe," to 1937, when "Indiana is in better condition than any other state in the Union." Expressing greatest pride in various liberal reforms—especially the steps taken toward developing a modern public welfare system—McNutt asserted that the crisis had passed and that the legislative program necessary to set the state on the proper path was "virtually complete," with only a few "refinements and improvements" yet required. McNutt left office on the same white horse on which he had arrived—riding off, he hoped, not into the sunset, but into the White House. Indeed, for the next four years his presidential ambitions played a significant part in Indiana politics.[29]

The man left sitting in the governor's chair was M. Clifford Townsend. Born in Blackford County in 1884, Townsend had been a teacher and county school superintendent, a state legislator, farmer, and in 1930 a major organizer and leader of the Indiana Farm Bureau. Although he appealed to anti-McNutt Democrats for their support in 1936 and promised to be his own man in the statehouse, Townsend ran entirely on McNutt's record and strongly endorsed McNutt and Roosevelt. He also shared McNutt's view that the Depression crisis was over and that adequate government programs were already in place. In an interview after the election Townsend stated, "I would like to serve four years now without doing much that is new. Trim up corners, give them a business administration and times of quiet contentment after the woeful days. It's time the government relaxed."[30] His inaugural address and first message to the General Assembly repeated this theme—advising the legislature that he had "no ambitious

[29] Indiana *House Journal*, 1937, p. 31. In February, 1937, McNutt accepted Roosevelt's offer to become high commissioner to the Philippines, where he remained until July, 1939. Neff, Paul V. McNutt, p. 470.

[30] Indianapolis *Times*, November 5, 1936. See also *ibid.*, November 2, 1936.

program of governmental reform" and that they should "hold
new legislation to a minimum . . . ."[31]

The 1937 Democratic-controlled legislature complied with the
new governor's wishes. Little significant legislation emerged.
The legislature approved some highway safety bills and established a new state labor division to arbitrate industrial disputes—a
partial response to labor's new power. They debated about taxes
without effect and killed the merit bill prepared by the League
of Women Voters, but they passed a bill exempting the 2 percent
club from the state's corrupt practices act.[32]

Although state government "relaxed" in 1937, as Townsend
hoped, partisan politics did not. Indeed, during 1937-1938 Townsend found himself in the midst of one of the Indiana Democratic
party's major feuds of the twentieth century, one that involved
traces of ideological differences as well as the usual personal
ambitions, McNutt's above all.

The chief protagonist in the 1937-1938 Democratic feud was
Senator Frederick Van Nuys. He had been active in Democratic
politics for decades before being first elected to the United States
Senate in 1932. The McNutt faction never accepted Van Nuys,
however, and the senator soon became the most powerful Indiana
Democrat independent of McNutt. Not only did he have support
among conservative, old-line Democrats, but his Senate seat gave
him considerable influence, including federal patronage appointments.[33] From this independent base Van Nuys began to threaten
first McNutt and eventually Roosevelt. He quarreled with Mc-
Nutt and, after 1934, with Senator Minton over federal patronage.
He attempted unsuccessfully to have gubernatorial and senatorial
nominations made in primary elections rather than party conventions—an effort to reduce McNutt's hold on the party. He

[31] Indiana *House Journal*, 1937, p. 112. See also Indianapolis *News*, January 11, 14, 1937.

[32] Indianapolis *News*, January 7, March 4, 8, 9, 10, 1937.

[33] Van Nuys's Senate patronage included United States attorneys and mar-
shalls, collectors of internal revenue, and customs collectors. Postmaster appointments were generally controlled by Democratic congressmen. Indianapolis *News*,
November 10, 1932; Notes on Appointments, 1933, Box 91, Emil Hurja Papers,
Franklin D. Roosevelt Library, Hyde Park, N.Y.

also supported the township trustees in their battles against state and federal centralization and control of public relief.[34] In 1936 he was the primary backer of E. Kirk McKinney's unsuccessful bid against Townsend, McNutt's candidate, for the gubernatorial nomination. Van Nuys eventually alienated himself not only from the state administration but from the national administration as well. His opposition to some New Deal legislation and particularly to the president's court-packing plan caused Roosevelt to include Van Nuys among those conservative Democrats to be "purged" in the 1938 campaign.[35]

McNutt and Townsend eagerly joined in this attempted purge, with Townsend publicly declaring from the White House steps that Van Nuys would not be renominated. For nearly a year Indiana politics bubbled over the flames of this intraparty feud. If denied the nomination Van Nuys threatened to run as an independent and to campaign on such issues as the 2 percent club, the liquor law operation, and other aspects of the party's machine politics. In addition to receiving encouragement from conservative and anti-McNutt Democrats, Van Nuys attracted Republican support. There was even some talk of Van Nuys's becoming the Republican nominee for the Senate. Townsend appeared eager to fight the issue to the last party vote, but McNutt feared the effects of party discord for the general ticket and for his planned presidential bid in 1940. And, it was commonly believed at least, McNutt was very much influenced by Van Nuys's "threats of telling what he knew on the State House Boys. . . ."[36] In early July, just before the party's state convention, McNutt

[34] Coy to Roosevelt, August 9, 1935, Box 14, OF 400, Appointments, Roosevelt Papers; Coy to Bruce McClure, May 28, 1935, Box 90, FERA, RG 69; Blake, *Paul V. McNutt*, pp. 155-156. Part of the friction over federal patronage grew out of McNutt's efforts to influence or control appointments usually made by federal congressmen or senators. John Day Deprez to Howe, December 10, 1934, Box 15, OF 400, Appointments, Roosevelt Papers.

[35] Patterson, *Congressional Conservatism and the New Deal*, pp. 120-121. Harold L. Ickes noted in his diary in November, 1937, that Roosevelt so much wanted to defeat Van Nuys that he was willing to risk losing a Democratic seat in the Senate. Ickes, *The Secret Diary of Harold L. Ickes*, II, 256.

[36] Jim Daugherty to Farley, December 9, 1938, Box 95, OF 300, Democratic National Committee Papers. See also New York *Times*, August 6, 31, November 21, 1937; Ade to James D. Rathbun, June 27, 1938, in Tobin (ed.), *Letters of*

surrendered and instructed the reluctant Townsend to welcome Van Nuys back into the party. Townsend complied, and he and Van Nuys, who had not spoken with one another for a year, embraced on the convention platform. Never before had the vaunted McNutt machine been so humiliated. To avoid further embarrassment to McNutt, Van Nuys, and the party, the platform and convention proceedings were bland and noncontroversial. In one of the shortest conventions in the party's history the only oratory to evoke delegate interest or enthusiasm was about McNutt's presidential bid. Soon afterward McNutt wrote Frank McHale, "It was the best solution of the most desperate situation in the history of Indiana politics . . . ."[37]

McNutt exaggerated, but the Van Nuys episode did not end with the convention embrace. Scenting the possibility of victory from a divided Democratic party and from reaction to the economic slump which began in late 1937, Republicans burst from their lethargy. The Republican revival in Indiana and throughout the nation was well illustrated by the Cornfield Conference, organized by Homer E. Capehart on his Daviess County farm in August, 1938. Enjoying the wealthy Capehart's hospitality, twenty thousand Republican precinct committeemen, county chairmen, and other leaders from Indiana and the Midwest ate barbecued chicken, steamed clams, corn on the cob, mashed potatoes, and country gravy, while listening to Capehart and others attack the New Deal in state and nation.[38] It was the beginning of hope for Republicans, and they campaigned hard. The fall elections in 1938 were a disaster for the Democrats. In the highest off-year turnout in the interwar years (72.6 percent), voters

---

George Ade, p. 205; Patterson, Congressional Conservatism and the New Deal, pp. 274-277. The intensity of interest in the Van Nuys split is reflected in the voluminous correspondence on the question to Governor Townsend. See Box B, Drawer 114, and Box A, Drawer 120, M. Clifford Townsend Papers, Archives Division, Indiana Commission on Public Records, Indiana State Library and Historical Building.

[37] McNutt to McHale, July 19, 1938, McNutt Papers, Lilly Library. See also Indianapolis News, July 12, 13, 1938; New York Times, July 3, 10, 1938.

[38] William B. Pickett, "The Capehart Cornfield Conference and the Election of 1938: Homer E. Capehart's Entry into Politics," Indiana Magazine of History, LXXIII (1977), 252-275.

returned Van Nuys to the Senate by only a 5,197 vote plurality compared to his 208,303 vote margin in 1932. And they elected the first Republican-controlled Indiana house in ten years, as the Democratic seats dropped from 77 in 1936 to 49. Of Indiana's twelve congressional races, Republicans won seven.[39]

After the election Democratic National Chairman Farley wrote party leaders asking for assessments of the loss. Partly, they responded, the Democratic defeats were the consequence of the usual decline in the vote for the party in power in an off-year election. But Hoosier Democrats provided Farley with a host of other reasons for the poor showing: low prices for agricultural products hurt the party with farmers, as did opposition to New Deal agricultural programs; the new Social Security system provided either too much or too little help to older people; WPA work relief was either too partisan or not partisan enough; and the state gross income tax continued to stir resentment.[40] But the party leaders were most insistent in blaming defeat on the Van Nuys episode. As one lamented, despite the attempt at unity, the intraparty feud "seriously affected the morale and ardor of the organization and alienated the so-called independent voters."[41] Indeed, low morale continued after the election as various party factions blamed each other for the poor November showing. Townsend supporters claimed that McNutt was the cause of defeat because he forced Van Nuys on the ticket, while the McNutt group claimed that Townsend's hard opposition to Van Nuys was the cause.[42]

[39] Pitchell (comp.), *Indiana Votes*, pp. 83, 87; Indiana Legislative Council, Indiana General Assembly, p. 56.

[40] Indiana responses to Farley's request for a postelection analysis are in Box 95, OF 300, Democratic National Committee Papers. For examples, see letters to Farley from Roy L. Barham, December 10, 1938; Joe J. Barbera, January 5, 1939; William A. Gutzwiller, December 9, 1938; R. D. Faust, January 24, 1939; Arthur H. Greenwood, December 3, 1938; and J. K. Burns, December 12, 1938.

[41] Val Nolan to Farley, January 4, 1939, *ibid.* Among many similar letters to Farley are those from Jim Daugherty, December 9, 1938, and Clarence A. Bertsch, December 22, 1938, *ibid.*

[42] James E. Percy to McNutt, November 13, 1938, McNutt Papers, Lilly Library; Peters to Farley, November 21, 1938, and Nolan to Farley, January 4, 1939, Box 95, OF 300, Democratic National Committee Papers.

By 1939 Democrats were in their weakest position since 1932. Although McNutt's growing presidential hopes promoted efforts toward harmony, so that a McNutt-Townsend split never fully materialized, the party was divided.[43] The serious economic downturn of 1937-1938 left many Hoosiers doubting that the New Deal really had succeeded and encouraged attacks on efforts to extend it. And Republicans controlled the lower house of the General Assembly. Townsend's message to the 1939 legislature was bleak: war threatened abroad while problems of relief and unemployment remained at home. Rather than the minor trimming he thought necessary in 1937, Townsend called for more social welfare legislation. The divided legislature did not respond. The Republican majority in the house presented a united front against any administration measure, while the Democratic-controlled senate thwarted Republican attempts to dismantle the legislation passed in the McNutt years. Except for passage of some public health bills, the 1939 session adjourned without enacting significant legislation.[44]

The 1940 election continued the Republican comeback that had begun in 1938. Republicans campaigned on the old issues of opposition to the New Deal—especially to its relief programs—and criticism of the 1933 state government reorganization, liquor control, patronage, and the 2 percent club. Republican candidates won eight of twelve Indiana seats in Congress, with Democrats winning only districts 1 (Lake County), 8 (southwestern Ohio River counties), 11 (Hancock, Madison, and Marion), and 12 (Marion). Republicans elected Angola newspaper publisher Raymond E. Willis over incumbent Senator Sherman Minton, a major defeat for state Democrats and for the Roosevelt administration. Minton won by approximately twenty-six thousand votes in Lake County and by ten thousand votes in St. Joseph and Vanderburgh counties, but he lost Marion and Allen counties.

[43] For a report on efforts at party harmony see McHale to McNutt, April 3, 1939, Box 11, Coy Papers.

[44] Indiana *House Journal*, 1939, pp. 15-17; Indianapolis *News*, November 29, 1938, January 6, March 8, 1939; Indianapolis *Star*, March 7, 1939; Bicker, The Assembly Party: Change and Consistency in Legislative Voting Behavior in the Indiana House, 1923-1963, p. 106.

Willis ran especially strongly in less populous counties in central and northern Indiana. Hoosier voters also cast a majority vote for native-son presidential candidate Wendell Willkie. Willkie had left the state in 1919 for a career in law and business in Ohio and New York, and his political aspirations received their major boost from eastern Republicans, not Hoosiers. Many professional Indiana Republicans thought Willkie was too liberal and too weakly tied to the party. Nonetheless, even though he failed in his attempt to deny Roosevelt a third term, Willkie doubtless helped the ticket in Indiana and contributed to the general Republican revival.[45] Republican strength in 1940 was most evident in elections to the state legislature, where the party captured control of both houses. The 1941 General Assembly had thirty Republicans in the senate and sixty-four in the house. Republicans also elected all state officeholders except one: Democratic gubernatorial candidate Henry F. Schricker defeated Kokomo Republican Glenn R. Hillis by fewer than four thousand votes, thereby denying Republicans a clean sweep in Indiana.[46]

Even Schricker's election was not a completely satisfying victory for his party. The Starke County Democrat had been a newspaperman, banker, and state senator before serving as lieutenant governor in the Townsend administration. But Schricker was far from being a liberal New Dealer and was never close to either Townsend or McNutt. Neither supported his nomination in 1940, and some of their supporters actively worked for other candidates. Schricker won the nomination nevertheless. He cam-

[45] Donald Bruce Johnson, *The Republican Party and Wendell Willkie* (Urbana, Ill., 1960), pp. 47-50; Justin H. Libby, "Wendell Willkie and the Election of 1940," in Ralph D. Gray (ed.), *Gentlemen from Indiana: National Party Candidates, 1836-1940* (Indianapolis, 1977), pp. 293-315; Herbert J. Rissler, Wendell Willkie and the Election of 1940 in Indiana (M.A. thesis, Indiana University, Bloomington, 1956), pp. 38-40, 58. The response of conservative, professional Indiana Republicans to Willkie's candidacy is illustrated in a remark supposedly made by former Senator James E. Watson when Willkie, a one-time Democrat and independent, asked him for his views: "Well, Wendell, you know that back home in Indiana it's all right if the town whore joins the church, but they don't let her lead the choir the first night." Warren Moscow, *Roosevelt and Willkie* (Englewood Cliffs, N.J., 1968), p. 70.

[46] Indianapolis *News*, May 24, November 7, 9, 1940; Pitchell, *Indiana Votes*, pp. 52-53.

paigned with little attention to the McNutt and Townsend administrations and the New Deal. Instead he relied on his personal popularity, especially in rural areas.[47] Schricker's independent route to the governor's office and Republican control of the legislature boded well for a change in state government and politics after 1940. The election also served to show the limitations of the liberal New Deal coalition of labor, ethnic, and black voters in Indiana.

Nineteen forty marked the end of a Democratic decade. It also marked a change in the issues that had dominated the state's politics. Economic prosperity returned as war defense production began to create more jobs. Issues of unemployment and relief took back seats to the Nazi invasion of France and to the question of America's role in the European war. The political closing of the decade was also marked by the outcome of the Democratic national convention in 1940. For ten years the presidential ambitions of Paul McNutt had greatly affected Indiana politics. After he left the governor's office and even while he served as high commissioner to the Philippines, McNutt and his advisers kept a close watch on Hoosier politics. By early 1939 the presidential effort was in full swing. McNutt campaigned as a successful but moderate New Deal governor and the heir to FDR, though critics accused him of having run a corrupt political machine in Indiana, and internal revenue agents interested in the 2 percent club investigated his finances. In July, 1939, Roosevelt appointed McNutt as head of the Federal Security Administration, a move interpreted variously as an effort to thwart McNutt's campaign for the presidential nomination and as a "laying on of hands" by Roosevelt. The president's decision to seek a third term and his choice of Henry A. Wallace as his running mate dashed McNutt's highest hopes. Although he supported the ticket and served loyally as director of the War Manpower Commission during the war, McNutt never again came close to national office. Without his ambition and power, Indiana politics changed after 1940.[48]

---

[47] Indianapolis *News*, June 27, 28, 1940; Indianapolis *Times*, June 28, November 6, 1940.

[48] McHale to McNutt, April 25, 1939, McNutt Papers, Lilly Library; Farley to Roosevelt, July 6, 1935, Box 35, OF 300, Democratic National Committee

152   INDIANA THROUGH TRADITION AND CHANGE

The 1930s was indeed an unusual decade. Politics and government became more important and more centralized at the state and federal levels. State and federal government assumed more responsibility, especially for the social and economic well-being of citizens. In Indiana and throughout the nation the Democratic party achieved majority status, shaped by the ambitions and liberalism of Roosevelt and McNutt and by the ability to mobilize new voters and convert Republicans to Democrats. Politics would never again be as it had been in the 1920s. McNutt's model of a powerful governor would cast a long shadow in Indiana, though none of his successors would achieve his enormous power. And yet, the 1940s and 1950s would witness the return of a Republican majority in Indiana and a repudiation of much, though by no means all, that had happened in the 1930s. Indiana after 1940 would experience a synthesis of some of the best and some of the worst from the state's political experiences of the 1920s and 1930s. Certainly for a long time Hoosiers would remember these decades —especially the 1930s—for they provided the reference points and the terms of debate that would persist well into the post-World War II era.

Papers; James A. Farley, *Jim Farley's Story: The Roosevelt Years* (New York, 1948), pp. 170, 214, 219, 301; Ickes, *The Secret Diary of Harold L. Ickes*, II, 394, 678-682, 684 and III, 66, 81, 261, 286, 368; Moscow, *Roosevelt and Willkie*, p. 74; New York *Times*, July 13, 1939, March 31, 1940; Indianapolis *Times*, May 1, 1940. For McNutt's career at the War Manpower Commission see George Q. Flynn, *The Mess in Washington: Manpower Mobilization in World War II* (Westport, Conn., 1979).

CHAPTER VI
AGRICULTURE AND FARM LIFE

INDIANA AGRICULTURE in the interwar years was characterized by an often jarring mixture of traditional and modern procedures and practices and by an often incongruous mingling of promise and failure. The application of science and technology to agriculture produced dramatic changes on many Indiana farms and seemed to promise a new prosperity for farmers. But the benefits of agricultural science and technology did not spread evenly across the state nor did they affect in the same way all types of farms, crops, or livestock. And although nearly all Hoosier farmers suffered from the nationwide depressions in agriculture in the immediate post-World War I years and again in the Great Depression of the 1930s, the exact effects of these economic storms varied, as did responses of farmers and politicians to them. By the eve of World War II, the Indiana landscape contained both modern farms little different from those of the late twentieth century and traditional farms more like those of the mid-nineteenth century.

There is one generalization about Indiana farming that continued to hold through the interwar years: corn and hogs were the economic mainstay of most Hoosier farmers, as they had been since the pioneer period. Indiana produced nearly $106.5 million worth of corn on 4,033,822 acres in 1939 (ranking fifth among the states) and $78.6 million worth of hogs. Following in value in 1939 were dairy cattle at $69.7 million and poultry and eggs at $36.3 million. This pattern of farm production changed only slightly through the first half of the twentieth century, with corn and hogs always dominant. In a sense, corn and hogs were even more important than their first- and second-place individual ranks would indicate: since most of the corn was fed to hogs, the two eventually became one. The alert farmer growing corn was always conscious of hog prices, and the farmer raising hogs always knew the price of corn. This was especially true in north-central Indiana, the heart of Indiana corn/hog production and the eastern edge of the national corn belt.[1]

Although corn and hogs remained supreme in Indiana agriculture, there were shifts in other crop and livestock production. The most significant trend in livestock was the decrease in numbers of horses, as tractors appeared on farms, and the increase in dairy cattle, as the markets for whole milk increased with the growth of cities. The number of horses and mules on Indiana farms declined from 717,233 in 1920 to 338,371 in 1940. Milk production increased steadily through the interwar decades, from 238.8 million gallons in 1919 to 348.4 million gallons in 1939. Among major crops, several declined in importance after World War I. Wheat acreage continued a downward trend begun at the end of the nineteenth century. Oat acreage increased until the late 1920s and then declined rapidly, partly because of the decline in the number of horses. Tame hay acreage remained at about the same level through the 1920s and 1930s. The most dramatic change in crop acreage was in soybeans, which were almost unknown in Indiana in 1920, the acreage devoted to them increasing rapidly from 267,268 acres in 1929 to 1,303,869 acres in 1939, ranking the state second in the nation in production of this crop.[2] In addition to the major crops of corn, wheat, oats, hay, and soybeans, Indiana began to produce more truck and fruit crops for market. The most notable change here was the rapid increase in the production of tomatoes. In the period 1929-1938, Indiana ranked first among the states in acreage devoted to tomatoes for commercial canning.[3]

[1] United States Bureau of the Census, *Sixteenth Census* (1940), I, *Agriculture*, Pt. 1, p. 538, III, 717; Lynn S. Robertson and Earl L. Butz, *Indiana's Agriculture: Its Output, Costs, and Trends* (Purdue University Agricultural Experiment Station *Bulletin, No. 523*, Lafayette, Ind., 1947), p. 4.

[2] United States Bureau of the Census, *Sixteenth Census* (1940), I, *Agriculture*, Pt. 1, p. 537, III, 760; Robertson and Butz, *Indiana's Agriculture*, pp. 18-19.

[3] Mervin G. Smith *et al., An Economic Analysis of the Production of Canning Factory Tomatoes in Indiana* (Purdue University Agricultural Experiment Station *Bulletin, No. 456*, Lafayette, Ind., 1940), pp. 3-5.

Knowing which crops and livestock Indiana produced in quantity is not as important, however, as understanding how, where, and by whom these crops and livestock were produced. Some of the answers to these questions are found in the application of science and technology to agriculture.

The most visible change in agriculture in the 1920s and 1930s was the increased use of machinery, much of it developed since World War I. More than any other single item, the tractor symbolized modern agriculture of the interwar years. In 1920 only 4 percent of Indiana farms had tractors, many of them Henry Ford's Fordson, which sold for $625, had metal wheels, and would, the advertisements proclaimed, take "the drudgery out of farm work and solve the labor problem." By 1930, 22 percent of Hoosier farms had tractors. By 1940 the figure had increased to 37 percent.[4] The tractors themselves changed during these years, becoming more efficient and versatile: they were made lighter but more powerful and by the 1930s ran on rubber rather than steel wheels. Using tractors enabled farmers to free many acres of land previously used for horse feed for other crops and to increase crop acreage because of the ability to perform more rapidly the critical operations of planting and harvesting. The increased drawbar power of tractors made it possible to pull wider and larger farm machines and to pull them faster than horses could. The power takeoff transmitted power from the tractor to machinery and made machine operations more efficient and dependable, while the belt pully provided a source of power that could be moved to farm equipment.[5]

The tractor spurred the development of new and more efficient machinery for planting, cultivating, and harvesting crops. The most important new machines for Hoosier farmers were the corn

<hr/>

[4] United States Bureau of the Census, *Sixteenth Census* (1940), I, *Agriculture*, Pt. 1, p. 543; Bluffton *Evening News*, April 29, 1921.

[5] Robert W. Schoeff and Lynn S. Robertson, *Agricultural Changes from 1910 to 1945 in a Central Indiana Township* (Purdue University Agricultural Experiment Station *Bulletin, No. 524*, Lafayette, Ind., 1947), p. 16; R. S. Kefer, B. H. Hurt, and Albert A. Thornbrough, "The Influence of Technical Progress on Agricultural Production," U.S. Department of Agriculture, *Yearbook of Agriculture, 1940* (Washington, D.C., 1940), pp. 512-514.

picker and the grain combine. Both began to appear in small numbers in the late 1920s. By 1930 there were about 1,500 corn pickers and 360 combines in use in the state. The number increased only slightly during the early years of the Great Depression—when it was cheaper to hire labor than buy a new piece of expensive equipment—but grew rapidly in the late 1930s. At the time of Pearl Harbor there were 11,900 corn pickers and 11,400 combines on Indiana farms.[6] Other tractor-powered machines included larger plows, disc harrows, grain drills, grain binders, mowers, and pickup balers. All allowed farmers to perform tasks more quickly and more efficiently, with less labor. Some traditional farm practices began to disappear, such as threshing by a crew of several dozen men who moved from farm to farm with a large threshing machine. Less common also for some farmers were the long, lonely days from early October to after Thanksgiving devoted to breaking off heavy ears of corn with numb hands. Farming still required hard work, even on the most modern farms, but the new machinery allowed the substitution of capital for some of the labor and the use of a different kind of labor. Farming became more of a business, but the farm family became an even more useful part of the labor force, not only in tending the garden, gathering eggs, and other chores but also in performing basic tasks of production. Farm women and children could and did drive the tractors that pulled the corn picker or combine. The new machinery influenced not only the use of labor and the quantity of possible crop acreage but also the kind of crop. The most notable example was the rapid increase in soybean acreage made possible because the combine allowed more efficient harvesting of this new crop.[7]

Two of the most important new pieces of machinery used in ag-

[6] Robertson and Butz, *Indiana's Agriculture*, pp. 24, 40.

[7] I. D. Mayer and J. C. Bottum, *The Adaptability of the Combine to Indiana Farms* (Purdue University Agricultural Experiment Station *Bulletin, No. 349*, Lafayette, Ind., 1931), pp. 46, 49; E. C. Young and George W. Collier, *Labor and Power Used in Crop Production in Central Indiana* (Purdue University Agricultural Experiment Station *Bulletin, No. 378*, Lafayette, Ind., 1933), pp. 26-27; Schoeff and Robertson, *Agricultural Changes from 1910 to 1945 in a Central Indiana Township*, pp. 16-21.

riculture were not intended for exclusive farm use. The automobile and motortruck appeared on Indiana farms early in the century. By 1920, 46 percent of Indiana farms had an automobile parked near the house or barn, often one of Henry Ford's Model Ts. By 1930, 78 percent of Indiana farmers had an automobile and by 1940 81 percent. The automobile helped farmers move about the farm, run to town for seeds or a new tractor part, and deliver eggs or, by attaching a trailer or wagon to the car, a load of hogs or hay. Motortrucks increasingly served farmers for transporting large volume or weight. At the end of World War I, 17 percent of the hogs received at the Indianapolis market arrived by truck. By 1929 the figure had risen to 63 percent. Less than 2 percent of Indiana farmers reported owning trucks in 1920. By 1930, 16 percent owned trucks, which was approximately the same figure reported in 1940. More important than farmer-owned trucks, however, was the rapid growth of commercial trucking, which provided farm delivery of supplies and equipment and farm pickup of agricultural products. Trucks and automobiles served to relieve many Indiana farmers of the long hours spent on the seat of a wagon that slowly moved from or to town, train station, or market.[8]

Farming in the interwar years was also changed by developments in agricultural science. Perhaps the most notable achievement was the development of hybrid corn seed, which in 1937 began to replace open pollinated varieties. In 1938 hybrid seed was used on about 33 percent of total corn acreage, and in 1939 on about 51 percent. Hybrid corn proved more resistant to plant disease and insects, and it was less susceptible to lodging, thus more adapted to harvesting by mechanical corn pickers. The most visible claim for the new hybrids was their greater yield: by the early 1940s hybrids yielded 25 percent more corn per acre than open pollinated varieties and had replaced the older seed on nearly all Indiana farms. Thus, even though corn acreage declined

[8] United States Bureau of the Census, *Sixteenth Census* (1940), I, *Agriculture*, Pt. 1, p. 543; James R. Wiley, *Motor Transportation of Hogs to the Indianapolis Market* (Purdue University Agricultural Experiment Station *Bulletin, No. 337*, Lafayette, Ind., 1930), p. 4; Robertson and Butz, *Indiana's Agriculture*, p. 30.

slightly in the interwar years, the introduction of hybrids and the mechanical corn picker served to increase total output, especially in the late 1930s, when yield per acre increased greatly. There were some new and improved seed varieties for other crops, but none were as spectacular as for corn.[9]

Some farmers also improved crop production through better use of fertilizer, although the most significant developments in this area occurred after World War II. By 1920 there was considerable evidence that the natural productivity of Indiana's soil was deteriorating rapidly, as decades of hard use by farmers had taken their toll. Some crop yields began to decline. Even manure, which was used by the most progressive farmers, was no longer sufficient alone, since it did not provide the phosphate necessary to retard soil depletion. Instead, farmers had to rely on commercial fertilizer if they wanted to maintain or improve their crop yields. The amount of commercial fertilizer used in Indiana increased rapidly in the interwar years, except for a large drop in the early 1930s; the proportion of plant nutrients used in the fertilizers also increased. Use of lime to reduce soil acidity likewise became more common, particularly in the mid- and late 1930s.[10]

Indiana farmers also benefited from improvements in livestock production. They increased their use of commercial livestock feeds—in years of relative prosperity—and decreased the amount of corn silage, so that the number of silos declined by about one-half during the interwar years. Farmers greatly increased their production of high protein hay—such as alfalfa and soybean hay—and decreased acreage in clover and timothy hay. Livestock production also benefited from considerable success in eradicating

[9] S. R. Miles, *Performance of Corn Hybrids in Indiana, 1937-1946* (Purdue University Agricultural Experiment Station *Bulletin, No. 526*, Lafayette, Ind., 1948), pp. 3-4; Robertson and Butz, *Indiana's Agriculture*, pp. 20, 22; United States Department of Agriculture, Agricultural Marketing Service, *Indiana Corn Acreage, Yield, and Production, 1928-1939, by Counties* (West Lafayette, Ind., 1940), pp. 3-4.

[10] *Indiana: The Land and the People* (Purdue University Agricultural Experiment Station *Bulletin, No. 496*, Lafayette, Ind., 1944), pp. 15-23; Robertson and Butz, *Indiana's Agriculture*, p. 22; A. T. Wiancko, G. P. Walker, and R. R. Mulvey, *Manure Increases Farm Income* (Purdue University Agricultural Experiment Station *Bulletin, No. 398*, Lafayette, Ind., 1935), p. 19.

or controlling major animal diseases, such as hog cholera, through improved farm sanitation practices, advances in veterinary medicine, and governmental involvement in quarantine and eradication procedures. Farmers also improved their livestock herds and poultry flocks through more attention to obtaining better breeding stock and more systematic crossbreeding. And, while labor efficiency did not improve as rapidly in animal as in crop production, there were some advances, as, for example, in the use of milking machines and other small farm machinery, which were made more practical by electrification in the late 1930s. Together these changes increased efficiency in livestock and poultry production: the average number of pigs saved per sow increased through the interwar years, for example, as did the number of eggs per hen and the gallons of milk per cow.[11]

The introduction of new scientific and technological innovations on Indiana farms was, in part, the consequence of aggressive education and promotion efforts by local, state, and federal governments and by Purdue University. Purdue's faculty and staff had begun a long tradition of research and service for Indiana agriculture soon after the school was established as the state land grant college in 1874. Purdue's agricultural research expanded considerably after 1905, when the state government joined the federal government in supporting the university's Agricultural Experiment Station. Hundreds of Station bulletins and circulars disseminated the results of Purdue and federal government investigations into nearly all aspects of agriculture, concentrating on practical methods to improve efficiency and productivity. Several Station bulletins that were published in the 1920s and 1930s, for example, extolled the nutritive value of soybeans and described the best methods of soybean production as determined by Purdue researchers. Other publications examined such subjects as commercial fertilizers, crop rotation, control of the European corn borer, and artificial heat and ventilation in poultry houses. The Purdue Experiment Station also studied farm management and

[11] Robertson and Butz, *Indiana's Agriculture*, pp. 21, 26; United States Bureau of the Census, *Sixteenth Census* (1940), I, *Agriculture*, Pt. 1, p. 538; *Indiana: The Land and the People*, pp. 35, 62.

marketing practices to improve the business efficiency of farmers. The state legislature assigned responsibility to the Experiment Station also for testing and inspecting feed, fertilizer, and veterinary medicine, in part because Indiana did not have a department of agriculture, which in many other states assumed these functions.[12]

The benefits of Purdue's experimentation in agriculture were disseminated to students enrolled in the university's school of agriculture as well as through Experiment Station publications. Purdue reached its largest audience through the activities of its agricultural extension service, which was established in 1911 and expanded greatly during the interwar years. The extension service published bulletins with practical farm advice and sponsored short courses and conferences for farmers at Purdue but had its largest impact in programs offered outside the West Lafayette campus. Special extension service trains carried the message of modern agriculture directly to Hoosier farmers. In April, 1925, for example, the extension service ran a soil improvement train on the Baltimore and Ohio tracks in the state and at each stop demonstrated the benefits of lime, tested soil samples, and provided enough lime free to farmers to treat one acre of their land. Similar trains continued to operate until 1947 as carriers of agricultural progress.[13] The extension department also sponsored off-campus short courses, field meetings, tours, and farmers' institutes, where experts demonstrated new farming techniques and discussed farm problems.

Perhaps the most important extension service activity was to supervise the work of the county agricultural agents, who coordinated extension programs at the local level and served, one

---

[12] Phillips, *Indiana in Transition*, pp. 142-143; E. C. Young and L. G. Hobson, *Costs and Profits in Producing Soybeans in Indiana* (Purdue University Agricultural Experiment Station *Bulletin, No. 306,* Lafayette, Ind., 1926); C. L. Shrewsbury and C. M. Vestal, *The Nutritive Value and Mineral Deficiencies of Soybeans* (Purdue University Agricultural Experiment Station *Bulletin, No. 420,* Lafayette, Ind., 1937); *Purdue University, 1922–1932* [West Lafayette, Ind., 1933], pp. 76-80.

[13] Purdue University Department of Agricultural Extension, *Annual Report, 1924-1925* (Lafayette, Ind., 1925), pp. 9-15, 42, 44.

historian has written, as the "foot soldiers of scientific agriculture."[14] The report submitted by the Shelby County agricultural agent in 1929 indicates the direction and variety of their work:

Three hundred five farmers attended ten meetings on seed corn selection. Nineteen completed the Five-Acre project. Two hundred nine boys and girls finished their projects in club work, 151 of these were in the Poultry Club. Farmers of the county used 2,100 tons of limestone during the past year. Twenty-six farmers attended the two lamb docking and castrating demonstrations. Swine, seed, and poultry extension schools were held. As a result of the swine school, six farmers are acting as demonstrators of the Hoosier Swine Sanitation system. A ninety per cent Chick Club was organized following the poultry school. Fifty-eight attended a tour to see the results of the members of this club. Last year six groups of rural women took part in the nutrition project. One hundred seventy-two completed the project and over 300 women attended the Achievement Day. This year twelve groups are taking part in the work. Nine Farmers' Institutes were held with a total attendance of 2,748 people.[15]

By 1929 similar work was underway in eighty-five of Indiana's ninety-two counties.

The great majority of county agents had studied at Purdue, and most doubtless looked to Purdue as their primary source of information and support. But county agents served other masters as well. Part of their financial support came from the federal government as a consequence of the Smith-Lever Act of 1914. County agents had important ties to the United States Department of Agriculture as a source of information and aid—ties which became stronger in the early 1930s when the agents were given primary responsibility for explaining and overseeing New Deal programs at the local level. The county agent was thus a conduit between Indiana farmers and the larger world, represented by Purdue's scientific agriculture and by the programs of the federal government. But the county agent was responsible not only to the outside world: in keeping with strong home rule sentiment in

[14] David B. Danbom, *The Resisted Revolution: Urban America and the Industrialization of Agriculture, 1900-1930* (Ames, Iowa, 1979), p. 87.

[15] Purdue University Department of Agricultural Extension, *Annual Report, 1928-1929* (Lafayette, Ind., 1929), pp. 96-97.

Indiana, each county board of education had responsibility for appointing the agent, and county government paid a large portion of his salary, with state and federal governments paying smaller portions. Not until 1937 did the state legislature transfer the power of appointment from the local level to Purdue in an effort to minimize patronage and politics in the county agent's office.[16]

Although the primary interests of the county agent and of Purdue's agricultural programs were crop and livestock production, there was also increasing attention paid to the quality of various other aspects of rural life such as the farm community and family life. In 1921, for example, the Vigo County agent sponsored a series of public meetings on the county's rural problems, with sessions devoted not only to soils and crops, livestock, horticulture, and markets, but also to the rural home, rural schools, and the rural church.[17] During the interwar years publications of the Agricultural Experiment Station and the extension service began increasingly to treat such subjects as rural schools, efficient kitchen arrangements, the benefits of electricity, and even good table manners.[18] The growing home economics division of Purdue's extension service sponsored many programs for women. Passage of the Capper-Ketcham Act in 1928 provided federal

[16] Lloyd H. Clark, The Present Status of County Agriculture Agents in Indiana (M.A. thesis, School of Education, Indiana University, Bloomington, 1930), pp. 28, 46-48; Purdue University Department of Agricultural Extension, Annual Report, 1933-1934 (Lafayette, Ind., 1934), pp. 8, 18; Dave O. Thompson, A History: Fifty Years of Cooperative Extension Service in Indiana (n.p., 1962), pp. 25-26; Gladys L. Baker, The County Agent (Chicago, 1939), p. 175.

[17] Vigo County's Rural Problems, Vigo, 1919-1921, Correspondence, Department of Public Instruction Papers, Archives Division, Indiana Commission on Public Records, Indiana State Library and Historical Building.

[18] W. C. Latta, Outline History of Indiana Agriculture (Lafayette, Ind., 1938), p. 346; Kathryne McMahon, The Farm Home Kitchen (Purdue University Agricultural Extension Bulletin, No. 141, Lafayette, Ind., 1926); Gail M. Redfield, A Study of Efficient Kitchen Arrangements (Purdue University Agricultural Experiment Station Bulletin, No. 418, Lafayette, Ind., 1937); May Masten, Food Preparation Club (Purdue University Agricultural Extension Bulletin, No. 161, Lafayette, Ind., 1930). The latter publication (p. 22) advised farm families that "Soup should be eaten from the side of the spoon and should be dipped from the body. Crackers should never be broken into the bowl but may be eaten with the soup."

support for these programs and especially for county home demonstration agents who supervised local projects in health and nutrition, clothing, home furnishing, kitchen improvements, and youth activities. The extension service gave special attention to young people through supervision of 4-H Club activities designed to teach scientific agriculture, to improve the attractiveness of rural life for farm youth, and to prepare them for a life on or off the farm that was vastly different from that of their parents or grandparents.[19] Purdue also encouraged vocational agriculture courses in public high schools and sponsored conferences for vocational agriculture teachers, the majority of whom were Purdue graduates. The number of high schools with vocational agriculture departments increased from 49 in 1919-1920 to 132 in 1929-1930.[20]

§ §

Research in agricultural science and technology led to improvements in machinery and production practices for crops and livestock in the interwar years. Purdue University, with federal, state, and local government support, carried the message and techniques of increased agricultural productivity and efficiency to farmers. Along with farm improvements, the county agricultural and home demonstration agents with their network of resources also promised a better quality of life for farm families. But the blessings of modern agriculture did not fall equally on all farmers. While some quickly abandoned horses and hired hands for tractors and corn pickers and perhaps rearranged the farm kitchen and adopted the new etiquette of table manners as well, others continued to farm and live much as their parents and grandparents had.

[19] Purdue University Department of Agricultural Extension, *Annual Report*, 1928-1929, pp. 15, 49-51; Z. M. Smith, *The Ninth 4-H Club Round-Up Held at Purdue University, May 3-7, 1927* (Purdue University Agricultural Extension *Bulletin, No. 151*, Lafayette, Ind., 1928).

[20] *Some Historical Data on Vocational Agriculture Education in Indiana* (Indiana Department of Public Instruction *Bulletin, No. 109*, Fort Wayne, Ind., 1931), pp. 51, 58-59; Purdue University Department of Agricultural Extension, *Annual Report*, 1928-1929, p. 17; Indiana State Board of Education, Minutes, January 18, 1924, Archives Division, Indiana Commission on Public Records.

Some farmers resisted modern agriculture because of an emotional attachment to traditional ways and a general distrust of change—especially change that came from outsiders or from books. Traditional farmers sometimes charged that county agents and Purdue staff were mere "book farmers." Often they simply ignored these evangelical missionaries.[21]

Some farmers continued traditional ways because, despite their desire to change, they could not afford the high cost of modern agriculture. The new machinery required amounts of capital that many Indiana farmers simply did not have and could not obtain. Nor could they afford to wait for the promised long-run returns from mechanization or new production practices. Getting by from year to year was their immediate and often only possible goal. Modernization was most difficult on small and medium-sized farms, where the volume of output often was not sufficient to finance the new equipment or methods. In addition, many smaller farms were unable to derive the economies of scale that came with the use of modern machinery and methods on large acreage. Not surprisingly, during the interwar years there was a strong correlation between the size of the farm and the degree of adoption of modern methods and machinery.[22]

Agricultural modernization thus widened the gap separating farms of different size: smaller farms had more and more difficulty competing in the same market with large farms. Although the average size of farms in Indiana increased in the interwar years, the magnitude of change was small: from 102.7 acres per farm in 1920 to 107.3 acres per farm in 1940. In fact, the early 1920s and early 1930s witnessed a decrease in average farm size. More impor-

[21] Thompson, *Fifty Years of Cooperative Extension Service*, p. 37. For a good illustration of this resistance to change see the sketch of Jack Wickard in Dean Albertson, *Roosevelt's Farmer: Claude R. Wickard in the New Deal* (New York, 1961), pp. 11, 16-17. The missionary-like quality of the extension service is evident in its publications and especially in the illustrations that accompany the text. One scholar has suggested that county agents generally had more support among local merchants, bankers, and businessmen than farmers. Danbom, *The Resisted Revolution*, p. 91. Further research is required to know the extent to which this was the case in Indiana.

[22] Mayer and Bottum, *The Adaptability of the Combine to Indiana Farms*, p. 49; Robertson and Butz, *Indiana's Agriculture*, p. 23.

tant than average farm size, however, was the increase in the percentage of large farms. The total number of farms in Indiana declined from 205,126 in 1920 to 184,549 in 1940, but the number of farms of more than 175 acres increased from 27,300 in 1920 to 31,022 in 1940. These large farms constituted 13.4 percent of the total number in 1920 and 16.8 percent in 1940, and they accounted for 34.1 percent of total farmland in the state in 1920 and 42.9 percent by 1940. Medium-sized farms of from 50 to 175 acres declined in number from 122,961 in 1920 to 97,107 in 1940. Small farms, under 50 acres, increased from 54,865 to 56,420 by 1940: many of them were operated by part-time farmers. As operators of larger farms adopted modern methods and technology, many of the smaller farmers held on in a subsistence or supplemental type of agriculture, relying on off-farm work for a portion of their family income. The most important change was the decline in the number of middle-sized farms, between 50 and 175 acres, which represented in many cases a recognition of the difficulties of competing with larger farms. For many families who owned middle-sized farms the necessary response was either to attempt to buy more land and increase the farm size or, as noted in Chapter I, to move to town or city and to jobs in an auto parts factory, a knitting mill, or a grocery store.[23]

The possibilities of agricultural modernization depended not only on a farmer's attitudes and on the size of his farm but also on the nature and location of farmland. Modern equipment and methods were of greatest utility on the relatively richer soil and more level topography of central and northwest Indiana. Tractors, combines, and corn pickers first appeared on the long straight rows of this cornbelt section. Farms here had a higher average investment in machinery than did farms in other parts of Indiana, and they were of larger average size.[24]

[23] United States Bureau of the Census, *Sixteenth Census* (1940), I, *Agriculture*, Pt. 1, p. 536; Robertson and Butz, *Indiana's Agriculture*, p. 27; Danbom, *The Resisted Revolution*, pp. 133-135.

[24] E. C. Young and F. F. Elliott, *Types of Farming in Indiana* (Purdue University Agricultural Experiment Station *Bulletin, No. 342*, Lafayette, Ind., 1930), pp. 3-13; Robertson and Butz, *Indiana's Agriculture*, pp. 5, 13; Mayer and Bottum, *The Adaptability of the Combine to Indiana Farms*, pp. 3-4.

The greatest contrast to the large mechanized farms of the cornbelt was provided by farms in southern Indiana and particularly in the unglaciated area of south central Indiana. During the interwar years, this region increasingly became the problem child of modern agriculture in Indiana. Thin, depleted, and eroded topsoil, rolling and hilly terrain, small farms, and, perhaps, a greater personal attachment to traditional ways combined to obstruct the modernization process in south central Indiana and to increase the difficulties of market competition with farmers elsewhere. From Brown and Monroe counties on the northern edge of the region, south to the Ohio River counties of Warrick, Spencer, Perry, Crawford, Harrison, and Floyd, many Hoosier farmers struggled to eke out a living, often on the edge of subsistence, much as their grandparents had before the Civil War. Average yield per acre for corn in these counties was nearly always far below the state average—more than 15 bushels below the state average of 51.5 bushels in most of these counties in 1939. Some farmers—those fortunate enough to own richer land along river bottoms—survived comfortably, and a few even prospered. Many others left their farms, especially in the 1920s. For the state as a whole, the amount of land in harvested crops declined by 1,641,545 acres or 13.8 percent during the 1920s. But in the twenty-three most hilly and unglaciated counties of southern Indiana, the decline in acreage was 24.7 percent compared to 11.4 percent in the remaining sixty-nine counties. Some of this land was converted to pasture, forest, and recreational use (including Brown County State Park), but most of it was simply abandoned, as farmers sought employment in towns and cities.[25]

[25] G. E. Young, *Marginal Farm Land in Southern Indiana* (Purdue University Agricultural Experiment Station *Bulletin, No. 376*, Lafayette, Ind., 1933), p. 4; United States Department of Agriculture, Agricultural Marketing Service, *Indiana Corn Acreage*, pp. 6-17. Unlike some other depressed agricultural areas, especially the southern United States, south central Indiana had a low percentage of tenant-operated farms (only 8 percent in 1940), compared to a state average of 28 percent. The highest percentage of tenancy was in the richest part of the Indiana cornbelt, with Benton County leading all Indiana counties at 56 percent tenancy. Percentage of tenancy for all east-north-central states in 1940 was the same as for Indiana, 28 percent, while the national average was 39 percent. G. G. Quackenbush and O. G. Lloyd, *Farm Tenure in Indiana by Type-of-Farming*

Farm abandonment and rural to urban migration in the 1920s, which was heaviest from southern Indiana, reversed temporarily in the back-to-the-land movement of the early 1930s. Fleeing massive unemployment, city dwellers flocked to rural areas throughout the state, moving into abandoned farmhouses, schoolhouses, poultry houses, and converted railroad freight cars. The most significant urban to rural migration of the early 1930s was to the abandoned farms of southern Indiana, where by 1932 nearly all available houses were again occupied, as well as some buildings never intended to house people. Here, on the least productive land in the state, families survived with a vegetable garden, a cow, and a few chickens, supplemented by occasional off-farm work and public relief. A study of a sample of 374 families who moved to southern Indiana from cities in the period 1930-1934 showed that 78 percent of the adults had grown up on farms or had owned or worked on farms before moving to the city and that 40 percent were returning to the home county of either the husband or wife. Almost all had been unable to find any work in the city after 1929.[26]

The back-to-the-land movement, brought about by the Great Depression, enabled many Hoosiers to ride out the economic storm, although often under considerable hardship. But the back-to-the-land movement greatly exacerbated long-standing public problems of rural and especially southern Indiana. Above all, the newcomers placed increased burdens on local schools and poor relief programs—shifting this burden from city to country. Prior to 1933, local property taxes largely financed schools and relief. Farm abandonment in the 1920s reduced the amount of taxable

---

Areas (Purdue University Agricultural Experiment Station *Bulletin, No. 488,* Lafayette, Ind., 1943), pp. 4-7, 30.

[26] H. E. Moore and O. G. Lloyd, *The Back-to-the-Land Movement in Southern Indiana* (Purdue University Agricultural Experiment Station *Bulletin, No. 409,* Lafayette, Ind., 1936), pp. 3, 6, 9, 16; Lynn S. Robertson, *The Economic Significance of the Non-Farming Rural Population in Northwestern Indiana* (Purdue University Agricultural Experiment Station *Bulletin, No. 388,* Lafayette, Ind., 1934), pp. 20-23; Young, *Marginal Farm Land in Southern Indiana,* p. 16. For favorable urban response to the back-to-the-land movement see Indianapolis *News,* November 1, 1932.

property, while the back-to-the-land movement in the early 1930s brought large numbers of poor, nontaxpaying city families to rural areas. An analysis of the poorest townships in southern Indiana showed that by 1934, 27 percent of the population had arrived since 1930. These newcomers paid less than 1 percent of the township taxes, but 26 percent of them received township poor relief, amounting to 18 percent of the total township relief, and their children greatly increased the size of the township school population. The back-to-the-land movement placed burdens on local schools and relief programs in other parts of rural Indiana—particularly near industrial areas in the north—but the problems were greater by far in southern Indiana.[27]

Passage of the state gross income tax, increased state aid to schools, and federal relief programs—all of which began in 1933—alleviated burdens placed by newcomers on rural relief and schools and helped the poorer townships of southern Indiana and their residents to struggle through the Depression. But the basic problem persisted even with the gradual return of prosperity by the end of the 1930s. Intensive use of the land and continued erosion and depletion during the Depression had left many parts of southern Indiana even more marginal as productive farmland. And, with limited industrial or other employment opportunities nearby, federal and state agricultural and land-planning experts began to argue for resettling the farm population elsewhere and shifting the submarginal land to forest and recreational use. Rather than continue to subsidize farming on this submarginal land, the experts argued, the farms should be converted to state or national forests, the schools and roads closed, and the township and county governments consolidated. In 1936 and 1937 land-use planning committees in each county studied and classified the land and designated tracts that could not adequately support farm families.[28]

[27] Moore and Lloyd, *The Back-to-the-Land Movement*, pp. 17-19; H. L. Hawley, *Small Agricultural Holdings in Two Industrial Areas in Indiana* (Purdue University Agricultural Experiment Station *Bulletin, No. 460*, Lafayette, Ind., 1941), pp. 30-34; Robertson, *The Economic Significance of the Non-Farming Rural Population*, pp. 23-28.

[28] Lynn S. Robertson *et al., A Guide to Agricultural Programs in South*

§ § §

That the benefits of agricultural modernization did not fall equally on Indiana farms is best illustrated by the marginal and submarginal farms of southern Indiana. But even modern, progressive farmers, who owned large acreages of rich flatland found that agricultural science and technology did not bring all they hoped in the interwar years. The early career of Claude Wickard is illustrative of the challenges facing even the most modern of Hoosier farmers.

Wickard was graduated from Purdue University in 1915, filled with zeal for scientific agriculture. His father, Andrew Jackson Wickard, known as Jack, was a traditional farmer who for decades had mined the fertility of his 280 acres in Carroll County and deeply mistrusted "book farmers." Yet Jack Wickard turned over management of the farm to young Claude, who, after the unusual years of World War I, began in 1920 a full-scale program to modernize Fairacre Farms. As his neighbors watched with amusement, Claude Wickard began to restore the fertility of the soil by use of commercial fertilizer and lime. He improved his crop strains and installed a seed-testing laboratory to determine germination of his corn stands, but he concentrated primarily on production of corn and hogs—buying thirty Hampshire brood sows, vaccinating them against cholera, a disease his father had not understood, and building sanitary, heated hog houses for winter farrowing. And he bought most of the modern farm equipment available, including a tractor and a new Ford car. The results were impressive. By the late 1920s Claude Wickard had won several awards from the agricultural extension service for single hog litters that after six months weighed more than a ton and for corn yields of more than one hundred bushels an acre, as much as 25 percent higher than his Carroll County neighbors. The capstone award was his designation as Master Farmer in 1927.[29]

Central Indiana (Type-of-Farming Area 8) (Purdue University Agricultural Experiment Station Bulletin, No. 480, Lafayette, Ind., 1942), pp. 29-30; Indiana State Planning Board, Preliminary Report on a State Plan for Indiana, pp. 101-119; Indiana: The Land and the People, pp. 11-13; Indianapolis Star, December 27, 1936.

[29] Albertson, Claude R. Wickard, pp. 19-39, 45-46.

Claude Wickard was a nearly pure example of the modern, scientific farmer of the 1920s. Yet, throughout the decade he remained deeply in debt, constantly in anxiety about his future prosperity, and little better off than he had been in 1920. Like most Hoosier farmers, Wickard was the victim of short- and long-term changes in post-World War I national and international economies. Farmers later remembered the decade-and-a-half before World War I as a golden age of unprecedented prosperity. The war years increased their returns, as high prices and government encouragement led farmers to plant to the fence-rows. The index of Indiana farm prices—using the period 1910-1914 as 100—climbed rapidly to a peak of 217 by 1919. The rapid fall began in 1920, and the bottom dropped out in 1921 when the Indiana farm price index plummeted to 121, as farmers produced far more than domestic or international markets could absorb. Indiana farm prices improved only slightly in the mid- and late 1920s, reaching a price index high of 151 in 1929 before the even more dramatic drop of the early 1930s. Moreover, along with lower farm prices in the 1920s went an increase in the relative cost of goods and services farmers had to buy. A bushel of corn or hundredweight of hogs bought considerably less in seeds, fertilizer, and clothing than they did in the prewar golden age. Despite hard work and progressive methods, farmers like Claude Wickard seemed no better off than their fathers. Indeed, in one of the cruel ironies of modern America, the increased yields attained by the progressive farmer served to add to the nation's agricultural production and further reduce farm prices.[30]

But it was not only the comparison of their post-1920 condition to the prosperity of the prewar golden age that caused anxiety for Hoosier farmers. They also worried when they compared agriculture to the rest of the economy of the 1920s. Although the post-World War I economic downturn affected all sectors of the economy, there was a general recovery after 1922, but it was

[30] Paul L. Farris and R. S. Euler, *Prices of Indiana Farm Products, 1841-1955* (Purdue University Agricultural Experiment Station *Bulletin, No. 644,* Lafayette, Ind., 1957); W. H. Settle, "Present Status of Agriculture," *Hoosier Farmer,* March 15, 1928, p. 6; Danbom, *The Resisted Revolution,* pp. 128-134.

a recovery not fully shared by agriculture. While much of the rest of the nation seemed to be enjoying unprecedented prosperity, many farmers continued to suffer severe economic hardships.[31]

The relative lack of prosperity for farmers in the 1920s was highlighted as never before by the perceived gap in the quality of life enjoyed by farm families compared to city families. The process of integrating countryside and city was hastened by new technology such as the radio and the automobile, but for many rural residents increased familiarity with town and city only served to underscore unfavorable features of rural life. Rural Indiana, it seemed to some, not only was not keeping up but instead was lagging further and further behind. Institutions that had formed the bedrock of rural life for decades seemed to be crumbling from within and attacked from without—above all, the rural one-room school and the small rural church. Certainly the physical facilities available in urban schools and churches made rural facilities seem shabby and inadequate (as will be noted in Chapter IX).

In their homes, farm and rural families often did not enjoy the material goods and comforts increasingly available to their town and city cousins. They lagged far behind urban Hoosiers in such modern home conveniences as running water, flush toilets, central heating, electricity, and telephones. In 1920, for example, only 10 percent of Indiana farm dwellings had electricity, and by 1930 the farm figure had increased to only 16.7 percent. Federal aid through the Rural Electrification Administration allowed for the rapid extension of electricity through rural Indiana in the late 1930s. By 1940 51.8 percent of farm homes enjoyed electric lights and some of the other electric conveniences, such as refrigerators, toasters, water pumps, and washing machines. Still, by 1940, when only half of Indiana farms had electricity, 98 percent of urban dwellings possessed this convenience. The changing percentage of Indiana farms with telephones shows not only a similar rural lag, but an actual decline in availability of a modern convenience. Farmers had eagerly installed telephones during the prosperity of the first two decades of the twentieth century. By 1920 66 percent of Indiana farm homes had telephones— helping considerably to assuage the loneliness and isolation of farm life. But from this peak in 1920 the number of telephones on farms actually decreased in the interwar years, reflecting more poignantly than perhaps any other factor the hardships experienced by many farmers and the lag in the benefits available to them in modern America. By 1930 only 61 percent of Indiana farms had telephones, and by 1940 the figure had fallen to 45 percent. Unsurprisingly, more prosperous farmers generally had greater access to such modern conveniences as electricity and telephones, while poorer farmers—particularly in southern Indiana—generally lagged farthest behind. Distribution of telephone service in 1940, for example, ranged from less than 15 percent of farm homes equipped with telephones in Brown, Orange, and Scott counties to more than 70 percent with telephones in the cornbelt counties of Boone, Clinton, and Carroll.[32]

After 1920, then, many Indiana farmers saw themselves less well off than they had been in the first two decades of the twentieth century and increasingly falling behind urban dwellers in material comforts. These sentiments and the conditions which prompted them came to be known in Indiana and the nation as "the farm problem." Like other problems, the farm problem evoked a variety of responses in the interwar years.

Perhaps the most important response advanced to solve the farm problem was organization. Beginning in the last decades of the nineteenth century Americans with similar economic, social, or cultural interests and goals had begun to organize into regional, state, and national associations to achieve common purposes. Farmers in Indiana had lagged behind other Americans in this search for a better life through organization. The Grange had

[32] United States Bureau of the Census, *Sixteenth Census* (1940), I, *Agriculture*, Pt. 1, p. 543; Robertson and Butz, *Indiana's Agriculture*, pp. 32, 42; Lynn S. Robertson and Keith Amstutz, *Telephone Problems in Rural Indiana* (Purdue University Agricultural Experiment Station *Bulletin, No. 548*, Lafayette, Ind., 1949), p. 4; *Indiana: The Land and the People*, pp. 43-44; Gail Redfield and Truman E. Hienton, *Electricity Serves the Farm Household* (Purdue University Agricultural Experiment Station *Circular, No. 214*, Lafayette, Ind., 1936), pp. 2-12.

Purdue University Agricultural Extension

Extension agent shows farmers a successful hog production project, circa 1931

Purdue University Agricultural Experiment Station

Mechanical corn picker, circa 1934

National guardsmen protect Columbian Enameling Company during
Terre Haute general strike, July, 1935

Workers and families outside General Motors plant in Anderson at end of
United Auto Workers sit-down strike, 1937

enjoyed popularity among some Hoosier farmers, but by the twentieth century it functioned largely as a social organization. The Farmers' Alliance and the Populist party, formed to express farm grievances in the 1880s and 1890s, gained only small and brief followings in Indiana.[33] The early twentieth century produced no significant third political party movement representing farmers in Indiana, so that by World War I, it seemed, no organization spoke for their economic and political interests. Then in 1919 an organization with such pretensions appeared at the local, state, and national levels.

The Indiana Federation of Farmers' Associations, later known as the Indiana Farm Bureau, was organized in March, 1919. By the end of the year, local organizations were formed in eighty-one of the state's ninety-two counties and affiliated with the state organization, which was part of the American Farm Bureau, also organized in 1919. By 1920 the Indiana Farm Bureau had 64,420 members. The number declined in the early 1920s and remained at slightly under 40,000 through the remainder of the decade. The Great Depression brought a large decline in membership, which reached a low point in 1933 of about 23,000. A gradual upswing in the late 1930s and a rapid increase in growth thereafter brought it to nearly 60,000 members by the end of World War II.[34]

From its beginning in 1919 the Farm Bureau was the most important agricultural organization in Indiana. Its strength derived not only from its numbers but also from a membership that generally included more successful farmers and from the organization's close ties to Purdue University. The Purdue staff played an important role in organizing the county Farm Bureau offices, and often the activities of county agriculture agents were much intertwined with those of the local Farm Bureau. In some counties the Farm Bureau office was located in the county agent's office, and doubtless many farmers did not fully realize which farm programs were supported by the public money and efforts of the

[33] Phillips, *Indiana in Transition*, pp. 169-178.
[34] Edna Moore Colby, *Hoosier Farmers in a New Day* (Indianapolis, 1968), pp. 20-28, 33-44, 127, 233.

extension service and which by the private money and efforts of the Farm Bureau.[35]

The state and local Farm Bureaus also derived strength from the formation of co-operative associations to market farm products and purchase farm supplies. Farmers had long co-operated on an informal local basis by borrowing or sharing equipment and labor and by organizing county fairs, and they had formed small local co-operative grain elevators and telephone companies. But by the early 1920s many believed that a wider, more formal, and more rigorously economic co-operation was necessary. According to William H. Settle, president of the Indiana Farm Bureau from 1923 to 1934, if farmers hoped to compete successfully with businessmen and industrial workers for a fair share of American prosperity, they had to form co-operatives, because "the rapid centralization which is taking place in the important industrial lines [is] eliminating competition and giving them an advantage over less closely-knit groups."[36]

The Indiana Farm Bureau played a major role in the growth of co-operatives, although many farmers also organized local co-operatives that were independent of the Farm Bureau. Despite opposition from some merchants, manufacturers, and suppliers, there were 420 co-operatives in the state by 1924: most of them were grain elevators and livestock shipping associations. Thereafter, the number of co-operatives declined, but the dollar volume of their business increased. By 1941 there were only 197 co-operatives in the state, but their dollar volume was more than three times that of 1924, and they handled one fifth of all products sold by Indiana farmers. Of the total of 197 farm co-operatives in 1941, 125 were affiliated with the Indiana Farm Bureau Cooperative Association, and they handled 75 percent of the dollar volume of co-operative business in the state. The Indiana Farm Bureau Cooperative Association engaged in an ever-widening range of activities in the late 1920s and 1930s—including not only pur-

[35] Phillips, *Indiana in Transition*, p. 179; Colby, *Hoosier Farmers*, pp. 33, 51-52; George Doup interview by Terry Anderson, July 29, 1977, transcript, Oral History Research Project Mss., Lilly Library, Indiana University, Bloomington.
[36] Settle, "Present Status of Agriculture," *Hoosier Farmer*, March 15, 1928, p. 5.

chasing but also producing and distributing such products as lubricating oil, gasoline, farm machinery, fertilizer, flour, baby chicks, and electricity. In all these activities farmers hoped to benefit from economies of scale, from increased bargaining power in negotiating with shippers, buyers, and sellers, and from more immediate and local direction of their economic activities.[37]

In the interwar years the co-operative movement did not produce the degree of efficiency, order, or profit that its supporters had hoped. It did not solve the farm problem, although it doubtless helped alleviate it. For some farmers and Farm Bureau leaders, the farm problem called for more than the self-help of economic organization. Solutions, they argued, could come only from political action.

Despite the traditions of rugged self-reliance associated with Jeffersonian agrarianism, farmers had long benefited from government aid. Cheap public land, government-sponsored transportation improvements, and land grant colleges were among the many ways in which the state and federal governments had helped farmers. In the 1920s the work of Purdue's extension service was perhaps the most visible evidence of public aid to agriculture. But to many Hoosiers the farm problem of the 1920s demanded new and more government aid.

Part of the political effort of farmers focused on the Indiana General Assembly. The 1923 legislative session marked the organization of what was probably the first formal farm bloc in Indiana (paralleling the national farm bloc formed in the 1921 Congress). Soon after the 1923 session began, the Indiana Farm Bureau called an evening meeting of farmer-legislators. Fifty-four attended and agreed upon the need for a united, bipartisan effort

[37] Verne Freeman interview by Terry Anderson, December 2, 1977, transcript, Oral History Research Project Mss., Lilly Library, Indiana University, Bloomington; T. L. Canada and E. H. Matzen, *An Economic Study of the History, Status and Operation of Agricultural Cooperatives in Indiana* (Purdue University Agricultural Experiment Station *Bulletin, No. 518*, Lafayette, Ind., 1946), pp. 4-15; Paul Turner, *They Did It in Indiana: The Story of the Indiana Farm Bureau Co-operatives* (New York, 1947), pp. 60-68; French M. Hyre, *Farm Co-ops in Indiana* (Louisville, Ky., 1940), pp. 1-14; I. Harvey Hull, *Built of Men: The Story of Indiana Cooperatives* (New York, 1952), pp. 31-37, 42-110, 180-185.

to increase state support for improved roads—funded by a gasoline rather than a property tax—and they decided to oppose the county unit education bill, which they concluded would reduce local township control of public education and increase its cost. The farm bloc achieved success in both areas in 1923. Thereafter, farmers continued their efforts to influence state legislation, largely through lobbying by the Indiana Farm Bureau. During the 1920s, the Farm Bureau successfully pushed for legislation to prohibit sale of low-grade seed, to foster co-operative marketing, to require tuberculin tests for cattle, and to regulate the sale of raw milk. But increasingly the Farm Bureau's legislative lobbying focused on taxation—on the need to substitute other forms of taxation for the property tax, which farmers argued fell unfairly upon them. The Farm Bureau gave strong support to Governor Paul McNutt's gross income tax bill in 1933 and played an important role during the 1930s in helping to resist efforts to repeal the tax.[38]

There is no doubt that the Farm Bureau achieved significant political influence in Indiana during the interwar years. Politicians consulted Farm Bureau leaders when they prepared state party platforms, shaped legislation, and made appointments to state committees and commissions.[39] The Farm Bureau was not a third political party, however; instead, it functioned as a bipartisan political pressure group, and its scope and effectiveness were generally limited to issues most directly affecting farmers.[40]

As Indiana Farm Bureau leaders worked to extend the co-operative movement and to influence state government, they became convinced that many of the components of the farm problem could be solved only by the federal government. As long as farmers bought and sold in a national and international market, there was little they could do at the state or local level to affect the basic problem of low farm prices. Indiana Farm Bureau Presi-

[38] Indianapolis *News*, January 4, 16, 23, 1923; Indiana Farm Bureau, *History of the Tax and Legislative Department of the Indiana Farm Bureau* (n.p., [1945]), pp. 5-13; "Marching Farmers Mean Business," *Hoosier Farmer*, March, 1939, p. 5.

[39] See, for example, Indianapolis *News*, June 5, 1930, June 3, 1932.

[40] See, for example, Lewis Taylor, "Measuring the Candidates," *Hoosier Farmer*, July, 1936, pp. 5, 28.

dent Settle soon became the state's strongest spokesman for federal aid to agriculture. Settle's efforts in the 1920s concentrated on support for the federal McNary-Haugen bill, which was designed to provide federal aid in disposing of agricultural surplus overseas and to protect a higher price for agricultural products in the domestic market. Settle looked like the stereotypical hayseed, but he was a sophisticated, energetic spokesman and lobbyist for a federal solution to the problems of agricultural surplus and low prices. To many of the farm experts at Purdue, however, the Indiana Farm Bureau president seemed to be a misguided radical. Led by the dean of the School of Agriculture, John Harrison Skinner, many Purdue staff members believed that the solution to the farm problem had to come from each individual farmer through the use of techniques developed and disseminated by Purdue. Mechanization, scientific production practices, and modern management were the proper solutions—not dangerous political interference with the laws of supply and demand. Settle's support of the McNary-Haugen bill was perhaps even more distasteful to the Purdue people because they had expected to dominate the Indiana Farm Bureau. Viewed from the offices and laboratories in West Lafayette, Settle was an independent and radical farm leader.[41]

Unwilling to wait for the laws of supply and demand, Settle armed himself in 1928 with bundles of petitions pledging Hoosier farmers to vote for the political party that supported the McNary-

[41] Settle, "Present Status of Agriculture," *ibid.*, March 15, 1928, p. 5; Albertson, *Claude R. Wickard*, p. 41; Wickard interview, 1952-1953, No. 7, pp. 305-307, No. 9, pp. 381-385, Wickard Papers; Colby, *Hoosier Farmers*, pp. 52, 119-124, 193. John Harrison Skinner grew up on a farm near Romney, Indiana, and entered Purdue in 1893, at the age of eighteen. He joined the Purdue faculty in 1899, and in 1907 became dean of the School of Agriculture. In 1928 he added to his duties the directorships of the Agricultural Experiment Station and the Department of Agricultural Extension, uniting the three agricultural departments at Purdue under one administrative head. Purdue University Department of Agricultural Extension, *Annual Report*, 1928-1929, pp. 11-14. Settle was far from radical compared to farm leaders in some other states. He strongly disavowed violence, farm strikes, and farm holidays in the early 1930s. William H. Settle, "This is Your Organization. Be Proud of Its Accomplishments," *Hoosier Farmer*, November, 1934, p. 5.

Haugen bill, and then he set off for the national party conventions. After both state and national Democratic party platforms endorsed the McNary-Haugen bill and the Republican party did not, the Indiana Farm Bureau—though carefully avoiding endorsement of either presidential candidate—pointed strongly to the satisfactory Democratic platform plank on agriculture and to the unsatisfactory Republican plank. But Republican candidate Herbert Hoover's resounding victory over Democrat Al Smith in 1928 in state and nation boded ill for McNary-Haugen. Although President Hoover made some tentative efforts toward increased aid to agriculture, the significant change did not come until 1933 with Franklin D. Roosevelt's New Deal.[42]

The New Deal agricultural programs attempted to raise farm prices by limiting production. The major effort was the Agricultural Adjustment Act (AAA) of 1933, which provided for acreage allotments, price supports, and marketing quotas to curtail production of specific products. The Indiana Farm Bureau supported passage of the act and worked hard to implement it in the state. Because of ties to the United States Department of Agriculture, the Purdue Extension Service and especially the county agents played major roles along with the Farm Bureau in educating farmers about AAA programs. County agents in Indiana devoted well over half of their time to this effort in 1933 and 1934. The largest AAA program in Indiana was directed toward limiting corn-hog production. In the twelve months from July 1, 1933, to June 30, 1934, the AAA sponsored 207 county and 6,457 township meetings to explain and implement the corn-hog program. As a result, Indiana farmers signed 85,651 corn-hog contracts and voluntarily agreed to limit to assigned levels both corn acreage and the number of hogs farrowed and produced for market in return for federal benefits totaling about $20 million. Although there were many complaints about the details of the program, both

[42] Albertson, *Claude R. Wickard*, p. 42; Democratic state platform, 1928, in Indiana State Platforms, I; New York *Times*, July 13, 1928. Democratic presidential nominee Alfred E. Smith's identification with Roman Catholicism and opposition to prohibition undoubtedly hurt the party among Hoosier farmers, counteracting favorable farm reaction to Democratic support of the McNary-Haugen bill.

from farmers who thought they deserved more and from those who objected to induced scarcity measures such as killing little pigs, Hoosier corn-hog producers showed strong support for AAA. In a 1935 referendum, 67,612 (89 percent) of the 75,669 Indiana corn-hog farmers who participated voted in favor of continuing the federal program. AAA also established smaller programs in Indiana in wheat, sugar beets, and tobacco.[43]

In 1936, the United States Supreme Court declared AAA unconstitutional, but other New Deal legislation soon continued and expanded federal efforts to raise farm prices, notably the Soil Conservation and Domestic Allotment Act of 1936 and the Agricultural Adjustment Act of 1938. These federal legislative shifts created confusion and anxiety for Indiana farmers, but many of the basic procedures and objectives of the early New Deal agriculture programs continued.[44]

The federal government undoubtedly helped many Indiana farmers survive the Great Depression, but the overall results were mixed. Indiana farm prices did rise after 1933, but during 1937-1938 they began a rapid decline, leading to strong farm anger expressed in the 1938 elections. Not until 1942 did Indiana farm prices rise to pre-Depression levels.[45] The New Deal farm programs were only moderately successful in curtailing agricultural

[43] "A Permanent Program," *Hoosier Farmer*, December, 1934, p. 4; Christiana McFadyen Campbell, *The Farm Bureau and the New Deal: A Study of the Making of a National Farm Policy, 1933-40* (Urbana, Ill., 1962), p. 64; Albertson, *Claude R. Wickard*, pp. 65-96; Purdue University Department of Agricultural Extension, *Annual Report*, 1933-1934, pp. 8-9, 18; *ibid.*, 1935-1936, pp. 19-20. For a general assessment of New Deal agricultural programs at the national level see Theodore Saloutos, "New Deal Agricultural Policy: An Evaluation," *Journal of American History*, LXI (1974-1975), 394-416.

[44] Purdue University Department of Agricultural Extension, *Annual Report*, 1937-1938, pp. 16-19.

[45] Farris and Euler, *Prices of Indiana Farm Products*, p. 26. For assessments that the farm vote was important in Democratic losses in Indiana in 1938 see Ed Wilken to James A. Farley, December 16, 1938, Roy L. Barham to Farley, December 10, 1938, and Joe J. Barbera to Farley, January 5, 1939, in Box 95, OF 300, Democratic National Committee Papers, Franklin D. Roosevelt Library, Hyde Park, New York. See also Indianapolis *News*, July 13, 1938. Nonetheless, the Indiana Farm Bureau continued to support New Deal agricultural programs through the 1930s. Hassil E. Schenck, "Talk to Your Congressman," *Hoosier Farmer*, January, 1940, p. 5.

production, and in working toward this goal they were aided by droughts in 1934 and 1936. By limiting acreage the federal programs encouraged farmers to seek the highest possible yields from the land they did farm, giving farmers more incentive to adopt modern production techniques, including soil improving efforts. But higher yields from the use of fertilizer and hybrid corn seed, for example, doubtless served to offset New Deal corn acreage limitations.[46] It is likely, moreover, that operators of larger, more efficient farms, who were generally more able to adopt modern production techniques, benefited more from the federal programs than did those with smaller farms. Such New Deal programs as the Resettlement Administration and the Farm Security Administration, as well as general federal relief programs, did provide some aid to small and marginal farmers in Indiana.[47]

§ § § §

Agriculture changed as much as, and perhaps more than, any other sector of the economy in the interwar years. Achievements in agricultural science and technology and the expansion of methods to disseminate these modern techniques changed the nature of farming and farm life, as illustrated by such developments as the rapid disappearance of horses from many Indiana farms, the introduction of mechanical corn pickers, the use of commercial fertilizers, the visits by county extension agents, and the electrification of rural areas. But, while science and technology improved productivity and perhaps the attractiveness of farm life, the benefits were not equally distributed, less frequently reaching southern Indiana and smaller farmers. Nor did science and technology produce the prosperity they promised. Even the most modern

[46] Robertson and Butz, *Indiana's Agriculture*, p. 20; Purdue University Department of Agricultural Extension, *Annual Report*, 1933-1934, p. 7; United States Department of Agriculture, Agricultural Marketing Service, *Indiana Corn Acreage*, pp. 1-4.

[47] E. H. Shideler, "Rural Rehabilitation Services for Indiana Farmers," *Hoosier Farmer*, July, 1937, pp. 11, 24; United States Department of Agriculture, *National Farm Program Data, 1932-1940: Indiana Highlights* (Washington, D.C., 1940), pp. 1-18. Scholars have generally concluded that the New Deal helped small farmers less than large farmers. Further research is necessary to determine the extent to which this was the case in Indiana. See Saloutos, "New Deal Agricultural Policy," *Journal of American History*, LXI, 403-413.

farmers experienced economic tribulations in the 1920s and 1930s. In response they organized economic co-operatives and joined the Indiana Farm Bureau to plead their case in the state and national legislatures. Farm interests in state government were directed toward lowering the property tax, but increasingly the focus of concern was the federal government. The New Deal agricultural programs largely bypassed state government and administration,[48] and farmers looked to Washington for solutions to the basic problems of farm surplus and low prices.

On the eve of World War II, many farmers and their families lived and worked much as they had at the close of World War I and much as their grandparents had at the close of the Civil War. For many others, life and work were vastly different. Jack Wickard still lived on the family's Carroll County farm in 1940, but it was a farm far removed from his nineteenth-century roots. His son's Purdue education had led to intensive adoption of modern agricultural techniques in the 1920s. But young Claude Wickard soon realized that his successful efforts at "book" farming could not alone solve the farm problem of the 1920s, and he increasingly moved to organized economic efforts—directing the Carroll County Farm Bureau Cooperative—and to political efforts—accompanying Indiana Farm Bureau President Settle to the Democratic National Convention in 1928. After serving one term in the 1933 state legislature, Claude Wickard went to Washington, where he worked in the corn-hog section of AAA, rising up through the ranks as one of the few genuine Democratic cornbelt farmers in Washington, until he became Secretary of Agriculture in 1940. Wickard continued to manage Fairacre Farms, returning often to Indiana. By the eve of World War II, his mortgage was paid off, and the farm was showing its first profit in more than two decades. In 1942 Jack Wickard finally decided that Claude should inherit the family farm. Like many traditional Hoosier farmers, Jack Wickard had little or no choice but to stand aside.[49]

[48] Patterson, *The New Deal and the States*, pp. 56, 102. By the late 1930s federal field agents had assumed much of the local responsibility for New Deal agricultural programs initially in the hands of the county agricultural agent. Purdue University Department of Agricultural Extension, *Annual Report, 1937-1938*, p. 16.

[49] Albertson, *Claude R. Wickard, passim.*

CHAPTER VII

TRANSPORTATION

DURING THE INTERWAR YEARS the hitching post and the stable stood in sight of the airport beacon, while interurban and steam trains competed with automobiles, buses, and trucks for movement of people and freight. These diverse and rapidly changing modes of transportation called forth a variety of political responses and also shaped significant social and economic features of life in Indiana between 1920 and 1940.

By far the most significant change in twentieth-century transportation was the rapid increase in automobile travel. Pioneer auto manufacturer Elwood Haynes tested his first successful horseless carriage along the Pumpkinvine Pike near Kokomo in 1894, but, despite the efforts of Haynes and others, Hoosiers were slow to adopt this new form of transportation. The ratio of population to motor vehicle registrations in Indiana lagged far behind the national average in 1900 and 1910. By 1920, however, Hoosiers had overcome their initial hesitancy and were purchasing automobiles as rapidly as their pocketbooks or credit standing would allow. The ratio of population to motor vehicles registered in Indiana in 1920 was 8.8:1 (i.e., there were 8.8 people for every car), compared to 11.4:1 for the nation as a whole, and the state figure declined rapidly thereafter, reaching 3.7:1 by 1930. During the early 1920s especially, first-time car owners caused the number of vehicles registered to more than double, from 333,067 in 1920 to 725,410 in 1925. By that year, the Indiana Highway Commission reported, "Horse drawn traffic has almost disappeared from our main highways. Such traffic has decreased rapidly in the past six years and now consists only of the local farm traffic."[1]

Although the number of cars continued to increase in the last

[1] Indiana *Year Book*, 1925, p. 1151; United States Department of Transportation, *Highway Statistics: Summary to 1975* (Washington, D.C., 1975), p. 59.

half of the 1920s, the rate of increase dropped rapidly as the automobile market became saturated, particularly among middle-class Hoosiers. By 1930, there were 874,963 vehicles registered in the state. The Great Depression brought only a slight absolute decrease in motor vehicle registrations, which dropped to a low of 770,071 in 1933, but rose slowly thereafter. Increased auto purchases at the close of the decade resulted in a state registration total of 1,000,306 in 1940—a ratio of population to motor vehicles of 3.4:1.[2] Even in the depths of the Depression most Hoosiers held on to their cars. In Muncie, Robert and Helen Lynd reported, car ownership "was one of the most depression-proof elements in the city's life. . . ."[3] Hoosiers kept their cars and continued to drive them. Annual motor fuel consumption in Indiana in the early 1930s never fell below the 1929 level of 433,503,000 gallons and rose rapidly in the last half of the decade to 721,951,000 gallons by 1940.[4]

The Hoosier's firm attachment to the automobile—which was formed in the post-World War I decade and survived even the onslaughts of the Great Depression—was based partly on the convenience and flexibility of the car compared to horse-drawn or rail transportation and also for many on the personal pride that accompanied automobile ownership. Many Hoosiers were first attracted to the new form of transportation by Henry Ford's practical Model T or by the Model A in the late 1920s. Ford's low-priced cars, which sold for under $500, accounted for 35 percent of total automobile registrations in Indiana in 1930. But Hoosiers, like other Americans, were increasingly fond of the colorful and more stylish models produced and heavily advertised by Ford's competitors. By 1930 Chevrolet was closing fast on Ford's new car sales in Indiana and accounted for nearly 16 percent of total registrations in the state, followed by Buick with

[2] United States Department of Transportation, *Highway Statistics*, p. 59; United States Public Roads Administration, *Highway Statistics: Summary to 1945* (Washington, D.C., 1947), p. 20.

[3] Lynd and Lynd, *Middletown in Transition*, pp. 265, 266-267.

[4] United States Department of Transportation, *Highway Statistics: Summary to 1975*, pp. 17-18.

nearly 7 percent and Dodge with almost 6 percent.[5] Everywhere, it seemed, were the enticements of car ownership—newspaper and magazine advertisements, radio commercials, even the state fair, where one newspaper in 1920 declared "the largest, most expansive, most complete, most brilliant display . . . was the automobile show."[6] And, of course, for many Hoosiers the ultimate display of the automobile was the Indianapolis 500-Mile Race, which provided new opportunities for competition among race car drivers and among manufacturers of cars and accessories. First run in 1911, under the sponsorship of several Indianapolis businessmen, notably Carl G. Fisher, an auto parts manufacturer, and James A. Allison, founder of Allison Engineering Company, the Indianapolis 500 was one of the major sporting events in America by the 1920s.[7]

The rapid increase in the number of automobiles in the 1920s affected nearly all aspects of society—so much so, one scholar has argued, that a "car culture" pervaded the decade.[8] For many Hoosiers, the automobile was the primary symbol of individual freedom and social progress achieved through technology. To a few others the car threatened the foundations of the society. The auto, critics argued, separated family members, especially adolescents from parents; provided opportunities for sexual license ("a house of prostitution on wheels," a Muncie judge reportedly charged);[9] led to a decline in church attendance and an abandonment of the traditional Sabbath;[10] and, with the enticements of

[5] Joseph A. Batchelor, A Statistical Analysis of the 1930 Passenger Car Registrations with Special Reference to Indiana (M.A. thesis, Indiana University, Bloomington, 1931), pp. 58, 59, 62, 76.

[6] Indianapolis News, September 6, 1920.

[7] Phillips, Indiana in Transition, p. 264; Al Bloemker, 500 Miles to Go: The Story of the Indianapolis Speedway (New York, 1961), pp. 145-175.

[8] James J. Flink, The Car Culture (Cambridge, Mass., 1975). Flink's book provides general background for the following discussion, along with Lynd and Lynd, Middletown, pp. 253-263. Flink and the Lynds may have exaggerated the negative features of the car culture. See Jensen, "The Lynds Revisited," Indiana Magazine of History, LXXV, 309-310.

[9] Lynd and Lynd, Middletown, p. 114.

[10] See, for example, Northwest Indiana Conference of the Methodist Episcopal Church, Minutes, 1925 (n.p., n.d.), p. 186.

advertising and installment buying, encouraged families to forego more important needs for the immediate gratification of car ownership. Others responded that the car brought families together for Sunday drives and auto vacations and provided new access to shopping, visiting, employment, and cultural and educational opportunities, especially for rural Hoosiers. The auto did make country and suburban living more possible for urban workers and opened urban employment to rural dwellers, but it also brought to towns and cities new forms of traffic congestion and conflict over downtown parking. In rural areas on Sundays traffic on narrow gravel and dirt roads swelled beyond reasonable capacity as Hoosiers descended on bucolic Brown County and cool Lake Michigan beach points.[11] The auto brought an end to the stench of horse manure on the town square: not until later did Hoosiers become aware that the gasoline engine brought its own pollution, though some did complain of the unsightly auto junkyards spreading over the urban and rural landscape.[12] And while the auto moved people rapidly and conveniently, it also resulted in increased highway deaths, which rose steadily from about 30 in 1920 to 307 in 1930. The steep curve of annual traffic fatalities in the interwar years dipped only in 1933, to 201, and then again rapidly climbed, reaching 447 by 1935. By then automobiles often traveled at speeds of fifty or sixty miles per hour. Highway traffic experts blamed the ever higher speeds as well as the greater number of cars for much of the increase in accidents and fatalities.[13]

Automobile owners and manufacturers proposed more and better roads as part of the solution to congested and dangerous highways. Responsibility for road construction and maintenance in Indiana traditionally rested with township and county governments. But as the auto replaced the horse and brought long-distance travel, higher speeds, and increased volume of traffic,

[11] Indiana State Committee on Governmental Economy, *Report*, pp. 646-647; Lynd and Lynd, *Middletown in Transition*, p. 307.

[12] Indianapolis *News*, October 8, 1921.

[13] Indiana *Year Book*, 1930, pp. 1165, 1172; 1935, p. 544; Indianapolis *Star*, March 17, 1940.

this local, decentralized arrangement seemed less and less adequate.

After a failed effort in 1917, the state legislature outlined in 1919 a modern highway system that was centrally planned, administered, and financed. The 1919 legislature created the Indiana State Highway Commission with responsibility to designate a system of state roads running to each county seat and each town of five thousand or more residents, all to be maintained by the state. In early 1920 the State Highway Commission and Governor James P. Goodrich designated a network of state roads, approximately 3,200 miles long. On April 1, 1920, the state took from local governments the responsibility for maintaining and improving these roads. Not only were nearly all these roads unpaved, but the combination of war and immediate postwar circumstances and county negligence had left them in unusually poor condition —so poor that in the spring of 1920 mud prevented many state highway trucks from reaching their assigned places of work. Nevertheless, a beginning had been made. By 1925 the state highway system consisted of 1,203 miles of paved roads and 2,658 miles of improved gravel and stone roads. At the end of the decade, twelve paved arteries led into Indianapolis, where only four had reached as late as 1923. Roads were paved with concrete and later asphalt, and additional county and township roads were incorporated into the state system. By 1940 the State Highway Commission was responsible for 10,099 miles of road, about half of which (5,065 miles) was paved.[14]

Construction and maintenance of state roads for high volume, high-speed motor traffic was an immensely expensive undertaking, second only to expenditures for public education in state and local government in Indiana.[15] Funding for the state highway system

[14] Indiana *Year Book*, 1920, pp. 1125, 1145; United States Public Roads Administration, *Highway Statistics: Summary to 1945*, p. 65; Wiley, *Motor Transportation of Hogs*, p. 7. For data on types of state road surface by county and maps of the highway system in 1940 see Indiana *Year Book*, 1940, pp. 639-645.

[15] In fiscal year 1924-1925, for example, state and local government expenditures for education were 23.3 percent of total expenditures and for highways and streets, 21.9 percent. *Statistical Report for the State of Indiana for the Year Ending September 30, 1925* (Indianapolis, 1926), p. 103.

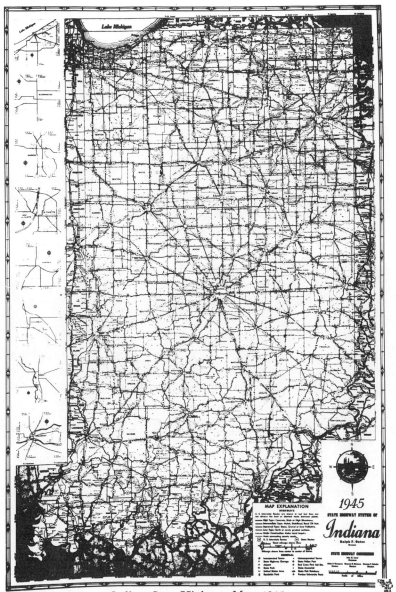

Indiana State Highway Map, 1945

came from several sources, but two were dominant: user fees and federal aid.

Federal money played a major role from the outset. The Federal Aid Road Act of 1916 provided matching grants to states for highway improvements and, very importantly, compelled states without highway departments to organize them in order to receive this aid. This federal legislation was a direct cause of the formation of the Indiana State Highway Commission in 1919. Federal aid and direction expanded further with passage of the Federal Highway Act of 1921, which laid the basis for a national highway system by providing increased aid to states for improvements of designated primary highways. In 1920 the Indiana State Highway Commission received its first federal aid, $484,999. The sum increased rapidly thereafter, reaching $3,704,940 in 1924, 24 percent of total Highway Commission receipts. This so-called normal federal aid continued through the 1930s and was greatly augmented by New Deal public works funds used for highway construction and maintenance. From 1934 through 1937 total federal aid accounted for between 30 and 47 percent of the total Highway Commission receipts, as the Commission eagerly sought this money. Because of this federal support, Highway Commission receipts were maintained at least at the level of 1929 through the Depression except for the years 1933 and 1934.[16]

The largest source of highway funding was user taxes, principally in the form of automobile license fees and the gasoline tax. Initially, the Highway Commission received funds from inheritance taxes and general property taxes, but popular objections to high property taxes in the early 1920s and a traditional belief that users should bear the primary burden for road construction and maintenance resulted in the institution of a tax on gasoline in 1923, all the revenues of which were slated for highways. The gasoline tax was set at two cents a gallon; it was raised to three cents in 1925 and four cents in 1929, when it accounted for 51

[16] John B. Rae, *The Road and the Car in American Life* (Cambridge, Mass., 1971), pp. 36-39, 74; Indiana *Year Book*, 1935, p. 479; 1940, pp. 570, 584, 587; Ellis L. Armstrong, Michael C. Robinson, and Suellen M. Hoy (eds.), *History of Public Works in the United States, 1776-1976* (Chicago, 1976), pp. 78-82.

percent of Highway Commission receipts. Beginning in 1925, one cent of the tax per gallon was diverted to cities and counties for local streets and roads. The state did not issue bonds for highways because of the provision in the state constitution prohibiting debt. All work was financed on a "pay-as-you-go" basis, with motorists and the federal government doing all the paying after 1923.[17]

The importance of the State Highway Commission's responsibilities and the large quantities of money and personnel involved in road construction and maintenance almost guaranteed that the Commission would become involved in controversy. As noted earlier, the State Highway Commission was a major source of political patronage, from the highest- to the lowest-ranking appointees. Apparently there was some job protection for professional highway engineers, but even they were not formally served by a merit system until 1941, and then it was not a fully effective protection. Since all construction work was done by private contractors, there were also occasional complaints about favoritism in awarding contracts and purchasing materials. Inefficiency and waste were unquestionably the consequences of this system, although there seem to have been no major public scandals involving the Highway Commission in the interwar years.[18]

As has traditionally been the case, there was conflict also over location and type of road improvements. The state exhibited less of the selfish or democratic localism that prevailed in the early nineteenth century, however, and concentrated initial efforts on a few main highways rather than on many secondary roads. In the 1920s federal government policy and financial aid encouraged this more centralized, arterial strategy. Conflict did erupt on

[17] Feightner, Our State Government, pp. 25, 80; Indiana Year Book, 1940, p. 587. It has been noted that because of the large portion of highway costs paid by users, the nation's highway transportation system was developed primarily to serve the needs of automobiles and trucks for fast, efficient travel, and perhaps too little attention was paid to other forms of transportation and the general social welfare. See Mark H. Rose, Interstate: Express Highway Politics, 1941-1956 (Lawrence, Kansas, 1979), p. 9.

[18] In addition to the sources cited in Chapter III see Lawrence H. Wendrich, The State Highway Commission of Indiana: A Study of Organization and Functions (Bloomington, Ind., 1942), pp. 23, 37; Indianapolis Star, March 17, 1940.

occasion, however, especially between urban and rural interests. Urban politicians objected to spending taxes collected from their constituents for improving backcountry roads. Questioning why "the city folk should pay for the country roads," legislators from Lake and Marion counties attempted in 1925 to revise state highway financing to guarantee that one half of the revenues collected in a local area would be used to improve streets and roads there. Although rural legislators were able to defeat this so-called "Road Grab" bill, the 1925 General Assembly did approve a complicated plan that allocated small portions of the gasoline tax to counties and cities on the basis of miles of streets and roads and on population.[19] While urban dwellers had a justified grievance, particularly since the state did not begin to maintain roads inside city limits until the 1930s, and then only selected main arteries, rural Hoosiers also demonstrated a legitimate need for increased state aid. In rural Indiana in 1920 and even as late as 1940, motorists often confronted a morass in the spring and fall and choking dust in the summer. It was not unusual for a motorist to suffer the humiliation of requiring horses to pull his automobile through a mudhole, sometimes for a fee, and on a few occasions for a fee charged by an unscrupulous entrepreneur who helped nature create the mud. The condition of rural roads caused special difficulties for farmers transporting products to market and for township trustees responsible for transporting children to school. A survey of one-room schools in 1935 showed that inadequate roads and bridges were primary deterrents to school attendance and school consolidation.[20]

[19] Indianapolis *News*, February 11, 1925; Feightner, *Our State Government*, p. 25; John D. Barnhart and Donald F. Carmony, *Indiana: From Frontier to Industrial Commonwealth* (4 volumes, New York, 1954), II, 468.

[20] Indiana *Year Book*, 1930, p. 1176; Ben H. Petty, *Why Our Road Maintenance Costs Are Increasing So Rapidly* (Purdue University Engineering Extension Service *Circular, No. 6*, Lafayette, Ind., 1924), p. 3; Nestle H. Voyles to L. N. Hines, September 14, 1920, Correspondence, Vigo-Foreign, Department of Public Instruction Papers, Archives Division, Indiana Commission on Public Records, Indiana State Library and Historical Building; "Schools Having A.D.A. in November 1935 Less than 11 Pupils," State Board of Education Papers, Archives Division, Indiana Commission on Public Records, Indiana State Library and Historical Building.

Most rural roads were the responsibility of the township and county governments and were financed by local property taxes. In 1925, for example, when the state controlled nearly 4,000 miles of highway, the counties were responsible for 37,530 miles and townships for 31,646 miles. Most township and county roads were dirt tracks; few boasted gravel or stone surfaces. Gradually in the 1920s county governments took control of township roads. In 1932 a special session of the state legislature relieved townships entirely of responsibility for roads, transferring authority for all township roads to the boards of county commissioners. Of the three traditional functions of township trustees—poor relief, education, and roads—the latter was the only one absorbed fully and permanently by the county, despite strong efforts for county units of administration in all three areas during the interwar decades. In addition to establishing a county highway unit system, the 1932 legislature prohibited counties from levying any taxes for road finance, thus making counties dependent on allocations from the state. The State Highway Commission also supervised the federal aid provided to counties in the 1930s to improve local farm-to-market roads. And just as counties absorbed township roads, the state gradually took over more miles of major county roads. In 1940 there were still 66,825 miles of county roads in the state, but most major routes of travel were under state authority.[21]

In the two decades between the World Wars, then, responsibility for roads and highways shifted from complete control by local government units to the dominant, though not complete, authority of the state. Here was one of the primary examples in twentieth-century Indiana of the trend toward centralization of administration and finance at the state level—a process much aided by the federal government. Unlike the long and intense conflicts

[21] Indiana *Year Book*, 1925, pp. 1029, 1135; 1940, pp. 567-568; *Laws of Indiana*, 1932, pp. 28-31; Sikes, *Indiana State and Local Government*, p. 44; John E. Stoner, *Comparative County Highway Administration: A Study of Steuben County, Indiana, Branch County, Michigan, Williams County, Ohio* (Lafayette, Ind., 1955), p. 13; Indianapolis *Star*, March 17, 1940. Despite the accomplishments prior to World War II, Indiana and the nation were far from developing a fully integrated highway system until the 1950s. See Rose, *Interstate: Express Highway Politics*, p. 2.

over public welfare and education, the process of centralization for highways provoked little opposition. The likely reason for this was that Hoosier motorists strongly favored road improvements and believed that the state could accomplish them better than local governments, especially for rural areas. Perhaps also, however, they found gasoline and license taxes and federal aid less visible or less objectionable than property and gross income taxes as sources of financial support for governmental services.

§ §

Accompanying the enthusiasm with which Hoosiers embraced the road and the car in the 1920s was a decline in other forms of transportation. Walking probably declined in importance; travel by horse-drawn vehicles certainly did. Although hitching posts remained on town squares, they were less and less frequently used and eventually were replaced by parking meters. But the most significant changes were in rail transportation, as steam locomotives and electric interurbans encountered the competition of automobiles, buses, and trucks.

There is no better symbol of late-nineteenth-century American economic progress than the steam locomotive. By the end of the century major trunk lines crossed the nation and, with short lines, provided Indiana farmers, businessmen, and travelers with inexpensive, rapid access to nearly all parts of the state and nation. In 1900, 6,471 miles of railroad track served most cities and towns in Indiana. Track mileage increased to 7,682 by 1920, when twenty-eight companies operated steam railroad lines in the state. Many of these lines were parts of the great trunk systems formed by consolidations and mergers in the late nineteenth and early twentieth centuries, providing routes across Indiana between Chicago and the East. Two trunk lines had major shares of track mileage in Indiana in 1920: the New York Central Railroad and its subsidiaries, which accounted for about 1,900 miles of track and was concentrated in the central and extreme northern parts of the state, and the Pennsylvania Railroad system, which controlled about 1,550 miles of track in Indiana. Next to these two behemoths, the largest mileage was controlled by the Chicago, Indianapolis and Louisville, popularly known as the Monon, with 601 miles of track in Indiana. Other lines operating several hundred miles of track in Indiana in 1920 included the Baltimore and Ohio, the only major trunk line extending across southern Indiana; the Chesapeake and Ohio; and the Wabash Railroad. Several roads served primarily the coal region of western Indiana, notably the Elgin, Joliet and Eastern and the Chicago and Eastern Illinois. And there were smaller companies, ranging in size all the way down to the seven-mile Ferdinand Railroad Company in Dubois County.[22]

The decline of railroads in importance in Indiana and much of America after 1920 is a complicated story and largely a part of nationwide changes. As revenues decreased, companies abandoned track and curtailed service. Some failed entirely. In Indiana the major lines continued to operate through the interwar years, though reducing the number of trains and abandoning track. Some smaller companies went into receivership or failed entirely. Track mileage in the state declined from 7,682 in 1920 to 7,346 in 1929 and to 6,929 in 1940.[23] Many of the forces causing this decline can be illustrated by the history of the Monon Railroad.

The Monon was *the* Hoosier line, holding a special place in the affections of many people in the state. Although the Southern Railway and the Louisville and Nashville jointly owned a majority of its stock after 1902, the Monon kept its own operating management. All but 27 of its 628 miles of track were located in Indiana, with one section running between Louisville and Michigan City and another line connecting Indianapolis and Chicago.

[22] For maps of the major railroad lines in 1920 and a detailed description of their formation see Phillips, *Indiana in Transition*, pp. 228-251. For a map showing lines in 1934 see Indiana State Planning Board, *Preliminary Report on a State Plan for Indiana*, p. 125. For annual operating statistics for each railroad as reported to the Indiana Public Service Commission see the Indiana *Year Book*.

[23] Data on Indiana track mileage are from reports of the Indiana Public Service Commission and do not include switching lines. Indiana *Year Book*, 1920, p. 872; 1930, p. 874; 1941, p. 244. Elmer Sulzer provides annual data on steam railroad abandonment, but, perhaps due to differences in defining the several factors involved, his figures are much lower than those of the Public Service Commission. Sulzer calculated abandoned mileage in the years 1920 to 1940 at 244 miles. Elmer G. Sulzer, *Ghost Railroads of Indiana* (Indianapolis, 1970), p. 11.

Chicago
LAKE MICHIGAN
Hammond
LAKE
Michigan City
Westville
LAPORTE
Lowell
Kankakee River
JASPER
STARKE
PULASKI
NEWTON
Medaryville
Francesville
Rensselaer
WHITE CASS
Monon (Bradford)
Reynolds
Monticello
Peru
WABASH
Ft. Wayne
ALLEN
Huntington
HUNTINGTON
Brookston
Delphi
MIAMI
Logansport
Wabash
Battle Ground
CARROLL
Lafayette
WARREN
CLINTON
Williamsport
TIPPECANOE
Frankfort
FOUNTAIN
MONTGOMERY
BOONE
HAMILTON
VERMILLION
Crawfordsville
Westfield
Ladoga
Bainbridge
PARKE PUTNAM
Indianapolis
MARION
Greencastle
Putnamville
Terre Haute
CLAY
VIGO
OWEN
Gosport
Bloomington
GREENE
MONROE
LAWRENCE
Bedford
Wabash River
DAVIESS
Mitchell
WASHINGTON
Orleans
White River
Salem
Borden (Providence)
CLARK
ORANGE
FLOYD
GIBSON
PIKE
New Albany
WARRICK
VANDERBURGH
Evansville
Ohio River

MAP OF
MONON RAILROAD
SYSTEM

——— Original New Albany and Salem (Now the Monon).
- - - The Monon.
===== Wabash & Erie Canal.

Frank Hargrave

Monon Railroad

The Monon carried coal and limestone from southern and western Indiana; tourists to French Lick and West Baden; farmers, businessmen, and weekend visitors to Indianapolis and Chicago; and students to and from the college towns of Bloomington, Greencastle, Crawfordsville, and Lafayette. For intrastate football games—such as the Indiana-Purdue contests—special Monon trains painted in school colors carried thousands of fans. Even for this popular Hoosier line, the interwar years were difficult. As always, it struggled for traffic with competing railroads, principally the New York Central and the Pennsylvania, the most powerful trunk lines in the state. In this struggle the Monon was handicapped by a route that included slow runs on town and city streets, such as the one through the center of Lafayette, and steep grades in southern Indiana, such as that through Bedford. The Monon's freight traffic increased only slightly in the 1920s, and coal, its largest single item of tonnage, remained stagnant through the decade at less than 1.5 million tons a year. Passenger traffic declined drastically, from 1,498,576 passengers in 1923, to 562,140 in 1929. Throughout the decade the Monon dropped more and more local trains; by 1930 all locals were gone. In the 1920s declining traffic began to force deferred maintenance of rails and ties. The advent of the Great Depression caused an already difficult situation to become desperate. In December, 1933, the Monon filed its bankruptcy petition, and the Interstate Commerce Commission began reorganization proceedings. The road continued to operate and provide important service, but passenger and freight traffic declined further and losses continued to grow. World War II did not significantly reverse the trend even temporarily, as it did for some railroads. Finally in January, 1946, the long reorganization was completed, and a new era of independent operation began, even though the major difficulties of the interwar years were never fully overcome.[24]

An important factor in the Monon's decline was competition

[24] George W. Hilton, *Monon Route* (Berkeley, Calif., 1978), pp. 124-163, 272; Leland S. Van Scoyoc, The History and Economic Significance of the Chicago, Indianapolis and Louisville Railway Company (Ph.D. dissertation, Indiana University, Bloomington, 1953), pp. 253-269, 321-399.

from other means of transportation. In addition to the rivalry with the Pennsylvania and New York Central, the Monon and nearly all steam railroads suffered from the competition of electric interurban railways.

Running on steel rails and powered from overhead electric wires, interurbans began in the first decade of the twentieth century to connect the towns and cities of the Midwest, often as extensions of street railways. By the beginning of World War I, Indiana had 1,825 miles of interurban track and ranked second only to Ohio. Interurban service reached every Indiana town with a population greater than five thousand except Bloomington, Madison, and Vincennes (reflecting the generally poorer transportation facilities in southern Indiana). Indianapolis, with its thirteen lines radiating to almost every city in the state, had the largest interurban network in the United States and boasted the nation's most impressive interurban station, the Indianapolis Traction Terminal. Designed by D. H. Burnham and Company of Chicago and built in 1904, the terminal included a train shed that covered nine tracks and a nine-story office building that housed waiting rooms, ticket offices, retail shops, and the general offices of several interurban companies. In 1918, 128,145 interurban trains carrying 7,519,634 passengers entered or left the Indianapolis Traction Terminal.[25]

The electric interurbans attracted travelers away from steam railroads and horse-drawn vehicles and encouraged more travel. Their frequent and convenient service and relatively low cost enabled more Hoosiers from small towns and farms to journey to such larger cities as Fort Wayne, Muncie, South Bend, and Indianapolis for social visits, jobs, and Saturday shopping and entertainment. During the 1920s, however, passenger traffic and revenue on Indiana interurbans declined steadily. Some of the companies made partly successful responses by encouraging freight traffic, such as by transporting milk, eggs, fruit, vegetables, poultry, and livestock to urban markets. As with the steam railroads, however, the difficulties evident in the 1920s turned to

[25] George W. Hilton and John R. Due, *The Electric Interurban Railways in America* (2d edition, Stanford, Calif., 1964), pp. 41-42, 69.

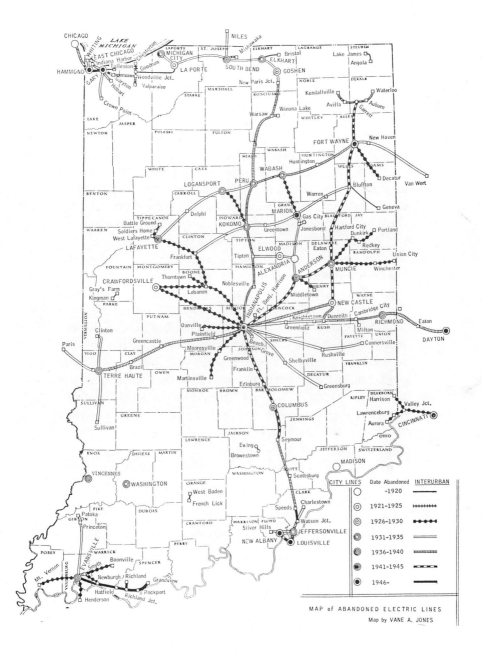

Interurban lines, with dates of abandonment

disasters with the Great Depression. Revenues fell drastically and, much more so than with steam lines, company after company abandoned service and failed. In the 1920s and early 1930s, Midland United Company, developed by Chicago utility tycoon Samuel Insull and associates, began acquiring interurban companies in Indiana. In 1930 the Insull group formed the Indiana Railroad Company, which eventually acquired every interurban in central and northern Indiana except the Northern Indiana Railways and the Indianapolis and Southeastern. By 1931 the Indiana Railroad Company had nearly one thousand miles of track, making it the nation's largest interurban company. Although the Insull management installed new equipment and made serious efforts to build a more integrated and efficient system, the Indiana Railroad Company failed in July, 1933. Thereafter, the lines were operated by a receiver, Bowman Elder, a close political adviser to Governor Paul McNutt. Elder showed some success and even an operating profit in 1936, but he could not reverse the decline. In September, 1941, Indiana Railroad transported its last interurban passengers, although the company continued and greatly increased the motor bus service that it had begun in the mid-1930s. By 1941 the state's once thriving interurban system was almost totally defunct—its end coming only four decades after it had begun.[26]

While interurban and steam railroads often competed with each other, their primary competition after World War I was from motor vehicles. As the highway system developed, the privately owned car increasingly surpassed rail travel in convenience and flexibility, particularly for shorter distances, giving Hoosiers un-

[26] *Ibid.*, pp. 91-92, 127-128, 200-201, 215-217, 275, 283-284; Jerry Marlette, *Electric Railroads of Indiana* (2nd edition, Indianapolis, 1980), pp. 15-25, 43-47. Operating statistics for interurbans in Indiana were published annually by the Indiana Public Service Commission in the Indiana *Year Book*. For maps of the interurbans in 1924 and 1934 see Indiana State Committee on Governmental Economy, *Report*, pp. 690-691. The South Shore was an exception to the general trend. Linking Chicago, the Calumet cities, and South Bend, it prospered during World War II and eventually gained the distinction of being the last interurban in America. William D. Middleton, *South Shore: The Last Interurban* (San Marino, Calif., 1970), pp. 37-80.

precedented mobility. In the 1920s commercial buses also began to attract passengers away from steam and interurban lines. By 1923 there were 128 bus companies operating to and from most cities in the state. As buses and cars transported more people, passenger traffic on steam and electric lines began to level off or decline, dropping rapidly in the late 1920s and early 1930s.[27] Because of the general economic prosperity, freight traffic on both steam and electric railroads in Indiana increased through 1929, but the rapid growth of private and commercial trucking after World War I attracted larger and larger shares of freight tonnage. The percentage of hogs delivered to the Indianapolis market by rail, for example, declined from 83 percent in 1918, to 63 percent in 1925 and to 37 percent in 1929, as trucks took the major portion of this business. By 1930 there were 122,197 trucks registered in the state, nearly quadruple the number in 1920.[28]

While motor vehicles and steam and electric railroads provided the most important forms of transportation, there were other modes of travel and transport. Water transport of freight continued to play an important role both on the Ohio River, where the federal government constructed a series of locks and dams between 1910 and 1929, and on the Great Lakes. By the 1930s the port of Indiana Harbor on Lake Michigan was the state's leading water access for goods. Pipelines provided another mode of transportation, especially for carrying crude oil to East Chicago refineries.[29] The newest form of transportation in the interwar

[27] Indiana *Year Book*, 1923, pp. 1123-1124; Indiana State Committee on Governmental Economy, *Report*, pp. 675, 696-697; Hilton and Due, *The Electric Interurban Railways in America*, pp. 226-228; Glen A. Blackburn, "Interurban Railroads of Indiana," *Indiana Magazine of History*, XX (1924), 426-436.

[28] Wiley, *Motor Transportation of Hogs*, pp. 4, 5, 30; Indiana *Year Book*, 1923, p. 1123; Sulzer, *Ghost Railroads of Indiana*, p. 9; United States Public Roads Administration, *Highway Statistics: Summary to 1945*, p. 20. For data on freight tonnage and revenues of steam and electric lines in the state see Indiana State Committee on Governmental Economy, *Report*, pp. 679-701.

[29] Charles K. Palmer, "Ohio Valley Commerce, 1787-1936," *Indiana Magazine of History*, XXXIII (1937), 153-170; Work Projects Administration, *The Calumet Region Historical Guide*, pp. 219-221; Moore, *The Calumet Region*, pp. 211, 244-246.

decades was the airplane. Commercial aviation in Indiana began in 1919 with the dedication in Kokomo of the state's first municipal airport. By late 1924 there were twelve airports in the state, and ten years later, fifty-nine, a growth that was partly spurred by Charles Lindbergh's spectacular flight in 1927, by federal airmail contracts, and later by New Deal public works programs that included funds for airport construction. Four major airlines operated in Indiana by 1934: United, Eastern, American, and Trans World. All had their main offices outside the state and depended largely on interstate traffic.[30]

§ § §

Growth and change in transportation in the twentieth century produced calls of various sorts and from diverse sources for new government regulations. Because many of the transportation lines and services existing in Indiana were interstate in character, the federal government played the dominant role in regulation. Federal influence was most evident in the regulation of railroads by the Interstate Commerce Commission (ICC), including the important powers of authorizing route changes and approving rates. The federal Transportation Act of 1920 first returned the nation's railroads to private control after a brief period of government operation necessitated by the wartime emergency and then expanded federal regulatory authority. The states continued to play a regulatory role, but it was an increasingly minor one. In Indiana the five-member Public Service Commission, established in 1913, had authority to ensure safety and approve rate changes and line abandonments for intrastate rail traffic. But even this intrastate authority proved impossible to exercise independently: because of competitive pressures, the Public Service Commission could ignore neither the interstate rates nor the intrastate rates that prevailed in contiguous states—particularly Illinois. In fact, the

---

[30] Indiana State Committee on Governmental Economy, *Report*, pp. 709-715. For an example of the conflict over construction of one Indiana airport see Frank, "Who Governed Middletown? Community Power in Muncie, Indiana, in the 1930s," *Indiana Magazine of History*, LXXV, 325-329.

Indiana regulatory commission often followed that state's lead as well as that of the ICC.[31]

Government regulations also affected motor vehicle traffic in the interwar years, although less so than railroads. The state first set speed limits and required vehicle registration in 1905. The rapidly increasing volume of traffic and highway accidents after World War I led to legislation designed to produce more order and safety on Indiana roads. Especially important was the Automobile Regulation Act of 1925, which established uniform speed limits and rules of the road. Enforcement of traffic regulations and the increase in auto-related crimes, which often crossed local boundaries, brought about a large expansion of state law enforcement efforts by the Indiana State Police, which was formed in 1921.[32] Also important was the movement, underway by 1925, to require state licensing of drivers as a means to remove irresponsible (particularly drunken) drivers from the roads by revoking their licenses. In 1929 the legislature approved the state's first driver license law. Not until 1939, however, did the state begin to require an examination for new drivers. By then, state officials strongly argued that driving on public highways was not a right but a privilege that should be withdrawn if abused.[33]

In 1925 the state also began to regulate highway common carriers by authorizing the Public Service Commission to hold hearings and grant "certificates of public convenience and necessity" for specified routes to bus companies. The Public Service Commission also received power to set safety and insurance requirements for buses.[34] Regulation of motortrucks proved to be a greater chal-

31 Indiana *Year Book*, 1920, pp. 806-809; 1930, pp. 854-855; *Public Service Commission of Indiana* v. *Atchinson, Topeka & Santa Fe Railway Company*, Cases 11388 and 13671, Interstate Commerce Commission *Reports*, LXXXIV (February-April, 1924), 709-724, 728-742.

32 Phillips, *Indiana in Transition*, p. 265; Indiana *Year Book*, 1925, p. 679; 1940, pp. 386-389; *Laws of Indiana*, 1925, pp. 570-607.

33 Indianapolis *News*, February 12, 1925; *Laws of Indiana*, 1929, pp. 499-513; Indiana *Year Book*, 1930, p. 28; 1940, pp. 426, 428-429. Vehicle registration and driver licensing provided new opportunities for political patronage. By 1935 there were 142 license branch offices in the state, and most were staffed by political party appointees. *Ibid.*, 1935, p. 220.

34 Indiana *Year Book*, 1925, pp. 234, 239; *Laws of Indiana*, 1925, pp. 138-139; Indianapolis *News*, February 13, 1925.

lenge. Much of this controversy centered around weight regulations for trucks. Automobile drivers and their political
representatives complained that heavy trucks caused intolerable
damage to Indiana streets and roads. And, as has often been the
case in controversies over government regulation, some business
interests also pressed for weight restrictions in order to limit
competition. Railroads and local grain dealers and elevator operators strongly urged stringent weight limits to reduce the increasing volume of grain trucked to Chicago and other markets.[35] In
1925 the legislature began to place various restrictions on trucks,
including a maximum weight of 22,400 pounds on any one axle. In
1931 the axle limit was lowered to 16,000 pounds, and even lower
limits were required for vehicles with hard rubber tires rather
than less destructive pneumatic ones. Despite these efforts at regulation, the Public Service Commission lamented in 1931 that the
trucking business in Indiana presented "a complicated and somewhat chaotic condition. . . ." The 1933 General Assembly apparently agreed: it passed a resolution asking Congress to authorize
the ICC to regulate trucks and buses just as it did railroads.
Nevertheless, the next session of the state legislature continued
the effort at state regulation, enacting two laws: one that granted
to the Public Service Commission the power to regulate rates
charged by motor carriers and one that placed a weight tax on
motor vehicles for hire.[36] City and town governments also began
to control truck routes: in 1931 they received power to limit
weights on designated streets and to prohibit truck traffic entirely
from certain residential streets.[37]

§ § § §

Changes in transportation in the interwar decades brought increased size and power to government. The state government

[35] An excellent view of this controversy is provided in many letters to state
legislator Claude Wickard in 1933. See, for examples, J. R. Nelson to Wickard,
February 11, 1933, Lee Evans to Wickard, February 11, 1933, and Fairfield Manufacturing Company to Wickard, February 18, 1933, all in Box 5, Wickard Papers.

[36] Indiana *Year Book*, 1931, p. 1003; *Laws of Indiana*, 1925, p. 600; 1931, pp.
237-238, 1484; 1933, p. 1238; 1935, p. 1416.

[37] *Laws of Indiana*, 1931, p. 238; Duncan, Control of the City Government in
Indianapolis, Evidenced by the Forces Determining Its Ordinances, 1925-1941,
pp. 329-334.

assumed greater responsibility for regulating the use of public highways by cars, trucks, and buses. And the state greatly expanded its role in construction and maintenance of highways, which thereby necessitated a more centralized administration by the State Highway Commission and a new state gasoline tax to finance the program. The federal government influenced state highway policy through federal aid and also played a major role in regulating transportation by steam and electric railroad, although the Indiana Public Service Commission continued to possess authority here, too.

Changes in transportation affected not only government but also social and economic conditions important to nearly all Hoosiers. In one lifetime Indianans could experience both the culmination of a transportation system of steam and electric trains and also its rapid decline—and in the case of the electric interurban its extinction. Above all, Hoosiers could watch in wonder, delight, or perhaps scorn as the automobile, bus, and truck rapidly invaded and changed the urban and rural landscape in the post-World War I years. Perhaps no other factor so affected the daily lives of so many Hoosiers as did the automobile. The Sunday drive and the gasoline tax, the newly paved road and the adolescent rebellion, the prosperity of the 1920s and the decline of religion— all these and a host of other changes were, rightly or wrongly, attributed to the automobile. Whether for better or worse, the car in the interwar decades came to play a dominant role not only in transportation but also in shaping social, political, and economic institutions, beliefs, and behaviors.

CHAPTER VIII
BUSINESS, LABOR, AND THE ECONOMY

ECONOMIC CHANGE has been a fundamental factor in the history of Indiana. The national prosperity of the 1920s after the brief postwar recession of 1920-1921 was an important feature of many of the social, political, and cultural developments of the decade. So, too, did the Great Depression of the 1930s have important effects far beyond the basic economic issues it raised. But there were other changes, often more important than the general ups and downs of the economy. The interwar decades saw a continuation and maturation of processes begun in the nineteenth century and often labeled "the industrial revolution." Manufacturing became increasingly important in the Indiana economy. Large business organizations became concentrated in a few cities and towns and replaced in importance the individual craftsmen and small firms that were located throughout the state. While the growth of big business brought concentrated economic power, it was a power that was increasingly limited if not balanced by the countervailing force of government regulation and labor organization. None of these changes was unique to Indiana, and none began or ended in the 1920s and 1930s, but all became in these decades basic features of the modern Hoosier economy. All of these factors would continue to grow in significance during World War II and in the postwar era.

Table I gives a summary view of manufacturing in Indiana from the end of World War I to the end of World War II and shows the rapid growth in value of manufactured product and value added by manufacture in the 1920s.[1] Because wartime conditions inflated the 1919 data, the actual increase was even

---

[1] Value added by manufacture is the value of product less the cost of materials, supplies, fuel, purchased electrical energy, and contract work. It is a useful indicator of the level and significance of manufacturing.

TABLE I
Manufacturing in Indiana, 1919-1947[2]

Year	Number of Establishments	Value of Product	Value Added by Manufacture
1919	7,916	$1,898,753,387	$ 723,802,819
1929	5,091	2,539,893,849	1,136,462,692
1939	4,337	2,227,648,011	970,211,797
1947	5,408	———	2,977,508,000

larger. The Depression in the early 1930s brought a sharp drop, but there was a sufficient recovery by the end of the decade to make the 1929 and 1939 figures roughly equal.

The size of Indiana's manufacturing is partly indicated by comparison with regional and national manufacturing data. Indiana was among the leading manufacturing states. In 1929 and 1939 Indiana ranked ninth among the forty-eight states in value of manufactured product and value added by manufacturing, slightly above its population rank of twelfth and eleventh in those years.[3] The state was part of the rapidly expanding industrial heartland that stretched from Pittsburgh to Chicago between the Ohio River and the Great Lakes. Here extensive trunk railroads tied abundant natural resources to factory towns and industrial cities. Here existed also the labor force and the consumer markets to produce and consume a growing share of the nation's manufactured product. Located in this expanding industrial belt, the Hoosier state could hardly have avoided the industrializing process entirely. Yet, in the late nineteenth and early twentieth centuries Indiana did lag behind its heartland neighbors. Comparisons of per capita value added by manufacturing from the Civil War onward show Indiana trailing Ohio, Illinois, and Michigan distantly until 1920, then gradually closing the gap and pulling even

[2] United States Bureau of the Census, *Fifteenth Census* (1930), III, *Manufactures*, 1929, p. 161; United States Bureau of the Census, *Sixteenth Census* (1940), III, *Manufactures*, 1939, p. 278; United States Bureau of the Census, *Census of Manufactures*, 1947 (3 volumes, Washington, D.C., 1950), III, 199. Data for 1947 are not comparable for value of product with earlier data.
[3] United States Bureau of the Census, *Sixteenth Census* (1940), III, *Manufactures*, 1939, pp. 42, 43.

with its neighbors by the post-World War II decade. (See Table II.)

TABLE II
Per Capita Manufacturing Value Added, 1860-1950[4]

Year	Ohio	Indiana	Illinois	Michigan	Wisconsin
1860	$ 20.9	$ 10.8	$ 11.9	$ 15.9	$ 13.5
1870	38.9	24.6	28.3	38.2	27.5
1880	38.7	22.3	37.3	32.4	30.0
1890	64.7	34.9	71.6	46.4	45.7
1900	84.7	59.9	99.2	58.9	68.0
1910	128.6	90.6	134.5	111.9	104.5
1920	378.7	246.3	297.5	421.0	271.9
1930	434.8	350.9	384.0	426.9	323.2
1940	307.7	283.0	278.8	342.2	218.8
1950	1002.6	974.2	910.2	1160.2	782.4

The pattern of manufacturing development in Indiana fits generally the regional and national patterns. The state's nineteenth-century reliance on simple food processing and on low-technology, resource-based industries became less important in the early twentieth century as newer, more technologically advanced, and more capital-intensive industries came to a dominant position. (See Table III.) Not coincidentally, these new industries attracted large national and even multinational firms that frequently manufactured in many locations and produced a variety of products.

Chief among these modern industries was iron and steel, which in 1919 assumed first place among all industries in the state in value of product—ranking Indiana third behind Pennsylvania and Ohio in iron and steel production. The most obvious feature of iron and steel production in Indiana was its location in the Calumet region, which became the nation's most concentrated steel-producing area in the 1920s. To the Calumet came iron ore via the Great Lakes and coal over the vast railroad network to be processed in the nation's largest and most modern steel

[4] Alfred Niemi, *State and Regional Patterns in American Manufacturing, 1860-1900* (Westport, Conn., 1974), p. 185.

TABLE III
Ten Leading Industries of Indiana, 1919, 1939
Ranked by Value of Product[5]

1919	Number of Estabmts.	Value of Products	Number of Wage Earners
Iron and steel	120	$242,972,517	28,861
Automobiles	530	182,416,894	26,658
Railroad cars	86	147,253,384	29,749
Meat	57	134,028,726	5,691
Food	1,369	108,967,767	11,948
Foundry and machine-shop products	395	85,359,946	18,828
Flour- and grist-milling	450	75,111,435	2,280
Printing and paper	915	58,275,123	10,937
Furniture	206	55,024,313	13,784
Clothing	142	46,844,939	12,106

1939	Number of Estabmts.	Value of Products	Number of Wage Earners
Iron and steel	289	$463,128,573	57,837
Automobiles	71	255,798,857	27,240
Petroleum refining	7	182,566,697	6,384
Food	855	160,772,480	18,122
Chemicals	46	84,532,930	3,539
Meat	78	83,719,316	4,498
Printing and paper	660	82,708,329	12,579
Electrical machinery	31	78,576,915	12,885
Clothing	126	71,009,682	21,621
Non-ferrous metals	56	61,710,705	6,348

[5] Barnhart and Carmony, *Indiana*, II, 436, 439.

plants by labor gathered from Europe, Mexico, and the American South as well as the Midwest. The 1920s was a boom decade for Calumet steel producers, as they benefited from the general prosperity and the rapidly growing demand for steel. The Calumet also may have benefited from the elimination in 1924 of the "Pittsburgh Plus" system, whereby all steel prices had been quoted f.o.b. Pittsburgh, regardless of where the steel had been produced. The major Calumet producer was United States Steel, whose Gary Works, the nation's largest, increased capacity from 2.3 million tons to 4.4 million tons during the 1920s. And, because the Gary Works were the largest, most efficient, and most modern in U.S. Steel's vast empire, they were kept running at near capacity through most of the decade, with the exception of the recession period of 1920-1921. Other Lake County steel companies also prospered during the 1920s. Inland Steel Company doubled capacity at its Indiana Harbor plant to 2.2 million tons, and the nearby plant of Youngstown Sheet and Tube Company reached almost 1 million tons capacity.[6]

Much of the steel produced in Lake County was used in the manufacture of automobiles. From the outset Indiana had a large share of this new and rapidly growing industry, which through the interwar years ranked second in the state behind iron and steel in value of product. During the first two decades of the twentieth century there were hundreds of different cars manufactured in more than fifty Indiana towns and cities. By the 1920s, however, the number of auto manufacturers in the state had declined to a handful, as the industry came to be dominated by three large producers—General Motors, Ford, and Chrysler—all based in Detroit. By 1930 only 4 percent of the automobiles registered in Indiana had been produced in the state.[7] The largest Indiana

[6] John B. Appleton, *The Iron and Steel Industry of the Calumet District: A Study in Economic Geography* (Urbana, Ill., 1927), pp. 14-16, 24; William T. Hogan, *Economic History of the Iron and Steel Industry in the United States* (5 volumes, Lexington, Mass., 1971), III, 811-812; Gertrude G. Schroeder, *The Growth of Major Steel Companies, 1900-1950* (Baltimore, 1953), pp. 114-115; Moore, *The Calumet Region*, pp. 330-331.

[7] Batchelor, A Statistical Analysis of the 1930 Passenger Car Registrations, p. 81. The percentage share of registrations in Indiana in 1930 among leading models

manufacturer to survive into the 1920s was Studebaker, which began in the mid-nineteenth century as a family-owned wagon business in South Bend. After World War I, under the presidency of Albert Erskine, Studebaker came close to joining the ranks of the major auto manufacturers, but the Great Depression brought disaster. In 1928 Erskine acquired the Pierce-Arrow Company; its high-priced luxury car soon became a white elephant. Like many other businessmen, Erskine refused to believe that the Depression would last. He continued to pay stock dividends, and in 1931 he brought out a new Studebaker model—the low-priced Rockne, named for Notre Dame's famous football coach. As the Depression deepened, so did Studebaker's red ink. In March, 1933, the company went into receivership, and a few weeks later Erskine committed suicide. Unlike many of its smaller competitors, Studebaker reorganized and recovered in the late 1930s and survived until the 1960s, but the South Bend company never again enjoyed the high position it had held prior to the Great Depression.[8]

Other Indiana car manufacturers were less successful than Studebaker. Several failed in the mid-1920s; others survived into the Depression. Perhaps the state's most well-known auto manufacturer was Elwood Haynes, who in 1894 had produced one of the nation's first cars. Haynes's Kokomo factory became the town's largest employer, and the company sold more than seven thousand cars by 1916. But the Haynes Automobile Company could never match the high volume, assembly-line production of Ford or General Motors. Detroit's competition and the recession of 1920-1921 forced the company into bankruptcy in late 1924.[9]

---

was: Ford, 34.7; Chevrolet, 15.5; Buick, 6.5; Dodge, 5.6; Essex, 3.9; Overland-Whippet, 3.8; Studebaker, 3.2. *Ibid.*, p. 58. For a listing of Indiana-produced cars and their places and dates of production see Wallace Huffman, "Indiana's Place in Automobile History," *Indiana History Bulletin*, XLIV (1967), 11-44.

[8] John B. Rae, *American Automobile Manufacturers: The First Forty Years* (Philadelphia, 1959), pp. 174-175, 196-197; Kathleen Ann Smallzried and Dorothy James Roberts, *More Than You Promise: A Business at Work in Society* (New York, 1942), pp. 269-301; Federal Trade Commission, *Report on Motor Vehicle Industry* (Washington, D.C., 1939), pp. 795-823.

[9] Ralph D. Gray, *Alloys and Automobiles: The Life of Elwood Haynes* (Indianapolis, 1979), pp. 167-202.

Haynes's fellow Kokomo residents and one-time partners Elmer and Edgar Apperson also manufactured cars, gaining some success with their Apperson Jack Rabbit. The Apperson Company failed in early 1925. Several moderately successful auto companies were located in Indianapolis, which up to World War I was a major center of the industry. The Cole Motor Car Company produced a highly regarded luxury car but never developed integrated, assembly-line production. The post-World War I recession and competition from the "big three" led the company to close in early 1925. The Marmon Motor Car Company began as a division of Nordyke and Marmon, one of the nation's major flour mill machinery manufacturers. In 1926 the company sold its mill machinery business to Allis-Chalmers in order to concentrate on automobiles. Its well-regarded luxury car, the Marmon, enabled the company to survive the 1920s but not the Depression. The last Marmon was produced in 1933. Another Indianapolis company, Stutz, attracted wide attention when Charles M. Schwab, Bethlehem steel tycoon, acquired controlling interest in 1922 and began efforts to build a large auto empire. The attempt to emulate General Motors failed, although the Stutz Bearcat became one of the premier sports cars of the 1920s. The company failed in 1936. Another effort to build a large auto company in Indiana in the 1920s began with Errett Lobban Cord, a young mechanic and race car driver who acquired the Auburn Automobile Company, located in Auburn in northeastern Indiana, and the Duesenberg Motor Company in Indianapolis. Cord did very well in 1926 and 1927 with his two luxury cars. In 1929 he offered a third model, the Cord, a front-wheel drive car of considerable engineering and aesthetic achievement. At the same time, he began an aircraft factory in Connersville. The company survived the initial blows of the Depression but finally closed in 1937.[10]

[10] Wallace S. Huffman, "The Apperson Brothers and Their Automobiles," *Indiana History Bulletin*, XLI (1964), 200-202; Huffman, "Indiana's Place in Automobile History," *Indiana History Bulletin*, XLIV, 11-44; Howard R. Delancy, The History of the Cole Motor Car Company (D.B.A. dissertation, Indiana University, Bloomington, 1954), pp. 234-278; Indianapolis *News*, August 11, 1922; Walter F. Peterson, *An Industrial Heritage: Allis-Chalmers Corporation* (Milwaukee, 1976), p. 199; Rae, *American Automobile Manufacturers*, pp. 118, 178-179, 180-183, 193.

The decline and near extinction of Indiana auto production was caused not only by national economic forces of the post-World War I recession and the Great Depression but also by the increasing difficulty of competing with the large auto companies. As in so many other areas of the twentieth-century economy, the benefits of sophisticated technology, of mass production for mass markets, of large bureaucratic organization, and of superior access to investment capital encouraged the development of a few big businesses that dominated the industry. None of the Indiana auto companies was part of this fundamental transition.

Although by 1940 only Studebaker survived from among Indiana auto producers, the auto industry continued to play a major role in the Hoosier economy during the interwar years and after. Many machine shops and factories in Indiana became major suppliers of parts and accessories for Detroit companies. In the production of motor vehicles, bodies, parts, and accessories, the 1939 manufacturing census ranked Indiana third (close behind Ohio though far behind Michigan) in value of product ($252,684,069), value added ($96,147,943), and number of wage earners (26,756).[11]

Auto-related companies were especially important in such central and northern Indiana cities as Indianapolis, Anderson, Muncie, New Castle, and South Bend.[12] Many of these companies began around the turn of the century as small machine shops that supplied parts to Indiana and out-of-state auto manufacturers. Some eventually became incorporated into the large Detroit companies. Others were established from the outset as branch plants of the big three—attracted to Indiana towns by transportation facilities, low prevailing wages, and limited labor union strength. The Remy Electric Company began in Anderson in 1901 as a locally owned, pioneer manufacturer of electrical equipment for automobiles. In 1919 the company became a part of General

[11] United States Bureau of the Census, *Sixteenth Census* (1940), II, *Manufactures*, 1939, Pt. 2, pp. 525, 528. This census category is very limited and does not include manufacture of automobile batteries, ignition apparatus, or lighting equipment, all of which were important auto-related industries in Indiana.

[12] Annual listings of manufacturers of auto parts and other products may be found in *Polk's Indiana State Gazetteer and Business Directory* and Indiana State Chamber of Commerce, *Directory of Indiana Manufacturers*.

Motors and by 1924 employed 3,672 workers. In 1926 GM transferred additional parts manufacturing to Anderson and changed
the name to Delco-Remy. Anderson's reliance on the auto industry increased in 1928 when GM purchased the Guide Lamp
Company, manufacturers of automobile lighting equipment, and
moved it from Cleveland to Anderson. Few, if any, towns in
Indiana were more dependent on automobiles and on a single
outside corporation, as is illustrated by Anderson's response to the
auto strike of 1937, which is discussed below. Nearby Muncie's
economic well-being also depended heavily on the automobile.
A locally developed machine shop, Warner Gear, which supplied
transmissions and other parts to several automobile manufacturers,
grew rapidly in the 1920s and in 1928 merged into the new
national corporation, Borg-Warner. Another machine shop of
similar name, the T. W. Warner Company, was organized in
1909 to supply transmissions and steering gears to auto manufacturers. By 1924 the company employed 2,200 workers. In 1929
it became the Muncie Products Division of GM, which constructed a large plant to manufacture all of Chevrolet's chassis
parts. For Muncie the gloomiest point in the Depression came in
April, 1932, when GM announced that it was closing its Muncie
factories and began stripping the floors of machinery and shipping
it to Flint and Pontiac, Michigan. But in mid-1935, amid joyous
celebration, GM returned to Muncie, seeking in the open-shop
town a haven from the labor union activity that was plaguing
plants in Ohio and Michigan. By the end of 1935, nearly half of
the town's factory workers again were employed by the auto
industry.[13] GM also began to play a significant though relatively
smaller role in Indianapolis, notably with its acquisition of the
Allison Engineering Company in 1929. Allison boasted a highly
skilled labor force and precision machinery designed to turn out

[13] Arthur Pound, *The Turning Wheel: The Story of General Motors through
Twenty-five Years, 1908-1933* (Garden City, N.Y., 1934), pp. 463-466, 487-488;
Will Oursler, *From Ox Carts to Jets: Roy Ingersoll and the Borg-Warner Story*
(Englewood Cliffs, N.J., 1959), pp. 148-156, 209-210; Lynd and Lynd, *Middle-
town in Transition*, pp. 13-14, 18-19, 35-41, 266; John Goldthwaite interview by
R. T. King, March 9, 13, 1979, transcript, p. 54, Oral History Research Project
Mss., Lilly Library, Indiana University, Bloomington.

airplane engines and other products; GM added sophisticated production and management techniques and more unskilled labor, enabling the company to evolve in the late 1930s from specialized machine shop to large-volume producer. In Indianapolis International Harvester also began production of truck motors in 1938 and by the end of the year employed 1,100 workers.[14]

Ranking behind automobiles and iron and steel in value of product in 1939 was petroleum refining, which supplied the ever-increasing amounts of gasoline and motor oil consumed by automobiles. The pattern in the oil industry was similar to steel and autos in that a few large companies dominated the industry. And like steel, but unlike autos, the industry's location in Indiana was concentrated in Lake County, where the Great Lakes and the network of railroads and pipelines provided the crucial transport facilities for crude oil and the refined products. The Indiana Harbor Ship Canal was lined with refineries, which included those of Standard Oil of Indiana, Sinclair, Cities Service, and Socony-Vacuum. The earliest and largest of the Calumet refineries was Standard Oil of Indiana's Whiting plant, which began production in 1890. By 1920 Standard of Indiana was one of the nation's largest companies—operating refineries in other parts of the country and overseas—but the Whiting refinery remained its primary facility and continued to be the location of the industry's most advanced technology. Standard of Indiana marketed its product in several midwestern states, often through company-owned gasoline stations. By 1924 the company accounted for 47 percent of the gasoline sales in Indiana, but its share declined in the 1930s and dropped to 21 percent by 1940.[15]

Indiana oil fields produced only a small portion of the nation's

---

[14] Goldthwaite interview, March 9, 13, 1979, pp. 20-33, Oral History Research Project Mss.; Pound, *The Turning Wheel*, pp. 460-461; History of the Indianapolis Works [of International Harvester] (Typescript, 1944, Indiana Division, Indiana State Library). Allison Engineering Company was organized in 1915 by James A. Allison, who was associated with Carl G. Fisher in the Indianapolis Motor Speedway.

[15] Work Projects Administration, *The Calumet Region Historical Guide*, p. 221; Paul H. Giddens, *Standard Oil Company (Indiana): Oil Pioneer of the Middle West* (New York, 1955), pp. 482, 582, 704.

petroleum by 1920, as nearly all the crude oil reaching the large Calumet refineries came from fields to the west and south of Indiana. The Lima-Indiana field in northwestern Ohio and northeastern Indiana reached its maximum production in 1904 with 11.3 million barrels and then declined rapidly. Small, scattered pools in southwestern Indiana became more important and by 1933 produced 97 percent of the Indiana crude oil. The Indiana Farm Bureau Cooperative began production of crude oil in Indiana in the 1930s and in 1939 built its own 3,500-barrel-per-day refinery near the Ohio River at Mt. Vernon. But the petroleum industry remained concentrated in Lake County and dependent on out-of-state crude oil.[16]

By 1940 iron and steel, automobiles, and petroleum refining were the three largest industries in Indiana, as measured by value of product. And they represented the most important trends in the modern development of American manufacturing and business. These industries were dominated by a few very large firms— in Indiana by U.S. Steel, the big three Detroit auto companies (particularly GM), and Standard Oil of Indiana. These kinds of big businesses appeared in industries that shared several characteristics: they required large amounts of capital, intense energy (especially heat), and complex machinery; they allowed economies of scale through continuous or large-batch production, such as the auto assembly line; and they needed large mass markets to sustain high-volume production.[17]

Iron and steel, automobiles, and petroleum refining were the most important of the modern big businesses in Indiana during the interwar years. There were other industries, however, which had some or all of the characteristics of these three giants and

[16] United States Congress, House of Representatives, 73d Congress, Committee on Interstate and Foreign Commerce, *Petroleum Investigation* (Washington, D.C., 1934), pp. 939-940, 951-952; Harold F. Williamson *et al.*, *The American Petroleum Industry: The Age of Energy, 1899-1959* (Evanston, Ill., 1963), pp. 17-18, 702.

[17] For general treatment of these themes and the growth of big business see Alfred D. Chandler, Jr., *The Visible Hand: The Managerial Revolution in American Business* (Cambridge, Mass., 1977), especially pp. 345-376; and Thomas C. Cochran, *American Business in the Twentieth Century* (Cambridge, Mass., 1972), pp. 1-138.

which also developed large industrial enterprises, though usually including a portion of smaller, more traditional companies as well.

One important industry which included both traditional and modern enterprises was glass manufacturing. This industry received its most significant stimulus from the natural gas boom in east-central Indiana in the 1880s and after. Although the Indiana natural gas supply dropped rapidly by the first decade of the twentieth century, many of the glass companies remained in the area, using coal and producer gas to provide the intense heat required in the production process. In 1919 Indiana produced 11.5 percent of the nation's glass and ranked fourth among the states in value of output and number of factories. Glass manufacturing evolved rapidly in the first three decades of the century, however, as new machines replaced skilled and unskilled labor. Many smaller companies failed or merged with large national companies, such as the Toledo-based Owens Bottle Company, which operated or controlled plants in Greenfield, Evansville, and Loogootee, Indiana, as well as in several other states in 1920. Probably the most widely known Indiana glass manufacturer was the Ball Brothers Company, established in Muncie in 1887. Although several attempts were made to consolidate it with other glass manufacturers, Ball Brothers by World War I had become one of the largest independent glass producers in the nation. Specializing in the manufacture of fruit jars, the company was a leader in technological innovation—rapidly adding new machinery before and after World War I. By 1930 one machine alone produced thirty fruit jars a minute. Like many modern companies Ball Brothers became more self-sufficient by acquiring zinc and rubber production facilities to produce lids and seals and three paper mills to produce corrugated paper boxes used to ship its jars in Ball-owned railroad cars. Although the company had five glass plants outside of Indiana by 1936, the Muncie factories remained the primary facility, covering seventy acres and employing twenty-five hundred workers.[18] Clearly a modern big business by

[18] Warren C. Scoville, *Revolution in Glassmaking: Entrepreneurship and Technological Change in the American Industry, 1880-1920* (Cambridge, Mass., 1948), pp. 113, 269, 304; Pearce Davis, *The Development of the American Glass*

the interwar years, Ball Brothers was still family owned and based largely in Indiana.

Another increasingly important industry was the manufacture of chemicals, which by 1939 ranked fifth in value of product in Indiana. Chemical companies evolved significantly in the interwar years, both as a consequence of scientific research and development stimulated by World War I and in response to other major industries such as oil, steel, glass, and automobiles. One of Indiana's major chemical companies was located in Terre Haute, where during World War I the United States government had purchased two whiskey distilleries to manufacture industrial alcohol. In 1919 the newly formed Commercial Solvents Corporation acquired control of these Terre Haute plants, which soon became major suppliers of butanol, a chemical used to produce a quick-drying lacquer essential for high-speed assembly-line automobile finishing. During the interwar years Commercial Solvents expanded its research and development efforts into a variety of chemical products and acquired additional production plants outside of Indiana.[19]

Important among chemical companies were the drug and pharmaceutical companies, which were increasing in significance in Indiana industry. Eli Lilly and Company provides a good example of changes in this industry. Begun in Indianapolis in 1876 by Colonel Eli Lilly (usually distinguished from his grandson of the same name by use of the Civil War title), the company's scientific research and development activities expanded greatly in the 1920s. Headed by George Henry Alexander Clowes, a Ph.D. in chemistry, the research staff made good use of developments in bio-

---

Industry (Cambridge, Mass., 1949), pp. 207-211; Frank Clayton Ball, *Memoirs of Frank Clayton Ball* (Muncie, Ind., 1937), pp. 93-95, 105-107. During and after World War II Ball Brothers suffered serious marketing and managerial problems, leading eventually to product diversification and the acquisition of management from outside the Ball family. Frederic A. Birmingham, *Ball Corporation: The First Century* (Indianapolis, 1980), pp. 143-145.

[19] Williams Haynes (ed.), *American Chemical Industry: The Chemical Companies* (New York, 1949), pp. 85-89; *Moody's Manual of Investments: Industrial Securities*, 1940, pp. 3102-3103; Fred C. Kelly, *One Thing Leads to Another: The Growth of an Industry* (Boston, 1936), pp. 18-19, 37-43. Corn from nearby counties was an important ingredient in many of Commercial Solvents' products, including, after 1933, whiskey.

chemistry that occurred during and after the Great War. Lilly's most notable success came with insulin, developed at the University of Toronto and first produced in high quality and large volume by the Indianapolis company in 1923. Lilly's insulin was soon in use worldwide and provided longer life to thousands of diabetics. Insulin also had an effect on the company that produced it: first-year sales were three times the dollar volume of any other single Lilly product. Insulin represented Lilly's most dramatic success resulting from increased attention to research and development. Another major source of change derived from attention to systematic production and management. After World War I, Colonel Lilly's grandsons, J. K. Lilly, Jr., and Eli Lilly, began major efforts to apply principles of scientific management to the production and distribution of pharmaceuticals. Young Eli Lilly concentrated on production. Attempting to eliminate or modify the inefficient hand production that predominated prior to 1920, he began a series of time-motion studies and by 1926 had installed a new straight-line production system housed in a new plant, thereby providing a constant and regulated flow of materials from entrance of raw product to exit of finished drug. Not surprisingly, Eli Lilly apparently derived part of his model for efficient, high volume production from a visit to a Ford assembly plant. The other young Lilly, J. K. Lilly, Jr., concentrated on similar methods to improve distribution. In 1922 he began a systematic study of distribution and sales patterns to replace the company's reliance on guesswork and tradition. Keeping a black notebook crammed with sales and other statistical data, J. K. Lilly, Jr., led the company into modern market research, not only in the United States but overseas as well.[20]

[20] E. J. Kahn, Jr., *All in a Century: The First 100 Years of Eli Lilly and Company* [Indianapolis, 1975], pp. 71-72, 82-86, 92-101; Roscoe Collins Clark, *Threescore Years and Ten: A Narrative of the First Seventy Years of Eli Lilly and Company 1876-1946* (Indianapolis, 1946), pp. 62-65. In 1932 Eli Lilly succeeded his father, J. K. Lilly, Sr., as president of the company, and J. K. Lilly, Jr., became executive vice-president. Another important Indiana pharmaceutical company was Miles Laboratories, located in Elkhart. Founded in 1880 as a patent medicine manufacturer, the company expanded rapidly in the 1930s, due largely to sales of its Alka-Seltzer, first marketed and heavily advertised in 1930. In the late 1930s Miles began major production of vitamins, introducing its One-A-Day brand in 1940. Haynes (ed.), *American Chemical Industry*, pp. 278-279.

None of these developments at Eli Lilly and Company in the 1920s was unique. The emphasis on systematic, high-volume production, on sustained statistical analysis of distribution and markets, on scientific research and development by technical staff and university researchers—all were hallmarks of modern business after World War I. Indeed, companies and individuals best able to adopt these more sophisticated and complex methods of modern business tended to prosper in the 1920s, to survive the Great Depression, and to grow to mammoth size during and after World War II. Such adaptation was as important for family-owned and managed companies, such as Lilly and Ball Brothers, as it was for the diversely held corporations based outside the state, such as GM or U.S. Steel.

There were other industries where change was less momentous. This was true of those with origins in the early nineteenth century and especially processors of grain, meat, and other food products from the surrounding countryside. On the eve of World War II some individuals and companies processed food much as had their predecessors on the eve of the Civil War. Yet even in these older, more traditional industries, there was change, including the development of large, modern business enterprises, as illustrated by several meat-packing, grain processing, and commercial canning operations.

Even though small meat-packers continued to operate in various parts of the state, big businesses increasingly dominated the industry in Indiana. Indianapolis continued to be the state's largest meat-packing center and was the fifth largest in the nation in 1919. Several large packers operated plants there, including Armour, Kingan, and Swift. In 1936 several former Armour employees founded their own Indianapolis-based company, Stark, Wetzel and Company.[21]

Milling of grain, which in the nineteenth century—even more than meat-packing—had been dispersed in small mills throughout the state, now came to be more concentrated in larger cities such as Indianapolis and Evansville, though small neighborhood flour

21 Barnhart and Carmony, *Indiana*, IV, 372.

mills still dotted the Indiana landscape. Some Indiana flour mills combined with larger corporations; for example, Phoenix Mills and Igleheart Brothers of Evansville both merged with General Foods in the late 1920s. Increasingly, however, the nation's major flour production shifted westward, closer to the supply of the hard wheat large commercial bakers considered more desirable than the soft wheat generally grown in Indiana. To survive, large Indiana mills began either to blend their own soft wheat flours with flour from hard wheat mills or to concentrate on differentiated and heavily advertised products, such as Igleheart Brothers' Swans Down cake flour or Acme-Evans' E-Z Bake flour.[22]

Indiana distilleries and breweries also processed grain, but, of course, their business was severely curtailed by the federal prohibition amendment. Upon its repeal in 1933 fewer breweries reopened—only seventeen, compared to thirty-nine in 1914, with the largest ones located in South Bend, Fort Wayne, Indianapolis, Terre Haute, and Evansville. Thereafter, the pattern was one of concentration, a smaller number of larger firms competing in larger market areas. Indiana breweries retained a significant share of the national beer output, ranking eleventh among the states in 1938. Indiana also resumed its place as a major producer of whiskey and other distilled liquors—ranking second behind Kentucky in 1940 with 20 percent of total national production. Much of this was produced at the Lawrenceburg plant of the large, multinational Seagrams Company.[23]

Perhaps the most rapidly changing food processing industry was commercial vegetable canning, where growth and change

[22] Federal Trade Commission, *Report ... on Commercial Wheat Flour Milling, 1920* (Washington, D.C., 1920), pp. 27, 108; Charles Byron Kuhlmann, *The Development of the Flour-Milling Industry in the United States with Special Reference to the Industry in Minneapolis* (Boston, 1929), pp. 186-191, 243, 284-287; "Acme-Evans Company Celebrates 150th Anniversary This Month," Indianapolis Chamber of Commerce, *Activities*, XL (December, 1926), 12-13.

[23] Allied Liquor Industries, Inc., *Beverage Distilling Industry Facts and Figures, 1934-1944* (New York, 1945), p. 35; Warren Milton Persons, *Beer and Brewing in America: An Economic Study* (n.p., 1938), pp. 9-11, 15; Manfred Friedrich and Donald Bull, *The Register of United States Breweries, 1876-1976* (Trubull, Conn., 1976), pp. 11-12, 97-104, 306. The latter source lists Indiana breweries with dates of closing.

accompanied the movement of people off farms and the decline in home-processed foods. Commercial canning expanded rapidly in early twentieth-century Indiana and especially during the 1930s. By 1935 the state had nearly three hundred canning factories, ranking it fourth in the nation in the number of canneries and second in the number of workers employed. Although most counties had at least one canning plant, the industry was concentrated in the central part of the state. Madison County with its forty-three plants ranked first. The Indiana canning industry included a wide variety of companies—ranging from large, partly integrated, multiplant and multiproduct companies to small, part-time, single product companies that were only a step beyond traditional household manufacturing. A few were organized and operated in some important ways much like General Motors or U.S. Steel. Stokely-Van Camp, for example, was one of the largest canning companies in the nation. Formed in 1933 by the merger of the Tennessee-based Stokely Brothers Company and the Van Camp Company of Indianapolis, the enterprise operated increasingly mechanized plants in more than a dozen states and marketed its expanding product line throughout the United States with the aid of extensive national advertising. Another major firm was the Morgan Packing Company, which was started by J. S. Morgan in Austin, Scott County, at the turn of the century. By the mid-1930s the company operated year-round in six Indiana plants and employed more than a thousand permanent workers and many more during the harvest seasons. This family-run company marketed its products across the nation through jobbers, operated its own fleet of trucks, and had a large printshop to produce its own labels. The company was not fully integrated: like most Indiana canners, it depended for its annual supply of fifty million cans on the huge American Can Company, which built a factory adjacent to the Austin plant. In addition to a few large companies such as Stokely-Van Camp and the Morgan Packing Company, there were dozens of small canning companies in Indiana. They might operate for only two or three months a year in a converted barn with little machinery. Many of them specialized in only one product, usually tomatoes, prepared with little capital and much unskilled labor, often female members of local families. Frequently they sold their product to large companies such as Heinz or Campbell for use in soups.[24]

There were other industries even less affected by changes in technology, organization, or size. These most traditional industries tended to be more dependent on natural resources, to use more labor than technology, and to rely on products that did not readily lend themselves to high-volume mass production and for which large consumer markets did not exist. One or more of these traditional characteristics were to be found in the furniture and limestone industries, where larger modern businesses seldom appeared or succeeded in Indiana and where the Depression of the 1930s was especially devastating.

Indiana furniture manufacturing was little affected by changing technology or business organization. And although the industry continued to be important and ranked fifth in the state in number of workers employed in 1939, many Indiana furniture and woodworking companies struggled for survival through the interwar years. All Indiana woodworking industries suffered as a result of the depletion of local timber resources. By World War I, Bloomington's Showers Brothers, probably the state's largest furniture company, acquired more than 75 percent of its wood from outside Indiana. In addition, Showers and other furniture manufacturers faced increasingly strong competition from the rapid growth of the industry in the southern United States, where manufacturers enjoyed lower wage and freight rates. Showers Brothers had expanded rapidly in the first quarter of the twentieth century, building several very large plants in Bloomington and smaller facilities in Bloomfield, Indiana, and Burlington, Iowa. By the mid-1920s this family-managed company claimed to be the largest furniture manufacturer in the country. The company exerted a dominant influence on the Monroe County economy, where it employed more than a thou-

[24] Lotys Benning, *The Vegetable Canning Industry* (Indianapolis, 1938), pp. 6, 11-14, 49-59, 65-67; Bernard F. Trimpe, The Stokely-Van Camp Company, 1898-1950: A Business History (D.C.S. dissertation, Indiana University, Bloomington, 1950), pp. 246-247, 378.

sand workers in the 1920s, many of them part-time or former farmers. After 1926, however, Showers's profits began to decline, and in 1929 the company suffered a deficit. The Depression greatly exacerbated the company's difficulties as sales dropped from $10 million in 1929 to $2 million in 1932. Company plants operated sporadically or not at all through the 1930s. World War II did not revive the ailing company. By the end of the war its work force of fewer than seven hundred consisted largely of older men, some in their seventies, and often endured layoffs. Showers struggled along until finally going out of business in the 1950s.[25]

Other woodworking manufacturers either failed prior to World War II or barely struggled through the interwar years. Like many wagonmakers, the Keller Manufacturing Company of Corydon faced extinction as demand for its product dropped rapidly after World War I. In the early 1930s the company in desperation began to manufacture furniture on a small scale, survived into World War II, and gradually recovered thereafter. Other similar small and medium-sized, family-owned woodworking companies also survived in southern Indiana, some by concentrating on producing radio cabinets, others by specializing in school and office furniture. Woodworking companies were especially numerous and important in Dubois County, where five businesses employed more than a hundred workers each in 1929. In northern Indiana the leading woodworking company was the South Bend plant of Singer Brothers, which made wood cabinets for the company's sewing machines. Although for a time a major

[25] Louis H. Orzack, Employment and Social Structure: A Study of Social Change in Indiana (Ph.D. dissertation, Indiana University, Bloomington, 1953), pp. 88-96, 113-127, 134-144; Dale Dillon, *Thoughts Concerning the 60th Anniversary of Showers Brothers Company* (Bloomington, Ind., 1928), pp. 5, 32-43. It is symbolic that Showers sold one of its Bloomington plants to RCA when the electronics company came to Bloomington in 1940. Within a year RCA employed more than a thousand workers, far surpassing Showers as the town's leading industry. Orzack, Employment and Social Structure, pp. 89, 143-145. For results of an oral history project centering on these two companies see R. T. King, "From Kitchen Cabinets to TV Sets," videotape, 1980, Indiana University Oral History Research Project.

South Bend employer, Singer gradually curtailed production and in the mid-1950s closed the South Bend plant.[26]

Woodworking industries did not generally prosper in Indiana during the interwar years, as declining natural resources and the nature of the industry adversely affected companies. The industry consisted of a large number of small firms that were frequently family owned and managed. There was little technological change to cut costs and increase productivity and apparently only very slight economies of scale to stimulate the growth of larger companies. Indeed, no company comparable to U.S. Steel, General Motors, or Standard Oil of Indiana emerged in furniture manufacturing. The closest versions, Bloomington's Showers Brothers and South Bend's Singer plant, barely survived the Depression, only to be boarded up in the post-World War II decade.

Limestone provides another example of a traditional industry struggling through the interwar years. Limestone is found in abundance and quality in south central Indiana, and the industry had concentrated there by the late nineteenth century. Limestone played an especially important role in the economy of Monroe and Lawrence counties, where quarries and mills dotted the countryside. The tremendous building expansion of the 1920s enabled Indiana limestone companies to prosper generally, but already there were difficulties that would be greatly magnified by the Depression. Because after 1920 architects began to favor less ornamental styles and more varied surface textures and colors, they turned to building materials other than limestone. At the same time, there were technological innovations in production of other materials that made them less costly and more readily available. Brick, cast stone, and later steel and glass all threatened the position of limestone as a major building material. Although the Indiana limestone companies undertook some promotional efforts

[26] Charles N. Kaufman, The History of the Keller Manufacturing Company (D.B.A. dissertation, Indiana University, Bloomington, 1964), pp. 131-163; Indiana State Chamber of Commerce, Directory of Indiana Manufacturers 1929 (n.p., n.d.); Barnhart and Carmony, Indiana, III, 234, 563-564, IV, 606-607; Robert N. Gold, Manufacturing Structure and Pattern of the South Bend-Mishawaka Area (Chicago, 1954), p. 110.

in the 1920s, their share of the building market declined. Increasingly the industry was plagued by excess capacity. A major merger in 1926 of twenty-four companies into the Indiana Limestone Company did not improve efficiency or provide the solution to the growing cutthroat competition among the large number of firms operating in the Bloomington-Bedford district. By 1929 the limestone companies were able to produce 30 to 40 percent more limestone than they were able to sell, even in their best sales years. Nor did their costs decline. Railroad freight rates for limestone rose rapidly, and, although refinements in production were made, no major technological innovations appeared to improve significantly the industry's productivity.[27]

The Depression brought disaster to the Indiana limestone industry. A large federal construction program in Washington, D.C., approved in the late 1920s, provided a temporary respite from the effects of the 1929 crash, since the program specified the use of Indiana limestone for the massive Federal Triangle, which was constructed in the period 1929-1933. Many observers attributed this use of Indiana limestone to the influence of Hoosier Republicans in national politics—above all Senator James E. Watson—a sentiment that grew after Democratic victories in 1932. It was indeed the case that Democratic control of Congress and the White House coincided with much less government use of limestone, despite efforts of Hoosier Democrats to lobby in favor of the material. But other factors doubtless affected the change, especially the objective of New Deal relief programs to spread employment by encouraging use of local materials in public buildings such as post offices. The precipitous decline in demand for limestone in public and private construction closed many of the mills and quarries in Monroe and Lawrence counties. There was some recovery in 1937 and 1938, but as late as 1939 employment was less than half the peak figure of the 1920s. The beginning of defense production in 1940 brought further decline instead of recovery. On the eve of World War II the limestone industry

[27] Joseph A. Batchelor, *An Economic History of the Indiana Oolitic Limestone Industry* (Bloomington, Ind., 1944), pp. 192-199, 209-214, 235-242, 264-268, 295-296.

suffered from excess capacity, intense competition from other building materials, changing tastes in architectural styles, and reliance on old-fashioned technologies, production methods, and business organization. Limestone, once the glory of Monroe and Lawrence counties, had become one of the state's long-term depressed industries.[28]

Another major natural resource industry to suffer during the interwar years was coal. Indiana's bituminous coalfields were located in the western and southwestern edges of the state, principally in the counties of Warrick, Pike, Vigo, Sullivan, Vermillion, Clay, Greene, Knox, and Gibson. Although Indiana retained its sixth-place ranking in coal production during the interwar years, the volume of production declined significantly. With increased use of substitute fuels, principally petroleum and natural gas, the nation's coal industry after World War I was plagued with too many mines and too many miners relative to demand for product—a condition that had very deleterious effects on Indiana coal producers. After World War I they faced difficult competition from new fields in Kentucky and West Virginia, where operators benefited from lower freight rates, lower, nonunion wage scales, and higher quality coal. Annual coal production in the state was erratic, but the trend was sharply downward.[29]

Unlike limestone, however, the structure of the coal industry changed considerably during the interwar years. At the end of World War I, small scattered mines produced much of Indiana's coal, often using part-time labor provided by farmers seeking extra income in winter. During the 1920s and 1930s, however, the number of mines decreased, as marginal producers failed, and a

[28] Ibid., pp. 22-23, 308, 324-351, 359-364; Sherman Minton, Memorandum for the President, May 2, 1940, PPF 2235, Franklin D. Roosevelt Papers.

[29] Osmond LaVar Harlin, Economics of the Indiana Coal Mining Industry (Ph.D. dissertation, Indiana University, Bloomington, 1958), pp. 81-90, 225, 285; Indiana State Chamber of Commerce v. Ann Arbor Railroad Company, Case No. 116138, Interstate Commerce Commission, Reports, CXV (July-October, 1926), 656; Carl M. Gray interview by R. T. King, April 12, 1979, transcript, pp. 20-25, Oral History Research Project Mss., Lilly Library, Indiana University, Bloomington.

small number of large mines and mining companies acquired an increasingly larger share of the production. By 1940 four companies produced about one third of the state's total.[30]

A major factor in this structural change was new technology. To reduce their relatively high labor costs and compete more efficiently, coal operators used machinery to replace or supplement traditional pick-and-shovel methods of cutting and loading coal. The proportion of underground coal production that was mechanically loaded increased from 4.8 percent in 1925 to 32.3 percent in 1930, to 62.5 percent in 1935, to 83.9 percent by 1940. The Indiana mines led all other coal areas in the nation in mechanization of underground mining. Even more significant was strip or open-cut mining, which expanded rapidly in the interwar years, from 4.7 percent of the state's total coal production in 1920 to 34.2 percent in 1930, to 43.1 percent in 1935, to 53.2 percent in 1940. For Indiana coal producers strip mining had several important advantages over underground mining. By using power machinery to strip away the overburden and then remove the coal, they generally achieved higher labor productivity, lower production costs, and higher profits. While some small coal operators engaged in strip mining in the interwar years, sometimes using only a horse-drawn scraper to remove the overburden, the returns from large capital investment in power machinery made strip mining especially attractive to larger companies. This attractiveness was demonstrated by the merger in 1939 of the Patoka Coal Company, a major investment of former Governor James P. Goodrich and his son Pierre F. Goodrich, with the Electric Shovel Coal Corporation. The new company, Ayrshire Patoka Collieries, was the state's largest coal company, operating four large strip mines in Indiana. Strip mining also proved more compatible with topographical and geological conditions in southwestern Indiana counties—especially Pike, Gibson, and Warrick—which chal-

[30] This estimate is made from railroad shipments from mines as reported in Coal Trade Association of Indiana, *Coal Production in Indiana, 1926-1950* (Terre Haute, Ind., n.d.), pp. 14-21. The companies with the largest coal shipments in 1940 were Ayrshire Patoka Collieries, Maumee Collieries Company, Enos Coal Company, and Princeton Mining Company.

lenged the earlier dominance of the western counties of Vigo and Sullivan, where underground mining continued to predominate. The dramatic, even revolutionary mechanization of underground and strip mining in Indiana during the interwar years changed forever the nature of the industry. The mechanized mines gained a large competitive advantage over nonmechanized, pick-and-shovel mines, and companies operating mechanized mines tended to consolidate and grow larger while their competitors fell by the wayside. And, while Indiana coal producers constantly fought competition from Kentucky and West Virginia producers, by the late 1930s they apparently were able to compete more successfully.[31] In coal, then, the mixture of traditional and modern characteristics that developed after World War I had moved rapidly toward the dominance of modern forms of enterprise even in this often "sick" industry.

The changes that occurred in industry in Indiana during the interwar years were part of the national pattern of increased emphasis on technology, high-volume production, and large-scale organization—a pattern that first developed in the late nineteenth century and persisted into the late twentieth century. Though the state's economic well-being continued to depend on abundant natural resources and on agriculture, that dependence played a relatively smaller role in shaping industrial and company growth and development than it had in the nineteenth century. Indeed, many Indiana companies that relied largely on local natural resources or agricultural products stagnated or failed during the interwar years. Some traditional enterprises held on in such areas

[31] Harlin, Economics of the Indiana Coal Mining Industry, pp. 95-97, 104-105, 229, 301-303, 387-390; John Hendrickson, The Development of Strip Coal Mining in Indiana (M.A. thesis, Indiana University, Bloomington, 1952), pp. 58, 71-76; Indiana Year Book, 1930, pp. 394-397, 405; Warren W. Parke interview by R. T. King, April 24, 1979, transcript, pp. 1-3, Oral History Research Project Mss., Lilly Library, Indiana University, Bloomington; Moody's Manual of Investments: Industrial Securities, 1940, p. 1817; Reed Moyer, Competition in the Midwestern Coal Industry (Cambridge, Mass., 1964), pp. 109-115; C. L. Christenson, Economic Redevelopment in Bituminous Coal: The Special Case of Technological Advance in United States Coal Mines, 1930-1960 (Cambridge, Mass., 1962), pp. 127-135; Coal Trade Association of Indiana, Coal Production in Indiana, pp. 14-21. For government regulation of strip mining see below, this chapter.

as woodworking, coal, limestone, and food processing, but increasingly even in these more traditional industries survival required the use of more sophisticated scientific, technological, or managerial skills. In other industries the trend was even more markedly toward technological change to achieve more efficient and productive use of capital and labor. Those industries that were more technologically sophisticated and more capital intensive tended to call forth large-scale manufacturing plants and large multiplant companies, requiring complex administrative co-ordination. And the emphasis on high-volume production for large markets often stimulated more attention to market research and advertising in order to forecast and influence demand. In Indiana the largest business organizations appeared in the steel, auto, and petroleum refining industries. Large companies developed in other industries as well. Though not as huge as U.S. Steel or GM, such companies as Ayrshire Coal, Eli Lilly, Ball Brothers, and Stokely-Van Camp exhibited some of the important features of modern twentieth-century business. Such companies also provided evidence that, while large corporations with corporate headquarters and decision makers located outside the state—in Detroit, Chicago, or New York City—were increasingly important, there did develop modern businesses that were owned and managed within the state.[32]

Whether locally managed or not, big business dominated industrial production in Indiana after World War I. The nineteenth-century industrial pattern of a large number of small firms changed to a twentieth-century pattern of a small number of large firms—especially in the most modern industries. In many ways the hundreds of small flour mills and woodworking enterprises that had best symbolized mid-nineteenth-century industry had given way in industrial significance to a handful of steel mills, oil refineries, automobile plants, and other modern enterprises. The general features of this industrial concentration are indicated in manufacturing census data. In 1919, 302 manufacturing establishments in Indiana produced more than $1 million worth of product.

[32] For a fuller discussion of these changes in their national context see Chandler, *The Visible Hand*, pp. 345-376, 469-476.

These 302 largest manufacturers, representing only 3.8 percent of the state total of manufacturers, produced 71.5 percent of the state's value of manufactured product and 65.8 percent of the value added by manufacturing. The dominance of the large producers increased as the total number of manufacturing establishments declined from 7,916 in 1919 to 4,919 in 1929, to 4,337 in 1939. At the same time, the number of firms producing more than $1 million worth of product changed only slightly, from 302 in 1919, to 339 in 1929, to 342 in 1939, yet this handful of million-dollar producers increased their share of value of product from 71.5 percent in 1919, to 76.4 in 1929, to 78.1 in 1939, and their value added from 65.8 percent in 1919, to 72.7 in 1929, to 75.3 in 1939. Both the prosperity of the 1920s and the hard times of the 1930s enhanced the importance of these major producers in the Indiana economy. The extent of concentration is indicated also by a census category first used in 1929—that of manufacturing establishments producing more than $5 million of product. Only sixty-nine Indiana establishments were in this category in 1929, representing 1.4 percent of the state total, but they produced 53 percent of the value of product and 47.8 of the value added by manufacturing. The figures for 1939 were almost exactly the same.[33]

Not only was manufacturing concentrated in a small number of firms, it was also concentrated in a few urban areas—above all, in Marion and Lake counties. Indianapolis and the Calumet cities of Gary, East Chicago, Whiting, and Hammond accounted for nearly half the state's total value of product by 1919, with Lake County's share at 27 percent and Marion County's at 21 percent. Expanding oil and steel production enabled Lake County to increase its share to 32 percent in 1929 and 33 percent in 1939, while Marion dropped to 17 percent in 1929 and 13 percent in 1939. Behind these industrial leaders were St. Joseph (South Bend-

[33] United States Bureau of the Census, *Fifteenth Census* (1930), III, *Manufactures*, 1929, p. 165; United States Bureau of the Census, *Sixteenth Census* (1940), III, *Manufactures*, 1939, p. 281. The nature of manufacturing census data makes such comparisons suggestive rather than exact. The Census Bureau's efforts to avoid publishing data that might reveal information on individual companies also reduce their utility.

Mishawaka), Vanderburgh (Evansville), and Allen (Fort Wayne), each with between 4 and 6 percent of total value of product in 1919 and between 5 and 7 percent by 1939. Next in order in 1919 were Madison (Anderson), Vigo (Terre Haute), La Porte (Michigan City), Delaware (Muncie), and Howard (Kokomo). The first ten counties changed only slightly in composition and rank order. (See Table IV.) The top ten accounted

TABLE IV

Ten Leading Manufacturing Counties in Indiana,
by Value of Manufactured Product, 1919 and 1939[34]

1919	Value of Product (in millions of dollars)	1939	Value of Product (in millions of dollars)
Lake	520.4	Lake	736.6
Marion	505.3	Marion	294.5
St. Joseph	103.7	St. Joseph	157.8
Allen	77.8	Vanderburgh	133.4
Vanderburgh	75.2	Allen	120.5
Madison	60.5	Madison	79.3
Vigo	54.7	Delaware	67.6
La Porte	53.3	La Porte	52.5
Delaware	42.4	Vigo	48.1
Howard	40.4	Elkhart	47.9
Total for above 10 counties	1,533.7	Total for above 10 counties	1,738.2
State Total	1,898.8	State Total	2,227.6

for nearly 81 percent of the state's total value of product in 1919 and 78 percent in 1929 and 1939. Clearly the state's industrial production depended on only a few urban areas.

All but one of the leading ten manufacturing counties in the interwar years were located in the central and northern parts of the state. The location of large manufacturers is indicated by Table V, which shows that companies with more than five hun-

[34] United States Bureau of the Census, *Sixteenth Census* (1940), III, *Manufactures,* 1939, pp. 278-279; George W. Starr, *Industrial Development of Indiana* (Bloomington, Ind., 1937), p. 41.

TABLE V
Location of Companies with More than
500 Employees, 1929[35]

Anderson (2)	Fort Wayne (11)	Lafayette (3)
Alexandria (1)	Frankfort (1)	Logansport (1)
Auburn (1)	Gary (5)	Mishawaka (2)
Bloomington (2)	Gas City (1)	Muncie (6)
Brazil (1)	Hammond (3)	Salem (1)
Columbus (2)	Hartford City (2)	South Bend
Connersville (3)	Goshen (1)	Terre Haute (2)
East Chicago (11)	Indianapolis (20)	Vincennes (1)
Elkhart (5)	Kokomo (3)	Whiting (1)
Evansville (5)		

dred employees predominated in Indianapolis, the Calumet Region, and several towns and cities of central and northern Indiana. Vanderburgh was unique among southern Indiana counties, as Evansville made good use of its river location and other resources to hold its large flour mills and furniture manufacturers, as well as attracting such new industries as manufacturers of electrical appliances and auto parts.[36] In most of southern Indiana, however, there were no large modern industries. This retardation of manufacturing in southern Indiana combined with increasing difficulties in competing with modern agriculture and declining employment in coal and limestone to bring considerable economic hardship to much of the area after World War I.

Also declining in relative industrial importance was Vigo County, which as late as 1900 had ranked third among Indiana counties in value of manufactured product. Terre Haute's reli-

[35] Indiana State Chamber of Commerce, *Directory of Indiana Manufacturers*, 1929. Numbers in parentheses indicate the number of companies with more than 500 employees. For reasons not known, data on employees were not included for South Bend.

[36] C. Walter McCarty (ed.), *Indiana Today* (Indianapolis, 1942), p. 55. The Indiana State Chamber of Commerce's *Directory of Indiana Manufacturers* lists companies by name and product for all towns and cities in the state and, combined with the federal manufacturing census, indicates the nature of industry in any locality. Information in this and following paragraphs comes from the 1922, 1929, and 1940 editions of the directories, copies of which are in the Indiana Division, Indiana State Library.

ance on railroads and railroad shops, iron and steel fabrication, and coal served the city and region less well after World War I than before. Though the city did attract some modern industries, such as Commercial Solvents, it dropped to seventh place among Indiana manufacturing counties in 1919 and to ninth place in 1929 and 1939.[37]

The industrial future after World War I seemed to belong to central and northern Indiana: to the Calumet cities, bursting with oil and steel production; to Indianapolis, continuing to use its transportation network to develop a mix of industries; to cities in the natural gas region that managed to adapt to the depletion of that natural resource by developing or attracting large companies, such as Muncie's Ball Brothers or Anderson's GM plants; to the northern industrial cities of Fort Wayne and South Bend, which combined home-grown enterprises in machine shops, automobiles, and agricultural implements with the ability—due in part to their transportation and location advantages—to attract branch plants of large industrial corporations such as International Harvester, General Electric, and Magnavox in Fort Wayne and U.S. Rubber and Bendix in South Bend-Mishawaka.[38]

There were, to be sure, modern industrial enterprises developing in other places, including some small towns in southern Indiana. In the 1930s the Cummins Engine Company in Columbus, for example, began its climb to leadership in the manufacture of diesel engines. RCA opened a major plant in Bloomington in 1940, attracted by the abundant labor supply.[39] And traditional firms which relied on labor intensive, low-volume production, simple technology, and small amounts of capital continued to play important roles, even in large cities such as Indianapolis. But the

[37] Alden Cutshall, "Terre Haute Iron and Steel: A Declining Industry," *Indiana Magazine of History*, XXXVII (1941), 242; Robert R. Drummond, Terre Haute, Indiana: A City of Non-Growth (Ph.D. dissertation, Northwestern University, Evanston, Ill., 1953), pp. 171-191.

[38] Gold, *Manufacturing Structure and Pattern of the South Bend-Mishawaka Area*, pp. 73-74.

[39] John W. Rowell, "The '30s: From 50 Engines a Year to 50 a Month," *Power Team*, July-August, 1979, pp. 4, 17; Richard H. Gemmecke, W. G. Irwin and Hugh Thomas Miller: A Study in Free Enterprise in Indiana (Ph.D. dissertation, Indiana University, Bloomington, 1955), pp. 284-316; Orzack, Employment and Social Structure, pp. 143-145.

interwar years marked the maturation and dominance of large, even gigantic, enterprises that depended increasingly on skillful administration, sophisticated research and development, large amounts of capital, complex technology, and wide markets, all combining to produce in large volume at high speed.

§ §

Changes in retailing were not as dramatic as in industry, but the pattern of change was similar. Throughout the interwar years the retail sector of the Indiana economy was composed of a large number of small stores. In 1929 nearly one half of the 39,402 stores in the state had less than $2,000 in assets. These small retail enterprises were most prolific in groceries (which represented more than one quarter of all retail stores), garage and auto sales, restaurants, women's clothing, and general stores. And these "mom and pop" stores tended to turn over rapidly through business failure or change of ownership. The other side of the high-turnover coin was the generally low barriers to entering these kinds of businesses: they required relatively small amounts of capital and tended to attract people with few technical or managerial skills, often relying instead on long hours of work for the proprietor and his or her family. Finally, these small retail businesses were spread across the urban and rural landscape—at muddy crossroads, on small-town squares, and throughout the neighborhoods of larger cities. The Great Depression may have intensified this pattern of small business: the 47,317 stores in Indiana in 1939 represented a 20 percent increase over 1929, yet total retail sales were down slightly from $1,200,458 in 1929, to $1,066,383 in 1939.[40]

While available data do not allow for precise delineation of the

[40] United States Bureau of the Census, *Sixteenth Census* (1940), *Census of Business*, I, *Retail Trade*, 1939, Pt. 3, p. 9; "Retail Turnover in Indiana, 1929 to 1937," *Indiana Business Review*, XIV (August 20, 1939), 6-7, XIV (September 20, 1939), 9-10; G. W. Starr and G. A. Steiner, "The Births and Deaths of Retail Stores in Indiana, 1929-1937," *Dun's Review*, XLVIII (January, 1940), 23-24. Competition from Chicago, Cincinnati, and other cities helped retard the development of wholesaling in Indiana, though Indianapolis did have a significant wholesale business by 1920. Benjamin Moulton, Indianapolis: Its Evolving Functions and Functional Areas (Ph.D. dissertation, Indiana University, Bloomington, 1950), pp. 78-80.

patterns of change, it does appear that retailing became more concentrated in the interwar years in larger businesses and in larger cities. First the railroad and interurban, then after World War I the automobile and paved roads enabled rural and small-town shoppers to travel greater distances for purchases and freed them from dependence on small local merchants. Urban retailers were acutely aware of the importance of improved transportation and made strong efforts to expand their city's hinterland. During the 1920s and 1930s, numerous studies of commuting and shopping patterns attempted to define and expand the geographic boundaries of Indianapolis's shopping area, which extended into the counties contiguous to Marion.[41] Small-town merchants struggled, often without great success, to keep and hold local trade away from the larger cities. The more ambitious small-town businessmen began to sponsor free movies, concerts, and drawings, and they combined with local newspapers to make emotional appeals to buy at home. Nonetheless, it appears that the attractions of Indianapolis, Fort Wayne, Evansville, and other large cities often pulled Hoosiers from their hometowns on Saturdays.[42]

Accompanying the increased pulling power of retailers in large cities was the growth of larger and different kinds of stores, which brought more variety, efficiency, and complexity to retailing. The full-line department store developed in larger cities in the late nineteenth and early twentieth centuries. In the variety of goods and services and in quality and price, department stores such as L. S. Ayres in Indianapolis or Root's in Terre Haute proved strong competitors to the crossroads general store or small-town clothing retailer. Downtown department stores were generally the major

---

[41] John Paver and Miller McClintock, *Traffic and Trade: An Introduction to the Analysis of the Relationship between the Daily Habitual Movement of People and Their Trade Activities in Markets* (New York, 1935), pp. 60-95; Indianapolis News, *A Concise Resumé of Selling Conditions in the Indianapolis Radius* ([Indianapolis], 1923), pp. 3-5; J. Walter Thompson, *Retail Shopping Areas* (n.p., 1927), pp. 60-64.

[42] Jasper *Herald*, March 6, 1925; Hartman, Brookston, p. 170; Miriam Joy Meloy, The Newspaper Editor as a Community Builder (M.A. thesis, Indiana University, Bloomington, 1940), pp. 32-40, 82-123. The Meloy study contains a very detailed picture of businesses in two unidentified small Indiana towns as they struggled in the late 1930s to keep shoppers away from Indianapolis.

attraction to shoppers, serving as the anchors of the central business district throughout the first half of the twentieth century. Another new form of retailing also challenged traditional small retailers. These were the chain stores, which grew rapidly after World War I by exploiting economies possible through high volume, multi-store retailing. Some of the chain stores, such as Sears, Roebuck and Montgomery Ward, began as mail-order houses catering to rural customers, then opened urban retail department stores in the 1920s, often competing with large department stores and small-town merchants. Chains also appeared in drugstores, gasoline stations, and low-priced variety goods, often as so-called five-and-ten-cents stores. Grocers probably formed the largest number of chain stores. In Indianapolis in 1934 there were 75 Kroger grocery stores, 73 Atlantic & Pacific stores, and 190 Standard stores. The latter chain was started in Indianapolis at the turn of the century by Lafayette A. Jackson, who opened stores in other Indiana towns as well. Although chain stores did not always succeed, they generally benefited from the economies of large-volume retailing and were able to attract customers away from more traditional retailers by extensive advertising, more up-to-date merchandise, and lower prices. The "mom and pop" grocery store, the village general store, and the small-town druggist all felt the competitive strength of the large modern retail enterprises.[43]

§ § §

Changes in business and the economy in the interwar years brought a variety of problems and conflicts which, some Hoosiers argued, should be ameliorated or solved by government. Earlier chapters have indicated the important role of government in transportation and agriculture. For other businessmen and labor, too, questions of government regulation and intervention in the econ-

[43] Indianapolis News, *Indianapolis Grocery and Drug Stores: Retail and Wholesale Listed in Routes, Department and Chain Stores* (Indianapolis, 1934); Indianapolis *News*, May 29, 1931; James H. Madison, "Changing Patterns of Urban Retailing: The 1920s," *Business and Economic History: Papers Presented at the Twenty-second Annual Meeting of the Business History Conference* (Urbana, Ill., 1976), pp. 102-111.

omy provided some of the most intensely controversial and significant political and economic issues of the 1920s and 1930s.

One example of government regulation was brought about by independent retailers in response to the growth of chain stores. Indiana became a pioneer among states in this area of government regulation. In the 1920s local merchants' associations and the Indiana Association of Retailers began to argue that chain stores competed in unfair and "unneighborly" ways with independent retailers. They presented their case to the Indiana General Assembly, which in 1929 responded with legislation placing a graduated tax on chain stores. The more stores in a chain, the higher the tax on each store: retailers with only one store paid a three dollar tax; those with two to five stores paid ten dollars for each store; six to ten stores, fifteen dollars; eleven to twenty stores, twenty dollars; and more than twenty stores, twenty-five dollars for each. Not only was Indiana one of the first states to pass a discriminatory tax on chain stores, but the Indiana law led to precedent-setting court action. Standard Grocery owner Lafayette Jackson brought suit to void the 1929 legislation. Jackson's taxes amounted to $5,443, whereas if his 225 stores had been independently owned the total tax for all 225 would have been only $675. With strong support from the National Chain Store Association, Jackson won a favorable judgment when the United States District Court in Indianapolis in 1930 declared the Indiana law unconstitutional. In 1931, however, the United States Supreme Court overruled the lower court and upheld the chain-store tax, thereby opening the door for similar anti-chain-store legislation in many other states and for higher tax rates. The Indiana legislature in 1933 increased the rates for chains composed of more than twenty stores from $25 to $150 for each store.[44]

44 *Laws of Indiana*, 1929, pp. 639-698; 1933, p. 1230; Boyd M. Ralston to Whiting Merchants Association, June 16, 1933, Boyd M. Ralston Papers, Lilly Library, Indiana University, Bloomington; Godfrey M. Lebhar, *Chain Stores in America 1859-1959* (New York, 1959), pp. 130-133, 171-172; Maurice W. Lee, *Anti-Chain-Store Tax Legislation* (Chicago, 1939), pp. 5-6, 12-14, 27-30, 40-48; Indianapolis *News*, February 1, 1930, May 29, 1931; Charles G. Daughters, *Wells of Discontent: A Study of the Economic, Social, and Political Aspects of the Chain Store* (New York, 1937), pp. 57-59.

Indiana Historical Society

Standard Grocery Store in 1930s

Auburn-Cord-Duesenberg Museum

1922 Auburns in Boston dealer's showroom

William A. Wirt

Herman B Wells

SHORTRIDGE DAILY ECHO
FIRST AMERICAN HIGH SCHOOL DAILY

VOL. XXVIII, NO. 174.   SHORTRIDGE HIGH SCHOOL, INDIANAPOLIS, TUESDAY, MAY 25, 1926.   TWO CENTS

Journalism Echo

S. H. S. DIAMOND SQUAD WINS FROM COLUMBUS

Last Inning Hit By Anderson Results In Blue and White Victory 7-6.

The Shortridge diamond squad staged a last inning rally yesterday afternoon at the Riverside diamond to win from Columbus 7-6.

Still mindful of the defeat at the hands of Manual last Friday the S. H. S. nine fought hard through the entire contest and in the last inning Anderson drove out a nice hit, which won the game for the blue and white.

Simms was on the mound for Shortridge and Holt was on the receiving end.

This game concludes the baseball schedule for this year and considering the material, the season has been very successful.

JEWELRY EXHIBITION ON STAIR LANDING

The annual jewelry exhibit of the jewelry and silversmithing classes started this morning, on the landing of the old building. All kinds of rings, silverware, metal boxes, bowls, tie pins and many other articles are on exhibition. Tomorrow the grade school teachers will be

GIRLS' EXHIBITION DEBATE TEAMS

Front Row: Julia Moriarity, Nellie Munson (Capt.), Helen McCoy.
Back Row: Valentia Meng, Belle Kaufman (Capt.), Ruth Lewis.

GIRLS' DEBATING TEAM PREPARED FOR EXHIBITION DEBATE TOMORROW

Resolved, That Public Opinion Should Favor the Million Population Plan for Indianapolis Is Question—Nellie Munson and Belle Kaufman Are Captains.

JOURNALISM ECHO

The second Journalism Echo for the year appears today, as a project of the second semester class in Journalistic Composition. We are indebted to Miss Pratt and the Tuesday staff for the opportunity to

Feminine Socrates and Demosthenes will exhibit their debating skill Wednesday at auditorium exercises. "Resolved, That public opinion should favor the million population plan for Indianapolis" is the subject for

Journalism Echo

MEREDITH NICHOLSON IN INTERVIEW GIVES HIS VIEWS ON WRITING

Receives Great Enjoyment When Writing "House of the Thousand Candles."

By Doris Bernstein

"I received more enjoyment writing "The House of the Thousand Candles" than I did in writing any other book," said Meredith Nicholson, prominent Indiana author of essays, poems, and novels, in a recent interview.

Mr. Nicholson said he had always been a great reader when a boy, as was also his father, and that was what gave him his first desire to become a writer.

Mr. Nicholson believes that the genius of writing must be in the person and that all the training in the world can not make that person write if he does not have the gift.

"Too many young people set their ambitions on becoming writers and nothing else, and then are badly disappointed in the end when they discover they are failures in that field of work."

Mr. Nicholson, himself, left high school during his first year, at the age of fifteen years.

"However," he declared, "that does not mean that one with the gift of writing has not the need of education

The chain-store legislation was part of an effort by independent retailers to preserve traditional forms and methods of business, an effort that also attracted general anti-big-business support during the depths of the Depression and benefited from the search by state government for new sources of tax revenue. In the mid- and late 1930s independent retailers also took their case against big business to the federal government. Congress passed some legislation in 1936 and 1937 that, while sympathetic to the cause of small retailers, did not adversely affect the competitive strength of large chains.[45] Indeed, it is likely that by the late 1930s most Hoosiers and other Americans had come to accept large chains as efficient mass distributors. Though small retailers continued to appeal for and receive some special government protection, the chains had proved their abilities to effect efficient, low-cost, mass distribution. By the eve of World War II Standard Grocery, J. C. Penny, Woolworth, Hook's Drugs, and the dozens of other large retailers were an accepted part of Indiana's main streets.

The chain-store legislation of 1929 and 1933 was an example, in part, of state government's attempt to regulate one kind of business for the benefit of another. State government also entered into efforts at business regulation to improve the quality of the environment. Strip mining of coal provides an example of an industry affected by this type of regulation and demonstrates some of the significant features of business-government relations.

Strip mining of coal was more efficient and profitable and less dangerous than underground mining, and, as noted above, it became the major form of coal production during the interwar years. But strip mining left behind a desolate landscape of ridges and valleys that were covered with soil of low fertility and prone to erosion. To counter adverse public reaction, coal operators and the Indiana Coal Producers Association began to encourage and sponsor voluntary tree planting on spoil banks, while at the same time lobbying against passage of a state restoration law. In

[45] The most important federal laws were the Robinson-Patman Act of 1936 and the Miller-Tydings Act of 1937. See Ellis W. Hawley, *The New Deal and the Problem of Monopoly: A Study in Economic Ambivalence* (Princeton, N.J., 1966), pp. 247-269.

1941, however, the Indiana Farm Bureau and others succeeded in persuading the General Assembly to pass a strip mining law. As the counsel for the Indiana Coal Producers, Carl M. Gray, later recalled, by 1941 "it was obvious we were going to get some regulations." To prevent more stringent legislation, Gray and his associates worked with legislators to write a law "we knew we could live with." The 1941 legislation required operators to plant grass or trees on all land that had been strip mined, under the supervision of the Indiana Department of Conservation. Although from the viewpoint of those most concerned with the environment it was a step forward, the issue was far from resolved and continued to be a source of conflict in the post-World War II decades.[46]

The tax on chain-store owners and the regulation of strip-mine operators are only two examples among many efforts at state government intervention in the economy that had limited effects on business. There were other attempts at government intervention that were more truly regulatory in purpose and result. Chief among these was the work of the Indiana Public Service Commission, which was established in 1913 to provide more careful and uniform regulation of utilities and transportation. As noted in Chapter VII, the commission had only limited influence on transportation because so much of this activity was interstate in character and therefore subject to federal regulation. The commission's role in utility regulation was more significant and more controversial. By the late 1920s there was a strong movement for abolition of the commission, a movement that came not from utility interests but from consumers and municipal government

---

[46] Gray interview, April 12, 1979, pp. 24, 51, Oral History Research Project Mss.; Indiana *Year Book*, 1941, p. 1002; 1942, pp. 104, 196-197; *Laws of Indiana*, 1941, pp. 172-181; Lee Guernsey, "Reclamation of Strip-Mined Lands in Vigo County, Indiana," Indiana Academy of Science *Proceedings*, LXVII (1957), 215-221. Many underground miners resented strip miners, who they believed took away jobs in the industry. In 1940 the convention of Indiana's District 11 of the United Mine Workers passed a resolution calling for state environmental legislation to regulate strip mining. Jack Foster, Union on Trial: The United Mine Workers of America, District No. 11 of Indiana, 1930-1940 (Ed.D. dissertation, Ball State University, Muncie, Ind., 1967), pp. 189-191.

officials seeking local control of companies providing electricity, gas, water, and telephone service, especially those that were municipally owned. The utility companies, including the large electrical holding companies represented in Indiana by the Insull interests, tended to support the Public Service Commission, doubtless because they preferred to deal with one established statewide agency rather than many local commissions or regulators. Critics charged that the Public Service Commission allowed rates that were too high, particularly after 1929, when general prices and wages fell rapidly. Part of the commission's difficulties reflected the inadequacy of its staff compared with the skilled lawyers and engineers who often represented the utility companies. In response to these arguments, Governor Paul McNutt in 1933 reorganized the commission and appointed a full-time counselor to represent consumers in rate cases. The first public counselor was Sherman Minton, who succeeded in bringing about some significant reductions in rates, thereby pleasing a sufficient number of Hoosiers to win a U.S. Senate seat for himself in 1934. Controversy over utility regulation did not end with the changes made in 1933, but the work of Minton and his successors combined with increasingly stringent federal regulation of public utilities to reduce some of the public discontent.[47]

Another area in which state regulation changed in the interwar years was finance and banking. Since the early nineteenth century Indiana government had regulated banks, generally under the assumption that these important businesses were entrusted with a large public interest and were especially susceptible to monopoly power and abuse. Despite the efforts of the state Department of Banking, created in 1919, many Indiana banks in the 1920s seemed plagued by poor management and were overly prone to failure: in 1927, twenty-eight failed; in 1928, twenty-four; in 1929, twenty-one. The Great Depression exacerbated the problem: sixty-four

[47] Indianapolis *News*, February 7, 1925, March 5, 1927, June 13, 1931; Feightner, *Our State Government*, pp. 76-77; Neff, Paul V. McNutt, pp. 159-161; Indiana *Year Book*, 1935, pp. 796-797; 1940, pp. 746-747, 949-950. Data on revenues and operating expenses of all utility companies in Indiana are provided annually in the report of the Public Service Commission, published in the Indiana *Year Book*.

Indiana banks failed in 1930, eighty-two in 1931. In 1931 Governor Harry G. Leslie appointed a commission to study the problem. The report of the Study Commission for Indiana Financial Institutions, submitted in 1932, concluded that many banks suffered from ruinous competition, poor management, and inadequate regulation. The commission's recommendations for codification and revision of existing laws were fully accepted by the McNutt administration and were enacted during the hectic legislative session of 1933 as the Indiana Financial Institutions Act. The Department of Financial Institutions which was created by this act had considerably expanded authority to regulate banks and other financial institutions by stricter control over applications for charters and by overseeing bank liquidations. The premier staff member of the new department was Herman B Wells, a young member of the Indiana University faculty who had served as research director of the 1932 study commission. Wells played a crucial role both in shaping the 1932 report and subsequent legislation and also in implementing it. The new regulatory structure he helped to create proved to be a model state agency. Reinforced by federal legislation, it remained in place far into the post-World War II years, providing a stable yet flexible banking system—one composed of a smaller number of banks with larger average resources than prior to the Depression and the 1933 legislation.[48]

Regulation of chain stores, strip mining, utilities, and banks indicates the many and varied ways in which state government affected business. By the time of Pearl Harbor, dozens of agencies

[48] Study Commission for Indiana Financial Institutions, *Report* (Indianapolis, 1932), is a model of government reports. It abounds with statistical data for Indiana and other states, includes a broad historical, comparative context, and discusses the significant issues. Readers of this report gain insight into why Herman B Wells became dean of the Indiana University businesss school and then president of the university before the decade was over. See also Neff, Paul V. McNutt, pp. 199-205; Joseph Aloysius Kehoe, *Some Financial Trends of National and State Commercial Banks in Indiana, 1915-1954* (Washington, D.C., 1956), pp. 7-9, 43-45; Edward E. Edwards and Gerald C. Fischer, *Banking Structure in Indiana with Recommendations for Change* (Bloomington, Ind., 1968), pp. 3, 8-11; Indiana Bankers Association, *Report of the Research Committee: 1937* (n.p., 1937), pp. 29-68; Herman B Wells, *Being Lucky: Reminiscences and Reflections* (Bloomington, Ind., 1980), pp. 48-61.

and boards existed in the state capital, ranging from the Alcoholic Beverages Division to boards licensing architects, beauticians, dentists, engineers, funeral directors, medical doctors, nurses, pharmacists, optometrists, podiatrists, and barbers, as well as agencies for state planning and health.[49] Some had been created prior to World War I, some after. Many extended their power in the 1930s. And yet, by 1940 state government's influence on business was minimal and seldom strongly regulatory. Doubtless even that limited regulation and intervention had some positive effects on the public welfare. Perhaps just as often it served to help one business obtain or maintain an advantageous competitive position over another. By setting standards for beauticians and banks, the state helped free them from the "ruinous" or "excess" competition of smaller, less skilled, or lower-paid entrepreneurs, just as the chain-store tax attempted to protect independent merchants from multiunit retailers. Often government regulation combined varying degrees of individual self-interest with always subjective definitions of the public welfare.

Local government also provided a small degree of business regulation, especially in the larger cities. Here, too, the objective often was to provide for the public welfare by preserving public health and safety. And here, probably more than at the state level, government was also responsive to the concerns of local business leadership. Indeed, the few available studies suggest that businessmen played the dominant role in local government, exerting their influence both individually and in organizations like chambers of commerce and other groups. Often they insured that regulation would be to their advantage.[50] The zoning laws which proliferated in the 1920s provide such an instance of local

[49] Reports of all these agencies are found in the Indiana *Year Book*, 1940. Public health agencies and legislation are treated in Chapter X.

[50] Lawrence H. Wendrich, Municipal Policy Determination in Kokomo, Indiana (Ph.D. dissertation, Indiana University, Bloomington, 1947), pp. 238-254; Duncan, Control of the City Government in Indianapolis, pp. 45, 157-162, 451-461. The theme of business dominance in Muncie pervades the *Middletown* studies, although it is likely Helen and Robert Lynd exaggerated the local power of business and especially of the Ball family. See Frank, "Who Governed Middletown? Community Power in Muncie, Indiana, in the 1930s," *Indiana Magazine of History*, LXXV, 321-342.

government regulation. In 1921 the state legislature passed an enabling act, and in November, 1922, Indianapolis became the first Indiana city to pass zoning legislation. The city ordinance established districts for residential homes, apartment houses, retail business, and industries and placed restrictions on lot sizes and building heights. This classification and restriction of land use was an attempt to reduce urban congestion and improve the quality of life. A noisy or dirty factory could be prevented from locating on a residential street. In addition to promoting the public welfare, zoning also promoted the interests of some business groups, notably real estate agents, who played a major role in passage of the Indianapolis ordinance. Other larger cities in Indiana adopted zoning ordinances in the 1920s also, although by 1935 there were still fifteen cities of more than ten thousand residents which did not have zoning regulations. It is likely that, as in most American cities, the zoning ordinances of the 1920s served less to advance the cause of urban planning than the interests of real estate agents and other businessmen, who often shaped the legislation and influenced its enforcement.[51]

Rather than regulating business, local government and citizenry often placed their primary efforts on attracting new businesses to their community. They raised money to recondition abandoned plants and to provide land free or at low cost for new factories. And, as noted below, they often sought to insure and publicize the existence of a harmonious, nonunion labor force. Especially during the Great Depression, local communities seemed more interested in attracting business than in regulating it.[52]

[51] Duncan, Control of City Government in Indianapolis, pp. 236-271; Garland August Haas, The Legal Background to the Preparation and Administration of Zoning Ordinances in Indiana (M.A. thesis, Indiana University, Bloomington, 1948), pp. 11-13; "Indianapolis Adopts Zoning," National Municipal Review, XII (1923), 43-44; Indianapolis News, November 27, 1922; Indiana State Planning Board, Preliminary Report on a State Plan for Indiana, pp. 23-24; Wendrich, Municipal Policy Determination in Kokomo, pp. 162-165; Seymour I. Toll, Zoned American (New York, 1969), pp. 188-210.

[52] Wendrich, Municipal Policy Determination in Kokomo, p. 9; Lynd and Lynd, Middletown in Transition, p. 366. In The Magnificent Ambersons (New York, 1918), Booth Tarkington noted "the new kind of young men in business

State and local government intervention in the economy was minimal during the interwar years, and adverse or coercive regulation of business was rare. Traditions of individual freedom and a laissez-faire economy maintained a stronghold in the state legislature and city councils during the 1920s. The 1930s saw a significant shift in business–government relations, but the major force for change came not from city halls or the state capitol but from Washington.

Federal government intervention in the economy—often to encourage economic growth—had begun with the new nation and, with shifting force and emphasis, was a part of American life throughout the nineteenth century. The Progressive movement of the early twentieth century brought an increase in efforts to expand regulatory legislation, which Franklin D. Roosevelt's New Deal amplified and extended in the 1930s. An initial New Deal concern was to stimulate business recovery through various programs of government aid. Most significant was the National Industrial Recovery Act of 1933, which sought to eliminate cutthroat competition, raise prices, and improve the conditions of labor by establishing codes of "fair competition" for different industries. Because the power of NRA extended only to industries engaged in interstate commerce, the federal government encouraged states to establish "little NRAs." Governor McNutt's strong New Deal support extended also to NRA, but not until the biennial session of the legislature convened in 1935 was he able to obtain the necessary state legislation. In March, 1935, Indiana became one of only a few states to pass a "little NRA" enabling bill. By then NRA had lost considerable support among business leaders and other elements of the public. To conservative businessmen like Benjamin Douglass, who owned a canning factory in Brown County, it was a "weird experiment in governmental meddling. . . ." To others it seemed to fail because it allowed too much power to business, especially big business and trade associations.

---

downtown." "They had one supreme theory: that the perfect beauty and happiness of cities and of human life was to be brought about by more factories" (pp. 388, 389).

The debate declined in importance when the Supreme Court declared the federal act unconstitutional in May, 1935.[53]

There were other New Deal efforts to bring about business recovery and, after 1935, to counter what New Dealers thought were excessive powers of big business. Federal regulation of banking, finance, and utilities was joined by modest efforts to attack monopoly or near-monopoly conditions in several industries. Historians differ over the meaning and significance of these measures and of the New Deal itself, but there is little doubt that the size and power of the federal government expanded considerably during the 1930s.[54]

Nor is there much doubt that President Roosevelt wished to save capitalism and avoid social or economic revolution. The economic structure of the nation was indeed modified by the New Deal, and the power of business was balanced by the increased power of federal government in a shift that would continue through the years of World War II and after. Yet the basic features of American business remained in place. Businessmen in Indiana and throughout the nation nonetheless were often vehement in their denunciation of Roosevelt and his "radical" New Dealers, particularly after the first year or two of his presidency. Robert and Helen Lynd reported that in 1935 Muncie businessmen thought their backs were "squarely against the wall," as there was " 'an insane man in the White House, . . .' "[55] Federal regulation of business, combined with New Deal social welfare

[53] Benjamin Wallace Douglass, *The New Deal Comes to Brown County* (Garden City, N.Y., 1936), p. 20; "State NRA Unsatisfactory to Big Majority of Members," Indianapolis Chamber of Commerce *Activities*, LI (March, 1935), 2; Lynd and Lynd, *Middletown in Transition*, pp. 22-24; Patterson, *The New Deal and the States*, pp. 112-117; Neff, Paul V. McNutt, pp. 251-253; Indianapolis *News*, March 12, 1935. For the complex relationships among the federal government, coal operators, and the United Mine Workers in the 1930s see James P. Johnson, *The Politics of Soft Coal: The Bituminous Industry from World War I through the New Deal* (Urbana, Ill., 1979).

[54] For the general nature of the controversy see Richard S. Kirkendall (ed.), *The New Deal: The Historical Debate* (New York, 1973).

[55] Lynd and Lynd, *Middletown in Transition*, pp. 498, 499. See also Douglass, *The New Deal Comes to Brown County*, and Samuel B. Pettengill, *Smoke-Screen* (New York, 1940).

programs, agricultural planning, and a burgeoning federal bureaucracy, appeared to deny the individual freedom that businessmen and others thought they had enjoyed traditionally in the past and ought to enjoy in the future. Others argued, in reply, that social, economic, and technological change had already made traditional definitions of individual freedom outmoded. Indeed, some argued, business itself was at the forefront of many of these changes.

§ § § §

The New Deal also effected a significant change in the conditions of labor. By its programs the Roosevelt administration expanded government influence over the conditions of work and, above all, over the propensity of labor to organize effective unions. For Indiana the consequences were of major, long-term significance.

Indiana's employed workers in 1920 numbered 1,117,032, a figure that rose slightly during the 1920s and dropped precipitously in the early 1930s. By 1940 the number of workers was still below the number in 1930. Within those aggregate numbers occurred changes in distribution of occupations as shown in Table VI. The major decline was in agriculture, a response to the important economic and technological changes on Indiana farms. In 1920 manufacturing for the first time in Indiana history employed a larger percentage of workers than agriculture, and it remained the largest category of employment through the interwar years. Though there was a drop in the percentage of workers employed in manufacturing in the 1930s, this sector of the economy continued to employ a much larger proportion of workers in Indiana than in the nation as a whole. The largest numbers of manufacturing workers were in the steel, automobile, and electrical and nonelectrical machinery industries, which together in 1940 accounted for 52 percent of the workers in this sector of the Indiana economy. There were substantial percentage increases in workers employed in wholesale and retail trade and in service and clerical jobs. The latter category included occupations ranging from domestic workers to medical doctors and

TABLE VI
Percentage Distribution of Workers,
Indiana, 1920-1940[56]

	1920	1930	1940
Agriculture	26.3	20.0	17.8
Mining	3.0	1.7	1.2
Manufacturing	33.8	34.6	30.0
Transportation	7.5	8.3	7.0
Wholesale and Retail Trade	10.3	12.2	16.3
Service, Clerical, and Other	19.1	23.1	27.7
Employed Workers Total Number	1,117,032	1,251,065	1,151,703

schoolteachers and had already begun its rapid twentieth-century growth. These latter two categories, trade workers and service and clerical workers, attracted 68 percent of the women employed outside the home in 1940, thereby helping account for the increasing ratio of female to male workers: in 1920, 16.6 percent of all Indiana workers were women; in 1930, 18.8 percent, and in 1940, 21.7 percent were women.[57]

Workers in Indiana experienced the challenges and difficulties that nearly everywhere were part of the industrialization process. Changes in technology and production methods created new jobs while modifying or eliminating others. Skilled shoemakers at U.S. Rubber in Mishawaka, limestone cutters in the Bloomington-Bedford mills, machinists at GM's Allison Division, and glass-blowers at Macbeth-Evans in Marion were among the many skilled workers whose jobs were increasingly performed by new machines operated by unskilled or semiskilled laborers. Jobs re-

[56] United States Bureau of the Census, *Fourteenth Census* (1920), IV, *Population*, p. 48; United States Bureau of the Census, *Fifteenth Census* (1930), IV, *Population*, p. 471; United States Bureau of the Census, *Sixteenth Census* (1940), III, *Population*, Pt. 2, p. 1016.

[57] *Ibid*. The largest employers of women in Indianapolis were Real Silk Hosiery Mills, L. S. Ayres department store, and Indiana Bell, each of which employed over a thousand women in 1929. *The Leisure of a People*, pp. 478-482.

quiring few or no skills were especially important in mass-production industries where they not only caused some displacement of skilled workers but also provided new sources of employment for women and young people—often the sons, daughters, and wives of farmers from Indiana and from Appalachia and the deep South.[58]

While displacement of workers and changes in the nature of work and the work force caused tension and conflict in factories and industries, most of the issues to which workers publicly responded were the more direct ones of wages and hours of work. In seeking increased material returns, workers, like managers and owners, found strength through large-scale organization.

The years immediately following World War I were beset with labor strife, as strikes and violence broke out in many areas of the state. Nineteen nineteen was an especially difficult year: violence and rioting accompanied strikes by telephone operators in Greene County, by employees of the Standard Steel Car Company in Hammond, and, most notable of all, by steelworkers in Gary and East Chicago. The failure of the 1919 national steel strike set the tone for the union movement during the next dozen years. Calumet region steelworkers surrendered to management in early 1920 without gaining union recognition, a reduction in their twelve-hour day, or any other concession. The steel companies, particularly U.S. Steel, emerged from the strike determined to resist collective bargaining and to protect and extend the open shop. In Indianapolis negative reaction to the 1919 strikes and general anti-union sentiment led the city council to enact an antipicketing ordinance, prohibiting picketing of any kind. Despite continued opposition from labor unions, the 1919 city ordi-

[58] Caroline Manning and Arcadia N. Phillips, *Wage-Earning Women and the Industrial Conditions of 1930: A Survey of South Bend* (Washington, D.C., 1932), p. 3; Batchelor, *An Economic History of the Indiana Oolitic Limestone Industry*, p. 244; Goldthwaite interview, March 9, 13, 1979, pp. 6-27, Oral History Research Project Mss.; Lynd and Lynd, *Middletown*, p. 31; Carl R. Dortch interview by R. T. King, February 9, 1979, transcript, p. 14, Oral History Research Project Mss., Lilly Library, Indiana University, Bloomington; Frank, Politics in Middletown: A Reconsideration of Municipal Government and Community Power in Muncie, Indiana, 1925-1935, pp. 38-40.

nance remained in effect until 1937. By 1923 the Associated Employers of Indianapolis—a powerful business group dedicated to destroying the closed shop—could claim that the city was the most successful open-shop town in the nation.[59]

There were sporadic strikes in Indiana after 1919—notably of coal miners and railway shopmen in the summer of 1922[60]—but the decade was generally peaceful, with few signs of organized labor strength. The decline of union power during the 1920s was due to several factors. The failure of unions to win the strikes of the years immediately after the war and the strong counteroffensive they inspired—often equating unions with radicalism—reduced worker support. Some unions were hurt by the changing economy and technology. The United Mine Workers—probably the state's most powerful and progressive union—suffered because of the decline of the coal industry and the shift to strip mining. Perhaps most important, the prosperity of the decade after 1922 removed basic incentives for labor agitation as many, though by no means all, workers began a short step toward some of the material pleasures of middle-class life—best symbolized by ownership of an automobile, even if only a used Model T. The decline in labor unrest and union strength was also a response to company paternalism during the 1920s, as management attempted to improve the conditions of work. Some companies installed cafeterias, sponsored athletic teams, and provided company picnics and entertainments. Some sponsored company unions to air grievances and remove incentives for formation of independent unions. And some improved more basic conditions of work. By 1924, for example, U.S. Steel had largely adopted the eight-hour day, which removed a major employee grievance.[61]

[59] Phillips, *Indiana in Transition*, pp. 347-348, 358-360; Moore, *The Calumet Region*, pp. 509-528; David Brody, *Labor in Crisis: The Steel Strike of 1919* (Philadelphia, 1965), pp. 112-178; Fred Witney, *Indiana Labor Relations Law* (Bloomington, Ind., 1960), pp. 22-26; New York *Times*, June 25, 1923; Associated Employers of Indianapolis, Inc., *Industrial Indianapolis 'Under One Roof': Souvenir of the Indianapolis Industrial Exposition . . . 1921* (n.p., n.d.); Martin, *Indiana*, pp. 271-272.

[60] Work Projects Administration, *Indiana: A Guide*, p. 95.

[61] *Ibid.*, pp. 94-95; Moore, *The Calumet Region*, pp. 529-530; Batchelor, *An*

By and large, the major political parties remained aloof from organized labor's concerns prior to the Great Depression. Both state parties' platforms in 1920 appealed to the labor vote by recognizing employee rights to form unions and to bargain collectively. Both supported a limited working day for women but said nothing of men. The Democratic platform was slightly more positive in its labor planks than the Republican platform, but neither party showed strong support for organized labor. Prior to World War I, the state legislature had provided for factory inspection, workers' compensation, and regulation of working conditions for women and children. But these moderately progressive labor laws were generally limited in scope and effectiveness, so that the workers' world was little influenced by state government.[62]

The onset of the Depression in 1929 served only to reduce further the power of organized labor. In the gloomy words of Indiana State Federation of Labor President T. N. Taylor, "apathy, discontent, unemployment and lack of confidence combined to weaken the morale of our membership."[63] At the same time, however, as companies cut back wages and began layoffs, some workers began to lose faith in the paternalism that had characterized the 1920s. Instead they became convinced that they could no longer rely on the professed good intentions of management to provide job or wage security but rather had to organize to protect themselves. In several plants workers went on strike in efforts to win recognition of their unions. Major strikes occurred

Economic History of the Indiana Oolitic Limestone Industry, pp. 242-262; Orzack, Employment and Social Structure, pp. 98-111; Richard F. Lythgoe interview by R. T. King, May 3, 1979, transcript, pp. 11-14, Oral History Research Project Mss., Lilly Library, Indiana University, Bloomington; Edward Andrew Zivich, From *Zadruga* to Oil Refinery: Croatian Immigrants and Croatian-Americans in Whiting, Indiana, 1890-1950 (Ph.D. dissertation, State University of New York, Binghamton, 1977), pp. 47-48; Stevens, Heartland Socialism: The Socialist Party of America in Four Midwestern Communities, pp. 226-228.

62 Democratic and Republican state platforms, 1920, in Indiana State Platforms, I; Indiana Democratic State Central Committee, *What Democratic Legislatures Have Done for Wage Earners of Indiana* (n.p., [1920]); Phillips, *Indiana in Transition*, pp. 328-338.

63 Indiana State Federation of Labor *Proceedings*, 1933, p. 11.

at the Real Silk Hosiery Mills in Indianapolis in April and May, 1934, at the Wayne Knitting Mills in Fort Wayne in June, 1935, and the garment factories of M. Fine & Sons in New Albany and Jeffersonville in the fall and winter of 1935.[64] The largest strike, involving about twenty-five thousand workers, occurred in Terre Haute in July, 1935. The relatively strong union tradition and sentiment in the city helped to escalate the strike at Columbian Enameling and Stamping Company into a general strike that nearly paralyzed the city. Governor McNutt declared martial law and sent one thousand national guardsmen. Peace returned after three days of violence and 185 arrests, although martial law remained in effect until February, 1936.[65] Strikes and violence in Indiana's coal mining region during the first half of the 1930s led McNutt to declare martial law in Sullivan County and to station National Guard troops at Shakamak State Park as a counter to violence.[66] Even at some plants with a tradition of good labor relations, such as U.S. Rubber's Mishawaka factory, the Depression brought bitterness and a rejection of the paternalism of the 1920s.[67]

The strikes and organizing activity in the first half of the 1930s were responses of workers not only to the Depression but also to new support from government. In 1933 the Indiana General Assembly passed an anti-injunction law, which prohibited courts from issuing injunctions against peaceful union activity (notably picketing). Combined with federal anti-injunction legislation passed in 1932, the state law was a boon to the labor movement,

[64] Work Projects Administration, *Indiana: A Guide*, p. 95; Neff, Paul V. McNutt, pp. 403-404.

[65] Work Projects Administration, *Indiana: A Guide*, pp. 95, 263; Neff, Paul V. McNutt, pp. 385-401. For indications of the intense reaction to the Terre Haute strike see the extensive correspondence in Box A, Drawer 102, McNutt Papers, Archives Division.

[66] Neff, Paul V. McNutt, pp. 376-384; Indianapolis *Star*, October 10, 1933; Foster, Union on Trial, pp. 112-149; Irving Bernstein, *The Lean Years: A History of the American Worker, 1920-1933* (Boston, 1960), p. 385.

[67] David Brody, "The Rise and Decline of Welfare Capitalism," in John Braeman, Robert H. Bremner, and David Brody (eds.), *Change and Continuity in Twentieth-Century America: The 1920s* (Columbus, Ohio, 1968), pp. 174-177; David Brody, "Labor and the Great Depression: The Interpretative Prospects," *Labor History*, XIII (1972), 242.

as it removed a major weapon of anti-union forces.[68] Even more important was section 7a of the National Industrial Recovery Act which was passed in 1933. A part of the early New Deal effort to bring economic recovery, section 7a guaranteed to labor the right to organize and bargain collectively without interference from management. "This is our big opportunity," Indiana State Federation of Labor President Taylor exclaimed.[69] Quickly workers formed local unions in several major plants, including the Bendix Products Corporation in South Bend and some of the automotive machine shops in Muncie. In most instances companies responded by refusing to recognize the new locals, often forming a company union as a counterforce. In some cases they threatened employees with loss of jobs if they joined the independent union. Some workers did gain experience in 1933 and 1934 in the mechanics of union organization, but their efforts had very limited results otherwise. Perhaps the most significant effect of section 7a was the intense opposition to the New Deal it generated among businessmen and others with anti-union sentiments.[70]

By 1935 even this limited union success seemed defeated when the Supreme Court declared the National Industrial Recovery Act unconstitutional. In the same year, however, Congress passed the National Labor Relations Act, often called the Wagner Act. The act prohibited employers from interfering with union organizers in their plants. It provided that the union could call an election, and, if a majority of employees voted in favor of the union, management had to bargain in good faith with the union as representative of the workers. This strong federal support was a major impetus to the dramatic changes of 1936 and 1937.[71]

Until the mid-1930s skilled workers enjoyed the greatest union

[68] Witney, *Indiana Labor Relations Law*, pp. 30-36; Charles C. Killingsworth, *State Labor Relations Acts: A Study of Public Policy* (Chicago, 1948), pp. 7-23.

[69] Indiana State Federation of Labor, *Proceedings*, 1933, p. 11.

[70] Sidney Fine, *The Automobile under the Blue Eagle: Labor, Management, and the Automobile Manufacturing Code* (Ann Arbor, Mich., 1963), pp. 205-206, 325-326; Lane, "City of the Century," p. 193; Lynd and Lynd, *Middletown in Transition*, pp. 26-34; Associated Employers of Indianapolis, Open vs. Closed Shop under NRA, September 25, 1933, mimeograph copy in Indiana Reformatory-Liquor Bill, 1933, McNutt Papers, Archives Division.

[71] Irving Bernstein, *Turbulent Years: A History of the American Worker, 1933-1941* (Boston, 1970), pp. 318-351.

strength, most of them in unions affiliated with the conservative American Federation of Labor (AFL), represented in Indiana by the Indiana State Federation of Labor. Much of the labor activity of the 1930s was directed toward organizing unskilled workers in the new mass-production industries, not on the basis of their craft or job but on the basis of their industry. In Indiana and the nation the Committee for Industrial Organization (CIO)— formed in 1935 and soon to be known as the Congress of Industrial Organizations—played a major role in organizing workers in mass-production industries, particularly steel and automobiles. Led by John L. Lewis of the United Mine Workers, the CIO's national efforts toward industry-wide organization in these newer industries had major effects on Indiana labor and business.[72]

The most significant efforts to organize workers throughout an entire industry were those in the automobile industry. The United Auto Workers (UAW) local at South Bend's Bendix plant was prominent in the drive to form an international union of all workers in the industry. The UAW became a full-fledged international union at its second annual convention, which was held in South Bend in April, 1936. Two months later the new international abandoned the more conservative, craft-oriented AFL in favor of affiliation with the CIO. At the same time the UAW and CIO launched a massive organization campaign directed at General Motors, the nation's largest manufacturer.[73]

GM operated plants in several Indiana towns, including Indianapolis, New Castle, Muncie, and Anderson. Often supported by the local community, both company officers and the individual plant managers strongly resisted UAW efforts to organize and win collective bargaining rights. When workers at GM's Toledo, Ohio, plant went out on strike, the company removed much of the machinery to Muncie. To attract the GM plant, Muncie's

[72] It is possible that the importance of the UMW in the growth of the United Auto Workers derived not only from Lewis's leadership but also from relationships among workers in the two industries. Indiana miners, with a long and strong tradition of union organization, may well have sought employment in the state's automobile factories after coal began to decline in the 1920s, bringing with them union experience and loyalty.

[73] Fine, *The Automobile under the Blue Eagle*, pp. 294-295, 327, 425-427.

political and business leadership eagerly promised that the city would remain an open-shop town. The mayor increased the size of the police force to prevent labor trouble, and the police picked up UAW organizers who attempted to distribute handbills downtown. The local radio station co-operated by refusing to air a paid UAW broadcast. There was little public sign of worker receptivity to union efforts. In January, 1937, when GM plants elsewhere were engaged in a bitter strike, nearly all Muncie's Chevrolet workers signed a letter sent to the GM president that assured him of their loyal support.[74]

The business and political response in nearby Anderson was similar but less peaceful. Two GM plants—Delco-Remy and Guide Lamp—employed eleven thousand workers in this city of about forty thousand. Local UAW membership in early 1937 was about four hundred. Anderson was a GM town, and the business leadership, mayor, police, radio station, and newspapers generally co-operated with the company's wishes. But they could not isolate Anderson from the nation during the crisis of 1936-1937. In late December, 1936, UAW members in GM's Flint, Michigan, plant began a sit-down strike, which quickly spread to other plants, including Anderson's Guide Lamp plant, where workers sought a reduction in their nine-hour day, pay for overtime, and an end to the company's speedup of their work. Nearly seventeen thousand of the town's residents responded to the sit-down by joining the Citizens' League for Industrial Security, an ad hoc group formed to resist the strike. Radio addresses and newspapers blamed outside agitators—UAW and CIO organizers—and condemned the small minority of strikers occupying the factory for keeping thousands of workers from their jobs. On several occasions violence broke out—in most cases initiated by anti-union forces. This was particularly the case on January 15, 1937, the so-called "night of violence," when a local mob drove union organizers from their downtown headquarters, ransacked the office, and drove away picketers at Guide Lamp. The plant

---

[74] Lynd and Lynd, *Middletown in Transition*, pp. 35-38, 44, 73, 366; Indiana State Federation of Labor, *Proceedings*, 1936, p. 37; Sidney Fine, *Sit-Down: The General Motors Strike of 1936-1937* (Ann Arbor, Mich., 1969), p. 49.

manager thanked the group for its work. The chief of police made no effort to interfere with their activity; the police blotter that night indicated there was "nothing to report." UAW efforts to obtain protection from Governor M. Clifford Townsend that violent night also failed.[75]

Despite the strength of anti-union forces in Anderson, the UAW eventually won. Governor Townsend sent seven hundred national guardsmen to Anderson, but only after the continued violence finally forced the mayor to request help. More important was help from outside the state. The UAW and CIO continued to send organizers to Anderson, including Victor Reuther and his wife, Sophie; the latter was given special responsibility to organize women at the GM factories. But it was the sit-down strike at Flint, Michigan, and the consequent agreement of GM in February, 1937, to regard the UAW as the collective bargaining agent for employees belonging to the union that provided the breakthrough. Although the door at GM was open, the Anderson local did not win immediate recognition. Not until April, 1940, did a majority of workers at Guide Lamp vote in favor of UAW representation, and not until 1941 did a majority vote for UAW at Delco-Remy. But 1936-1937 was the turning point in Anderson because of the effects of events outside Anderson. Only by the aid of federal labor legislation and by union activities and support from outside Indiana could Anderson union members and sympathizers overcome the great hostility and resistance in their community. The UAW succeeded in Anderson only because auto workers there were part of a national industry and national company that behaved with little regard for state or community

[75] Fine, *Sit-Down*, pp. 95, 212-216, 313-315; Indianapolis *Times*, February 16, 1937; National Labor Relations Board, *Decisions and Orders*, August, 1939 (Washington, D.C., 1940), pp. 119-160; Victor G. Reuther, *The Brothers Reuther and the Story of the UAW* (Boston, 1976), pp. 172-182; Claude E. Hoffman, *Sit-Down in Anderson: UAW Local 663, Anderson, Indiana* (Detroit, 1968), pp. 45-46; UAW Local 146 to M. Clifford Townsend, February 12, 1937, Box A, Drawer 109, Townsend Papers; Rex E. Roberts interview by R. T. King, August 13, 1979, transcript, Oral History Research Project Mss., Lilly Library, Indiana University, Bloomington.

boundaries.[76] Success came despite the opposition of local political and business leadership and perhaps despite the opposition or indifference of many other members of the public as well.

The General Motors sit-down strike of 1936-1937 had important effects outside the company. Without striking, South Bend's Studebaker workers shared the benefits of union organization. The managers of the small, independent auto company decided that it could not afford a strike and would have to follow in GM's wake. In May, 1937, Studebaker signed a bargaining agreement with the local UAW. Stronger resistance to unions at International Harvester in Fort Wayne kept the UAW from gaining recognition at the company's truck plant until 1941.[77] Workers at the Cummins Engine Company in Columbus also benefited from the growing strength of the UAW, but they rejected the large union in favor of their own Diesel Workers Union, which was organized in 1938. As one local organizer later recalled, "we thought we could run it better than those guys in Detroit."[78] In South Bend, Fort Wayne, Columbus, and elsewhere, Hoosier workers derived considerable strength from the power of the new industrial union whether they were members or not.

Union organization in the auto industry also influenced labor developments in the Calumet region's steel plants. The failures of 1919 were not repeated. The CIO's Steel Workers Organizing Committee (SWOC) was hard at work in 1936 and 1937. Its major victory came in March, 1937, when U.S. Steel—influenced by anticipation of a profitable year and by the settlement at GM—signed a collective bargaining agreement. Inland Steel and Youngstown Sheet and Tube refused to sign an agreement, how-

[76] Fine, *Sit-Down*, pp. 216, 317; Hoffman, *Sit-Down in Anderson*, pp. 68-77, 84-85.

[77] Frederick H. Harbison and Robert Dubin, *Patterns of Union-Management Relations: United Automobile Workers (CIO)—General Motors—Studebaker* (Chicago, 1947), pp. 122-136; Robert Ozanne, *A Century of Labor-Management Relations at McCormick and International Harvester* (Madison, Wis., 1967), pp. 149-151, 207, 233-234.

[78] John W. Rowell, "From the Depression to War, and How Employees Organized," *Power Team*, September-October, 1979, p. 9.

ever, and in May, 1937, SWOC called a strike. The "little" steel strike of 1937 was mostly a verbal and legal battle in Indiana. Helped by Governor Townsend's active mediation efforts, the plants reopened in July, 1937, although SWOC and the little steel companies did not sign union contracts until 1942.[79]

By 1939 Indiana's union members numbered 176,700, ranking the state eleventh in size of organized labor. Nearly 22 percent of Indiana's nonagricultural employees belonged to unions by 1939. While available data do not allow for precise delineation of the growth of membership during the 1930s, 10 percent of Indiana union members belonged to the newly organized steel and auto unions by 1939 and 30 percent to these and other unions affiliated with the CIO. The CIO and especially its steel and auto constituents would continue to grow rapidly in Indiana after 1939.[80]

The growing union membership in Indiana's major mass production industries should not obscure the fact that on the eve of World War II the great majority of the state's workers did not belong to unions. Resistance to unions in smaller towns and in smaller companies and industries was especially strong. Union organization made little or no headway in small canning factories, for example.[81] But resistance occurred also in larger cities and industries. Not until 1943 did the UAW succeed in organizing workers at GM's Allison Division in Indianapolis, in part because older, skilled machinists there resisted this large industrial union. And in some large, modern companies, such as Eli Lilly, a successful policy of benevolent paternalism, which included makework to avoid layoffs, helped influence workers to reject union

[79] Lane, *"City of the Century,"* pp. 194-196; Robert L. Tyler, "The Little Steel Strike of 1937 in Indiana: An Episode in the Continuing Conflict over a Philosophy of Labor Relations," Indiana Academy of the Social Sciences, *Proceedings,* II (1957), 115-122; Brody, *Labor in Crisis,* pp. 179-188; Townsend to Van A. Bittner, July 10, 1937, Box F, Drawer 111, Townsend Papers; Bernstein, *Turbulent Years,* pp. 496-497.

[80] Leo Troy, *Distribution of Union Membership among the States: 1939 and 1953* (New York, 1957), pp. 4-5, 14, 18.

[81] Benning, *The Vegetable Canning Industry,* p. 40; National Labor Relations Board, *Decisions and Orders,* July-September, 1938 (Washington, D.C., 1939), pp. 705-712.

organization efforts.[82] By the late 1930s the growing strength of labor unions led more progressive businesses to move away from head-on resistance to labor organizers and toward a more subtle and sophisticated response. By 1940 major companies employed specialists in personnel and industrial relations, who themselves met in local and state conferences to exchange ideas for improving employee-employer relations.[83] Workers themselves often resisted union appeals—perhaps in part because they were content simply with the right to organize—which, when combined with growing union membership elsewhere, may have been sufficient sometimes to win concessions from management for unorganized workers. And doubtless many workers resisted unions because of attachments to traditional concepts of individual freedom.

Even though most Hoosiers did not join unions, the 1930s was the decade of the great transformation for labor. Organized labor's newfound strength was reflected clearly in the increasing attention it received from politicians. McNutt's relations with unions were mixed, starting off rather well but souring later, especially when he declared martial law during the Terre Haute general strike. The Indiana Federation of Labor at its 1935 convention accused McNutt of strikebreaking and denounced "this attempt to establish a Fascist-Military-Dictatorship in our state . . . ."[84] Townsend made a special effort to win the votes of organized labor in 1936 and to maintain good relations with the unions after the elections. Because of labor's growing strength, Townsend was particularly cautious in using the National Guard or martial law in any way that might appear to be strikebreaking. Instead, with legislative support, Townsend organized the Indiana Division of Labor in 1937 to settle labor disputes through voluntary mediation rather than strikes.[85]

[82] Goldthwaite interview, March 9, 13, 1979, pp. 105-106, Oral History Research Project Mss.; Kahn, *All in a Century*, pp. 42-44.

[83] "What's New in Personnel and Industrial Relations," Personnel and Industrial Relations Institute, Purdue University, *Program*, 1940 (Lafayette, 1940).

[84] Indiana State Federation of Labor, *Proceedings*, 1935, pp. 110-111. For earlier warm approval of McNutt see *ibid.*, 1933, p. 32.

[85] *Ibid.*, 1936, pp. 41-44; 1937, pp. 39-40; Witney, *Indiana Labor Relations Law*, pp. 49-51; Indianapolis *News*, March 10, 1937.

Not all Hoosier Democrats shared Townsend's moderate sympathies with labor. By the late 1930s some believed that pro-labor legislation and sympathies had gone too far. The Democratic chairman in Ripley County lamented in 1938 that "there was no need for the National Administration, nor the State, to give labor everything, and persecute the employer and kill business."[86] Such attitudes would continue in Indiana, but, nonetheless, the power of organized labor in the economy and in politics expanded considerably and continued to grow after 1940.[87]

Labor's new strength did not generally reflect a rejection of American capitalism or democracy. Though some businessmen and newspapers professed to fear that labor unions were bringing radical ideas and objectives to Indiana, there is only slight evidence to justify such concerns. There were indeed socialists and communists in the labor movement, and they played a role in some Indiana strikes, including the Terre Haute general strike of 1935, but the numbers and strength of radical labor leaders were not large in Indiana.[88] Perhaps the most significant example of more radical response to labor's problems in Indiana came at the Columbia Conserve Company.

Columbia Conserve was a family-owned Indianapolis canning company operated by William P. Hapgood. In 1917 Hapgood began an experiment in industrial democracy by allowing workers to decide how the plant would be run. In 1929 he offered a profit-sharing plan in which workers' salaries were based on individual needs, the amount to be decided by a workers' committee. Married workers received more than single workers, and those with children received a two-dollar-a-week extra allowance for each child. Hapgood also gradually transferred company stock to employees; by 1930 the 151 workers had collective control of 51 percent of Columbia Conserve's voting stock. Columbia Con-

86 William A. Gutzwiller to James A. Farley, December 9, 1938, Box 95, OF 300, Democratic National Committee Papers. See also Pettengill, *Smoke Screen*, pp. 54-57, 109-112.

87 For business opposition to the Wagner Act and its enforcement see "Hope Seen for Some Change in Wagner Act," Indianapolis Chamber of Commerce, *Activities*, LVI (March 27, 1940), 1, 4.

88 Neff, Paul V. McNutt, pp. 292-294; Foster, Union on Trial, pp. 146-149.

serve gained nationwide attention; it was praised as a model of industrial democracy and denounced as an example of dangerous radicalism. Critics doubtless took solace in the company's troubles that came with the Depression. In addition to the usual problems facing business, Columbia Conserve was plagued with internal conflict after 1930. To William Hapgood's great consternation, his son Powers Hapgood and John Brophy, both of whom also played major roles in CIO organizing elsewhere, led some workers to agitate for a union. The company struggled through the 1930s, but a strike in 1942 and an adverse court order in 1943 led to the end of the experiment in industrial democracy.[89]

Columbia Conserve is significant in its uniqueness. Workers' ownership and other deviations from capitalism were the exceptions, despite the new strength among labor. Although many businesses emerged from the 1930s with slightly reduced power within and without the plant, the general nature of their organization and operation was not radically changed either by unions or government. Labor had more power, to be sure, but it was power used mostly to improve the material rewards and conditions of work within the context of the capitalist system, not to alter the system. Even the workers at Columbia Conserve ended up in that moderate position: in 1942 they organized a local AFL union.[90]

§ § § § §

It is not possible to delineate precisely the extent to which Hoosier workers, businessmen, or the Indiana economy generally benefited or suffered as a consequence of the economic changes in the interwar years. It is apparent that the state, which had

[89] William P. Hapgood, *An Experiment in Industrial Democracy: The Results of Fifteen Years of Self Government* (Indianapolis, [1933]); Kim McQuaid, "Industry and the Co-operative Commonwealth: William P. Hapgood and the Columbia Conserve Company, 1917-1943," *Labor History*, XVII (1976), 510-529; Russell E. Vance, Jr., An Unsuccessful Experiment in Industrial Democracy: The Columbia Conserve Company (Ph.D. dissertation, Indiana University, Bloomington, 1956); Michael D. Marcaccio, *The Hapgoods: Three Earnest Brothers* (Charlottesville, Va., 1977), pp. 165-188.

[90] Vance, Columbia Conserve, p. 314. Columbia Conserve went out of business in 1953.

lagged behind neighboring states in economic and especially manufacturing development, began in the interwar years to narrow
the gap. Comparisons of per capita value added by manufacturing
support this conclusion, as noted in Table II. So also do data on
per capita income. Through the 1920s and 1930s, Indiana ranked
in per capita personal income far behind the other east-north-
central states of Ohio, Illinois, Michigan, and Wisconsin and far
below the national average. The Depression brought a steep decline in per capita income everywhere, but for Hoosiers the drop
was more precipitous—declining from 87.1 percent of the nation's
average per capita income in 1929 to only 77.6 percent in 1932.
Indiana emerged from the Depression relatively better off than
before, however: per capita income dramatically increased after
1935. By 1941 the state had surpassed the national average in per
capita income, and its $726 figure was considerably closer to the
east-north-central states' average of $783 than it had been in 1929,
when Indiana's per capita income had been $612 compared to the
five-state average of $765. That Indiana was catching up with its
neighbors was even more apparent by 1945, when the state's per
capita income of $1,248 was nearly equal to the five-state average
of $1,314.[91] No doubt Indiana's improving income position rela-
tive to neighboring states was due to many factors, but it is likely
that the extensive growth and modernization of manufacturing
provided the primary base.[92]

[91] Frank A. Hanna, *State Income Differentials, 1919-1954* (Durham, N.C.,
1959), pp. 38-40. Considerably more study of income distribution and patterns
of social mobility is necessary before it is possible to estimate the effects of this
relative improvement in Indiana's economy on the state's population. Studies of
social mobility in Marion County for the periods 1905-1912 and 1938-1941 suggest
at least that the economic changes of the interwar years did not adversely affect
prospects for social mobility. Otis Dudley Duncan, "Methodological Issues in
the Analysis of Social Mobility," in Neil J. Smelser and Seymour Martin Lipset
(eds.), *Social Structure and Mobility in Economic Development* (Chicago, 1966),
pp. 51-97; Natalie Rogoff, *Recent Trends in Occupational Mobility* (Glencoe,
Ill., 1953); James N. Baron, "Indianapolis and Beyond: A Structural Model of
Occupational Mobility across Generations," *American Journal of Sociology*,
LXXXV (1980), 815-839.

[92] For an introduction to the debate among economists on this point see
Conference on Research in Income and Wealth, *Studies in Income and Wealth*.
Vol. XXII: *Regional Income* (Princeton, N.J., 1957), especially pp. 113-193.

The interwar years brought no thoroughgoing revolutions to labor or business. Spread across the state in large cities, small towns, and dusty crossroads were small stores, shops, and factories where conditions for owners and workers in 1940 were little different from those in 1920 and in some cases even 1880. But in many of the larger and most important industries, change was fundamental after World War I. In steel, automobiles, and oil, and also in smaller industries such as glass and chemicals, modern techniques of production and organization accompanied the productive and profitable flowering of big business and often big labor as well. There remained important traditional industries in 1940, including furniture, limestone, and coal. The extent to which they could survive and prosper would depend increasingly on their ability to adopt the technology and organization of modern big business. To be sure, there continued to be opportunities for the individual entrepreneur—the man or woman who built a new business from the bottom up. Perhaps the best example of this kind of success was the Madame C. J. Walker Manufacturing Company, established by a black woman in Indianapolis in 1910 to produce cosmetics for blacks. The company became the largest black-owned business in the state and one of the very few large companies in which a woman played a prominent role.[93] There also continued to be room for the traditional skilled craftsman who worked alone.

But modern big businesses, increasingly joined by organized labor and state and federal government, directed the center of the Hoosier economy and established the conditions of economic life for workers and managers. Increasingly, Hoosier workers and managers were parts of large organizations—organizations that were often parts of national and even multinational enterprises whose loyalties and concerns transcended local and state boundaries. The changes in business and labor combined with develop-

Indiana's manufacturing economy after 1940 was especially stimulated by war production. See Chapter XII.

[93] Mrs. C. J. Walker moved to New York in 1915, and thereafter black attorney Freeman B. Ransom directed much of the company's business affairs. Thornbrough, *Since Emancipation*, pp. 73-74.

ments in transportation and agriculture to bring to Indiana during the interwar years an economy much more like the economy of the late twentieth century than that of the late nineteenth century. Although these economic transformations were often gradual and uneven, they had momentous and long-term effects on the way nearly all Hoosiers worked, lived, and thought.

CHAPTER IX

EDUCATION AND RELIGION

SCHOOLS AND CHURCHES were fundamental institutions, functioning as the anchors of Hoosier communities and transferring
to youth the values and beliefs of the society. Because of their
importance, education and religion often became the battle-
grounds on which conflicts over broader social, political, and
cultural beliefs and issues were staged. During the 1920s and 1930s
schools and churches became important points of debate between
Indianans who wanted change and those who wished to leave
unchanged these institutions and their ways.

Few areas of life reflected major concerns and conflicts of
Indiana's citizens more clearly than public education. During the
interwar years there was widespread support for improving and
expanding the education available to the state's half million public
school students,[1] and considerable progress was made. Diagram 1
shows that higher levels of education had been reached by
younger Hoosiers on the eve of Pearl Harbor than those achieved
by their parents and grandparents. Not all Indianans agreed on
the kinds of education desirable or on the nature of changes necessary, however. Those citizens attuned to the demands of an
increasingly modern society argued for considerable improvements in Indiana's public schools. In particular, they saw the
need for more active direction from the state capitol in order
to provide a more centralized and standardized system of public
education. As justification, they cited Article VIII of the Indiana Constitution, which charged the state legislature with provid-

---

[1] Total public school enrollment in Indiana in 1919-1920 was 566,288; in
1929-1930 it was 667,379; in 1939-1940, 671,364. United States Office of Education,
Statistics of State School Systems 1945-46 (*Biennial Survey of Education in the
United States, 1944-46*, Washington, D.C., 1949), p. 41.

Median Years of School Completed
by Persons Twenty and Over, by Age:
1940, Indiana[2]

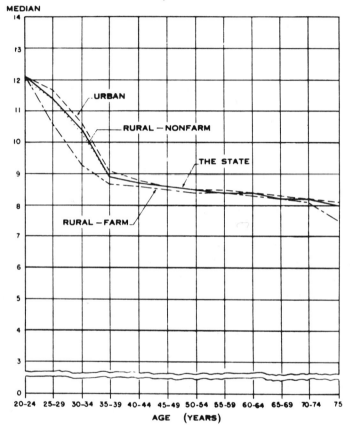

United States Bureau of the Census

ing "for a general and uniform system of common schools."[3]

Although there was no formal association of educational reformers or modernizers, the Indiana State Teachers Association
and several state superintendents of public instruction strongly

[2] United States Bureau of the Census, *Sixteenth Census* (1940), IV, *Population,*
Pt. 2, p. 680.

[3] See, for example, Commission for a Survey of the Problem of State Aid for
Public Schools, *Report* (Indianapolis, 1931), p. 8.

advocated more standardized, centralized public education. More broadly, Republicans and urban Hoosiers tended to favor change in the schools, often drawing support and ideas from sources outside the state.[4] Democrats and rural Hoosiers, especially in southern Indiana, were more likely to oppose change, arguing for a continuation of the tradition of local financing and control of public schools. They feared centralization would result in higher taxes and in school policies and programs that would not reflect the wishes of the local community. An anonymous country dweller wrote the Indianapolis *News* in 1925, clearly stating this position: "We ruralists who pay the tax to keep up our schools, etc., are to be told what we should have and do by the city intellectuals who do not help us in any way, for the amount of state tax that comes to the country from the cities and incorporated towns is and will be infinitesimal."[5] Although the specific issues in education during the 1920s and 1930s seldom evoked clear-cut battles between rural and urban Hoosiers, provincials and cosmopolitans, traditionalists and modernists, or Democrats and Republicans, they often reflected these orientations.

Those seeking changes in the educational system took the offensive in the years immediately after World War I, aided by agencies outside the state. In 1920 the Indiana Department of Public Instruction published a pamphlet titled *Why Does Indiana Rank 17?* The pamphlet was a response to a study of the nation's schools by the New York-based Russell Sage Foundation.[6] The report's conclusion that Indiana's schools ranked only seventeenth in the nation in quality of education was, the Department of Public Instruction pamphlet reported, "a shock of surprise to many Hoosiers, who had assumed Indiana's schools stood in the

---

[4] Support for these generalizations follows in this chapter. It might be noted here that differences between the two major political parties' positions on education appear in their party platforms during the 1920s. See Indiana State Platforms, I.

[5] Indianapolis *News*, January 1, 1925.

[6] Leonard P. Ayres, *An Index Number for State School Systems* (New York, 1920). See also John M. Glenn, Lilian Brandt, and F. Emerson Andrews, *Russell Sage Foundation 1907-1946* (2 volumes, New York, 1947), I, 284.

front rank."[7] A second pamphlet, also published by the Department of Public Instruction in 1920, called for a statewide effort to advance Indiana schools from seventeenth to first place. In November, Superintendent of Public Instruction L. N. Hines organized a ten-day series of conferences and public meetings across the state to consider the low ranking and respond to it.[8]

In March, 1921, doubtless reacting to this activity, the General Assembly passed a resolution recognizing that "public attention has been directed to the low rating of the Indiana school system. . . ." The legislators instructed the governor to appoint a five-member commission to study and evaluate public education "with a view to standardizing, unifying and correlating the various policies and agencies of such system in order that they may be in harmony with the educational requirements of the State."[9] The Indiana Education Survey Commission was soon at work—staffed and financed by the General Education Board of New York City, a philanthropic organization funded by John D. Rockefeller and oriented toward the goals of professional educators. The Survey Commission's report appeared in 1922; it documented in detail the shortcomings of Indiana schools and provided a formal statement of the issues and problems that would dominate the debate over education in the next several decades.[10]

[7] [Indiana Department of Public Instruction], *Why Does Indiana Rank 17?* [1920]. According to the study, Indiana's schools ranked sixteenth in 1900 and seventeenth in 1910. Ayres, *An Index Number for State School Systems*, p. 47.

[8] [Indiana Department of Public Instruction], *State Wide Campaign to Advance Indiana's Schools from Seventeenth to First Place* (n.p., [1920]); L. N. Hines to Jesse Greene, August 26, 1920, Vigo-Foreign, Correspondence, Department of Public Instruction Papers; Indiana *Year Book*, 1920, p. 604.

[9] Indiana *Senate Journal*, 1921, pp. 818-819, 903. Commission members were J. A. Van Osdol, lawyer, Anderson; Byron Somers, president of the Fort Wayne Board of Education; Carolyn Shoemaker, dean of women, Purdue University; William O. Schanlaub, county superintendent of schools, Kentland; and Charles M. Curry, professor of literature, Indiana State Normal School, Terre Haute.

[10] Indiana Education Survey Commission, *Public Education in Indiana: Report* . . . (New York, 1923), p. vii; General Education Board, *Annual Report*, 1922-1923 (New York, 1924), pp. 24-27. Not published until 1923, the Survey Commission's report was released in late 1922 and thus was available to the 1923 General Assembly. Indianapolis *News*, November 23, 1922.

The major theme of the Indiana Education Survey Commission's report was the inadequacy of Indiana's small rural schools and the consequent need to consolidate, centralize, and standardize the state's education system, particularly where it affected rural education. The state's forty-five hundred one-teacher schools, most of them located in rural townships, were not always the idyllic places of learning portrayed in art, poetry, and prose, or later recalled in the fading memories of former students. To the Survey Commission they were instead localist bastions of backwardness that were resisting the needs of a modern society. Using the recently developed tool of achievement tests, the Survey Commission found that pupils in one-teacher township schools scored significantly lower than pupils in city schools. Part of the fault for lower scores lay with the teachers: the commission concluded that "rural teachers are as a body immature, unprepared, inexperienced, and deficient in teaching skill."[11] In city schools, 52 percent of the elementary teachers had a high school degree and two or more years of teacher training. In the township schools only 7 percent of the elementary teachers met these standards. Rural teachers also had less experience. In the largely rural one-teacher schools, 65 percent of the teachers had less than five years' experience, while in the city schools the figure was only 23 percent. Less experience was matched with lower salaries in the one-teacher schools, where 69 percent of the teachers were paid only the state-mandated minimum of $800.[12]

The Survey Commission criticized other features of Indiana's schools, in almost every case finding conditions most deplorable in rural schools. Short terms generally handicapped Indiana schools. More than 70 percent of the state's high schools had terms of only 160 days or less, with shorter terms prevailing in small

[11] Indiana Education Survey Commission, *Public Education*, p. 21. See also William F. Book, *The Intelligence of High School Seniors as Revealed by a State-wide Survey of Indiana High Schools* (New York, 1922), pp. 229-230, 234.

[12] Indiana Education Survey Commission, *Public Education*, pp. 43-46. For general background on the criticism of rural education see David B. Tyack, *The One Best System: A History of American Urban Education* (Cambridge, Mass., 1974), pp. 14-27.

rural high schools.[13] The inadequacies of the school buildings also hindered education—again particularly in rural areas. The Survey Commission judged the majority of one-teacher schoolhouses to be in acute disrepair: "Roofs leak, the weather-boarding is missing here and there, doors are broken. . . ." Inside, "the walls are covered with dust and soot." Nearly all had outside toilets, which were "as a rule so ill kept and so filthy as to be a menace to the health and morals of the children."[14]

The many shortcomings of Indiana's public schools, especially in rural areas, were due, the Survey Commission reported, to the local and decentralized administrative and financial structure of the state's public school system, making "continuous state-wide leadership . . . impossible."[15] Indiana public schools were largely financed and administered at the local level. During the 1920s local property and poll taxes accounted for approximately 90 percent of school revenues, while state support amounted to less than 10 percent.[16] Federal support was virtually nonexistent. Because of this heavy dependence on local taxation and because of the wise disparity in population and wealth among communities in Indiana, there was considerable variation in the amount of money available to schools. In general, rural schools enjoyed less local tax revenue than urban schools, particularly in southern Indiana, even though the tax rate in the rural district might be higher.[17]

In response to the inequalities in local school revenue and the presumed variation in quality of education that resulted, in 1905 the General Assembly had passed a school relief or deficiency act, which allowed the state superintendent of public instruction

[13] Indiana Education Survey Commission, *Public Education*, pp. 99-100. Only Florida and North Carolina had average shorter high school terms than Indiana. At the same time, however, Indiana had a larger percentage of its population enrolled in high school than most states, ranking fourth in this statistic. *Ibid.*, pp. 98-100.

[14] *Ibid.*, pp. 88-89.

[15] *Ibid.*, pp. 264-265.

[16] Indiana State Committee on Governmental Economy, *Report*, p. 440.

[17] Indiana Education Survey Commission, *Public Education*, p. 183. Local school tax rates in 1922 varied from 8¢ on $100 of taxable property in Jordan Township, Warren County, to $1.82 in Boonville, Warrick County. *Ibid.*

Lawrenceburg in the January, 1937, flood

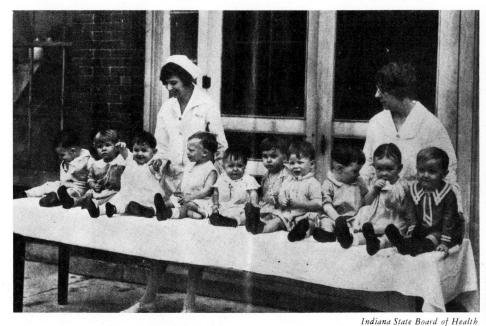

Better Babies Contest, 1927 State Fair

John Dillinger

Dr. Ada Schweitzer

to apportion 5.2 percent of the state school tax to poorer school corporations in addition to the regular per pupil apportionment. After 1905 the percentage of state school tax moneys set aside for the deficiency or relief fund gradually increased, so that by the 1920s, 30 percent of the total state school tax was allocated as extra aid to poorer school corporations, most of them in rural and southern Indiana. The 1933 State School Relief Act provided for even more aid to poorer school corporations. By 1940 nearly half the school corporations were receiving state relief funds, which on the average amounted to more than one fourth of their total operating costs.[18]

Compensatory financial aid to poorer schools helped, but it alone was not sufficient to overcome their shortcomings, especially if the aid was accompanied by few uniform standards or controls. In the late nineteenth and early twentieth centuries the state legislature had endeavored to establish uniform standards in several areas, including recommended and later required courses of study and textbooks.[19] Local communities continued to exercise great control after World War I, however, either through elected or appointed school boards in city and town schools or through the elected trustee in the township schools. It was the township trustee who caused reformers the greatest concern. Indeed, most of the significant debates over the public schools sooner or later came to focus on rural schools and the township trustee.

The Indiana Education Survey Commission reported in 1923 that the township trustee "possesses almost autocratic power over the schools."[20] According to critics, the trustee often exercised that power in ways not conducive to improving the quality of education. He often behaved like a partisan politician with only a

[18] *Ibid.,* p. 182; Indiana Rural Education Survey Committee, *Report,* March, 1926 (Indianapolis, 1926), p. 96; Edwin B. McPheron and Pressly S. Sikes, *Indiana's Program of Relief to Common School Units* (Bloomington, Ind., 1943), pp. 8-27; J. W. Jones and R. W. Holmstedt, *The Distribution of State Funds for the Purpose of Equalizing Educational Opportunity in Indiana: A Report to the Commission on State Aid for Public Schools in Indiana* (Terre Haute, Ind., 1930), pp. 11-23; Indiana *Year Book,* 1935, pp. 331-334; 1941, pp. 724-726.
[19] Phillips, *Indiana in Transition,* pp. 387-394.
[20] Indiana Education Survey Commission, *Public Education,* p. 134.

common school education—which he usually was—rather than like a professional educator—which he usually was not. His decisions in locating and constructing school buildings and purchasing school supplies often reflected his politically partisan and local orientation and sometimes his own economic self-interest as well. And critics asserted that the trustee used his power of appointing and dismissing teachers to reward friends and punish enemies, whether personal or political.[21]

The strength of the township trustee was matched by the weakness of the county superintendent of schools, who was elected by township trustees throughout the county in what was usually a partisan election. The office of county school superintendent was generally considered to be a political office, and the incumbent was expected to contribute to the party that elected him. In 1922 the majority of superintendents were natives of the county in which they were employed, and nearly half were serving their first terms. Few met the state requirement of a college degree and three years of teaching experience. Rather than being experienced, independent professionals overseeing the schools, therefore, county superintendents too often were the powerless errand boys of the trustees.[22]

By the early 1920s critics of Indiana's public education had concluded that the system's primary weakness was the low quality of rural schools and that the township trustee was the primary cause of this weakness. Thus, the Survey Commission concluded in its 1923 report: "The only way to correct the defects of the trustee system is to abolish the township as the local unit."[23] In-

[21] *Ibid.*, pp. 141-142; Indiana Rural Education Survey Committee, *Report*, p. 51; Indiana State Committee on Governmental Economy, *Report*, pp. 457-458. For additional discussion of the role of township trustees generally and particularly in poor relief see Chapter IV.

[22] Indiana Education Survey Commission, *Public Education*, pp. 135-140; William A. Baker, The Status of the County Superintendent of the State of Indiana (M.A. thesis, Indiana University, Bloomington, 1933), p. 98; Mark R. Gray (ed.), *Historical Resumé of the Indiana State Association of Township Trustees* (Indianapolis, 1930), p. 32.

[23] Indiana Education Survey Commission, *Public Education*, p. 144. See also "Ten Advantages of City Schools over Country Schools," *Indiana Teacher*, LXXIII (March, 1929), 16-17.

stead of the township, the Survey Commission proposed that the
county be made the primary unit of school administration and
financing as a necessary prelude to consolidation and centralization of public education.

Replacing the township with the county as the primary unit
in the public school system was supported by five former state
superintendents of public instruction and by many professional
educational organizations, including the Indiana State Teachers
Association, the Indiana County Superintendents Association,
the Indiana Parent-Teacher Association, and the Indiana State
Board of Education.[24] One of the leading spokesmen for the
county unit was Benjamin J. Burris, state superintendent of public
instruction from 1921 to 1924. Burris argued the advantages of
the reform, which would provide a county board of education
elected on a nonpartisan ticket to administer all schools except
city schools. The county board would have responsibility for
locating schools, purchasing supplies, appointing teachers, electing the county superintendent, and levying a uniform school tax.
In short, it would assume the functions of the independent township trustees. The advantages, according to Burris and others,
would include centralized purchasing of school supplies, more
efficient use of teachers, economy in location of schools (irrespec-
tive of township lines), a uniform and fair tax rate throughout
the county, and more uniform quality in schools throughout the
county and the state. Apparently mindful of the success of large-
scale, systematic organization and management in the modern
American business community, Burris concluded that the county
unit reform would allow for "the application of a well-established
business principle of organization and administration to a system
of rural education."[25]

In response to these arguments the Indiana Senate in January,

[24] Indianapolis *Star*, March 1, 1923; "State News," *Educator Journal*, XXIII
(1922-1923), 232.

[25] Benjamin J. Burris, "Necessity of the County Unit for the Efficient Administration of Rural Schools," National Education Association, *Address and Proceedings of the Sixty-first Annual Meeting, 1923* (Washington, D.C., 1923), pp.
789-795. The quotation is on page 789. See also Benjamin J. Burris, "The County
Unit of School Administration," *Educator Journal*, XXIII (1922-1923), 160-162.

1923, began debate on a bill that compelled schools to reorganize along county lines. Opposition to the original bill was strong, especially from the Indiana Farm Bureau, leading supporters to agree to an amendment that allowed voters in each county to decide by referendum whether to adopt the county unit plan. Even this major concession was not sufficient: the bill was defeated in the senate by a vote of seventeen to twenty-nine. All seventeen favorable votes were cast by Republicans, with the negative votes split almost equally between Democratic and Republican senators. The vote did not split exactly along rural-urban lines, although there was a tendency in that direction, most noticeable in the votes cast by all six senators from Marion County in favor of the bill. There was general agreement, according to the Indianapolis Star, that the bill was strongly opposed in rural Indiana.[26]

Opposition to the county unit plan continued after 1923. The Democratic party, with its strength in rural and southern Indiana, went on record in the mid-1920s in opposition to the plan.[27] Township trustees, not surprisingly, resisted a change that would deprive them of their responsibility in education—a responsibility that accounted for most of their duties. Parents and taxpayers in rural Indiana also showed reluctance to support the county unit plan. Some, almost certainly, simply were not interested in the issue of improving the quality of education, believing that what had been good enough for them was good enough for their children and perhaps distrusting the modernizing influence of education. Many feared that the county unit plan would result in higher property taxes, particularly to support transportation costs that would accompany school consolidation. And some viewed their local schools, especially their small high schools, as community centers, sources of local pride and identity—a sentiment most visible in the attachment to the local basketball team. A county unit plan, they feared, would bring larger, more distant schools

---

26 Indiana Senate Journal, 1923, p. 721; Indianapolis Star, March 1, 1923; Indianapolis News, January 16, 17, 1923.

27 Democratic party platform, 1924, in Indiana State Platforms, I. The Republican party platform of 1924 avoided the county unit issue, although it indicated general support for progress in education. Republican party platform, 1924, in ibid. See also Indianapolis News, May 9, November 3, 1924.

and perhaps a greater cost. They also feared the plan would reduce local control. One small-town newspaper succinctly stated
the case against the county unit reform: "Centralization always
militates against the rule of the people. Centralization always
means higher taxes. . . ." Another country editor was more expansive:

Now comes the theorists and reformers, led by the well paid experts
from the East and the self appointed prophets from the state university
and Purdue, ably re-enforced by the school book drafters and cheered
on by the politicians with a mania for centralization . . . . The taxpayer
has his belly full of centralized government. The trustees are particularly precious, for they represent the last vestige of the fading right of
the voter to have a personal hand in the management of local affairs.[28]

Proponents of the county unit plan were well aware of these
traditional and local concerns, and during the interwar years they
mustered data and arguments in response. They asserted that any
added cost in consolidated schools, such as higher transportation
costs, would be offset by economies in administration and purchasing and in more efficient grouping of pupils with teachers.
Most important, the educational reformers argued, the county
unit plan would improve the quality of education by allowing for
broader curricula and better-supervised teaching. In an effort to
demonstrate these benefits, the Department of Public Instruction,
with funds provided by the General Education Board, established
in 1924 a model countywide purchasing, accounting, and teacher
supervision project in Johnson and LaGrange counties. The centralized purchasing and accounting feature of the demonstration
project was judged as "almost a complete failure, since it was
impossible to get the necessary cooperation from all the [town-
ship] trustees." But the countywide teacher supervision experi-

[28] Winchester *Democrat*, January 8, 1925; Monticello *White County Democrat*, January 26, 1923. See also Roland E. Young, The History of School District
Reorganization in the State of Indiana (Ed.D. dissertation, Indiana University,
Bloomington, 1968), p. 98; Indiana Rural Education Survey Committee, *Report*,
p. 86; Gray (ed.), *Historical Resumé of the Indiana State Association of Township Trustees*, pp. 8-9; "Victorious—and Keeping Our Powder Dry," *Indiana
County and Township Officer*, III (February, 1935), 12; Indianapolis *Star*, January 4, 1925; Crawfordsville *Journal*, February 7, 1925.

ment was deemed successful in improving teaching and learning in the two demonstration counties, especially as evidenced by pupil scores on achievement tests. Whether the data, conclusions, and arguments were valid or not, they failed to convince opponents of the county unit plan. Not until the post-World War II years did Indiana move closer to county-organized schools.[29]

Educational reformers failed in their efforts to achieve their primary goal of the county unit plan. School consolidation did occur during the interwar years, however, but largely within the townships and at local initiative. Some township trustees and taxpayers recognized the advantages in sharing costs and facilities with their neighbors across township or town lines and formed joint schools, although each party retained its legal existence. This local co-operation and consolidation accounted for a reduction in the number of one-teacher schools from 4,500 in 1920 to 616 in 1945.[30] In a 1929 act the legislature provided for the formation of new school corporations in which a township could merge with a school town of less than fifteen hundred people, combining assets and liabilities to form a new entity. Although this act was an important precedent for the movement toward countywide school reorganization in the post-World War II years, it was little used during the period before 1945.[31]

While educational reformers failed to force radical change in the basically local organization and administration of public schools, they were successful in bringing about some increase in centralized state controls and, they hoped, in raising the quality of public education. One such area was teacher education and preparation.

[29] *Value of Rural School Supervision: Results of Two-Year Demonstration in Indiana* (Indiana Department of Public Instruction *Educational Bulletin No. 84,* Indianapolis, 1926), pp. 5, 6, 8, 11, 13. The quotation is on page 6. See also Indiana Rural Education Survey Committee, *Report,* p. 86; Indiana State Committee on Governmental Economy, *Report,* pp. 428-431, 461-478; Joint and Consolidated School Survey Commission, *Report* (Indianapolis, 1931).

[30] United States Office of Education, *Statistical Summary of Education, 1945-46 (Biennial Survey of Education in the United States, 1944-1946,* Washington, D.C., 1950), p. 16; Indiana *Year Book,* 1930, p. 931.

[31] Young, The History of School District Reorganization, pp. 89-91.

Reformers in the early 1920s concluded that Indiana's teachers, especially in the township schools, were woefully lacking in formal training.[32] Part of the explanation for the minimal training of teachers was the licensing system. Teacher licenses were issued on the basis of either credentials for academic work or an examination given by the state or county superintendent. Most elementary teachers in 1922 had licenses issued by county superintendents. It was commonly assumed that county licenses were easier to obtain than state licenses and that there was considerable room for the discretion of the county superintendent and particularly the township trustee in issuing a license.[33] The Teacher Licensing Law of 1923 closed the door of easy entry by county examination and reduced the level of trustee or superintendent capriciousness. The law marked a significant step toward standardization and professionalization of teacher training, as it required that all new licenses and renewals be issued by the State Board of Education and only for academic work completed in approved teacher-training institutions. The law required a minimum of one year of formal training beyond high school and encouraged prospective teachers to specialize in preparation for teaching either in rural schools, primary schools, or high schools. From this point on, the State Board of Education, not local individuals, would decide on the requirements for teacher training and would gradually raise those requirements.[34]

The reformers also achieved some success in reducing the arbitrary power of township trustees to dismiss teachers for personal or political reasons or to avoid paying salary increases to more experienced teachers. In 1927, over strong opposition from the township trustees, the legislature passed a teacher tenure law,

[32] Indiana Education Survey Commission, *Public Education*, pp. 35-36.
[33] *Ibid.*, p. 54.
[34] *Laws of Indiana*, 1923, pp. 36-50; Indiana *Year Book*, 1923, p. 283. The vote in the house on the teacher licensing bill was sixty-five in favor and twenty-nine opposed. With the exception of one Republican maverick, all negative votes were cast by Democrats; fourteen Democrats did vote in favor of the bill. Indiana *House Journal*, 1923, pp. 212-213. Democratic opposition to the Teacher Licensing Law continued after passage. The party's 1924 platform called for repeal of the law. Indiana State Platforms, I.

which granted all teachers a permanent contract after five years of service. Tenured teachers could be dismissed if the number of teaching positions declined but not for personal or political reasons.[35]

Efforts to improve the quality of education by means of standard and state-centered regulations also produced a more stringently written and enforced compulsory school attendance and child labor law in 1921. Most strongly advocated by the Republican party, the law required children under age sixteen to complete the eighth grade before leaving school.[36] The percentage of children aged five to seventeen attending school in Indiana increased from 79 percent in 1919-1920, to 85 percent in 1929-1930, and to 90 percent in 1939-1940, although factors other than the compulsory attendance and child labor law also influenced this change.[37]

While many of the legislative reforms affecting public schools in the 1920s and 1930s had as part of their general purpose the preparation of children for a more modern society, some innovations were very specifically oriented toward the assumed needs of the society and clearly mirrored the transformations and sometimes the conflicts of twentieth-century Indiana. One such area was modification of the school curriculum—a subject about which many professional educators had waxed enthusiastic since the late nineteenth century. Influenced by the progressive education movement led by John Dewey, many Indiana schools endeavored to make their curricula more practical and more flexible, especially at the high school level. Rather than concentrating on preparing students for college, as many high schools had done in the nineteenth century, educators focused on vocational training, preparation for daily living, and promotion of good character and citizenship. In the 1920s the Indiana Department of Public

35 Republican party platform, 1920, in Indiana State Platforms, I; *Laws of Indiana*, 1927, pp. 259-262. As noted below, financial considerations during the Depression led to repeal of tenure for teachers in the township schools in 1933. *Ibid.*, 1933, pp. 716-719.

36 Charles E. Gibbons, *School or Work in Indiana?* (New York, 1927), pp. 5, 11-12, 20; Ellen Nathalie Matthews, *Children in Fruit and Vegetable Canneries: A Survey of Seven States* (Washington, D.C., 1930), pp. 61-84.

37 United States Office of Education, *Statistics of State School Systems*, p. 50.

Instruction recommended a curriculum that placed "strong emphasis upon those objectives contributing to the social, moral and civic life."[38] The department became particularly interested in "character education," sponsoring statewide conferences in Indianapolis to promote this elusive objective. Courses in American history and civics were increasingly popular in the 1920s and 1930s, for, as the Department of Public Instruction's history manual advised, the study of the past allowed children to "note the conditions of success and failure and learn how to fashion [their] own lives for community service." Through history, civics, and other courses, the schools became primary agents in efforts to instill good citizenship, patriotism, and respect for law and order— to serve as stabilizing forces in a rapidly changing society.[39]

The school curriculum also moved toward other practical concerns in the interwar years—preparing students not to enter college or the professions but simply to get a well-paying job. Foreign languages, a staple of the late-nineteenth-century curriculum, continued to be taught, with Latin enjoying the largest enrollment. But there was a pronounced decrease in the ratio of foreign language enrollment to total enrollment during the 1920s and 1930s, as new courses in bookkeeping, manual arts, home economics, health, and physical education, as well as history and civics, were added, especially in urban schools. Vocational education courses received an important stimulus from the federal government, which began in 1919 to provide financial support for these programs.[40] The Evansville school system achieved national

[38] Indiana *Year Book*, 1928, p. 767. See also Indiana Education Survey Commission, *Public Education*, p. 106.

[39] Indiana Department of Public Instruction, *History Manual; United States History, Indiana History* (Indianapolis, 1926), p. 4; Indiana State Board of Education, Minutes, March 19, 1920, p. 226. See also Lynd and Lynd, *Middletown*, pp. 196-198; Indiana *Year Book*, 1926, p. 713; Errol Wayne Stevens, "Indiana History in the Junior High and Secondary School Curricula," *Indiana Magazine of History*, LXXVII (1981), 57-68.

[40] Berry, A Survey of Foreign Language Teaching in Schools of Indiana in 1935-1936, pp. 49-50; Lynd and Lynd, *Middletown*, pp. 193-196; Indiana State Board of Education, Minutes, January 18, 1924, p. 2; Feightner, *Our State Government*, pp. 46-47. Rural schools began to introduce vocational agriculture and home economics courses, with support from the Indiana Farm Bureau. Z. M. Smith to Frank E. Allen, December 27, 1934, Indiana State Board of Education Papers.

recognition as a pioneer in curriculum development. Among many changes and experiments undertaken in the 1930s, Evansville educators at Lincoln High School (where there was a black student body) introduced a course of study centering around housing. Offered partly in response to the opening of a new federal low-income housing project for black families, the new course was to be "an integrating-experience curriculum" and included units in the history of housing, in home life, home management and budgeting, and in home safety and disease prevention. The objective, in the words of an Evansville educator, was "to help the student learn through reality."[41]

Indiana's most widely known progressive curriculum program was that of the Gary schools, headed by Superintendent William A. Wirt, a native of Bluffton, Indiana, and a graduate of DePauw University. Beginning in 1907, Wirt developed the Gary Plan, in which a system of rotating classes allowed students to alternate between vocational and academic courses and between different sections of the school building. Sometimes labeled the work-study-play school or the platoon school, Wirt's system was designed to prepare large numbers of students for the business of living and to provide this preparation as efficiently and thoroughly as possible. Not coincidentally, the Gary Plan mirrored the practical needs and methods of the modern industrial society, especially as it had taken form at United States Steel's Gary Works in the early twentieth century. Seldom had school and society so clearly come into conformity.[42]

Indiana's public schools also reflected the broader society's attitudes, vacillations, and conflicts in race relations. In some schools, particularly in such northern Indiana cities as Fort Wayne,

[41] Harold Spears, *The Emerging High-School Curriculum and Its Direction* (New York, 1940), pp. 179-183. The quotation is on page 179. See also "Revolution in Evansville," *School and Society*, April 6, 1935, p. 479.

[42] Moore, *The Calumet Region*, pp. 471-485; Work Projects Administration, *The Calumet Region Historical Guide*, pp. 179-183. The Gary Plan fared less well in the 1930s, particularly after William A. Wirt's death in 1938 and after a critical report on the city's schools by investigators from Purdue University. See Cohen and Mohl, *The Paradox of Progressive Education*, pp. 123-159; Lane, "*City of the Century*," pp. 202-203.

South Bend, and East Chicago, black and white students sat side by side in integrated classrooms. In the southern part of the state, public schools were generally segregated and remained so until after passage of a state law in 1949 prohibiting segregation. The crucial changes and developments in race relations in the schools occurred in Indianapolis and Gary, cities which accounted for more than one half of Indiana's black population by 1930.[43] In both cities the trend during the period from 1920 to 1945 was toward greater segregation of white and black students.

In Gary nearly every black child attended segregated neighborhood elementary schools, which usually reflected the segregated residential patterns of the city. During the 1920s most black high school students attended Froebel School, where they accounted for about one third of the school's graduating class in 1930. Froebel, as one scholar has noted, was "Gary's 'token' melting pot school," containing in addition to its black population a large proportion of immigrant children. Froebel was also the Gary school that concentrated most heavily on educating future blue-collar workers.[44] The melting process at Froebel was token in part, because many school activities were segregated or were denied altogether to black students. Black students had a separate prom and commencement, and they were excluded from the yearbook, band, and most extracurricular activities. Blacks could use the school's swimming pool only on Fridays, the day before it was cleaned.

As Gary's black population increased, new space for black students had to be found. In 1927 school officials transferred eighteen black students to Gary's Emerson School. In protest, twelve hundred white students boycotted classes, chanting in front of the school: "We won't go back until Emerson's white." Whether or not the striking students represented the sentiments

[43] Thornbrough, "Segregation in Indiana," *Mississippi Valley Historical Review*, XLVII (1960-1961), 595, 608; Thornbrough, *Since Emancipation*, pp. 53-54, 57.

[44] Balanoff, Black Community of Gary, pp. 271-277. See also Neil Betten and Raymond A. Mohl, "The Evolution of Racism in an Industrial City, 1906-1940: A Case Study of Gary, Indiana," *Journal of Negro History*, LIX (1974), 55; Cohen and Mohl, *The Paradox of Progressive Education*, pp. 110-122.

of the larger Gary community, school officials surrendered four days after the strike began. They gave white students excused absences from class and removed black students to a temporary all-black school. Moreover, the Emerson School strike of 1927 led Gary officials to decide on the construction of a new high school exclusively for blacks. Roosevelt School opened in 1931 as one of the largest all-black schools in the Midwest, marking a new stage of more intense segregation in Gary.[45]

Black responses to the changes brought by the Emerson strike and the opening of Roosevelt varied. A large number resisted, arguing for integration of the public schools. The local chapter of the National Association for the Advancement of Colored People (NAACP), with financial support from national head-quarters, filed an unsuccessful suit to prevent the construction of a separate black school. Some blacks made the best of segregation and even welcomed it as an opportunity to teach black culture, foster race pride, and develop Roosevelt as an anchor of Gary's black community. Indeed, blacks generally showed more concern and involvement in Roosevelt and its policies during the 1930s than did whites for their schools.[46]

The opening of Roosevelt kept most of Gary's other schools white but did not stop the increase in the numbers of blacks at Froebel. In 1945, when nearly half of Froebel's students were black, a strike by the school's white students produced a crisis similar to that at Emerson nearly two decades earlier. Nationwide attention focused on Froebel after young singing idol Frank Sinatra came to Gary to perform and to denounce the student strikers. With support from school administrators and some civic leaders, the strike was settled without giving in to the demands of white students. Instead, tentative steps were taken to begin integration of Gary's other schools, including by the late 1940s, Emerson.[47]

[45] Moore, *The Calumet Region*, p. 393; Lane, "*City of the Century*," pp. 142-147.

[46] Balanoff, Black Community of Gary, pp. 286-287, 296; Lane, "*City of the Century*," p. 146; Cohen and Mohl, *The Paradox of Progressive Education*, pp. 154-158.

[47] Lane, "*City of the Century*," pp. 232-239.

Indianapolis also experienced racial conflict over its public schools. Indianapolis elementary schools were generally, but not entirely, segregated in 1920, reflecting patterns of residential segregation. The high schools were integrated. During the early 1920s, however, as the number of blacks in Indianapolis continued to increase, frightened whites responded with demands for segregation. Under pressure from such organizations as the Indianapolis Chamber of Commerce, the Federation of Civic Clubs, and the Mapleton Civic Association, the Indianapolis Board of School Commissioners moved to divide the races in the city's schools. New boundaries for elementary schools further segregated white and black children. In late 1922 the school board recommended construction of a separate high school for blacks. Black opposition to segregation led to an unsuccessful suit against construction of the new high school, supported as in Gary by the NAACP, though with some internal conflict between the organization's black lawyers and their white colleagues. In 1927, as the school was nearing completion, the school board announced that every black high school pupil in the city would attend the new school— a policy that lasted until the passage of the state desegregation law of 1949. The only victory blacks could claim in Indianapolis was the successful fight to change the proposed name of the school from Jefferson High School to Crispus Attucks.[48]

In addition to functioning as arenas for racial conflict, public schools also had to respond to the Great Depression. During the difficult years of the 1930s, Indiana schools suffered from the demographic and economic shifts accompanying the Depression. As the birthrate declined in the 1930s, total public school enrollments remained nearly stable: the total Indiana enrollment for school year 1941-1942 was almost exactly the same as that for

[48] August Meier and Elliott Rudwick, "Attorneys Black and White: A Case Study of Race Relations within the NAACP," *Journal of American History*, LXII (1975-1976), 932-933; Mohraz, *The Separate Problem*, pp. 123-130; Thornbrough, "Segregation in Indiana," *Mississippi Valley Historical Review*, XLVII, 601-606. It is important to note that the move toward increased segregation in Indianapolis cannot be attributed to the Ku Klux Klan. As Emma Lou Thornbrough demonstrates, segregation efforts preceded the Klan's emergence and attracted broader support than the Klan. See *ibid.*, pp. 594-618.

282 INDIANA THROUGH TRADITION AND CHANGE

1929-1930. The enrollment in the state's elementary schools in 1941-1942 was 9 percent below the level of 1929-1930—reflecting the lower birthrate of the Depression years. The dramatic change occurred in the high schools, where the enrollment for 1941-1942 was 35 percent above that of 1929-1930.[49] This large increase in high school enrollment was due mostly to the bleak employment opportunities for young people, which encouraged them to remain in school even after passing the age of compulsory education.[50]

Although the Depression increased the formal education level of Indiana youth, large high-school enrollments placed a heavy burden on schools at a time when school revenues were greatly declining. During the first three years of the Depression decade, school revenues declined by one fourth of the 1929 level, necessitating a drastic reduction in school expenditures. Expenditures decreased from $91.66 per pupil in 1929-1930 to $60.20 in 1933-1934, then rose slowly thereafter to $86.13 by 1939-1940.[51] The general price decline offset some of these reductions, but the Committee on Governmental Economy noted in 1934 that "educational programs have been curtailed in a drastic fashion, school terms have been shortened, teaching positions have been eliminated, salaries have been reduced, and school buildings and equipment have been allowed to deteriorate."[52]

For students the Depression meant not only an increase in the quantity of schooling but also a possible decline in quality. For

[49] United States Office of Education, *Statistics of State School Systems*, p. 17.

[50] Indiana State Committee on Governmental Economy, *Report*, p. 428. An exception to this general trend was in the poorer areas of southern Indiana, where parents sometimes kept older and younger children out of school during the Depression. Moore and Lloyd, *The Back-to-the-Land Movement in Southern Indiana*, p. 20.

[51] Indiana State Committee on Governmental Economy, *Report*, p. 428; United States Office of Education, *Statistics of State School Systems*, p. 24. See also *Your Schools: A Report of a Survey of the Public Schools of Evansville, Indiana, 1936* (n.p., 1936), p. 42; "Economies in the Indianapolis School System," *School and Society*, December 30, 1933, p. 861; Cohen and Mohl, *The Paradox of Progressive Education*, pp. 144-146.

[52] Indiana State Committee on Governmental Economy, *Report*, p. 428. See also Indiana League of Women Voters, *Indiana Schools and the Depression* (Indianapolis, 1935), pp. ii-iii.

many teachers it meant an increased student-teacher ratio, a lower salary, and sometimes a deferred salary. For even less fortunate teachers, the Depression meant a loss of job or at best only a short-term appointment. The teacher tenure law, passed in 1927 in an effort to provide job security and improve the quality of teaching, was repealed for township schools in 1933. Though teachers in city schools might receive tenure, they too faced insecurities, best demonstrated by the formation in 1937 of an American Federation of Teachers' local in Gary.[53]

A significant long-term effect of the Great Depression on public education was the shift toward a greater proportion of state funding. Prior to 1933 local property and poll taxes provided more than 90 percent of school revenues, and the state provided the remainder. A dramatic shift occurred in 1933, when Governor McNutt and the legislature increased state support to approximately 30 percent of total school revenues—an increase made possible by McNutt's gross income tax. By 1945-1946 the state was providing 38 percent of school revenue, a level of support that would provide a strong case for increased state-directed standardization and centralization in the post-World War II years. The federal government's support remained at less than 1 percent.[54]

§ §

Higher education also changed during the interwar years as young Indianans responded to the increasing demand for more education in business and the professions. One measure of this change was that the number of students attending colleges and normal schools in the state doubled. Student registrations increased from 17,612 in 1922, to 26,893 in 1930. The Depression brought only a slight falling off in college attendance, reaching a low point of 23,374 in 1933 and rapidly rising in the late 1930s to a peak of 34,352 students in 1939.[55]

[53] Laws of Indiana, 1927, pp. 259-262; 1933, pp. 716-719; Cohen and Mohl, The Paradox of Progressive Education, pp. 146-147.
[54] Indiana State Committee on Governmental Economy, Report, pp. 440-441; United States Office of Education, Statistical Summary of Education, p. 16.
[55] Indiana Year Book, 1923, p. 333; 1931, p. 575; 1934, p. 475; 1940, p. 1043.

Accompanying the increased numbers of college students was a change in the nature of institutions of higher education. State-supported schools began to play a relatively more important role, especially in the education of teachers. Private normal schools for teacher education proliferated in Indiana in the late nineteenth century, and many of them were of very low academic quality. Part of the trend toward professionalization of education after World War I included the state's assumption of enlarged responsibilities for teacher training and certification, notably at the State Normal School at Terre Haute, founded in 1870, and its Eastern Division in Muncie, opened in 1918. The combination of a shortage of teachers after World War I and increased financial support from public and private sources caused both teacher training institutions to grow rapidly, then to evolve and eventually separate in 1929 as the Indiana State Teachers College and Ball State Teachers College—the Muncie institution acquiring its name from the glass-jar manufacturing family that made large financial contributions. In 1922 total enrollment for both institutions was 1,610. By 1929 it was 4,632, 64 percent of which represented female students.[56] As the state teachers colleges grew and as the state increased requirements for teacher certification, the private normal schools continued a decline begun in the early twentieth century. Tri-State College in Angola, Valparaiso University, and Central Normal College in Danville hung on through World War I as private normal schools. Valparaiso fell on especially hard times in the early 1920s. Following an abortive attempt by the Ku Klux Klan to take over the institution in 1923, the Lutheran Church of the Missouri Synod purchased the school in 1925 and gradually restored it to academic health. Tri-State survived, but it ended its teacher-training program in the 1920s. Central Normal continued to train teachers through the interwar years. By the time of its demise in 1951, the school claimed that nearly one third of the teachers in Indiana had taken courses at

[56] *Ibid.*, 1923, p. 333; 1930, p. 1001; Glenn White, *The Ball State Story: From Normal Institute to University* (Muncie, Ind., 1967), pp. 46-51; William O. Lynch, *A History of Indiana State Teachers College* (Terre Haute, Ind., 1946), p. 297.

Central Normal. With the passing of the private normal schools, increasingly more of Indiana's teachers received their training at the state schools in Terre Haute and Muncie.[57]

Despite the growing importance of Indiana State and Ball State, the two major institutions of higher education in Indiana remained Purdue University and Indiana University. The school in West Lafayette continued its specialization in engineering and agriculture (see Chapter VI), while the Bloomington school concentrated on the liberal arts and sciences, law, business, and medicine, with the university's facilities for the latter field of study located largely in Indianapolis. Only slowly did Indiana University expand its teacher-training program. Together Purdue and Indiana accounted for 35 percent of total college enrollment in the state in 1922 and 42 percent by 1939.[58]

Although the state assumed an expanded role in higher education, critics charged that such state support was far from adequate. Surveys of the four state institutions of higher education in 1922 and 1926 found Indiana lagging behind its neighbors in the north-central region (Ohio, Illinois, Michigan, Wisconsin, Minnesota, and Iowa) in proportion of tax dollars spent for higher education, in faculty salaries, and in size of libraries. The 1926 survey was also most critical of insufficient support for research and publication at all four state schools. The state normal schools were judged especially deficient in scholarship—perhaps not surprisingly, in that only 3 percent of the faculty at Terre Haute and 2 percent at Muncie had Ph.D.s in 1926, and most were graduates of the Terre Haute school. This lackluster academic record caused

[57] Eber W. Jeffery, History of Private Normal Schools in Indiana (Ph.D. dissertation, New York University, 1932), pp. 211-215; Indiana Education Survey Commission, *Public Education*, p. 86; Moore, *The Calumet Region*, pp. 465-471; Kent D. Beeler and Philip C. Chamberlain, " 'Give a Buck To Save A College': The Demise of Central Normal College," *Indiana Magazine of History*, LXVII (1971), 117-119.

[58] Indiana *Year Book*, 1923, p. 333; 1940, p. 1043. For criticism of Indiana University's alleged lack of attention to teacher training and its "bias in favor of college studies of the older classical or conventional type" see Indiana Education Survey Commission, *Public Education*, p. 80. Nonetheless, by 1931, when there were 13,624 living graduates of the university, 4,073 were engaged in teaching or educational administration. Clark, *Indiana University*, II, 313.

the North Central Association of Colleges and Secondary Schools to threaten in 1928 to deny accreditation to both teachers schools. The academic environment at Purdue and Indiana universities was judged higher in quality than at the teachers schools but low in relation to other midwestern state universities.[59]

Indiana University had made considerable progress in the 1880s under President David Starr Jordan, but then it settled into mediocrity. Although there were some very good teachers and scholars on the Bloomington campus after World War I, they were part of a faculty that was generally undistinguished and sometimes provincial. The 1926 survey concluded that Indiana University was "losing its best young men" to campuses elsewhere that supported academic and professional distinction and offered higher pay.[60] The Bloomington administration, joined by other state school administrations, worked hard to convince a parsimonious legislature of the need for more financial support but met only limited success.[61] Blame rested not only in the state capitol, however, for the leadership at Indiana University too often thought of the school as though it was and should be a simple, rural, nineteenth-century institution. According to Thomas D. Clark, historian of the university, William Lowe Bryan, president from 1902 to 1937, and some of his administrative colleagues "were

[59] *Financial and Statistical Studies of Indiana University, Purdue University, and Indiana State Normal: A Preliminary Report to the Indiana Education Survey Commission* (New York, 1922), pp. 9-10, 12; Charles H. Judd et al., *Report of a Survey of the State Institutions of Higher Learning in Indiana* (Indianapolis, 1926), pp. 117, 141, 158, 199-201. The 1922 study was done by the General Education Board as part of the survey of state education authorized by the General Assembly in 1921. The 1926 report was prepared by a commission of professional educators from outside Indiana appointed by Governor Ed Jackson. See also White, *The Ball State Story*, pp. 73-75; Lynch, *A History of Indiana State Teachers College*, pp. 290-292, 314. Annual data on faculty, library, and income by college are found in the report of the Department of Public Instruction in the Indiana *Year Book*.

[60] Judd et al., *Report of a Survey of State Institutions of Higher Learning*, p. 132.

[61] Frank K. Burrin, *Edward Charles Elliott, Educator* (Lafayette, Ind., 1970), pp. 90-93; Clark, *Indiana University*, II, 239-249; Joint State Schools' Alumni Commission, *Statewide Endorsement of the State School Program Now before the Indiana Legislature* (Indianapolis, 1929).

limited in perspective if not eccentric in the hiring, discharging, and encouragement of faculty members."[62] A great change began in the late 1930s through a combination of self-help, outside aid, and serendipity. In 1937 a university self-study committee concluded that "the faculty of the University is far from a distinguished one" and suggested that "it is clear that Indiana does not deserve to be classed with the other state institutions in the Middle West (except Purdue), much less the leading endowed schools of the country."[63] The committee criticized support for research as inadequate and charged that parochialism had produced nepotism and inbreeding of faculty and administration. The committee's negative assessments fell on responsive ears. In 1937 Herman B Wells replaced Bryan and began vigorously to recruit the best teachers and scholars in the nation, aided by a new pension plan that allowed many of the older faculty to follow Bryan into retirement. By 1942, 94 of the 225 faculty members in Bloomington had arrived since 1937, bringing with them new ideas for research and teaching. The recruitment of new faculty, the imaginative leadership of Wells, the commitment to quality apparent in the self-study report, and the improvements in the physical plant made possible by New Deal work relief—all combined to free Indiana University from its less relevant nineteenth-century traditions and to place it on a path toward respectability among major universities in the nation.[64]

The important changes initiated at Indiana University in 1937 did not obviate the judgment that the state institutions of higher education were generally not of high quality during the interwar years. Such a situation would have been less significant if the state had boasted many outstanding private colleges. There were a few such institutions, to be sure, but only a few. The 1926 study found that Indiana was the only state in the north-central region in which financial support for *both* private and public colleges was below the region's average. Indiana's private colleges, the study noted, did not have a single scientist of national distinction. Per-

---

[62] Clark, *Indiana University*, II, 308.
[63] *Ibid.*, p. 377.
[64] *Ibid.*, pp. 363-397, III, 13-17, 30; Wells, *Being Lucky*, pp. 96-112.

haps most revealing was the implication that Hoosier youth "voted with their feet" by going elsewhere to school. The 1926 report found that of the 15,548 college students from Indiana in 1920-1921, 28 percent were attending schools outside the state. No other state in the north-central region lost more than 21 percent of its college students to other states.[65]

Nearly all of Indiana's private colleges were affiliated with a religious denomination. The University of Notre Dame was the largest—growing rapidly in the 1920s—and the best known, though as much for its football team as for its academic standing. In 1929 the South Bend school spent $15,400 on football uniforms, about the same sum budgeted for new library books. The Methodist church supported Evansville College and DePauw and Taylor universities, though ending its formal affiliation with the latter in 1922. DePauw, located in Greencastle, seems to have maintained its position during the interwar years as one of the Midwest's better liberal arts colleges. It adopted a more flexible curriculum in 1926 and attracted increasingly larger proportions of students from outside the state and from non-Methodist families. The major school associated with the Disciples of Christ was Butler University in Indianapolis, which also enjoyed a good reputation in the interwar years. The Indianapolis institution was plagued in the 1920s with an overly ambitious athletic program, however, leading to its expulsion from the North Central Association of Colleges and Secondary Schools in 1930 and 1931. Both Butler and DePauw suffered administrative conflicts in the 1930s as the Depression forced retrenchment.[66] These were the largest private schools in Indiana: Notre Dame enrolled 3,128 students in 1930; Butler, 2,006; DePauw, 1,651. Other private colleges in Indiana that year had fewer than 500 students, except for Man-

[65] Judd *et al., Report of a Survey of State Institutions of Higher Learning,* pp. 45-47, 52.

[66] Thomas J. Schlereth, *The University of Notre Dame: A Portrait of Its History and Campus* (Notre Dame, Ind., 1976), pp. 129, 147; William C. Ringenberg, *Taylor University: The First 125 Years* (Grand Rapids, Mich., 1973), p. 114; Flynn (ed.), *The Indianapolis Area of the Methodist Episcopal Church,* pp. 19, 118; George B. Manhart, *DePauw through the Years* (2 volumes, Greencastle, Ind., 1962), II, 329-332; Shaw, *Hoosier Disciples,* pp. 347-353, 376-379, 382.

chester College, which enrolled 652 students. The smaller schools included, in addition to those already mentioned, Earlham, Franklin, Hanover, Indiana Central, Oakland City, Rose Polytechnic Institute, St. Mary's-of-the-Woods, and Wabash.[67]

Student life varied greatly on Indiana college campuses in the interwar years. On many campuses a new social freedom for high jinks and pranks, more intense social life, and expanded extracurricular activities followed World War I. Intercollegiate athletics became increasingly important, as did fraternities and sororities. Some colleges, especially those affiliated with Protestant religious denominations, continued to hold tight rein on student life. Dancing and smoking were frequently troublesome issues for college deans and presidents in the 1920s. In 1926 DePauw surrendered to student pressure to permit dancing at college events. Earlham began to allow dancing in 1930, by which time most other Indiana colleges had also surrendered, though faculty supervision was still considered necessary. At Indiana University the issue was not dancing but student violation of prohibition, a problem which pitted the deans of men and women against the Book Nook, the major site of student conversation, music, and frivolity. Such social issues paled during the Depression, when more students sought part-time jobs off campus or with the National Youth Administration on campus. Throughout the interwar years neither college administrators and faculty nor students ignored the practical world beyond the campus, especially as they engaged increasingly in teaching and learning that would provide direct preparation for a career in the professions or business. After World War I both Purdue and Indiana University took important steps to meet the demands of modern businesses for trained managers, with the Bloomington campus opening a School of

[67] Indiana *Year Book*, 1931, p. 575. For other institutions classified by the Department of Public Instruction as normal departments and special schools see *ibid*. For an example of an Indiana Bible college see William C. Ringenberg, "A Brief History of Fort Wayne Bible College," *Mennonite Quarterly Review*, LIV (1980), 135-155. It is regrettable that so few of Indiana's colleges have been well served by historical scholarship. With the exceptions of the histories of DePauw and Indiana University, cited above, such college histories that exist generally are not of high quality, especially for the twentieth century.

Commerce and Finance in 1920. Colleges also reflected the attitudes of the society beyond the campus toward women and blacks. Women were referred to as "coeds," and their dormitory hours were monitored and their career choices directed to teaching, nursing, and social welfare work. The rapid growth of college attendance favored more male than female students. Women represented 40 percent of college students in Indiana in 1922, 38 percent in 1930, and 35 percent in 1939, a decline due in part to limited opportunities for public school teachers after 1929. Blacks were represented in colleges in much smaller proportions than in the general population and were often restricted or segregated once they arrived on campus. Butler apparently had the largest number of black students, even though social life was entirely segregated. In 1929 the Indianapolis university adopted a quota system to limit the number of blacks admitted. In Bloomington the university cafeteria and many restaurants in town were closed to the few blacks on campus, while at Purdue the lines of color were even more clearly drawn.[68]

Efforts to change schools and colleges in the years 1920-1940 met many and varied obstacles. The desire for local control, the force of tradition and resistance to change, and the ever-present concern about higher taxes—all provided major sources of frustration for those seeking change. Issues related to taxation and finance were probably most significant. There was, to be sure, evidence of unprecedented enthusiasm for education and particularly for the practical benefits it promised in better jobs and higher incomes. In Muncie, for example, the Lynds concluded that education "evokes the fervor of a religion, a means of salvation, among a large section of the working class."[69] At the same time that many

[68] Manhart, *DePauw through the Years*, II, 493-494; Opal Thornburg, *Earlham: The Story of the College, 1847-1962* (Richmond, Ind., 1963), p. 349; Clark, *Indiana University*, II, 138-139, 265-283, III, 59-60; Shaw, *Hoosier Disciples*, p. 377; Indiana *Year Book*, 1923, p. 333; 1931, p. 575; 1940, p. 1043; Indianapolis *News*, April 29, 1929; William Luther Howard, A Personnel Study of NYA Students of Indiana University (Ed.D. thesis, Indiana University, Bloomington, 1940), pp. 31-78; Thornbrough, *Since Emancipation*, pp. 67-68; Wells, *Being Lucky*, pp. 214-221.

[69] Lynd and Lynd, *Middletown*, p. 187.

Hoosiers were taking pride in their schools and colleges, they remained ever watchful of extravagance. The State Superintendent of Public Instruction could report proudly in 1925 that "more than thirty-one per cent of the funds available for use of the State Department of Public Instruction during the fiscal year ending September 30[, 1925,] was not spent and reverted to the general funds of the state."[70] Tensions between economy and quality in education were omnipresent, reflecting the many ways in which schools and colleges belonged to the broader society.

§ § §

Religion continued to occupy a prominent place in Indiana during the 1920s and 1930s. Hoosiers generally assumed that an individual belonged to one or another of the major religious denominations. The Lynds reported that newcomers to Muncie were often greeted with the question, "What church do you go to?"[71] Membership in a major Christian denomination was often a prerequisite for acceptance in the community. In 1927, for example, Noblesville officials withdrew an offer of the school superintendency because the individual was a Unitarian and refused to join a more orthodox congregation.[72]

Although the importance of traditional religion continued in post-World War I Indiana, and although religion was in many ways among the most stable of social and cultural forces, religious forms and behaviors did change in these years, as the churches confronted new problems in an increasingly secular society. In some ways, in fact, the 1920s and 1930s stood apart as a period in which organized religion in Indiana and the nation seemed especially threatened.[73]

The period was one first of slight growth and then of stability in membership for Indiana churches (see Table I). Indiana church membership numbered 1,382,818 in 1926, which was an increase

[70] Indiana *Year Book*, 1925, p. 909.

[71] Lynd and Lynd, *Middletown*, p. 315.

[72] Howard K. Beale, *Are American Teachers Free? An Analysis of Restraints upon the Freedom of Teaching in American Schools* (New York, 1936), p. 514.

[73] For a general overview of this period see Robert T. Handy, "The American Religious Depression, 1925-1935," *Church History*, XXIX (1960), 3-16.

TABLE I

Church Membership of Major Denominations in Indiana, 1916-1936[74]

Denomination	1916		1926		1936	
	Number	Percent of Total	Number	Percent of Total	Number	Percent of Total
Catholic	272,288	23.1	312,194	22.6	315,185	23.3
Methodist Episcopal	261,228	22.2	288,181	20.8	252,803	18.7
Disciples of Christ	137,727	11.7	154,067	11.1	130,004	9.6
Northern Baptist	75,374	6.4	82,394	6.0	80,498	6.0
United Brethren in Christ	59,955	5.1	68,482	5.0	61,504	4.6
Presbyterian Church in the U.S.A.	59,209	5.0	66,574	4.8	67,694	5.0
Lutheran (Missouri Synod)	38,309	3.3	54,870	4.0	59,100	4.4
Negro Baptist	10,412	0.9	30,388	2.2	41,746	3.1
Total Church Membership	1,177,341		1,382,818		1,350,288	

[74] United States Bureau of the Census, *Religious Bodies*, 1916 (2 volumes, Washington, D.C., 1919), I, 109; *ibid*, 1926, I, 172-174; *ibid*, 1936 (2 volumes, Washington, D.C., 1941), I, 745-749. These are the eight largest denominations except for 1916 when there were seven denominations in rank order between Negro Baptist and Lutheran (Missouri Synod).

of 205,477 above the 1916 membership figure and somewhat more than the general population growth. The hardships of the Depression did not produce a surge of new members: total church membership declined slightly to 1,350,288 by 1936, even though the total state population had increased.[75] Judged by church membership, Indiana was not significantly more or less religious than other states. In both the 1926 and 1936 censuses of religious bodies, Indiana ranked thirteenth among the states in church members, only slightly behind the state's rank in total population, which was twelfth in 1926 and eleventh in 1936.[76]

Within this general pattern of church membership, Indiana's major religious denominations showed considerable stability. The rank order of the largest denominations was nearly the same in 1936 as in 1926 and 1916. The Roman Catholic Church continued to have the largest number of members, with the Methodists close behind. Catholic membership figures often included children, however, whereas those of many of the Protestant denominations did not. If only members thirteen years of age and over are counted, the Methodists could claim 203,303 Hoosiers in 1936 compared to the 208,591 Catholics.[77] Following Catholics and Methodists, those denominations with more than forty thousand members in Indiana were the Disciples of Christ, Northern Baptists, Presbyterians, United Brethren in Christ, Missouri Synod Lutherans, and Negro Baptists. Smaller Protestant denominations, with between ten and forty thousand members in Indiana in 1936, included the Evangelical and Reformed Church, United Lutheran Church in America, the Congregational and Christian Churches,

[75] Though census data on church membership are subject to some qualifications, they reflect general trends. See United States Bureau of the Census, *Religious Bodies*, 1936, I, 20. Comparisons of church membership to the general population are approximate, because the population count was made at the beginning of the decade and the religious census was taken midway in the decade. The state's total population increased by 8.5 percent in the 1910s, 10.5 percent in the 1920s, and 5.8 percent in the 1930s. United States Bureau of the Census, *Sixteenth Census* (1940), II, *Population*, Pt. 2, p. 675.

[76] United States Bureau of the Census, *Religious Bodies*, 1926, I, 32; *ibid.*, 1936, I, 35.

[77] *Ibid.*, 1936, I, 206.

Church of the Brethren (Conservative Dunkers), Society of Friends, Church of Christ, Evangelical Church, Protestant Episcopal Church, Church of the Nazarene, American Lutheran Church, and the Mennonite bodies. Jewish congregations in the state had 25,494 members in 1936. There were other smaller denominations and many independent churches with no denominational affiliation. In Indianapolis, for example, there were approximately fifty independent churches in 1940—most of them of the Pentecostal variety.[78]

Church denominations were not evenly distributed across the state. Most of rural and small-town Indiana was overwhelmingly Protestant, with Catholic strength concentrated in the cities. More than 77 percent of the Roman Catholic Church's membership in Indiana in 1926 was found in urban churches, with more than a third of all Hoosier Catholics living in Indianapolis, South Bend, Gary, Fort Wayne, and Evansville. Large expanses of the state were far removed from a Catholic church. In forty-three counties in 1926 less than 10 percent of the total church membership was Catholic. While most of these heavily Protestant counties were in rural Indiana, there were a few rural counties with large Roman Catholic populations. Rural Dubois and Perry counties were two of only three counties (the third was Lake County) with more than 50 percent of church members belonging to the Catholic church. A few small communities were almost exclusively Catholic. The village of Ferdinand in Dubois County, for example, had a population of 986 in 1938, and all but 16 were Catholics.[79]

Members of Jewish congregations, who represented less than 2 percent of the Hoosier religious population, were almost exclusively urban. The census of 1926 listed only one rural congregation among the forty-six in the state. Forty-two percent of the state's Jewish population lived in Indianapolis in 1926, with other

[78] *Ibid.*, I, 745-749; Indiana Historical Records Survey, Work Projects Administration, *A Directory of Churches and Religious Organizations in Indiana* (4 volumes, mimeographed, Indianapolis, 1940-1941), I, 35-38.

[79] United States Bureau of the Census, *Religious Bodies*, 1926, I, 360-576, 601-606, II, 1256; Albert Kleber, *Ferdinand Indiana, 1840-1940: A Bit of Cultural History* (St. Meinrad, Ind., 1940), p. 197.

relatively large communities in South Bend, Gary, Fort Wayne, and Evansville.[80]

Indiana's major Protestant denominations were generally distributed more evenly across the state, with a few smaller denominations settled in scattered pockets. The Brethren, for example, were heavily concentrated in the northern Indiana counties of Elkhart, Huntington, and St. Joseph. Black churches were concentrated in black neighborhoods in urban areas, where they often functioned as major social and cultural institutions. Most Negro Baptists lived in Indianapolis and the Calumet cities, with two thirds of the state membership of 30,338 in 1926 in Marion and Lake counties. The African Methodist Episcopal Church ranked second among black denominations, with 7,486 members. Other black churches in 1926 had a total of 11,830 members in the state.[81]

Of the many causes of concern for religious leaders and members, few received as much attention as the condition of Indiana's rural churches. The small rural church standing in a grove of trees, the cemetery nearby, was a primary focus of nineteenth-century community life. In the twentieth century, however, some observers came to fear that the small rural church no longer adequately met the religious and social needs of society. The most thorough statement of concern came from a survey made in 1922 of rural church life in Jennings County in southern Indiana. Conducted by the Reverend Marion C. Bishop of the liberal Interchurch World Movement, the survey found Jennings County's churches declining in material and spiritual resources. The report stated that narrow denominational rivalry had spawned too many rural churches—churches that were too small and too poor to serve their members adequately.[82] Three fourths of the

[80] United States Bureau of the Census, *Religious Bodies, 1926,* I, 360-576, II, 647.

[81] *Ibid.,* I, 601-603; United States Bureau of the Census, *Negroes in the United States, 1920-1932,* p. 542; James Comer, "The Functions of the Urban Black Church," in A. L. Lazarus (comp.), *The Indiana Experience: An Anthology* (Bloomington, Ind., 1977), pp. 69-72.

[82] Organizers outside the churches also complained of the retarding influence of denominational rivalry. One of the leaders in the Farm Bureau Cooperative movement in Indiana later recalled that "in many rural communities where two or three denominations existed, the social life of the community was divided into

forty-nine churches in Jennings County had only one room and thus were unable to provide the diverse educational, social, and recreational activities that were increasingly available in multi-room urban churches. Instead, the churches were "hold-overs from the day in which the Church stressed preaching and the individualistic gospel." Perhaps more important, the 1922 survey found a lack of spiritual and community leadership in Jennings County. Ministers were inadequately trained and paid. Twelve of the twenty-three ministers in the county followed second occupations in order to earn a living. The average length of stay in a charge was only two years, as ministers quickly moved on, presumably to better-supported positions. Young men in training for the ministry were particularly reluctant to move to rural churches like the ones in Jennings County or to remain there long.[83]

The 1922 survey of rural churches concluded that "many churches deserve extinction. They are sectarian in spirit, lack community vision and exist for the worship of a mere handful of individuals."[84] Whether they deserved it or not, Indiana's rural churches did decline in number, from 4,579 in 1926, to 3,716 in 1936.[85] In many cases two or more rural congregations merged, sometimes consciously following in the wake of local school mergers by building a new church adjacent to the consolidated township school. Denominational leaders lamented the rural church problem—often discussed on conference programs. In the 1930s Indiana Baptists, Disciples of Christ, Lutherans, and Methodists established rural church commissions to study the problem

---

small groups and it was sometimes difficult to persuade these various factions to work together on common economic problems." Hull, *Built of Men: The Story of Indiana Cooperatives*, pp. 193-194.

[83] Benson Y. Landis, *Rural Church Life in the Middle West as Illustrated by Clay County, Iowa and Jennings County, Indiana with Comparative Data from Studies of Thirty-five Middle Western Counties* (New York, 1922), pp. 51, 53-54, 58-61. The quotation is on page 53. See also Hartman, Brookston, pp. 148-155.

[84] Landis, *Rural Church Life*, p. 70.

[85] United States Bureau of the Census, *Religious Bodies*, 1926, I, 132; *ibid.*, 1936, I, 156. Rural population declined by 7.0 percent in the 1920s and 0.3 percent in the 1930s. United States Bureau of the Census, *Sixteenth Census* (1940), II, *Population*, Pt. 2, p. 675.

and promote the training of ministers and lay leaders for work in rural congregations. Such efforts met with only limited success.[86]

The problems of young people attracted as much attention as those of rural churches, doubtless in response to the observed or feared changes in social and moral behavior of youth. During the 1920s the churches expanded activities for directing youthful religious and social behavior. Part of the effort involved control or elimination of temptations in the broader society, especially liquor, but also gambling, smoking, dancing, and indecent motion pictures and literature. The 1926 Indiana Conference of the Methodist Church directed special attention to "the youth problem," and resolved that "by agitation, education, and, if necessary, legislation, we must have clean motion pictures, decent pleasures, normal recreations. . . ."[87]

The churches' primary efforts to influence youth were not through censorship or other legal measures, however, but through religious education. The major institution of youth education was the Sunday school, which was usually held during the hour before the morning preaching service. Here children learned Bible stories and verses and songs and symbols of their parents' religion, often organized around a weekly "lesson." The Sunday school was also important as one of the few religious institutions that transcended denominational lines. Township, county, and state Sunday school conventions and institutes provided nondenominational inspiration and education for thousands of Hoosier Protestants. In 1925 the Indiana Council of Religious Education reported more than

[86] Flynn (ed.), *The Indianapolis Area of the Methodist Episcopal Church*, pp. 65, 72; Henry G. Waltmann (ed.), *History of the Indiana-Kentucky Synod of the Lutheran Church in America: Its Development, Congregations, and Institutions* (Indianapolis, 1971), p. 17; Cady, *The Origin and Development of the Missionary Baptist Church*, p. 311; Shaw, *Hoosier Disciples*, p. 369; Indiana Annual Conference of the Methodist Episcopal Church, *Minutes*, 1931 (n.p., n.d.), p. 516; *ibid.*, 1938 (n.p., n.d.), p. 418; Jack J. Detzler, *The History of the Northwest Indiana Conference of the Methodist Church 1852-1951* (Nashville, Tenn., 1953), pp. 155-156; C. R. Defenderfer, *Lutheranism at the Crossroads of America: A Story of the Indiana Synod of the U.L.C.A.* (n.p., [1948]), p. 63.

[87] Indiana Annual Conference of the Methodist Episcopal Church, *Minutes*, 1926 (n.p., n.d.), p. 388. See also Northwest Indiana Conference of the Methodist Episcopal Church, *Minutes*, 1925, p. 187.

a thousand conventions and conferences attended by one hundred and fifty thousand people. These programs and the formation in 1930 of the Council of United Church Women were important preparations for the ecumenical spirit among Protestants that led to the founding of the Indiana Council of Churches in 1943.[88] The churches also provided religious and social instruction for young people in vacation Bible schools and in summer church camps, which became very popular in the 1920s. The church camps provided not only religious education but also, in the words of one Methodist, "the finest social contacts under healthful surroundings. . . ."[89] Various denominations also supported young people's organizations, scout troops, and Young Men's and Young Women's Christian Associations.[90]

The most thoroughgoing effort to provide religious instruction was in the parochial school. Although several religious and ethnic groups supported their own schools in the interwar years, the Roman Catholic Church was most active in this area. The *Indiana Catholic and Record* expressed the church's strongest sentiment on education: "The Catholic school is the only fit school for the Catholic child." Roman Catholic schools enrolled 46,576 pupils in 1920, 57,058 in 1932, and 53,829 in 1937. The largest growth

[88] Grover L. Hartman, *A School for God's People: A History of the Sunday School Movement in Indiana* (Indianapolis, 1980), pp. 71-96; Grover L. Hartman, Retrospect and Prospect—The Indiana Council of Churches at Age Thirty Five (Mimeographed, 1977, copy in author's possession), pp. 1-2. Hartman's preface to *A School for God's People* is a wonderfully evocative description of his own youthful experiences in the Sunday school of Liberty Chapel, United Brethren Church, in Tippecanoe County. See also Walter S. Athearn *et al.*, *The Indiana Survey of Religious Education* (3 volumes, New York, 1923-1924), I, 57, 508, 513. This survey of Sunday schools was conducted in 1920 under the auspices of the Interchurch World Movement. The report focused on the need for application of professional and progressive education methods to the Sunday schools. It is worth noting that none of the Sunday school superintendents of the six largest Protestant churches in Muncie had read Athearn's report two years after it appeared. Lynd and Lynd, *Middletown*, p. 384.

[89] Flynn (ed.), *The Indianapolis Area of the Methodist Episcopal Church*, p. 110. See also Shaw, *Hoosier Disciples*, pp. 330-331; Cady, *The Origin and Development of the Missionary Baptist Church*, p. 320; Hartman, *A School for God's People*, pp. 85-86.

[90] Lynd and Lynd, *Middletown*, pp. 336-337, 393-398; *The Leisure of a People*, pp. 106-111.

came in high school enrollment, which was 2,886 in 1920, 4,639 in 1932, and 6,128 in 1937. This increase reflected the consolidation of Catholic high schools in Indiana cities in the 1920s, including Cathedral in Indianapolis, Reitz Memorial in Evansville, and Gibault in Vincennes, and the general increase in high school enrollment in the 1930s. Catholic schools generally admitted blacks. Cathedral in Indianapolis enrolled black students in the 1920s, but at least one of the elementary schools in the city (St. Rita's) was designated "colored."[91]

Most churches chose not to sponsor parochial schools. Some did work to promote religious instruction within the context of public education, however. Protestant churches in Gary established a released-time program in 1914 which later spread to other Indiana communities. Children were excused from their classes for one period a week for religious instruction with denominational representatives.[92]

Concern for youth was part of church involvement in a variety of secular activities during the interwar years. Some of the progressive reforms that characterized the social gospel movement around the turn of the century continued into the post-World War I era. The churches' social reform efforts were most evident in programs to help immigrant and black newcomers adjust to a new life in Indiana cities. Various Protestant denominations supported neighborhood settlement houses and mission churches in Fort Wayne, Indianapolis, and Gary. Yet there was little other evidence of active progressive reform among Indiana churches. The proceedings and publications of the major denominations during the 1920s were generally silent or vaguely noncommittal on the kinds of social and economic issues that attracted Christian

[91] *Indiana Catholic and Record*, August 31, 1945; Humbert P. Pagani, *200 Years of Catholicism in Indiana* (Indianapolis, 1934), p. 35; Sister M. V. Naber, A Study of Certain Phases of the Present Status of Catholic Secondary Education in Indiana (M.A. thesis, Indiana University, Bloomington, 1935), pp. 24-34; *The Leisure of a People*, pp. 304-305; Thornbrough, *Since Emancipation*, p. 63. Data on enrollment are from *Directory of Catholic Colleges and Schools* (Washington, D.C., 1921), pp. 190-191; *Directory of Catholic Colleges and Schools, 1932-1933* (Washington, D.C., 1932), pp. 193, 246; *Catholic Colleges and Schools in the United States* (Washington, D.C., 1940), pp. 63, 69.

[92] Shaw, *Hoosier Disciples*, p. 319.

progressive reformers of the previous generation. During the Great Depression the churches made some general statements calling for a more humane and ethical capitalism, but little else.[93]

Instead of direct efforts to eliminate social injustice or change society, Indiana's churches tended to focus on individual moral behavior, often in an effort to preserve the status quo against the forces of modernity and secularism. The motion picture, for example, was an outstanding cause of concern and drew strong criticism from denominational leaders. At their 1933 state convention the Baptists' resolution on movies declared that "the standards of life there presented are for the most part unchristian, unamerican and a menace to our social and moral life."[94] In a show of interdenominational co-operation, ministers throughout the state joined together one Sunday in the fall of 1934 to alert their congregations to the evils emanating from Hollywood.[95] Protestant churches—especially the Methodists—also directed criticism toward the increased tendency of "prostituting the Christian day of rest and worship into a day of unrestrained amusement and pleasure."[96] The churches placed part of the blame on commercial amusements and recreation at swimming pools, parks, golf courses, and motion picture theaters—all increasingly enjoyed on Sundays —but they assigned much of the cause of Sabbath-breaking to the automobile, which one Methodist conference criticized as "a means for taking people away from, rather than to, the Church."[97]

[93] Flynn (ed.), *The Indianapolis Area of the Methodist Episcopal Church*, p. 96; Cady, *The Origin and Development of the Missionary Baptist Church*, pp. 294, 317; Annual Conference of the Methodist Episcopal Church, *Minutes*, 1933 (n.p., n.d.), p. 211; Lynd and Lynd, *Middletown in Transition*, pp. 32, 312-313. For the earlier social gospel movement in Indiana see Phillips, *Indiana in Transition*, pp. 440-444.

[94] Indiana Baptist Convention, *Proceedings of the One Hundredth Anniversary*, 1933 (n.p., n.d.), p. 30; Cady, *The Origin and Development of the Missionary Baptist Church*, pp. 296-297.

[95] Indiana Annual Conference of the Methodist Episcopal Church, *Minutes*, 1934 (n.p., n.d.), p. 391.

[96] North Indiana Annual Conference of the Methodist Episcopal Church, *Minutes*, 1923 (Cincinnati, Ohio, 1923), p. 450.

[97] Northwest Indiana Conference of the Methodist Episcopal Church, *Minutes*, 1925, p. 186. See also Indiana Annual Conference of the Methodist Episcopal Church, *Minutes*, 1921 (n.p., n.d.), p. 200; Lynd and Lynd, *Middletown*, pp. 342-343.

But concerns such as Sabbath-breaking and motion pictures paled when compared to the attack on liquor and the defense of prohibition. During the 1920s Protestant churches led efforts to enforce and retain the prohibition laws. The Methodists were probably the most consistently aggressive and vehement in defending the cause, though their numbers in Indiana gave them in any case a louder voice than that of other denominations. Within the Methodist churches, prohibition came close to being the principal issue of secular reform—the apparent solution to many of the ills of the society. Methodists had especially strong ties with the Indiana Anti-Saloon League and vigorously supported its leader, E. S. Shumaker, a Methodist minister. (See also Chapter II.) Many of the Anti-Saloon League field workers were Methodists, and in 1928, for example, twenty-seven of the forty-five field day meetings sponsored by the League were held in Methodist churches.[98] Although Methodists and members of other denominations greatly lamented the repeal of prohibition in 1933 and campaigned to reinstitute it, their efforts lacked the earlier intensity. By 1944, the resolution on temperance at the annual conference of Indiana Methodists signaled an accommodation with modern life hardly imaginable only two decades earlier: "With many evils threatening the present-day civilization, we recognize that the church must not become unbalanced by giving all of its attention to the removal of one of these evils."[99]

Not all Indiana churches supported prohibition, even at its peak in the immediate post-World War I years. Some of the Lutheran congregations, particularly those with large German-American membership, did not join the crusade. The major dissident was the Roman Catholic Church, which had traditionally

[98] Flynn (ed.), *The Indianapolis Area of the Methodist Episcopal Church*, pp. 88, 111-112; Frederick A. Norwood, *History of the North Indiana Conference 1917-1956: North Indiana Methodism in the Twentieth Century* (Winona Lake, Ind., 1957), p. 173. Indiana Baptists also consistently supported prohibition but perhaps with less organized intensity than Methodists. See, for example, Indiana Baptist Convention, *Proceedings of the Ninety-fourth Anniversary*, 1926 (n.p., n.d.), pp. 32, 41.

[99] Indiana Annual Conference of the Methodist Church, *Minutes*, 1944 (n.p., n.d.), p. 84. See also Cady, *The Origin and Development of the Missionary Baptist Church*, p. 314.

refused to support prohibition, as many of its members—especially those with European backgrounds—strongly opposed this kind of reform.

Roman Catholics' reluctance to join the prohibitionist parade did not endear them to many Protestants. This difference was part of the traditional anti-Catholicism of many Protestant Hoosiers. By the 1920s the Protestant churches were not outwardly anti-Catholic in their formal denominational proceedings, even though the support given to the anti-Catholic Ku Klux Klan indicates that individual congregations and ministers may have been.[100] The Catholic church itself began to respond more effectively to anti-Catholic sentiment. Most notable was the publication of *Our Sunday Visitor* beginning in 1912, edited in Huntington by Father John Francis Noll. In this weekly newsletter Father Noll devoted considerable attention to challenging anti-Catholic prejudice and always with due consideration for his Protestant readers. *Our Sunday Visitor* soon became one of the most successful Catholic publications and enjoyed a large national audience.[101]

Like businesses and individuals, many Indiana churches during the 1920s embarked on efforts to construct new buildings and to remodel and enlarge their old structures. In this building boom there was a rush to display material affluence. Rather than duplicating the usually simple frame or brick structures of nineteenth-century Indiana, Methodists and other nonliturgical churches constructed new buildings in more expensive and elaborate styles, often employing features of Gothic architecture. This trend was most evident in the larger towns and cities. Aggressive building campaigns sometimes used the methods of the wartime Liberty Loan fund drives to raise money for the new churches and for church community buildings that were equipped with kitchens, classrooms, and recreational areas. The new structures also carried

---

[100] Shaw, *Hoosier Disciples*, p. 332; Cady, *The Origin and Development of the Missionary Baptist Church*, p. 295.

[101] Richard Ginder, *With Ink and Crozier: A Biography of John Francis Noll, Fifth Bishop of Fort Wayne and Founder of* Our Sunday Visitor (Huntington, Ind., 1952), pp. 112-115.

large mortgages, which contributed to the financial difficulties of many congregations during the 1930s.[102]

But Gothic architecture, community buildings, and the flurry of church activities did not hide the malaise that threatened organized religion in the interwar years. The changing American lifestyle, with its increasingly secular and material preoccupations, surely affected the churches, though their spokesmen only occasionally voiced concern. A Methodist report from the Greencastle district in 1925, for example, lamented that "the backwash of the war, with its worldliness, materialism, and religious indifference has at times almost engulfed us," while a South Bend district reported three years later that "in spite of our efforts to keep the church in forefront of this progress it often seems that industrial life is outrunning religion."[103] It is possible that some religious leaders, threatened and perplexed by these changes, were inclined to dig in deeper in efforts to resist change and to focus more narrowly on campaigns to control individual moral behavior, as exemplified in the prohibition crusade and the support for the Klan—both of which looked to past traditions.

But the threats to the churches did not come entirely from the outside. One of the most serious problems that confronted Protestant churches during the 1920s came from within, as some members and leaders split along lines usually labeled as "fundamentalist" and "modernist." The differences were varied and complex, but at its simplest the fundamentalist-modernist controversy centered on varying responses to science and to the place of the Bible in Christian theology and life. Modernists asserted their acceptance of science generally and of Darwinian evolution specifically. They were receptive to the new higher criticism of the Bible, which did not insist on acceptance of the Scriptures as the literal word of God. Modernists also tended to be more liberal

---

[102] Flynn (ed.), *The Indianapolis Area of the Methodist Episcopal Church*, pp. 103, 107; Cady, *The Origin and Development of the Missionary Baptist Church*, p. 293; Shaw, *Hoosier Disciples*, pp. 357-360; Indiana Baptist Convention, *Proceedings of the Ninety-first Anniversary*, 1923 (n.p., n.d.), p. 22.

[103] Northwest Indiana Conference of the Methodist Episcopal Church, *Minutes*, 1925, p. 173; Flynn (ed.), *The Indianapolis Area of the Methodist Episcopal Church*, p. 77. See also Lynd and Lynd, *Middletown*, pp. 406-407.

in their social and political attitudes. Fundamentalism developed rapidly in the 1920s—largely as a reaction against modernist beliefs. Fundamentalists insisted on a literal interpretation of the Bible as divine authority, specifically rejecting Darwinian evolution and the scientific base on which it rested. This position was observed nationally in 1925 in the confrontation between William Jennings Bryan and Clarence Darrow over the Tennessee anti-evolution law. In addition to their orthodox view of evolution and the Bible, fundamentalists tended to oppose pluralism and diversity of opinion in nonreligious areas of life, holding to more traditional social, economic, and political beliefs. Finally, fundamentalism was strongest in Indiana's small towns and rural areas, although it also found followers in the cities, especially among working-class urban dwellers.[104]

The fundamentalist-modernist controversy affected most of the major denominations. Protected by liturgy, creeds, and confessions, Catholic and Lutheran churches were generally less troubled, but Methodists, Disciples, Presbyterians, and Baptists suffered conflict and division. Indiana Baptists were especially split in the 1920s. Some modernist Baptists relaxed their traditional opposition to dancing, the theater, and breaking the Sabbath. They experimented with worship services that included sensational sermon topics and syncopated hymns, and, above all, they showed an openness to scientific evolution and to an historical, critical approach to the Bible. These tentative expressions of modernism evoked a strong counterattack from some Indiana Baptists and other Protestants. Indeed, historian John Cady wrote, "So strong was the initial impact of the fundamentalist attack that it looked for a time as if a new conservative sect of large dimensions was in the process of formation, breaking directly across Protestant denominational lines."[105]

104 For general treatment of the controversy see Robert T. Handy, *A History of the Churches in the United States and Canada* (Oxford, [Eng.], 1976), pp. 381-386; Martin E. Marty, *Righteous Empire: The Protestant Experience in America* (New York, 1970), pp. 215-220; Willard B. Gatewood, Jr. (ed.), *Controversy in the Twenties: Fundamentalism, Modernism, and Evolution* (Nashville, Tenn., 1969), pp. 3-46.

105 Cady, *The Origin and Development of the Missionary Baptist Church*, pp. 303-309. The quotation is on page 309.

The old denominational lines generally held, of course, but various fundamentalist sects enjoyed increasing popularity in the 1920s and 1930s. Holiness and Pentecostal churches apparently grew more rapidly than the major Protestant churches, perhaps because of their eagerness to offer traditional religious certainty and salvation in an increasingly complex society and perhaps also because of their social and spiritual warmth, often displayed in intense revival meetings rather than in Gothic architecture or community buildings.[106] Among the most rapidly growing of the Pentecostal churches was the Church of the Nazarene, whose membership in Indiana increased from 1,141 in 1916, to 5,302 in 1926, to 12,277 in 1936. Independent Pentecostal congregations appeared throughout the state in rural areas and in storefronts of urban working-class neighborhoods. Most of the forty-nine independent churches in Indianapolis in 1940 were of the Pentecostal-Holiness variety, and most were located in working-class neighborhoods. In Bloomington by 1940 newly organized churches included three Pentecostal assemblies, two Nazarene churches, an Assembly of God, and a Church of God, with others located in the countryside. Many drew their members from families dependent on work in the stone mills and quarries.[107]

The 1920s and 1930s were difficult years for Indiana churches. Although material prosperity marked the early years of this period, the churches suffered economically along with everyone else during the 1930s. Even more troublesome were the efforts to resist or adjust to the increasingly secular concerns and changing

[106] Handy, *A History of the Churches,* p. 387; Hartman, Brookston, p. 156; Anton T. Boisen, "Divided Protestantism in a Midwest County," *Journal of Religion,* XX (1940), 359-381. The latter study is an excellent analysis of religious and denominational change in Monroe County, Indiana, comparing the 1930s with the 1890s and showing the extent to which the major churches (Methodists, Baptists, and Disciples of Christ) had achieved middle-class formality and respectability by the 1930s, while newer churches sprang from grass-roots religious fervor of the common people.

[107] United States Bureau of the Census, *Religious Bodies,* 1916, I, 109; *ibid.,* 1926, I, 172-174; *ibid.,* 1936, I, 745-749; Indiana District Church of the Nazarene, *Proceedings of the Ninth Annual Assembly,* 1923 (Kansas City, Mo., 1923), pp. 39-40; Indiana Historical Records Survey, A Directory of Churches and Religious Organizations in Indiana, pp. 35-38; Boisen, "Divided Protestantism," *Journal of Religion,* XX, 367-368.

moral standards of the larger society. Some observers detected a spiritual decline, a lethargy and malaise in which most of the forms of traditional religion lost meaning. The fundamentalist-modernist controversy further hurt the churches, causing internal division and perhaps lowering their prestige in the public mind. Although these challenges would continue into the 1940s and after, a resurgence of interest in religion and support for the churches marked the years during World War II and its immediate aftermath. Even though the 1920s and 1930s constituted a period of religious depression, churches during these years played a major role in the society of which they were a part, especially as they responded to change in that society.

CHAPTER X

PUBLIC HEALTH AND PUBLIC SAFETY

THERE IS CONSIDERABLE EVIDENCE to suggest that health care and the actual health of Indianans improved significantly during the interwar decades. The death rate for the state's population dropped from 13.5 deaths per 1,000 persons in 1920, to 12.1 in 1930, to 11.8 in 1940. Even more indicative of improving health was the drop in death rates for younger Hoosiers: rates for those in the age group fifteen to twenty-four, for example, declined from 5.0 in 1920, to 3.4 in 1930, to 1.9 in 1940. Infant mortality rates (the number of deaths under one year of age per 1,000 live births) also showed dramatic improvement, dropping from 81.8 in 1920, to 57.7 in 1930, to 41.9 in 1940. The maternal death rate declined, too, from 8.1 deaths per 1,000 births in 1920, to 6.2 in 1930, to 2.9 in 1940.[1]

These aggregate statistics only begin to suggest the changes occurring in the physical well-being of Hoosiers after World War I. They do not indicate the source of improvements in health and health care. Nor do they suggest the very important challenges and conflicts that questions of health care posed for a variety of professions, agencies, and institutions in Indiana. In fact, while Indiana clearly made progress in this area, there was also evidence of challenges unmet and relative backsliding.

The traditional source of health care in nineteenth-century Indiana was the family. Health was the special responsibility of mothers and grandmothers, whose knowledge of folk medicine was backed by a collection of herbs, teas, patent medicines, and other remedies. By the late nineteenth century, medical science

[1] United States Bureau of the Census, *Vital Statistics Rates in the United States, 1900-1940* (Washington, D.C., 1943), pp. 152, 572-573; Indiana *Year Book,* 1930, p. 824; 1935, p. 704; 1941, p. 481. The reported national infant mortality rate was 85.8 in 1920, 64.6 in 1930, and 47.0 in 1940. The national maternal mortality rate was 8.0 in 1920, 6.7 in 1930, and 3.8 in 1940.

and trained physicians had begun to displace family folk medicine with new knowledge about the diagnosis and treatment of disease. By the 1920s, the professional physician had achieved wide, though not complete, acceptance as the primary source of medical care. The variety of types of medical training had narrowed: practitioners of the interwar years increasingly were graduates of regularly accredited medical schools—especially the Indiana University School of Medicine, founded in 1908. Research and professional training in the university's classrooms and laboratories and in its Robert W. Long Memorial Hospital, James Whitcomb Riley Memorial Children's Hospital, and William H. Coleman Hospital for Women—the latter two founded in the 1920s—represented important medical progress. Nonetheless, remnants of traditional medicine remained. The popularity of chiropractors was a cause of special concern to physicians and to the Indiana State Medical Association. In order to compete with other forms of health care, many medical doctors made house calls and often provided more care in home visits than in their offices. Many also supplemented their incomes by dispensing prescription medicines from their own office stock.[2]

Although the medical profession greatly extended its role in health care in the first decades of the twentieth century, that influence was neither exclusive nor unchallenged. Not only did various traditional or "irregular" medical practices and beliefs continue to compete with medical doctors, but new forms of professional health care developed, sometimes to be challenged or resisted by medical doctors. At the same time, adequate health care for rural, black, and poor Hoosiers remained an especially serious challenge.[3]

[2] Clark, Indiana University, III, 381-385; Burton D. Myers, The History of Medical Education in Indiana (Bloomington, Ind., 1956), pp. 176-179; "The Recent Legislature and the Medical Profession" and "Fighting the Chiropractors," Journal of the Indiana State Medical Association, XIV (1921), 125-127; E. M. Shanklin to Robert Benjamin Jones, February 20, 1936, Patronage File, Drawer 94, McNutt Papers, Archives Division; Allon Peebles, A Survey of the Medical Facilities of Shelby County, Indiana: 1929 (Chicago, 1930), pp. 29, 33-34, 73-74; Lynd and Lynd, Middletown, pp. 435-443.

[3] For health of the sick poor see Shaffer, Keefer, and Breckinridge, The Indiana Poor Law, pp. 103-191, especially for the role of the Indiana University hospitals.

§ §

One of the outstanding changes in American medicine in the first half of the twentieth century was the rapid expansion of public health services. Public health extended beyond the individual to community-wide health concerns, such as communicable diseases, infant and child hygiene, sanitation, food and milk control, and school health supervision. Public health agencies also emphasized preventive medicine through health education and through community programs directed by private and public agencies. The various forms and objectives of public health and preventive medicine held only slight attraction for many private physicians and in some instances generated their intense disapproval and opposition. The general public, too, responded often with apathy or hostility.[4]

The primary focus of public health in Indiana was the Indiana State Board of Health. Founded in 1881, the board greatly expanded its activities in the first two decades of the twentieth century, guided after 1896 by Dr. John N. Hurty, one of the nation's most energetic public health crusaders. A study of the effectiveness of state public health boards, sponsored by the American Medical Association in 1914-1915, ranked Indiana's board sixth in the nation. The study noted that Indiana's public health education work "is especially prominent and effective. Dr. Hurty has devised many new details which have been copied by others . . . ."[5] Hurty resigned in 1922, but the board continued and expanded its pursuit of improved health. Its record during the interwar years included considerable achievement mixed with conflict and some important failures.

One of the State Board of Health's most notable areas of activity was its effort to control diseases transmitted by impure water, milk, and food. For a long time scientists had known the

[4] George Rosen, *Preventive Medicine in the United States, 1900-1975: Trends and Interpretations* (New York, 1975), pp. 46, 50-54; Peebles, *A Survey of the Medical Facilities of Shelby County*, p. 145.

[5] Charles V. Chapin, *A Report on State Public Health Work Based on a Survey of State Boards of Health* (Chicago, 1916), pp. 21, 196-197. See also Thurman B. Rice, *The Hoosier Health Officer: A Biography of Dr. John N. Hurty* (n.p., [1946]), *passim*; Phillips, *Indiana in Transition*, pp. 469-473.

importance of contaminated food and drink in spreading such diseases as tuberculosis and typhoid, but the will or means to act on such knowledge often proved inadequate, in part because traditional individual solutions usually did not apply to community problems of communicable diseases.

Much of the State Board of Health's work in the interwar years was an attack on impure water, including efforts to improve the purity of municipal and private water supplies, extend modern sewage treatment facilities, and reduce the incidence of stream and lake pollution. By the 1920s there could be no doubt of the unfortunate ability of modern civilization to foul its own nest, as clean, safe water seemed to be going the way of horse-drawn carriages in Indiana.[6] Lakes, rivers, and streams were grossly polluted by domestic waste and by industrial wastes from canneries, oil refineries, meat-packing plants, and factories. Perhaps the most obviously offensive sources of pollution were the many city and town sewer systems which simply discharged raw waste directly into the closest river. By 1941 approximately 200 of the 280 Indiana communities with sewer systems still did not treat their waste. Untreated sewage in the White River—especially from Muncie—led the State Board of Health to report in 1930 that "the water at the Anderson intake is so polluted that . . . it is almost impossible to treat the water to the point where it is safe, and it is impossible to render it palatable." In general, the report concluded, "White River for several miles below Muncie has the appearance and odor of an open sewer."[7] The St. Joseph River received the untreated waste of South Bend, Elkhart, and Misha-

[6] Air pollution received little attention from Indiana public health agencies, undoubtedly because they saw no obvious connections to health. Nonetheless, air pollution was a problem in cities like Indianapolis, where burning of soft coal led to "a choking, rasping, stifling, depressing, suffocating smog. . . ." Indianapolis *News*, October 24, 1924. See also *ibid.*, November 3, 1922, January 9, 1923, and March 5, 1925; and Tarkington, *The Magnificent Ambersons*, pp. 111-112, 389-393.

[7] Quoted in Frank, Politics in Middletown: A Reconsideration of Municipal Government and Community Power in Muncie, Indiana, 1925-1935, pp. 323-324. The pollution of White River was exacerbated by a precipitous decline in water flow during the interwar years. John E. Stoner and Pressly S. Sikes, *Water and Sewerage Systems in Indiana: The Planning of Future Construction Now* (Bloomington, Ind., 1944), pp. 23-24.

waka throughout the interwar years.[8] Whiting, Hammond, East Chicago, and Gary discharged their industrial waste and raw sewage directly into Lake Michigan, which was, in turn, the source of their public water. An investigation of Lake Michigan in 1925 concluded that water received at the lake intakes for Hammond, Whiting, and East Chicago "showed such high bacterial content as to impose what is considered an excessive load upon even a modern purification plant . . . ." The public water supply at Gary was deemed only slightly better.[9] On the southern border of the state, many towns and plants disposed waste into the Ohio River, which usually served also as the source of public water supplies. Pollution of the Ohio was exacerbated by the federal government's construction of sixty dams between Pittsburgh and Cairo, which, although improving navigation, often obstructed water flow in summer months and turned the river into "60 cesspools."[10] Pollution of rivers and lakes throughout Indiana not only killed fish and created unpleasant odors, but also constituted a dangerous health hazard by contaminating the water supply of many communities. Though such conditions existed prior to World War I, by the interwar years it was apparent to many that these conditions were worsening and that they could not be remedied by continued reliance on individual responsibility or local governments. Particularly since water pollution was often produced by many communities and industries, the problem called for action at the state level.

The state government began major efforts during the interwar years to encourage municipal governments to construct sewage treatment and water purification plants. The 1921 General Assembly approved legislation allowing municipal governments

[8] Stoner and Sikes, *Water and Sewerage Systems in Indiana*, p. 25.

[9] H. R. Crohurst and M. V. Veldee, "Report of an Investigation of the Pollution on Lake Michigan in the Vicinity of South Chicago and the Calumet and Indiana Harbors 1924-1925," *Public Health Bulletin*, CLXX (April, 1927), 41, 132-133. The quotation is on page 132.

[10] Indiana *Year Book*, 1939, pp. 688-689. For useful maps showing distribution of public sewers and outdoor sanitation facilities and the location of stream and lake pollution see Indiana State Planning Board, *Preliminary Report on a State Plan for Indiana*, pp. 27-29.

greater flexibility in financing construction of waterworks by sale of revenue bonds; revenue from the new facility rather than local tax moneys could be used to pay off the bonds.[11] The 1927 legislature passed a Stream Pollution Law that gave the State Board of Health responsibility for improving the quality of streams and lakes. This new program was aided considerably by a grant of money from the Rockefeller Foundation to enable the State Board of Health to survey Indiana rivers and to plan for improvements in water quality. The 1927 legislation exempted Lake Michigan and the streams that flowed into it, however, and gave the State Board of Health only moderately effective enforcement powers. Nonetheless, along with increasing local recognition of the necessity for responsible action, these modest efforts by the state government stimulated construction of new water and sewage treatment facilities. In 1920 less than 2 percent of the state's urban population was served by sewage treatment facilities. By 1930 the percentage had increased to 24.[12]

The early years of the Depression brought a near halt to the construction of public works. In the mid- and late 1930s, however, dramatic changes occurred, as the percentage of urban population served by sewage treatment facilities increased from 24 percent in 1933, to 47 percent by 1936, to 72 percent by 1940. The State Board of Health played an important role in this progress. Armed with information on the extent of stream and river pollution and on the quality of water supplies for every community in the state, health officials intensified their pressure on local governments. In this effort they were significantly aided by the 1935 Stream Pollution Law, which gave the state board increased authority to control municipal sewage disposal, especially by denying approval for any new sewer construction that did not include provision for adequate sewage treatment. But the more stringent activities

[11] *Laws of Indiana*, 1921, pp. 205-215; Stoner and Sikes, *Water and Sewerage Systems in Indiana*, pp. 35-38.

[12] *Laws of Indiana*, 1927, pp. 126-128; Indiana *Year Book*, 1928, pp. 541, 574; B. A. Poole, "Progress in the Control of Stream Pollution in Indiana," Purdue University *Engineering Bulletin*, XXIV (July, 1940), 143-145. For progress in Indianapolis see C. K. Calvert, "The Sanitary Works of Indianapolis," *American Journal of Public Health*, XXIV (1934), 739-742.

of state government were possible only because of the support of the federal government. The United States Public Health Service became increasingly active in providing information and aid. Its publicity campaign against the traditional outhouse in urban and rural areas combined with federal money to bring about the installation of more than a hundred thousand sanitary privies in Indiana between 1933 and 1939. Most important were the federal public relief funds allocated by the Public Works Administration, Works Progress Administration, and other New Deal agencies for constructing water and sewage treatment plants. Without this federal money and support it would have been foolhardy for state government to press Depression-era local governments to undertake expensive public works programs.[13]

Progress during the interwar years in construction of water purification and sewage treatment plants in Indiana was important to the health of Hoosiers. And yet the challenges confronting state public health officials and local governments were similar to those of Alice in Wonderland, who had to run faster simply to stand still. The increased availability of clean water at the turn of a spigot resulted in increased use of water, thereby creating larger amounts of waste to be treated and disposed of. By the eve of World War II, many municipal plants were inadequate to the demands made upon them. The Ohio River provided special problems, since Kentucky owned the river and since more than half a dozen states contributed to its pollution. Although a beginning in interstate co-operation was made when Indiana and several states ratified the Ohio River Valley Water Sanitation Compact in 1939, little real progress was made on the Ohio prior to 1945. Moreover, Indiana made only limited responses to problems of

[13] Poole, "Progress in the Control of Stream Pollution," Purdue University *Engineering Bulletin*, XXIV, 143-147; Stoner and Sikes, *Water and Sewerage Systems in Indiana*, p. 43; *Laws of Indiana*, 1935, pp. 537-550; Indiana *Year Book*, 1935, pp. 596-597; 1939, p. 682. For two case studies of the ways in which state pressure and federal money combined to construct municipal sewage treatment plants see Frank, "Who Governed Middletown? Community Power in Muncie, Indiana, in the 1930s," *Indiana Magazine of History*, LXXV, 335-342; Harrold E. Norris, "Control of Stream Pollution as Applied to the City of Peru, Indiana," Purdue University *Engineering Bulletin*, XXIV (July, 1940), 149-152.

industrial pollution. Hesitation here was doubtless due to the desire not to harm or offend industries that provided needed jobs, but it was also a result of the New Deal focus on public rather than private causes of pollution. During World War II there was little improvement, and problems of water pollution would continue to provide major challenges to federal, state, and local governments in the post-1945 era.[14]

In addition to playing an increasingly important role in improving water quality, government also assumed more responsibility for reducing food contamination. The pre-World War I Progressive era had produced federal and state legislation designed to provide inspection and control of food processing, but major problems persisted, especially in enforcement. Milk was the most important problem in the interwar years, not only because it was an ideal medium for transmitting disease, notably typhoid and tuberculosis, but also because milk consumption increased as its nutritional value became more widely publicized. State legislation passed in 1925 and strengthened in 1937, requiring either pasteurization of milk or tuberculin testing of cattle, and increased inspection by state health officials were important responses in the interwar years. Many cities also passed ordinances to prohibit sale of unpasteurized milk, though some local governments did not provide for adequate enforcement. Positive change also followed the Milk Control Act of 1935, which provided for licensing dealers and setting minimum prices in order to eliminate unfair competition from "backyard dairies" and to promote cleaner milk by protecting high quality producers.[15]

[14] Stoner and Sikes, *Water and Sewerage Systems in Indiana*, pp. 20-24; John E. Stoner and Oliver P. Field, *Public Health Services in an Indiana Defense Community* (Bloomington, Ind., 1942), pp. 34-35; Indiana *Year Book*, 1939, pp. 688-689; Poole, "Progress in the Control of Stream Pollution," Purdue University *Engineering Bulletin*, XXIV, 144-148; Armstrong, Robinson, and Hoy (eds.), *History of Public Works in the United States*, p. 416.

[15] *Laws of Indiana*, 1925, pp. 608-611; 1937, pp. 1231-1233; 1935, pp. 1365-1394; Lamar Lyn Kirven, State Regulation of the Milk Industry in Indiana and Texas from 1929 to 1939 (M.A. thesis, Indiana University, Bloomington, 1942), pp. 63-81; Peebles, *A Survey of the Medical Facilities of Shelby County*, pp. 136-137; Lynd and Lynd, *Middletown in Transition*, p. 399; John Taylor to

In addition to encouraging clean water, food, and milk, public health workers also concentrated on specific communicable diseases. One of the most important responsibilities of the State Board of Health was the collection of statistics on morbidity and mortality. During the interwar years the board published such statistics annually and used them as guides and evidence for various public health strategies. Among the most disheartening statistical information gathered was the death rate from typhoid, which during the 1920s was higher in Indiana than in any other northern state. This consideration played a significant role in shaping the State Board of Health's sanitary campaigns, since typhoid epidemics were associated with contaminated water and unpasteurized milk. Considerable progress was made, as the typhoid death rate dropped steadily from 9.6 deaths per 100,000 people in 1920, to 3.7 by 1930, to 1.0 by 1939. Nonetheless, typhoid epidemics continued to plague the state throughout the interwar years.[16]

There were high incidences of other communicable diseases, even though remedies were relatively simple. Indiana was among the states with the highest numbers of smallpox cases during the interwar years, though the death rate from the disease was low. Diphtheria was also a public health problem. In both cases medical science had developed simple remedies in the form of preventive immunization, which partly accounted for a dramatic twentieth-century decline in the incidence of these diseases compared to the nineteenth century. But full success in vaccination or immunization required either public understanding or state control. Indiana lacked both compulsory vaccination and immunization laws during the interwar years, and parents often had their children protected only when an epidemic threatened—or immediately after. In 1941, 53 percent of schoolchildren in Indiana under the age of

John H. Hare, June 26, 1933, Meetings-Pamphlets, 1934, McNutt Papers, Archives Division; Indiana *Year Book*, 1932, pp. 663-684; Stoner and Field, *Public Health Services*, pp. 60-65.
    [16] Walter W. Lee, "Typhoid Fever in Indiana," *Journal of the Indiana State Medical Association*, XX (1927), 388-390; Indiana *Year Book*, 1925, p. 640; 1929, pp. 893-894; 1930, p. 803; 1940, p. 830.

ten did not have smallpox vaccinations, and 57 percent did not have diphtheria immunizations.[17]

There were other communicable diseases that were more difficult to combat, since prevention involved not so much biological and medical as social, economic, and cultural remedies. Tuberculosis and venereal diseases were two such cases in Indiana. Both stimulated intense public health campaigns.

Known as consumption in the nineteenth century and often referred to as the "Great White Plague," tuberculosis was an especially difficult disease to control, even in the post-World War I years. Patent medicines, often containing narcotics or alcohol, continued to be advertised and used as cures, doubtless because there was no simple single remedy. Instead, effective treatment consisted of rest, fresh air, sunlight, and good nutrition, along with various other measures. The tubercle bacillus was especially communicable where living conditions included malnutrition, contamination of food and water, and overcrowding in unsanitary housing. But the disease also infected middle- and upper-class Hoosiers; Paul McNutt's daughter fought a long battle against it. Because tuberculosis was an infectious disease and one so difficult to treat, it attracted the energies of the public health movement to prevent its transmission. During the 1920s tuberculosis became one of the major concerns of public health in Indiana and the nation.[18]

The campaign to control and prevent tuberculosis in Indiana began in the second decade of the twentieth century and included a feature that was unusual in public health efforts. The Indiana Tuberculosis Association, a voluntary health group founded in 1907, played the major role in launching and carrying out the crusade, although often working closely with the State Board of Health, the medical profession, and other groups such as the Red Cross and the Visiting Nurse Association. Financed by private

[17] Indiana *Year Book*, 1942, pp. 365-368; Peebles, *A Survey of the Medical Facilities in Shelby County*, pp. 124-127.

[18] Rosen, *Preventive Medicine*, pp. 25-37; Harry F. Dowling, *Fighting Infection: Conquests of the Twentieth Century* (Cambridge, Mass., 1977), pp. 70-81; Neff, Paul V. McNutt, p. 28.

donations, largely through the sale of Christmas seals, the Indiana Tuberculosis Association mounted extensive campaigns to teach methods of control and prevention. The voluntary agency was most effective through its county associations, which played critical roles in education programs by publicizing the importance of child nutrition, supporting public health nursing programs, and establishing tuberculosis clinics and other testing programs.[19]

The Indiana Tuberculosis Association also pressured state and local governments to take more responsibility in the campaign. In 1919 the legislature authorized the creation of the Division of Tuberculosis within the State Board of Health, which immediately began a public education program of exhibitions, lectures, and conferences—complete with a moving picture machine and a stereopticon to show vividly the nature of the disease. But the state never took the lead in tuberculosis public education programs, probably because state and county voluntary associations were already doing considerable work. However, the State Board of Health administered the program for reporting tuberculosis cases and for testing cattle for bovine tuberculosis. State government also played an important role in treatment offered through a state sanatorium, located in Parke County. Opened in 1911, the institution performed a useful function, but the number of beds was always grossly inadequate for the number of cases. Some local governments worked with county tuberculosis associations and other civic groups to build sanatoria, but most served only the largest cities. In 1930 Governor Leslie appointed a state tuberculosis committee to study these problems and the state's responsibility. The committee's report not only showed that the number of beds for tuberculosis cases was insufficient, but also pointed out wide sectional differences in the state. The disease was most prevalent in rural southern Indiana, the region least able eco-

[19] Harriett Salinger Iglauer, *The Program for the Control and Prevention of Tuberculosis in Indiana* (Indianapolis, 1943), pp. 72-86; Rice, *The Hoosier Health Officer*, pp. 266-268, 298-301; Madelyn Kearney, A History of the Marion County Tuberculosis Association, 1924-1936 (M.A. thesis, Indiana University, Bloomington, 1954). The Indiana Tuberculosis Association published the monthly *Hoosier Health Herald*, containing articles and editorials on control and prevention of the disease.

nomically to provide either public or private care. Although health officials agreed that the minimum requirement was one bed per annual death, in northern Indiana there were only five beds available to care for tuberculosis cases for every seven tuberculosis deaths a year; in the central section of the state there were five beds for every ten tuberculosis deaths; in the southern section there were five beds for every twenty-five deaths. Only the state could remedy this sectional problem, the 1930 commission concluded, and it drafted a bill proposing state financial aid to help counties construct and maintain sanatoria. Because of the Depression, no action was taken until 1938, when a special legislative session approved construction not of county institutions but of a state sanatorium to serve southern Indiana. With nearly half the construction costs coming from the Public Works Administration, the state's second sanatorium opened near New Albany in 1940.[20]

As a partial consequence of these government and voluntary efforts, the death rate from tuberculosis declined impressively, from 107.7 deaths per 100,000 people in 1920, to 65.9 in 1930, to 39.1 in 1940. The continued decline during the 1930s was especially significant, since it might be expected that deteriorating conditions in nutrition and housing available to a large portion of Depression-era Hoosiers were conducive to an increase in the tuberculosis rate. That the downward trend in the death rate did not reverse in the 1930s was doubtless due to the existence of a firmly established institutional framework that continued its benefits through the Depression. While considerable progress was made, it is important to note the lag for certain groups. Rural Hoosiers continued to have a high death rate from tuberculosis: in 1940 a rate of 48.0 compared to 41.2 for the urban population. And blacks suffered at appalling levels. In 1940 the tuberculosis death rate for blacks was 188.2 compared to 34.1 for the white

[20] Iglauer, *The Program for the Control and Prevention of Tuberculosis*, pp. 12-61; Indiana Tuberculosis Commission, *Report*, 1930 (n.p., 1930); Indiana State Committee on Governmental Economy, *Report*, pp. 290-293. In 1929 there were in Shelby County thirty-six tuberculosis cases and nineteen suspected cases. The county's quota in the state sanatorium was two patients. Peebles, *A Survey of the Medical Facilities of Shelby County*, p. 129.

population, a major factor in raising the total tuberculosis death rate for Indianapolis and Gary, with their large black populations, above the state's urban average.[21]

As with tuberculosis, the public health campaign against venereal diseases extended of necessity beyond the boundaries of biological and medical science, indeed farther beyond, since combating syphilis and gonorrhea stirred traditional attitudes regarding sexual morality. Venereal disease was traditionally correlated with morality, even among some doctors and health officials.[22] Social disapprobation associated with venereal diseases led many doctors to refuse to treat cases, and those who did often refused to report the information to the State Board of Health. The response of the general public often was to ignore the problem, sometimes out of ignorance of its magnitude as well as moral concerns.[23] During World War I, a modification of these traditional attitudes began. Wartime leaders realized the degree to which venereal diseases could limit military strength and began an intense campaign of publicity, some of which carried over after the war. In 1919 the State Board of Health added a Bureau of Venereal Diseases, with responsibility for education programs, especially among adolescent males, and for testing and treatment. With half its support coming from federal appropriations, the new bureau in its first year supervised nine clinics and conducted more than fifteen thousand Wasserman tests at the state laboratory.[24] While the campaign against venereal diseases continued thereafter, there was a new burst of activity in the mid- and late 1930s. This nationwide effort included articles and reports in magazines and newspapers on the once-taboo subject, and in 1938 new federal legislation (the LaFollette-Bulwinkle Act) increased aid to the United States

[21] Indiana *Year Book,* 1925, p. 638; 1935, p. 687; 1941, pp. 496, 505, 514; Rosen, *Preventive Medicine,* p. 36.

[22] For the linking of morality and venereal disease by an official of the State Board of Health see A. G. Long, "The Sociology of Venereal Diseases in Indiana," *American Journal of Public Health,* XIII (1923), 489.

[23] Peebles, *A Survey of the Medical Facilities of Shelby County,* p. 128; Indiana *Year Book,* 1920, pp. 497-499; Rosen, *Preventive Medicine,* p. 37.

[24] Rice, *The Hoosier Health Officer,* pp. 273-276; Indiana *Year Book,* 1920, pp. 494-499.

Public Health Service and state health agencies in the campaign. The $60,000 the Indiana State Board of Health received the first year was a major factor in increasing its dissemination of pamphlets, radio scripts, movies, and other educational materials. Many local health agencies also developed publicity campaigns and opened more clinics for testing and treatment. In 1939 the General Assembly passed the Premarital Health Examination Law, which required a blood test for syphilis before a marriage license could be issued. In the same session members also approved legislation that required physicians attending pregnant women to test for syphilis. The Indiana State Medical Association participated in the campaign through symposia and other programs for educating doctors. The results of this broad effort to control venereal diseases are impossible to ascertain. Reported mortality rates for syphilis in the 1930s ranged between 6.2 and 7.3 deaths per 100,000, but problems of reporting make sure figures suspect, while estimates of morbidity were little more than guesses. There is no doubt that the anti-venereal disease campaign was important, but it is likely that of the major diseases attacked by public health campaigns during the interwar years, this particular problem remained furthest from solution.[25]

Although the public health campaigns against specific diseases and the attention to food and water were directed to the general population, there was often special emphasis on the health of children. Contaminated water and milk worked their most malevolent effects on children, while smallpox, diphtheria, typhoid, venereal diseases, and other communicable diseases all grimly produced poor health and death for young Hoosiers. A wide-ranging campaign for improving the health and welfare of children was a major part of progressive reforms at the local, state, and federal

[25] "Fort Wayne Starts Fight on Social Diseases," *American City*, LII (April, 1937), 19; *Laws of Indiana*, 1939, pp. 513-516, 21-22; "Publicity Concerning 'Social Diseases,'" *Journal of the Indiana State Medical Association*, XXIX (1936), 343-344; "Our Syphilis Control Program," *ibid.*, XXX (1937), 536-537; "Control of Syphilis," *ibid.*, XXX (1937), 419-428; Indiana *Year Book*, 1935, pp. 612-617, 697; 1939, pp. 611-615; 1941, pp. 472-478, 505.

levels prior to World War I.[26] This was also one of the few significant cases of a program that continued through the 1920s, thereby linking progressive and New Deal reform.

The state legislature first made important commitments to child welfare in 1919. It provided for a special commission to study the subject, which reported in 1920 and prepared bills passed by the 1921 General Assembly regarding child labor, school attendance, and other child welfare objectives.[27] More specifically in the realm of public health, the 1919 legislature authorized and funded the Division of Infant and Child Hygiene of the State Board of Health. The division got off to an active start and greatly expanded its work after passage of the Sheppard-Towner Act of 1921. This federal legislation, one of the first major ventures of the national government into social welfare, responded to lingering progressive sentiments and to the political influence of newly enfranchised women and women's groups. Sheppard-Towner provided direct and matching funds to states for educational programs in maternal and infant hygiene. Under strong pressure from the Indiana League of Women Voters, the 1923 legislature and Governor McCray passed and approved the funding and enabling legislation necessary to receive this federal money.[28]

Directed by Dr. Ada E. Schweitzer, the new Division of Infant and Child Hygiene became the most active center of public health in Indiana during the 1920s. Schweitzer received her medical degree in 1907 from the Indiana Medical College. Thereafter she concentrated on public health work—especially with children—

[26] For this work in Indianapolis see United States Department of Labor, Children's Bureau, *Baby-Saving Campaigns: A Preliminary Report on What American Cities Are Doing to Prevent Infant Mortality* (Washington, D.C., 1913), pp. 26-27, 40.

[27] Albion Fellows Bacon and Edna Hatfield Edmondson, *Child Welfare Legislation: Work of the Indiana Sub-commission on Child Welfare of the Commission on Child Welfare and Social Insurance* (Indiana University Extension Division, *Bulletin*, VII, September, 1921), pp. 1-94.

[28] Stanley J. Lemons, *The Woman Citizen: Social Feminism in the 1920s* (Urbana, Ill., 1973), pp. 153-159; Indiana *Year Book*, 1925, pp. 568-569; Greenough, *A History of the League of Women Voters of Indiana*, p. 8; *The Indiana League of Women Voters, 1923* (n.p., n.d.).

working for the State Board of Health and the federal government. She developed a national reputation that led in 1928 to her election as president of the American Association of Women in Public Health. In Indiana Schweitzer was careful to co-operate with leading women's groups, including the League of Women Voters, American Association of University Women, Indiana Federation of Clubs, Tri Kappas, and other philanthropic organizations. By 1925 Schweitzer's staff included four physicians and five registered nurses—all female. They gave dozens of lectures and demonstrations on maternity and infant care, sponsored child health conferences, conducted baby clinics, and publicized their cause throughout the state with pamphlets, movies, and extremely popular baby contests at the Indiana State Fair. Schweitzer and her associates encouraged prenatal care by a physician or nurse, hospital care for childbirth,[29] and postnatal medical checks. They instructed mothers in nutrition and emphasized the importance of orange juice, cod-liver oil, safe milk, and balanced diets. By the late 1920s Schweitzer was able to point to statistical evidence of improved health in Indiana: the proportion of underweight children declined by half between 1922 and 1929; infant diarrhea, a major cause of infant death, dropped by more than 50 percent in the period from 1917 to 1927; and, perhaps most impressive, the infant mortality rate declined from 81.8 deaths under one year of age per 1,000 live births in 1920 to 57.7 in 1930. Schweitzer did not claim full credit for these changes, but she argued that her division's work was an important factor in improving the health of children, mothers, and the general population as well.[30]

In addition to being the most active public health agency, the Division of Infant and Child Hygiene was also the most controver-

[29] It was still customary in the 1920s for many women to receive little or no prenatal care and for babies to be born at home, though there was a trend toward hospital births. Births in the Muncie hospital as a percentage of total city births increased from 12 percent in 1925 to 39 percent by 1935. Lynd and Lynd, *Middletown in Transition*, pp. 389-390. See also Peebles, *A Survey of the Medical Facilities of Shelby County*, pp. 130, 147.

[30] Hubbard (ed.), *A Book of Indiana*, pp. 191, 356; Indiana *Year Book*, 1925, pp. 566-600; 1929, pp. 835-840; 1930, pp. 718-774; Rice, *The Hoosier Health Officer*, pp. 315-316.

sial. Some of the controversy resulted from conservative opposition to the Sheppard-Towner Act as an unwarranted, even radical, interference of government in individual and private concerns. The American Medical Association (AMA) led this national opposition, while the Indiana State Medical Association (ISMA) was among the most active state organizations in opposition. Organized medicine's antagonism was important in bringing an end to Sheppard-Towner in 1929. ISMA also focused its attack on Schweitzer, charging that she did not provide a sufficiently large role for organized medicine and that this publicly-supported work interfered with the private practice of physicians in Indiana. This attack on the Division of Infant and Child Hygiene was part of a broader campaign against the State Board of Health and part of the first major battle against what the ISMA and AMA labeled "state" or "socialized" medicine. Under state medicine, the *Journal of the Indiana State Medical Association* declared in 1927, "the rank and file of the people are to be herded like cattle and given their medical and surgical attention by government employees, and the rank and file of the medical profession are to be mere cogs in a great machine that renders impersonal and perhaps poor service to the people." In addition to attacking child and maternal public health activities, ISMA criticized the use of the state laboratory for testing, especially Wasserman tests for syphilis, and the publicly-supported venereal disease clinics—all of which the executive committee of ISMA reported in 1933 "put the state in competition with the practitioners of medicine."[31]

Apparently under strong pressure from organized medicine, Governor McNutt responded soon after taking office in 1933.

[31] "State Medicine," *Journal of the Indiana State Medical Association*, XX (1927), 23; "Reorganization of the Indiana State Board of Health," *ibid.*, XXVI (1933), 209. See also "Misguided Zeal for Public Welfare," *ibid.*, XIV (1921), 50-51; "The Sheppard-Towner Bill," *ibid.*, XIV (1921), 192-193; Dorothy Ritter Russo (ed.), *One Hundred Years of Indiana Medicine, 1849-1949* (n.p., 1949), pp. 17-18, 47; Rice, *The Hoosier Health Officer*, pp. 313-314, 324; Lemons, *The Woman Citizen*, pp. 160-165, 173. It is possible that some of the opposition from the largely male medical profession to governmental work in child and maternal health and to public health nursing derived from resistance to women in leadership roles. For a suggestion of this tension see Rice, *The Hoosier Health Officer*, p. 299.

His government reorganization plan included changing the State Board of Health to the Division of Public Health. In the process he got rid of Schweitzer and her associates, abolished the Division of Infant and Child Hygiene in the name of government economy, and responded to general medical discontent with the old State Board of Health by firing Dr. William F. King, who had succeeded Hurty as secretary in 1922 and on whom the ISMA laid much of the blame for state medicine. McNutt accepted ISMA's recommendation of Dr. Verne K. Harvey as King's successor, and the governor promised that thereafter the Division of Public Health would work closely with ISMA, its county medical societies, and the Indiana University School of Medicine. McNutt also promised that the state laboratory would curtail work that competed with private practitioners and that the state would end its support of venereal disease clinics. These and other changes led the ISMA executive committee to report that "the organized physicians of the state have gotten pretty nearly everything that they can reasonably ask" and that McNutt's actions constituted "the biggest step that has ever been taken in Indiana away from state medicine."[32]

Harvey's tenure as director of the Division of Public Health from 1933 to 1940 was much less controversial than his predecessor's, since he carefully worked with physicians and ISMA. The compromises of 1933, which ISMA proudly labeled "the Indiana Plan," remained in place and allowed state and local medical societies more leadership in preventive medicine. Their support of the campaigns against venereal disease in the 1930s is indicative of that role.[33] And yet there were changes in public health in the

[32] "Reorganization of the Indiana State Board of Health," *Journal of the Indiana State Medical Association*, XXVI (1933), 212. See also "Dr. King Should Be Retained," *ibid.*, XX (1927), 229; "The Indiana State Board of Health," *ibid.*, XXVI (1933), 280; "The Indiana Plan," *ibid.*, XXVI (1933), 381; Russo (ed.), *One Hundred Years of Indiana Medicine*, pp. 48-49; Ruby Roten Absher, The History of the Indiana State Board of Health from 1922 to 1954 (Doctor of Health and Safety thesis, Indiana University, Bloomington, 1978), pp. 66, 82.

[33] *Journal of the Indiana State Medical Association*, XXXII (1939), 511; Indiana *Year Book*, 1935, p. 594; Iglauer, *The Program for the Control and Prevention of Tuberculosis*, pp. 69-70.

mid- and late 1930s that revived some of the programs of the 1920s and created new programs. Even more than in the 1920s, the initiative came from the federal government.

Major change in public health resulted from passage of the Social Security Act of 1935. Title V of that federal legislation provided federal aid for maternal and infant health, which revived the purposes of Sheppard-Towner. The McNutt administration eagerly co-operated with the new social security program. The special session of the General Assembly in March, 1936, passed the Public Health Act in order to receive Title V money. In April, 1936, the new Bureau of Maternal and Child Health, with half its funding derived from this federal source, began a program of public education and field work similar to that of the Division of Infant and Child Hygiene of the 1920s. However, the new director, Dr. Howard B. Mettel, unlike Schweitzer, was careful to work closely with private physicians, local medical societies, and a special liaison committee of ISMA.[34]

The second change in the late 1930s derived from Title VI of the Social Security Act of 1935, which provided federal support for full-time professional local health officers. By the 1920s Indiana was one of only a few states that did not authorize full-time county health officers. State Board of Health secretaries Hurty and King both campaigned hard for full-time county public health officers. They argued against Indiana's exclusive reliance on part-time officers, who, although they were practicing physicians, were often untrained in preventive medicine and were usually able to devote only limited time to this important work. In his 1925 report King asserted that

because of the obsolete and impractical system of public health administration in Indiana, with part time and poorly paid local health officials, it is necessary for the State Health Department to not only take the initiative in but to undertake to actually perform to the best of its ability whatever constructive health work is carried out in most communities of the state.

[34] Howard B. Mettel, "Evaluation of Maternal and Child Health Services in Indiana," *Journal of the Indiana State Medical Association*, XXX (1937), 433-434; Indiana *Year Book*, 1936, p. 594; 1939, pp. 618-620; 1940, pp. 864-868; Lemons, *The Woman Citizen*, pp. 175-176.

The problem was especially acute in rural areas, while in some cities local health departments and voluntary agencies provided much of the necessary public health service.[35]

The 1935 session of the General Assembly responded to these concerns by allowing but not requiring counties to appoint full-time public health officers. Title VI of the Social Security Act provided money for these officers, stimulated a movement toward a merit system for their appointment, and led to the establishment in late 1936 of the Bureau of Local Health Administration in the Division of Public Health. With federal and state money, the new bureau embarked on an effort to create district public health departments that served several counties to provide full-time professional public health services at the local level. Major impetus to the bureau's work came with the devastating Ohio River flood of January, 1937, which created a potentially disastrous threat to public health in communities along the river. In response, the bureau established four district health departments to serve the river counties. Others were added later, and by 1941 there were eight district health offices that served all of southern Indiana, where the need was assumed to be greatest. The Bureau of Local Health Administration provided the compromise solution to conflicts that had long beset official health work in Indiana. Promoted as a move toward decentralization and greater control by local government and by local medical societies, the bureau also allowed for full-time professional health work at the local level with some supervision from the state. The new system neither solved all controversies nor provided the level of health care some public health officials wished, but it represented a step toward solving a difficult and complex problem.[36]

[35] Indiana *Year Book*, 1925, p. 523. See also 1920, pp. 487-488; Peebles, *A Survey of the Medical Facilities of Shelby County*, p. 117; Indiana State Committee on Governmental Economy, *Report*, p. 289; Rice, *The Hoosier Health Officer*, pp. 321-323. For city health efforts in Gary, Muncie, and Terre Haute see American Child Health Association, *A Health Survey of 86 Cities* (New York, 1925), pp. 363-365, 440-442, 528-530.

[36] *Laws of Indiana*, 1935, pp. 1027-1034; Stoner and Field, *Public Health Services*, pp. 14-15, 31; Iglauer, *The Program for the Control and Prevention of Tuberculosis*, pp. 61-62, 66-69; "The New Health Officer Set-Up," *Journal of the*

There were major improvements in the quality of health care available to Hoosiers in the years between the two world wars. New medical knowledge, better-trained physicians, and more and better hospitals led to improved private health care. Expanded and new responsibilities characterized preventive and public health efforts. The public health movement included voluntary associations, Red Cross, Community Chest, and Visiting Nurse Associations, which made major contributions. In 1939, for example, the 508 public health nurses in Indiana included 232 nurses employed by these and other nongovernmental agencies, the remainder being employed by state and local government, often with federal money.[37] Broad-based public health programs also came from state government, which in the interwar years conducted campaigns to improve water quality, provide pure food and milk, and combat communicable diseases. The federal government, too, made important contributions throughout the period, but especially after 1933.[38]

There were notable achievements in these public health efforts, yet they were achievements mixed with disappointments and failures. New health problems appeared just as some old ones seemed near solution. By the eve of World War II, polio had begun to alarm medical and public health officials. The 682 cases reported in 1940 alone constituted almost half the total reported in the entire period 1920-1939.[39] And noncommunicable and chronic diseases such as cancer and heart disease presented new challenges.

More important, perhaps, old problems remained unsolved as Hoosiers' traditional attachments to individualism and self-help obstructed change. The gap between whites and blacks in health and health care apparently narrowed—especially in the late 1930s

---

Indiana State Medical Association, XXX (1937), 640-641; Indiana *Year Book,* 1935, p. 594; 1942, pp. 355-356; Thurman B. Rice, "Suggested Plans for the Development of Public Health in Indiana," *Journal of the Indiana State Medical Association,* XXXVIII (1945), 60-61.

[37] Indiana *Year Book,* 1939, p. 544. There were 242 public health nurses in Indiana in 1920. *Ibid.,* 1940, p. 800.

[38] In 1939 the State Board of Health received $405,870 in federal appropriations and $406,444 in state appropriations. *Ibid.,* 1940, p. 792.

[39] *Ibid.,* 1941, pp. 437, 452.

—but it remained distressingly large. By 1940 the infant mortality rate for black Hoosiers had dropped considerably, but it was still 60.5 compared to 40.8 for whites, and the maternal death rate for blacks was 4.0 compared to 2.4 for whites. The death rate for the state's entire black population was 18.0 compared to 11.5 for whites.[40] In cities, problems of dilapidated and unsanitary housing for blacks and whites plagued efforts to improve health. The New Deal brought federal money for construction of some public housing for poorer families, including Sunset Park in Vincennes and Lockefield Gardens in Indianapolis.[41] But these efforts were only small steps toward solving the problems they addressed.

Health care for rural Hoosiers presented special problems, also, perhaps best indicated by the continuing high tuberculosis rate in rural and especially southern Indiana. The public health district setup begun in 1937 was an important step toward providing full-time public health services to rural Indiana, but Indiana continued to rank far behind other states in this important area. Indeed a nationwide study of local public health, conducted by the American Public Health Association in 1942, found Indiana seriously lagging. The report for the state concluded:

it cannot be maintained that Indiana has at present anything approaching adequate local health service . . . . Only 4 states, none of them as rich as Indiana, have reported smaller per capita expenditures for local health service. Indiana apparently has availed itself of neither its local resources nor the federal subsidies for building up a creditable statewide local health service.[42]

The Indiana State Board of Health echoed this indictment in a report prepared at the end of World War II. Concluding on the basis of several indicators that Indiana ranked thirty-seventh among the states in public health generally, the state agency lamented that "the essentials for a bare minimum health service have not been provided."[43] From a different perspective, the

40 *Ibid.*, 1941, p. 505; 1935, p. 697.

41 *Ibid.*, 1935, p. 624.

42 Haven Emerson, *Local Health Units for the Nation* (New York, 1945), p. 94.

43 Indiana State Board of Health, *Public Health in Indiana* (n.p., [1946]), pp. 3-18. The quotation is on page 17. See also Russo (ed.), *One Hundred Years of*

Lynds concluded in their study of Muncie in the mid-1930s that "the slowly cumulating debits of rachitic children, abscessed teeth, and tuberculosis are readily overlooked in this go-as-you-please culture in which the onus for keeping healthy is placed traditionally on the individual."[44] These indictments were perhaps exaggerated, especially as they did not indicate the progress made during the interwar years. Yet, given the foundation laid in the first two decades of the twentieth century and comparing the state's progress with that of others, Indiana could have achieved a better system of health care for its citizens.

§ § §

In addition to changes in the ways in which Hoosiers protected themselves from disease, there were also during the interwar years transformations in the ways in which they protected themselves from crime. Local responsibility remained an important feature in public safety as in public health, but increasingly the state played a larger role, especially in effecting a transition toward a more modern, professional system of crime prevention and control.

Enforcement of law had traditionally been the responsibility of local law authorities in Indiana—of township constables, town marshals, city police, and county sheriffs. Many worked under severe hardships. A special census in 1934 showed that the large majority of Indiana law enforcement officers had no experience or training before assuming their positions and that only one third had attended school beyond the eighth grade. Most had no job security but rather were dependent on either their own election, in the case of county sheriffs, or the election of a political superior, in the case of city police. Partisan politics had a large and sometimes demoralizing influence upon the majority of local law enforcement officers, and there were more than occasional instances of corruption.[45]

Indiana Medicine, p. 50, for an argument that Indiana's involvement in the area of public health declined between the world wars.

[44] Lynd and Lynd, *Middletown in Transition*, p. 400.

[45] A study, done in 1934, provides detailed data on the characteristics of law

This local, unprofessional method of law enforcement was increasingly unsuited to the needs of twentieth-century Indiana. Hoosiers and other Americans perceived a rapid increase and a change in the nature of crime during the 1920s. Demand for bootleg liquor provided new opportunities for criminal entrepreneurs, both large and small, while opposition to prohibition stimulated disrespect for the law. Bank robbers were distressingly successful, particularly after 1929 when the Depression provided new incentives for this form of crime. Many authorities also believed that the press, radio, and movies sensationalized and sometimes even romanticized crime, which further encouraged its growth. By the close of the 1920s, these concerns were prominently noted, not only in the annual reports of the Indiana State Police Bureau but also in both major party platforms.[46] In his 1929 annual message Governor Leslie lamented "the constant and most alarming increase in crime within our state the past few years . . . ."[47] The General Assembly authorized the Conference on Law Observance and Enforcement, which met in October, 1929, and led to the appointment of a special committee which reported its recommendations in 1931. Noting the changing nature and increased incidence of crime, the committee asserted that "crime is organized as never before, and, until the agencies having to do with apprehension and punishment of the criminal are better coordinated and their equipment modernized, the state will remain under a serious hardship in its efforts at law enforcement." And, the committee concluded, because "coping with crime is a state-wide problem . . . the state should be the unit of control."[48]

---

enforcement officials by type of officer. Indiana State Committee on Governmental Economy, *Report*, pp. 382-391. See also Indianapolis *News*, October 14, 1929.

[46] Annual reports of the State Police Bureau are in the Indiana *Year Book*. See, for example, Indiana *Year Book*, 1928, p. 31. See also Democratic and Republican state platforms, 1930, in Indiana State Platforms, I.

[47] Indiana *House Journal*, 1929, p. 52.

[48] Indiana Committee on Observance and Enforcement of Law, *Report* (n.p., 1931), pp. 12, 16. See also Minutes of the Committee on Observance and Enforcement of Law, October 11, 1929, Box E, Drawer 45, Leslie Papers; Indianapolis *News*, October 12, 1929.

The Leslie administration studied the problem and recommended solutions, but no doubt because of the Depression the legislature did not act. Crime seemed to increase as the economy worsened. Bank robberies, particularly in small towns, led the Indiana Bankers Association and local banks and merchants to begin a program of volunteer or vigilante police associations to aid hard-pressed county sheriffs and town police.[49]

By far the most dramatic illustration of the problem of crime and the inadequacy of local law enforcement by 1933 was provided in the career of John Dillinger. Born in 1903 in Indianapolis to a middle-class family, Dillinger experienced a rebellious and troubled childhood. In his teens the family moved to a farm near Mooresville, south of Indianapolis. In 1924 Dillinger robbed a local grocer and earned the harsh sentence of ten to twenty years in the state reformatory at Pendleton. Transferred to the state prison at Michigan City in 1929, he made the personal associations through which he received advanced training in criminal behavior. Paroled in May, 1933, Dillinger and his comrades soon began a long series of robberies that included Indiana banks in Daleville, Mason City, Greencastle, East Chicago, Montpelier, Indianapolis, and South Bend. To supply their need for machine guns, bulletproof vests, and other equipment, the Dillinger gang robbed police stations in Auburn, Peru, and Warsaw, and stole dozens of cars to provide for their transportation. Their daring holdups resulted in injuries and death to several law officials and bystanders.

The Dillinger gang was the most notorious of many gangs that spread terror through Indiana and the Midwest during the early years of the Depression. At the same time, John Dillinger himself became a widely admired folk hero for his occasional Robin Hood-like chivalry, his haughty impudence toward law and prison officials, and his dash and flair in executing bank robberies (particularly in jumping over bank counters). Captured in January, 1934, Dillinger was placed in the Lake County jail at Crown Point. His dramatic escape in March brought nationwide scorn and ridicule to Lake County Sheriff Lillian Holley, who

[49] Bruce Smith, *Rural Crime Control* (New York, 1933), pp. 111-112; Indiana *Year Book,* 1932, pp. 1449-1450.

had assumed the job after her husband was killed in the line of duty; to Sam Cahoon, the jailer, who had himself served several jail terms for public intoxication; to Robert Estill, the county prosecutor, who had posed with his arm around Dillinger in a photograph distributed nationwide; and to Governor McNutt, who had signed Dillinger's parole a year earlier. Dillinger's career ended in July, 1934, when Federal Bureau of Investigation agents, with the aid of East Chicago police and the famous "woman in red," tracked him to the Biograph Theater in Chicago and shot him dead when he emerged.

The myth and romance associated with Dillinger, even after his death, should not obscure the important role he played in pointing out the deficiencies in law enforcement. Dillinger made a mockery of small-town banks, local police, and county sheriffs. Though Captain Matt Leach of the Indiana State Police became nearly obsessed with capturing Dillinger, he and his handful of associates worked under great handicaps. After Dillinger's escape from the Crown Point jail, no one even thought to call the state police, doubtless reflecting the limited expectations held for Leach and his colleagues.[50]

The McNutt administration began efforts to create a modern state police force even before Dillinger began his escapades. In early 1933 the General Assembly expanded state police authority from that of highway patrol to general statewide law enforcement. But Dillinger's dangerous and embarrassing career produced calls for significant change and improvement in the state police.[51] The administration's governmental study committee of 1934 placed major emphasis on law enforcement. The committee's report concluded that township constables and county sheriffs were "out of place in a system of crime control as needed in this decade." While they recognized a legitimate and necessary role for city police departments, the committee recommended greater responsibility for state police generally, particularly in rural areas,

[50] John Toland, *The Dillinger Days* (New York, 1963), *passim*; Neff, Paul V. McNutt, pp. 320-326; Lane, "*City of the Century*," pp. 177-181.
[51] *Laws of Indiana*, 1933, pp. 473-477; Indianapolis *News*, March 8, 12, 1934; Indianapolis *Star*, March 9, 1934.

Hoagy Carmichael orchestra, Columbia Club, Indianapolis, winter 1928-1929

Theodore Dreiser

Richard Lieber

Indianapolis Star

Purdue-Indiana football game, 1932 (Purdue won, 25 to 7)

Paul Gass

Washington (Ind.) High School
state basketball champions, 1930

and a decreased role for local law enforcement authorities, especially county sheriffs. To carry out new responsibilities, the committee concluded that the state must provide a larger, better-trained, and better-equipped state police, for "the system and scientific technique in criminal gangs must be matched by scientific methods on the part of the police." The committee also recommended a reduction of political influence and patronage at all levels, from the city to the state police.[52]

Governor McNutt and the 1935 General Assembly responded to these recommendations with money and legislation that doubled the number of state police personnel, created a state police training school, and provided, with financial support from the Indiana Bankers Association, a state police radio system that placed radios in all state police cars and motorcycles. Like many other McNutt-era reforms, the 1935 state police act also gave the governor greater authority over appointment, removal, and policy. Expansion in the state police force continued after 1935, so that by 1940 Indiana boasted nearly two hundred state policemen, compared to the forty employed in 1930. The annual report of the state police for 1940 pointed with pride to the creation of "a single modern department" and the great decline in bank robberies in the preceding five years.[53]

The development of a modern state police system was not completed in the 1930s, however, as partisan politics continued to play a part. At least some applications for the state police still included a sign-off by precinct committeemen and the county party chairman. A long conflict between the professionally oriented superintendent of the state police, Al Feeney, and McNutt's patronage secretary, Pleas Greenlee, ended with Feeney's dismissal in mid-1935. Though there was progress toward a state police merit system after 1935, it was not completed prior to 1940.[54]

[52] Indiana State Committee on Governmental Economy, *Report*, pp. 381-426. The quotations are on pages 421 and 419.

[53] *Laws of Indiana*, 1935, pp. 1463-1465; Indiana *Year Book*, 1935, pp. 2-5; 1940, pp. 386-388; 1930, p. 8; Neff, Paul V. McNutt, pp. 334-339.

[54] Walter Rader to Greenlee, April 24, 1935, Box A, Drawer 86, McNutt Papers, Archives Division; Indianapolis *News*, March 9, 1934, March 4, 1935; Neff, Paul V. McNutt, pp. 318-339.

The safety of Hoosiers required a modern police system. So, too, did it require a modern prison system—one that successfully kept dangerous offenders behind bars and also increased the possibility that once they were free they would not again be a threat to public safety and welfare. Dillinger's career indicates the consequences of failure. Indiana prisons apparently served to harden his commitment to a criminal career, and later they proved embarrassingly easy for him and his associates to escape, as newspaper stories and editorials prominently noted.[55]

The prison problem in Indiana was familiar and long-standing. At the base was inadequate financial support, which resulted in overcrowding and poor facilities in local jails and state prisons. Many county jails remained poorly financed and administered through the early twentieth century, but the state farm at Putnamville, opened in 1915, provided a more efficient and often more humane means of incarceration for misdemeanants and relieved some of the burdens on county governments.[56] A fire at the state's Jeffersonville facility resulted in construction of a new and more modern reformatory at Pendleton, opened in 1923. But Pendleton and the other state penal institutions suffered from serious overcrowding during the interwar years. In 1930 Pendleton, with a capacity of 1,200 prisoners, had a population of 1,981, while the state prison at Michigan City, with a capacity of 1,550 prisoners, held 2,331.[57] Under such conditions it was difficult not only to guard and control prisoners but also to provide the kinds of individual attention and help that encouraged rehabilitation. A 1936 survey of Indiana penal institutions by F. Lovell Bixby, assistant director of the Department of Justice, led to very negative criticisms. Pendleton, Bixby concluded, had twice as many prisoners as desirable and required a "modern, constructive program aimed at restoring the prisoner to society rather than keeping

[55] Indianapolis *Star*, March 5, 1934; Indianapolis *News*, March 8, 1934.

[56] Helen Wilson, *The Treatment of the Misdemeanant in Indiana, 1816-1936* (Chicago, 1938), pp. 46-56, 74-82; John H. Klinger and Thomas G. Hutton, *Indiana and the Adult Offender: A Study of the Crime Problem* (n.p., [1939]), p. 42.

[57] Indiana Committee on Observance and Enforcement of Law, *Report*, p. 14.

him quiet during his period of imprisonment . . . ." Bixby found conditions even worse at Michigan City, where "a lack of skill and aptitude on the part of the management is evidenced in many ways." A full-scale federal study of Indiana's prisons in 1938 reached similar damning conclusions.[58]

Part of the difficulty was partisan politics, an omnipresent feature of nearly all state institutions. Prison guards and wardens were usually patronage appointees with little or no job security. Several members of the Dillinger gang escaped from the state prison at Michigan City in 1933 only a few months after the change from Republican to Democratic control in the governor's office had produced a new warden and 69 new guards out of the total 120 at the prison. Democratic prison guards, though less experienced, were probably no worse than their Republican predecessors, but patronage in the state prisons was a major obstacle to the kinds of professionalism critics thought necessary. Though McNutt's governmental reorganization in 1933 and the creation of the Department of Public Welfare in 1936 attracted some increased attention to rehabilitation and also to questions of probation, parole, and juvenile delinquency, it did not create a merit system in state penal institutions. An institutional building program begun in 1937 with state and federal money resulted in improvements and expansion of prison facilities, but here, as elsewhere, major challenges remained.[59]

---

[58] F. Lovell Bixby to Wayne Coy, July 30, 1936, Box 18, Coy Papers; United States Prison Industries Reorganization Administration, *The Prison Problem in Indiana* (Washington, D.C., 1938).

[59] Toland, *The Dillinger Days*, p. 113; United States Prison Industries Reorganization Administration, *The Prison Problem in Indiana*, pp. ii, 5-7; Klinger and Hutton, *Indiana and the Adult Offender*, pp. 79-80; John H. Klinger, *Indiana's Convicted Criminals: A Discussion of Prison and Parole Problems as They Appear in 1938* [Indianapolis, 1938]; Indiana *Year Book*, 1940, pp. 522-526.

CHAPTER XI

LEISURE, SPORTS, AND CULTURE

HOOSIERS worked in factories, offices, kitchens, and farms, politicked and voted, attended schools and churches; but after World War I many discovered that they had more time for leisure activities and greater opportunities to pursue a wider range of such activities than ever before. In 1929 a major survey of leisure in Indianapolis determined that the average workday in the city was eight hours and forty minutes compared to the common ten-hour day in 1915 and that the average workweek had dropped from sixty hours to forty-eight hours. While factory and office hours decreased, many women who spent long hours in house-work and cooking also benefited from commercially prepared foods, such as bread, and from new electrical appliances, such as vacuum cleaners, washing machines, refrigerators, and ranges, all of which became increasingly available, especially in urban mid-dle-class homes. As with other areas of life, greater leisure and wider opportunities for recreation, entertainment, and culture were not equally available to all: differences between urban and rural Hoosiers, blacks and whites, men and women, youth and adults were sometimes reflected in leisure activities.[1]

The increased time free from work presented new challenges and opportunities. Some leisure-time activities required special clothing, for example, as L. S. Ayres department store in Indian-apolis suggested when in 1923 it proudly opened a new depart-

[1] *The Leisure of a People*, pp. 55-56, 464-467; Wisehart, "Is This Your Family Too?" *American Magazine*, CXI, 55; Lynd and Lynd, *Middletown*, pp. 155–158, 172, 225-226. *The Leisure of a People* report was directed by Eugene T. Lies, a representative of the Playground and Recreation Association of America. It is another example of an outside, professionally prepared report on a social problem in Indiana. The report is wonderfully detailed, 571 pages in length, an excellent source for a wide range of social and leisure activities in Indianapolis during the 1920s.

ment "devoted entirely to sports wear."[2] Using leisure well became increasingly important, not only for the intrinsic satisfactions this could provide but also for the social status it conferred. The Indianapolis *News* noted critically the new fad of men and women "punishing themselves in the sun" to darken their skin, "all because tan [skin] indicated a trip to lake or seashore, a vacation, the expenditure of money and social standing."[3] A few observers worried that the increased leisure would be wasted, particularly by young adults, in "idling, meandering, gambling, trash-reading, razzy, jazzy-joy-riding, illicit sex-practices. . . ." As a preventive, an Indianapolis report on leisure emphasized family activities and encouraged adults "to keep up the play spirit in themselves, get some hobbies, throw dignity to the winds at times and romp with those children."[4]

Family trips and vacations were high on the list of ways to spend leisure time, particularly as the automobile gave Americans in the post-World War I era a new mobility, facilitating Sunday drives, weekend trips, or cross-country expeditions—all as a family unit.[5] Hoosiers were especially fortunate, for in their cars they had access to one of the nation's most rapidly developing state park systems.

The movement to build state parks in Indiana took hold during the state's centennial celebration in 1916 and the following year led to the acquisition of tracts of land on McCormick's Creek in Owen County and Turkey Run in Parke County. In 1919 the General Assembly created the Indiana Department of Conservation to administer the parks and to oversee the state's interests in fisheries and game, forests, geology, and other natural resources. The architect and prime mover of the new direction in conservation generally and in state parks specifically was Richard Lieber,

[2] Indianapolis *Star*, March 1, 1923.
[3] Indianapolis *News*, June 30, 1931.
[4] *The Leisure of a People*, pp. 83, 85.
[5] Paid vacations were a luxury not generally available to the working class in the 1920s. Factory workers who took vacations were not paid for days missed. Of 122 working-class families interviewed in Muncie in 1925, only 24 had taken a week or more of vacation in the previous year. Lynd and Lynd, *Middletown*, p. 262. See also *The Leisure of a People*, pp. 467-468.

who became the first director of the Department of Conservation, serving from 1919 to 1933. Lieber had been born in Germany in 1869, emigrated to America in 1891, and eventually entered business in Indianapolis.[6]

Like many others in the Progressive era, Lieber became interested in preserving the natural beauty of the land threatened by modern development and destruction. To Lieber such preservation was necessary not simply for its own sake, though that was important, but also for the emotional and physical health of individuals and for the order and stability of the society. In his 1925 annual report, for example, Lieber argued that "State Parks are a partial antidote for our social ills caused by industry. With the increased congestion of population in small spots the state parks have become 'social safety valves.' " In them, Lieber argued, visitors could find the "physical expression of life, liberty and the pursuit of happiness."[7] In radio addresses, lectures, and his annual reports, Lieber energetically taught Hoosiers the varied benefits of conservation and state parks. And while he often waxed romantic, Lieber was a strong proponent of organization and administrative efficiency and economy. His policy of charging a ten-cent admission to the parks was designed to insure "an appreciation of the park by the visitor and materially assist in the maintenance and capital outlay," so that the parks could become self-sustaining.[8] And Lieber was a professional conservationist, who was active not only in putting Indiana in the vanguard of park development but also in wider arenas through the National Conference on State Parks.[9]

To McCormick's Creek and Turkey Run, Lieber's department added other state parks in the 1920s: Clifty Falls (1920), Muscatatuck (1921), Indiana Dunes (1925), Pokagon (1925), Spring Mill (1927), Brown County (1929), Shakamak (1929), and Mounds (1930). The Department of Conservation also managed

[6] Phillips, *Indiana in Transition*, pp. 220-223; David M. Silver (ed.), "Richard Lieber and Indiana's Forest Heritage," *Indiana Magazine of History*, LXVII (1971), 45-55.

[7] Indiana *Year Book*, 1925, p. 322.

[8] *Ibid.*, p. 323.

[9] Frederick, Colonel Richard Lieber, pp. 271-272, 346-356, 365, 376.

the Nancy Hanks Lincoln Burial Ground, Tippecanoe Battleground, Bass Lake Beach, the James F. D. Lanier House, Pigeon Roost Monument, and the Corydon State Capitol. Popular support for the parks and memorials was best shown in the number of paid admissions, which increased from 45,297 in 1920 to 508,073 in 1929. The Depression brought only a slight drop in paid attendance, followed by an increase to 770,040 in 1935 and 1,212,449 in 1940.[10]

Despite these successes, Lieber's Indiana career ended on a sour note when he became a victim in part of the Democratic victory in 1932 and Governor McNutt's patronage policy, which was extended with new vigor to the state parks. Under political pressure Lieber resigned in July, 1933. But like many builders Lieber had made other enemies as well, including some among Republicans and the Izaak Walton League. He retired to Brown County, close to the natural environment he had done so much to preserve and to make available to millions of Hoosiers.[11]

§ §

In addition to enjoying the growing number of state parks and memorials, Indianans also engaged as participants or spectators in a wide range of organized sports, as the 1920s witnessed a flowering of athletic activity. In Indiana there was no doubt about which sport was pre-eminent.

Hoosiers played and watched basketball with an avidity un-

[10] Indiana *Year Book*, 1941, p. 953. Brief descriptions of the facilities of each park and monument are found in the annual reports of the Department of Conservation, published in the Indiana *Year Book*. In 1940 the department acquired responsibility for the George Rogers Clark Memorial, which became a National Memorial operated by the National Park Service in 1966. *Ibid.*, 1941, pp. 973-975; Indianapolis *Star*, July 12, 1966. For the Indiana Dunes Park see also Frederick, Colonel Richard Lieber, pp. 257-267, and Moore, *The Calumet Region*, pp. 598-601.

[11] Frederick, Colonel Richard Lieber, pp. 333-340; H. H. Evans to Governor Harry Leslie, December 31, 1930, January 1, 1931, Leslie Papers; L. G. Bradford to Paul McNutt, March 16, 1933, Congressmen-Executive Orders, 1933, McNutt Papers, Archives Division. For a statement of Lieber's mature thought see Richard Lieber, *America's Natural Wealth: A Story of the Use and Abuse of Our Resources* (New York, 1942).

matched anywhere else. "Indiana madness," "Hoosier hysteria," "a state religion"—these were the terms used to describe basketball. While participants ranged from grade school children to college teams and industrial leagues, major attention focused on high school teams. Basketball was a team sport suited for small-town Indiana, and each community intensely concentrated its civic loyalty on the high school team. Often in the 1920s they built large gymnasiums as monuments to their attachment to team and community. Gyms in some towns held more people than lived in the town. A few were enormous: Martinsville, Muncie, and Vincennes each provided seating for more than five thousand basketball fans. Town council, club, and church meetings could never be scheduled on basketball nights, and anyone who missed the game was a social oddity, or at least suffered for days the punishment of being unable to participate in the dozens of conversations that reviewed the game. Youths could learn the sport easily, since it required relatively little equipment and few players. And even only one or two outstanding players gave a high school the chance to win, not only in contests with the schools in the area but in statewide matches.[12]

A large part of Indiana's enthusiasm for basketball was generated by the state high school basketball tournament, first played in 1911. By the 1920s more than seven hundred teams competed, the winners progressing from sectional tournaments to regionals, semifinals, and the finals, where the state champion emerged. And that team was the true state champion, for, unlike states where schools were classified according to size, Indiana had only one tournament. The smallest schools played the largest, and always with the possibility of winning. Franklin won three times in a row, in 1920, 1921, and 1922, and Frankfort, under Coach Everett Case, won four state championships between 1925 and 1939. Indeed, the small-town and rural high schools did better than the large city schools in the state tourney. The only state champion from any of the five largest cities in the state in the years

12 Kyle Crichton, "Indiana Madness," *Collier's*, February 6, 1937, pp. 13, 38; McFadden, *Shelbyville*, p. 298; Lynd and Lynd, *Middletown*, p. 485; Bowman, *Hoosier*, p. 277.

from 1920 to 1940 was Fort Wayne South in 1938. Overseeing
the state tournament and high school basketball and other sports
was the Indiana High School Athletic Association (IHSAA),
founded in 1903, and headed from 1913 to 1944 by Arthur L.
Trester, a former school principal who had studied with John
Dewey at Columbia University. With skill and firm control
Trester and his colleagues helped make basketball and the state
tournament the premier sporting phenomenon in Indiana.[13]

In their study of Muncie Robert and Helen Lynd asserted the
power of the Muncie High School basketball team to unite the
community: "North Side and South Side, Catholic and Kluxer,
banker and machinist—their one shout is 'Eat 'em, beat 'em,
Bearcats!' "[14] But Indiana basketball was not everywhere and always as all-encompassing as the Lynds or the sport's avid boosters
proclaimed. Like other features of the society, basketball reflected
social distinctions of race, sex, and religion. The Indiana high
school basketball tournament was for males, most of whom were
white and Protestant. Black high schools such as Crispus Attucks
in Indianapolis and Roosevelt in Gary were not allowed to join
the IHSAA and not allowed to enter the tournament. Their
teams traveled to other black schools, often out of state, and to
Catholic high schools. Catholic schools also were denied entry in
the IHSAA and founded their own state athletic association and
basketball tournament. In 1941, two weeks after Pearl Harbor,
the IHSAA at last agreed to accept private, parochial, and black
schools into membership. These schools first competed in the 1943
tournament. Girls had far fewer opportunities to play basketball
than boys. Only about fifty high schools had girls' teams that
played other schools, and there was no state tournament. And to

[13] Crichton, "Indiana Madness," *Collier's*, February 6, 1937, pp. 13, 38; Indianapolis *News*, February 25, 1930; G. Dale Glenn, The History of the Indiana
High School Athletic Association (Ed.D. dissertation, Indiana University, Bloomington, 1975), pp. 63-65, 81. Data on state tournaments are found in the published
annual handbook of the Indiana High School Athletic Association. A useful
compilation of data, including tournament games, is in Herbert Frederic Schwomeyer, A History of Indiana High School Basketball (D.P.E. thesis, Indiana
University, Bloomington, 1970).

[14] Lynd and Lynd, *Middletown*, p. 485.

make the game less strenuous, IHSAA required special girls' rules of play.[15]

Hoosiers did not speak with one voice on the subject of basketball. Some were very critical because they believed that "in basketball community spirit is manifested with such intensity that the game is magnified beyond all reason . . . ."[16] The clearest examples of the magnified spirit were cases in which local boosters recruited outstanding players from elsewhere—encouraging the boy and his family to move into the school district by special enticements, often in the form of a job for the father. Anderson High was suspended from the state tournament in 1933 because local fans paid the moving expenses of a player and his family from Ohio. Each year the IHSAA board heard several cases alleging such violations and meted out punishment to those it found guilty.[17] Indeed, Commissioner Trester made strenuous efforts to keep Indiana basketball a fair and competitive sport for amateurs. His sometimes high-handed methods, however, earned the enmity of the press, which joined others—especially blacks protesting the exclusion of black schools—in unsuccessful attempts to shift control of athletics from the IHSAA to a state government agency.[18]

In addition to controversy and criticism over recruitment of players and the powers of IHSAA, a few educators charged that

[15] Glenn, The History of the Indiana High School Athletic Association, pp. 109-111; Indianapolis News, March 24, 1939; Indianapolis Recorder, February 15, 1941. The degree to which black students in integrated schools were allowed to participate in team sports has been largely ignored by those who have studied sports or schools. At least one black basketball player, Jack Mann, starred at Muncie High in the 1930s, and blacks participated in other sports, especially track. Among the difficulties they faced were social barriers that prevented them from accompanying their teammates into restaurants or hotels on trips. Goodall and Mitchell, A History of Negroes in Muncie, pp. 27, 34.

[16] Indianapolis News, November 9, 1931.

[17] Ibid., March 11, 1933; Crichton, "Indiana Madness," Collier's, February 6, 1937, p. 38. Reports of charges and findings are included in the annual handbook. See, for example, Indiana High School Athletic Association, Thirty-second Annual Handbook, 1935 (n.p., n.d.), pp. 162-163.

[18] Indianapolis Times, March 1, 1933; Indianapolis Star, March 13, 1939; Indianapolis Recorder, February 15, 22, 1941; Glenn, The History of the Indiana High School Athletic Association, pp. 117-124.

basketball interfered with the educational purposes of the schools. Gary's school superintendent, William A. Wirt, went so far as to recommend abolition of the state tournament, a factor in his declining popularity in the 1930s. And in 1936 the editor of the *Journal of the Indiana State Medical Association* charged that basketball "is quite overdone in our state," that the tournaments placed on players "a physical and mental strain that would seem too great for their years," and that, because of the focus on basketball, too little attention was paid in schools to the general physical education of all students.[19]

Such voices of criticism were a small minority, however, as basketball continued to be the major sport in Indiana—the sport that went beyond play to essential matters of community identification and pride. Those who criticized the intensity of the sport and its fans, as well as education reformers who intended in the name of efficiency and progress to destroy a high school team by consolidation of schools, did not always fully understand the importance and meaning of this simple game to many Hoosiers.

Though basketball reigned supreme, Indianans enjoyed other sports as well. High school teams competed in baseball, golf, track, wrestling, and football. Because many regarded football as too expensive, too dangerous, and requiring too many players, the sport was slow to grow in Indiana high schools. It increased in popularity in the 1920s, however, with about one hundred high schools playing the sport by 1930. Most obvious was the rabid interest in college football in the 1920s, such as that generated by Knute Rockne and his teams at Notre Dame and by the annual Purdue-Indiana games.[20] Baseball received less attention in high schools and colleges, partly because the climate kept the season short. But in summer leagues, organized at levels reaching from youngsters to professionals, the national sport was very popular in Indiana. During the month of July, 1929, Indianapolis newspapers listed the games of 113 different local teams, including

[19] Meister, A History of Gary, Indiana: 1930-1940, pp. 104-105; "Basketball Insanity," *Journal of the Indiana State Medical Association*, XXIX (1936), 579.
[20] Glenn, The History of the Indiana High School Athletic Association, pp. 32-33, 111-113; Indianapolis *News*, March 17, 1923.

30 that participated in the Indianapolis Amateur Baseball Association. Professional baseball became the major spectator sport in America by the 1920s, best symbolized by the heroic image of Babe Ruth. Though Hoosiers joined enthusiastically in listening to games on radio and following the box scores and stories in daily newspapers, there were no major league professional teams in the state. Loyalties focused on Cincinnati, St. Louis, or Chicago teams or on minor league teams such as the Indianapolis Indians.[21] Professional boxing also attracted Indiana fans, though church groups and others vehemently objected to the sport's "brutality, bloodshed and gambling." The Indiana State Athletic Commission, established in 1931, provided some regulation and control of professional boxing and wrestling.[22]

The most widely known professional sporting event in Indiana was the Indianapolis 500-mile race, first run in 1911. Its organizers, notably Carl G. Fisher and James Allison, were particularly interested in testing and promoting the automobile, in which they had business interests. By 1925 all cars in the race were custom-built, and the winners averaged more than one hundred miles an hour on the brick track. Auto accessory companies rushed to promote their tires, batteries, and spark plugs. World War I aviator Eddie Rickenbacker bought the Indianapolis Speedway in 1927. He was able to continue the race through the 1930s, with entries of cars powered by modified stock engines, including those of Indiana's Studebaker Company and Cummins Engine Company. During World War II, however, the race was not run. It resumed in 1946 under the new ownership of Anton Hulman, Jr., a Terre Haute businessman. While the 500-mile race attracted large crowds, not all Hoosiers took delight in the event. Prior to 1945 some of the "better families" in Indianapolis tended to regard the race as a vulgar spectacle, while church groups and the American Legion objected to its being run on Memorial Day. In 1923 the

---

[21] *The Leisure of a People*, pp. 443-446.
[22] Charles H. Winders to Emmett F. Branch, June 16, 1924, Branch Papers. See also F. A. Hayward to Warren T. McCray, August 10, 1923, McCray Papers; Indiana *Year Book*, 1932, pp. 1013-1015. The state athletic commission was limited entirely to professional boxing and wrestling.

General Assembly passed a resolution prohibiting commercial sports on the day set aside to honor war dead, but Governor McCray vetoed the act because he thought it unconstitutional.[23]

Sports in the interwar years—especially the 1920s—became more important to Hoosiers, and they came to be more organized, more professional, more national in scope. Even individual exercises, once acquired in the course of daily work or in an evening walk, came for some to be a part of organized activity. Urban middle-class businessmen joined athletic clubs, such as the Indianapolis Athletic Club, opened in 1924, or the local YMCAs. And they flocked to play golf at country clubs and public courses, as the game became the most popular leisure activity among middle-class men in the 1920s. Tennis also became more popular in the postwar years. Traditional games and individual physical activities remained, of course. Children still played hopscotch, duck on davy, tag, and andy over, and adults played croquet, fished and hunted game, swam, and pitched horseshoes. But for many, sports became organized team sports, complete with uniforms, programs, and scoreboards, as thousands watched and hundreds of thousands listened to radios and read in the newspapers about the play of a handful of increasingly skilled and highly paid professional athletes. Babe Ruth, Jack Dempsey, and Bobby Jones came to represent the mainstream of modern sports.[24]

§ § §

Hoosiers also spent leisure time participating in nonathletic group activities. Increasingly important after World War I were the variety of clubs and other social organizations that existed in every town and city. Newspaper notices in Indianapolis for one month in 1929 showed more than 400 meetings of 171 organizations, ranging from the Kiwanis Club to the Hoosier Kennel Club. In the small town of Brookston there were thirty-nine clubs

[23] Bloemker, *500 Miles to Go: The Story of the Indianapolis Speedway*, pp. 145-210; Peckham, *Indiana: A Bicentennial History*, pp. 175-182; North Indiana Annual Conference of the Methodist Episcopal Church, *Minutes*, 1923 (Cincinnati, 1923), p. 450; Clutter, The Indiana American Legion, 1919-1960, pp. 123-130.

[24] *The Indac: Indianapolis Athletic Club* (n.p., 1924); Indianapolis *News*, March 17, 1923; *The Leisure of a People*, pp. 95, 265-266, 442-443.

functioning in 1939, not counting several church groups. Clubs in Brookston and elsewhere differed in purpose, function, and membership. The most obvious difference was that most were intended exclusively for men or for women. The men's clubs tended to be business- and service-oriented. Rotary was generally the oldest and most prestigious—its members often the leading businessmen in the town—but men also joined Kiwanis, Lions, and other civic clubs in the 1920s. And the American Legion post often performed important social functions in many communities. There were also the older fraternal lodges, such as the Masons and Knights of Pythias, though some of these seemed to have diminished in appeal after World War I.[25]

In most communities women's clubs outnumbered men's and performed more important civic and social functions. Twenty-five of Brookston's thirty-nine clubs were exclusively for women. In Brookston and elsewhere these groups ranged from less formal bridge and Mah-Jongg gatherings, to mothers' clubs, home economics clubs, art, music, and literary organizations, and philanthropic sororities. The most popular of the latter was Tri-Kappa, described by one writer as "Indiana's greatest sorority, a kind of rural Junior League in purpose and social position among the county seats."[26] Many of the women's clubs also had a voice at the state level through the Indiana Federation of Clubs, which included nearly six hundred local clubs representing thirty thousand members by the mid-1920s. The Indiana Federation of Clubs did engage in some social reform and political activity in such areas as Americanization, movie censorship, and public health, but it was not as active in government and politics as the Indiana League of Women Voters. Women's clubs proliferated most among urban middle-class women, with rural and working-class women often lacking the time and money for this form of leisure and service. The clubs enabled women to seek like-minded

[25] *The Leisure of a People*, pp. 62, 450-453; Hartman, Brookston, pp. 159, 176; McFadden, *Shelbyville*, p. 291; Lane, *"City of the Century,"* p. 106; Lynd and Lynd, *Middletown*, pp. 301, 306-307; Lynd and Lynd, *Middletown in Transition*, pp. 280-285.

[26] Bowman, *Hoosier*, p. 286.

social companionship in formal organizations rather than only through the more traditional vehicles of family, church, and neighborhood.[27]

§ § § §

As had always been the case, Hoosiers could also spend leisure time reading. An increasing variety of magazines, newspapers, and books were available in stores, newsstands, and libraries. Newspapers represented the most consistently available reading material in Indiana homes. From the pioneer period onward newspapers served as disseminators of information and as focal points of community social, cultural, and political life. Like everything else, newspapers changed in the twentieth century. Evolving technology and organization provided fuller and more immediate access to national and international news, so that readers generally received more and better news from beyond the local community. As wire service stories and syndicated editorials and features became increasingly important, there was less space for the local editor and reporter, and some observers detected a declining influence in the individuality and power of editors and reporters. In 1928 Louis Ludlow, former Indiana and Washington newspaperman and congressman from Indiana, addressed the changes in newspapers: "Individuality has become sunk in an amazing growth of standardization," he lamented. "Publishing newspapers has become a great business—a tremendous business—with its spiritual edge somewhat dulled, I fear, in the zeal for counting room success."[28] Another Indiana newspaperman, Benjamin F.

[27] Hartman, Brookston, pp. 159-162; Indianapolis News, November 6, 1924; Lynd and Lynd, Middletown, p. 285; The Indianapolis Local Council of Women, 1892-1924 (n.p., n.d.); Grace Gates Courtney (comp.), History: Indiana Federation of Clubs (Fort Wayne, Ind., 1939), pp. 323, 398. Additional information on the Indiana Federation of Clubs is available in the organization's yearbook, published in the interwar years, and in the Luella F. McWhirter Papers, Lilly Library, Indiana University, Bloomington. McWhirter was very active in the Federation and in many other women's organizations.

[28] Louis Ludlow, A Plea for Greater Idealism and Individualism in Our Newspapers (Remarks to Sigma Delta Chi, Bloomington, Ind., March 18, 1928, mimeograph copy in Indiana University Library, Bloomington), pp. 2-3. See also Guido

Lawrence, also called attention to "The Changing Order:" Speaking to the Indiana Republican Editorial Association in 1925, he asserted that "the day of a great writer being the mainspring of a paper has passed. The people don't want to be preached too [sic]. They want to be amused, entertained. That is why we must have the comic strips."[29] Lawrence himself was part of the changing order, for he was general manager of the Indiana Star League, a business combination formed in 1903 to publish papers in Indianapolis, Terre Haute, and Muncie. Other Indiana newspapers were also parts of larger organizations. Most notable after World War I was the sale in 1922 of the Indianapolis *Times* to the Scripps-McRae, later Scripps-Howard, newspaper chain.

Whether owned by local or outside interests, many Indiana newspapers were less tightly bound to a political party in the twentieth century than they had been in the nineteenth century, when they were often party organs. Nonetheless, partisan bias was often apparent on the front page as well as the editorial page. The Indianapolis newspapers were most important in this regard as they circulated far beyond the city limits and functioned as state as well as city papers. They carried local reports from Indiana communities and were thorough in coverage of state politics. The Indianapolis *News* was generally fuller in its coverage of state issues than the Indianapolis *Star* or Indianapolis *Times*. And the *News* became more Republican in its politics, especially after the death of its longtime publisher Delavan Smith in 1922. Warren F. Fairbanks, son of Republican politician and Vice-President Charles W. Fairbanks, who had been a silent partner in the *News*, assumed the leadership of the *News* company. Warren and his brother Richard Fairbanks swung the paper more strongly in the

Stempel, III, A Study of Content, Make-up, and Bias of Editorial Pages of Small and Medium Indiana Daily Newspapers for the Period of 1912 to 1948 (M.A. thesis, Indiana University, Bloomington, 1951); Lynd and Lynd, *Middletown in Transition*, p. 376. Some local editors continued to express individuality in their papers, notably George R. Dale, muckraking editor of the Muncie *Post-Democrat*. Frank, "Who Governed Middletown? Community Power in Muncie, Indiana, in the 1930s," *Indiana Magazine of History*, LXXV, 326-327.

[29] Indianapolis *News*, January 24, 1925.

Republican direction, culminating in its support by the late 1920s of old guard conservative Senator James Watson, whom the paper had earlier opposed.[30] The Indianapolis *Times* was more independent and liberal and more likely to support Democratic candidates than was the *Star* or *News*, but the *Times* was not entirely free in its political preferences. Its editorial support of Republican candidate Herbert Hoover in the 1928 presidential election was directed by the Scripps-Howard chain, which dictated choice of presidential candidates on the basis of a vote by all editors in the chain.[31]

The political outlook in Indianapolis was generally matched elsewhere. Most Indiana newspapers, as elsewhere outside the South, tended to support Republicans, a situation much lamented by Democrats. As one wrote in 1936: "Indiana is handicapped by a lack of Democratic newspapers. The press is very biased . . . against the New Deal."[32] Paul McNutt characterized the paucity of Democratic papers as "the greatest problem the party has faced in the last half century."[33] On learning of Warren Fairbanks's death in 1938, McNutt and some Democratic friends began an unsuccessful effort to purchase the Indianapolis *News*. They had succeeded four years earlier in buying the bankrupt Fort Wayne *Journal-Gazette*, making it one of only a handful of newspapers that supported the state Democratic administration in the 1930s. Others included the Michigan City *Dispatch*, South Bend *News Times*, and, generally, the Indianapolis *Times*.[34]

To some degree the political partisanship of Indiana newspapers represented a continuation of individualism—a partial re-

[30] Hilton U. Brown, *A Book of Memories* (Indianapolis, 1951), p. 236. For examples of the fuller and more favorable coverage given to Republican than to Democratic candidates see Indianapolis *News*, November 3, 1924, October 6, 1932.

[31] Gildea, The "Religious Issue" in the 1928 and 1960 Presidential Elections, pp. 23-27.

[32] William H. Larrabee to James A. Farley, August 14, 1936, Box 1094, Democratic National Committee Papers.

[33] McNutt to Frank M. McHale, August 15, 1938, McNutt Papers, Lilly Library.

[34] Neff, Paul V. McNutt, pp. 330, 447-448; Norma Jean Thiele, A History of the Fort Wayne News-Sentinel (M.A. thesis, Indiana University, Bloomington, 1958), p. 51.

jection of the blandness and standardization many observed or feared in the press. Many Indiana newspapers also retained or expanded their local color features, especially those that touched Hoosier traditions, often presented in nostalgic and sentimental form. The Indianapolis *News* ran many such stories and features, including Frank McKinney (Kin) Hubbard's Abe Martin sketches and the folksy poetry of William Herschell. The Indianapolis *Star* featured Kate Milner Rabb's "Hoosier Listening Post." As the WPA guide to Indiana noted in 1941, Indiana's "modern newspapers have continued the task of [James Whitcomb] Riley in raising to self-consciousness the home-grown qualities of the people of the State."[35]

The trend toward standardization was also relieved by the survival of small-town and country newspapers, often weeklies, whose pages were filled with news of birthday parties, marriages, sickness and death, social visits, church services, basketball scores, and club activities. But here, too, there was change, for the small newspapers found it increasingly difficult to compete with telephones, radios, and big city dailies.[36] Indiana weekly papers declined in number from 398 in 1920 to 298 by 1940, and the number of towns with at least one newspaper dropped from 320 in 1920 to 293 in 1940. The number of daily papers in the state declined from 126 in 1920 to 98 in 1940, usually as smaller circulation papers merged or went out of business. Newspapers with circulations of more than twenty-five thousand increased in number from 7 in 1920 to 13 in 1940, and those with circulations between five thousand and twenty-five thousand increased from 21 in 1920 to 25 in 1940, doubtless reflecting urban population growth and the decline or merger of smaller newspapers.[37]

[35] Work Projects Administration, *Indiana: A Guide*, p. 115.

[36] George Ade noted in 1933 that "the happenings which were events in 1900 are now trivial incidents and yet the average weekly gives most of its space to tedious routine news. . . . In every community there are burning local issues and these are mostly ignored." Ade to Carl F. Ackerman, August 25, 1933, in Tobin (ed.), *Letters of George Ade*, p. 170.

[37] N. W. Ayer & Son's American Newspaper Annual & Directory 1921 (Philadelphia, 1921), pp. 10, 259-288; N. W. Ayer & Son's Directory of Newspapers and Periodicals 1941 (Philadelphia, 1941), pp. 264-292. Newspapers with circulations of more than twenty-five thousand in 1920 were located in Fort Wayne (2), Indianapolis (3), Muncie (1), and Terre Haute (1). In 1940 they

There were also special-interest newspapers, such as the foreign language press. A German language paper *(Freie-Presse Staats-Zeitung)* survived in Fort Wayne until 1927, and a Polish and a Hungarian paper still existed in South Bend in 1940. But the small and declining number of foreign-born residents in Indiana could not support many foreign-language papers. Religious newspapers serving the state's readers included the *Indiana Catholic and Record*, founded in 1910, and the *Indiana Jewish Chronicle*, founded in 1921, both published in Indianapolis. Gary and Indianapolis also had several important black newspapers, though only two survived into World War II—the Gary *American*, founded in 1927, and the Indianapolis *Recorder*, founded in 1896. Both were major voices within the black communities of the two cities, and the Indianapolis paper also made an effort to report news regarding blacks in other Indiana communities.[38]

Indianans could also read a variety of periodicals. Here especially there was a trend toward nationally oriented publications, as Hoosiers read the same material that Americans in Massachusetts or Wyoming read. Nearly half the magazine subscriptions in Brookston in 1939 were for farm magazines,[39] and a quarter were for women's magazines, including *McCall's*, *Household*, and *Woman's Home Companion*. The best-selling magazine in the Brookston drugstore was *True Story*. The same magazines were also read in Muncie, but this larger, less agriculturally oriented community showed more interest in publications such as the *Saturday Evening Post* and *American Magazine*. Muncie in 1925 had fewer than twenty-five subscriptions to *Harper's* and the *New Republic*.[40]

---

were located in Evansville (2), Fort Wayne (2), Gary (1), Hammond (1), Indianapolis (3), Lafayette (1), South Bend (1), and Terre Haute (2).

[38] Karl J. R. Arndt and Mary E. Olson, *German-American Newspapers and Periodicals 1732-1955* (2nd edition, New York, 1965), pp. 111-130; *Ayer Directory, 1941*, pp. 276, 1241; Balanoff, Black Community of Gary, p. 257; Hartence Harlin, The Indianapolis Recorder: A History of a Negro Weekly Newspaper (M.A. thesis, Indiana University, Bloomington, 1951).

[39] At least two of the most popular farm magazines were Indiana publications: the *Indiana Farmer's Guide* and the Indiana edition of the *Prairie Farmer*. The latter claimed circulation in Indiana of 110,000 by 1937. James F. Evans, *Prairie Farmer and WLS: The Burridge D. Butler Years* (Urbana, Ill., 1969), pp. 71, 86.

[40] Hartman, Brookston, pp. 163-164; Lynd and Lynd, *Middletown*, pp. 239-240.

§ § § § §

Indianans also read books in their leisure time, the same books that Americans everywhere read, many of them written by fellow Hoosiers. Indiana authors achieved an immense popularity not only at home but throughout the nation in the first decades of the twentieth century. At the end of World War II the librarian at Purdue University ascertained what many Hoosiers knew to be true. Using the top ten best-selling novels for each year from 1900 to 1940 he "assigned the score of ten for each top best seller during those years. The second novel on the list was scored as nine, the third as eight and so on . . . . The birthplace of each author was next ascertained . . . . The various states were then credited with the scores of the novelists born in them." Indiana's score was 215, just behind the leader, New York, with 216, and far ahead of third-place Pennsylvania with 125, even though the eastern states had more people and potential authors.[41] In a general history of American literature, published in 1930, only one state received a separate chapter—"The Emergence of Indiana," it was titled. By the turn of the century Hoosiers had developed a reputation as a writing people, a reputation that grew in the next several decades and one that many cherished and promoted. When in 1922 the Indianapolis *News* asked its readers to vote for the ten greatest living Hoosiers, five of the top ten choices were professional writers: Booth Tarkington, George Ade, Gene Stratton Porter, Meredith Nicholson, and Kin Hubbard.[42] But for his death in 1916, James Whitcomb Riley would surely have been on the 1922 list and at the top, for the poet was the most widely admired writer

[41] John H. Moriarty, "Hoosiers Sell Best," *Indiana Quarterly for Bookmen*, III (1947), 7-8. No one has yet fully explained why Indianans wrote so many popular books. For attempts see Arthur W. Shumaker, *A History of Indiana Literature with Emphasis on the Authors of Imaginative Works Who Commenced Writing Prior to World War II* (Indianapolis, 1962), pp. 8-15; Peckham, *Indiana: A Bicentennial History*, pp. 158-163.

[42] Fred Lewis Pattee, *The New American Literature, 1890-1930* (New York, 1930), Chapter 6; Indianapolis *News*, August 19, 1922. The *News* counted 802 ballots. The results and votes were: Booth Tarkington (531); Elwood Haynes (433); Albert Beveridge (358); A. B. Anderson (357); George Ade (327); Thomas Marshall (327); Gene Stratton Porter (258); Meredith Nicholson (256); Kin Hubbard (231); and John N. Hurty (212).

the state had ever produced. His images of rural and neighborly Indiana cast a bright light over much of the state's literature.

While it is misleading to place all of Indiana's authors in a single category or to conceive of a Hoosier school of literature, there were important similarities among many Indiana writers. Much of the literature produced in early twentieth-century Indiana was romantic rather than realistic, sentimental rather than grim or satirical, nostalgic rather than shockingly modern or daring. Indiana authors tended to be traditional in their choice and treatment of subject, to emphasize the virtues and positive features of the present and past, and sometimes to resist change or the threat of change. In treating these themes, many often used Indiana settings and reflected there the values and characters of hometown people they knew.[43]

The best and most popular of the Indiana hometown authors was Booth Tarkington. Born in 1869 in Indianapolis, he set many of his novels and stories in the upper North Meridian-Pennsylvania Street neighborhood where he lived most of his life. Beginning with *The Gentleman from Indiana* (1899), Tarkington produced a stream of well-written and immensely popular stories, books, and plays, including his widely read children's books, *Penrod* (1914) and *Penrod and Sam* (1916). Perhaps his best novels were *The Magnificent Ambersons* (1918) and *Alice Adams* (1921), both of which were set in Indianapolis and both of which won Pulitzer prizes. Like much of his work, both studied in masterful detail middle- and upper-class families facing change in their society. By the 1920s Tarkington was acutely sensitive to social and economic change, often implicitly and explicitly comparing the simpler, smaller, quasi-industrial town of post-Civil War Indianapolis to the rapidly growing, sometimes alien, and often smoky and congested post-World War I city: "It was heaving up in the middle incredibly; it was spreading incredibly; and as it heaved and spread, it befouled itself and darkened its sky. Its boundary was mere shapelessness on the run."[44] The title and contents of his partial autobiography, *The World Does Move*

[43] Shumaker, *A History of Indiana Literature*, pp. 22-31, 440-442, 585-587.
[44] Tarkington, *The Magnificent Ambersons*, p. 386.

(1928), reflected his concern for change: "In nature all is change, and so there is no such thing as a fixed point, which can be only an abstract conception. Looking forth upon the examples apparently set by the rest of the universe, we are encouraged to surmise that the world moves, not as a pendulum, but in an ascending spiral."[45] While Tarkington was too hopeful to deny the possibility of progress—of an ascending spiral—and while he remained to his death in 1946 hopeful that change was for the better, he often lamented the direction in which the world was moving, clinging to the ideals and traditions of the late nineteenth century. He expressed disdain for new directions in literature, art, economics, and politics, and he was especially critical of the New Deal, which he saw as denying individual freedom. Throughout the interwar years his work was widely read, though less so by the 1930s. Five of his books appeared on the top ten best-seller lists from 1920 to 1932. None was a bestseller thereafter, though he continued to write novels and short stories, notably *The Heritage of Hatcher Ide* (1941). Perhaps the best of his later work, the novel shows his gentlemanly distaste for the changes occurring in Indianapolis and the nation during the interwar years, yet ends with a hopeful affirmation of progress, again using the imagery of the ascending spiral.[46]

Tarkington was a giant among his literary contemporaries in Indiana, but others also achieved widespread fame. Meredith Nicholson (1866-1947) was much like Tarkington, though as a moderate Democrat he had less trouble accepting the new political directions of the 1930s. Nicholson tended toward a romantic and optimistic view, especially in his novels, the most popular of which was *The House of a Thousand Candles* (1905). Often also he showed a strong sentiment for his native state and region, as in his historical essays in *The Hoosiers* (1900) and *The Valley*

[45] Tarkington, *The World Does Move*, p. 280.

[46] James Woodress, *Booth Tarkington: Gentleman from Indiana* (Philadelphia, 1954), pp. 242-318; Alice Payne Hackett, *Fifty Years of Best Sellers, 1895-1945* (New York, 1945); Booth Tarkington, *The Heritage of Hatcher Ide* (New York, 1941), especially pp. 298-299.

of Democracy (1918) and in many later essays. Particularly notable is his "Stay in Your Own Home Town," written in the
1920s, in which he advised that "home remains a word of power,
even in these restless times." Though he claimed to be "an irre-
deemable hick," who much preferred Indianapolis to New York
and enjoyed buying his "neckties of clerks at home who call me
Nick and tell me about their babies and how Uncle Jim came in
from Scott County last week and brought a bushel of sheepnose
apples,"[47] Nicholson was a highly literate and widely knowledgeable man, a strong proponent of democracy but an equally
intense critic of its excesses and failures, and a writer who understood Hoosiers and Americans as few have. And, unlike many of
his literary colleagues, he showed a sympathetic understanding
of women in the 1920s, defending the woman who "quite natu-
rally is bored by the senile whimper that her place is in the home"
and asserting that "it's a distinct gain for civilization that woman
has ceased to be a clinging vine."[48]

One writer who wandered from Indiana but always came back
home was George Ade (1866-1944). He began a journalistic
career in Lafayette, near his hometown of Kentland, but in 1890
he moved to Chicago where his humorous stories and fables began
to win wide popularity as commentaries on human nature, especially his *Fables in Slang* (1900). In 1903 Ade returned to his
native Newton County and spent the next four decades shuttling
between there and Florida, entertaining a wide circle of friends
and writing plays, stories, and books, most of them humorous,
many very popular, and many attempting to explain Indiana and
the Midwest to others. His biographer described him as "a good,

[47] Meredith Nicholson, "Stay in Your Own Home Town," in *Old Familiar
Faces* (Indianapolis, 1929), pp. 148, 154-155. See also Shumaker, *A History of Indiana Literature*, pp. 325-337. Nicholson did leave home, serving from 1933 to 1941 as
American diplomatic representative in several Latin American countries, though
he hungered for news of Indianapolis while away. See especially his correspondence with Carleton B. McCulloch, in McCulloch Papers.

[48] Nicholson, "Should Nellie Stay at Home?" in *Old Familiar Faces*, pp. 167,
170. Tarkington, too, commented on the "new" woman of the 1920s, though
characteristically his emphasis often was on changing fashion. See Tarkington,
The World Does Move, pp. 250-265.

simple man with a magnificent gift that he packaged for the market place."[49]

Another important Indiana humorist was Frank McKinney Hubbard, known as Kin Hubbard (1868-1930). He spent most of his career with the Indianapolis *News*. Like Ade, Hubbard's fame spread beyond Indiana, largely through the syndicated newspaper column and collected sayings of the fictional Abe Martin and his Brown County neighbors, whose comments on human character and commonplace events were often insightful as well as humorous: "We used t'call a feller a durned crank that devoted all his time an' attention t' one thing, but t'-day he's a specialist." Or, " 'The reason I hate to pay an income tax is that nobuddy ever says thank you, come agin, or nothin'. You don't even see who gits it, . . .' "[50] One of the most knowledgeable students of Indiana literature concluded that no one else has succeeded better than Hubbard "in catching the exact flavor of the humor and philosophy native to Indiana . . . ." Like many of his contemporary Hoosier writers, Hubbard noted that "I've had a couple of chances to go to New York and make something of myself, but . . . I'd rather stay here where I can get in the band."[51]

Gene Stratton Porter (1863-1924) differed only slightly from her Indiana contemporaries. An amateur naturalist, she set her novels in rural Indiana and gave much attention to the natural environment, especially birds and the area of the Limberlost Swamp near Geneva in Adams County where she lived for many years. Beginning with *Freckles* (1904) and *A Girl of the Limberlost* (1909), she wrote novels of romantic sentimentality and

[49] Lee Coyle, *George Ade* (New York, 1964), p. 138. Ade's earlier biographer was a personal friend and most sympathetic critic. Fred C. Kelly, *George Ade: Warmhearted Satirist* (Indianapolis, 1947). See also Jean Shepherd's very good essay on Ade in Jean Shepherd (ed.), *The America of George Ade (1866-1944): Fables, Short Stories, Essays* (New York, 1960), pp. 9-22; and Shumaker, *A History of Indiana Literature*, pp. 444-473.

[50] Kin Hubbard, *Abe Martin: Hoss Sense and Nonsense* (Indianapolis, 1926), p. 13; Kin Hubbard, *Abe Martin's Broadcast* (Indianapolis, 1930), p. 20.

[51] R. E. Banta (comp.), *Indiana Authors and Their Books 1816-1916* (Crawfordsville, Ind., 1949), pp. 160, 162. See also Shumaker, *A History of Indiana Literature*, pp. 475-485.

simple moralizing that were very popular: by 1924 ten million copies of her books had been sold. Though not a highly skilled writer and often demonstrating more sweetness than substance, Porter contributed to furthering interest in nature and conservation just at the time that Indiana's state park system was developing.[52]

There was another major Indiana author between the world wars who was vastly different from his Hoosier contemporaries—in many ways their antithesis. Some have denied Theodore Dreiser (1871-1945) the label "Indiana author," although he was born in Terre Haute and spent the first two decades of his life in Indiana, including a year at Indiana University. Dreiser often drew on his youthful experiences in his novels and wrote about the state directly in *A Hoosier Holiday* (1916) and in his fascinating autobiography, *Dawn: A History of Myself* (1931). His literary fame began with *Sister Carrie* (1900) and continued through *An American Tragedy* (1925). Dreiser's fiction was realistic in the grimmest manner, dealing with corruption, immorality, poverty, and suffering, and it often devoted great attention to sexual attractions and conflicts. Unlike Tarkington and most other Indiana authors, who ignored or only alluded to such matters, Dreiser confronted the world as he had known it in the shabbier neighborhoods of Terre Haute and Sullivan, the waterfront of Evansville, and the streets of Chicago. To many readers in Indiana and elsewhere he was "only a gloomy and dirty-minded man whose prose was tortuous," a "writer who could find a rotten spot in every apple."[53] George Ade described him as "a very grim and disagreeable and cantankerous individual who is 'agin' almost every thing. He lacks [a] sense of humor . . . ."[54] Always he seemed out of step with his times, as William E. Wilson has noted:

[52] Shumaker, *A History of Indiana Literature*, pp. 405-413; Roderick Nash, *The Nervous Generation: American Thought, 1917-1930* (Chicago, 1970), pp. 137-138.

[53] Banta (comp.), *Indiana Authors*, p. 91.

[54] Ade to James D. Rathbun, January 24, 1934, in Tobin (ed.), *Letters of George Ade*, p. 178.

It was characteristic of Dreiser that he publicly hated the British in
World War I and got himself accused of anti-Semitism at the beginning of Hitler's tyranny, that he praised the Communists in the boom-
ing 1920's when "Bolshevik" was a dirty word, shied away from them
in the depressed 1930's when Party-joining and "fellow-traveling"
were not only acceptable but fashionable among the intelligentsia, and
finally became a member of the Party in 1945, the year of his death,
when American ex-Communists were beginning to scurry for cover
behind constitutional amendments.[55]

But to many serious readers and critics, Dreiser remains by far the
most creative and thoughtful of Indiana authors, the one whose
literary reputation is most enduring.

These were Indiana's most important writers in the interwar
years—Tarkington, Nicholson, Ade, Hubbard, Porter, and
Dreiser. There were others, many others, for the Indiana literary
tradition encouraged Hoosiers to write.[56] They wrote stories,
novels, plays, poetry, and children's literature, sometimes published on small hometown presses, sometimes by New York
publishers, and sometimes by the Bobbs-Merrill Company of Indianapolis, which showed special interest in Indiana authors. Some
Hoosiers wrote nonfiction. A few achieved distinction, especially
in history. Albert Beveridge's biographies of John Marshall and
Abraham Lincoln and Claude Bowers's books about politics in the
1790s and 1860s were popular history at its best. Logan Esarey's
studies of Indiana's past, especially his essays in *The Indiana Home*
(1943), and his editorship of the *Indiana Magazine of History* in
the 1920s marked the flowering of a rich tradition in state history,
combining scholarly and popular interests. Work in state and
local history was furthered by two important institutions: the
privately supported Indiana Historical Society and the state gov-

55 William E. Wilson, *Indiana: A History* (Bloomington, Ind., 1966), p. 226.
Wilson provides a very interesting comparison between Dreiser and Tarkington.
See *ibid.*, pp. 218-227.

56 For discussion of hundreds of other Indiana writers, including biographical
details, lists of publications, and some evaluations, see Shumaker, *A History of
Indiana Literature*; Banta (comp.), *Indiana Authors*; Donald E. Thompson
(comp.), *Indiana Authors and Their Books, 1917-1966* (Crawfordsville, Ind.,
1974); and Donald E. Thompson, *Indiana Authors and Their Books, 1967-1980*
(Crawfordsville, Ind., 1981).

ernment's Indiana Historical Bureau, both expertly led from 1924 to 1944 by Christopher B. Coleman.[57]

But most Indiana authors tended toward fiction and, with the exception of Dreiser, toward romantic fiction, often combined with nostalgia and sentimentality, and sometimes with a distrust or distaste for the direction in which society was moving. It was these Indiana writers who came to be considered as the builders of the state's golden age of literature—a period of literary prominence that began with Edward Eggleston's *Hoosier School-Master* (1871) and peaked in the first decades of the twentieth century. These golden age authors often produced the typical, sometimes the best, and certainly the most popular literature in America. The 1920s and 1930s were the tail end of this golden age or perhaps, as Shumaker suggests, its afterglow. Many of these authors continued to write after World War I, and their books continued to sell well. Yet there were signs and fears that they represented a fading generation, a style of literature whose time was passing. Dreiser's critical success was closest to home in providing such evidence, but important also was the different kind of literature represented by such American authors as F. Scott Fitzgerald, Ernest Hemingway, and Sinclair Lewis—writers who seemed more attuned to the complex concerns of the new modern age of post-World War I America and less attuned to the rural and small-town values and ideals of the nineteenth century.[58]

With the exception of Dreiser, Indiana authors lost their critical

[57] Jack O'Bar, A History of the Bobbs-Merrill Company, 1850-1940: With a Postlude through the Early 1960s (Ph.D. dissertation, Indiana University, Bloomington, 1975), pp. 79-82; Lorna Lutes Sylvester (comp.), "No Cheap Padding": Seventy-five Years of the Indiana Magazine of History, 1904-1979 (Indianapolis, 1980), pp. ix-xi; Lana Ruegamer, A History of the Indiana Historical Society, 1830-1980 (Indianapolis, 1980), pp. 135-173.

[58] Shumaker, A History of Indiana Literature, pp. 21-30; Richard A. Cordell, "Limestone, Corn, and Literature: The Indiana Scene and Its Interpreters," Saturday Review of Literature, December 17, 1938, pp. 3-4; Wilson, Indiana, pp. 206-207; Suzanne Ellery Greene, Books for Pleasure: Popular Fiction, 1914-1945 (Bowling Green, Ohio, 1974), pp. 117, 142-154; Heath Bowman, "Those, Those, Hoosiers," Saturday Review of Literature, January 6, 1945, pp. 6-7.

appeal as the twentieth century reached midpoint.[59] However, their books remained secure on the shelves and in the minds of many Hoosier and other American readers. And they continued to be worth reading: Tarkington most importantly, but the others, too, provide good insights into the age in which they came to maturity. Literary critics may denigrate these writers because they "always played to a little knot of the folks from back home,"[60] yet in their attachments to Indiana and with their often acute sense of change, they provided enduring connections between the generations before and after and useful insights into the dynamics of tradition and change.

Hoosiers not only bought books but also borrowed books from expanding public libraries. Often aided by the generosity of Andrew Carnegie, every respectable town acquired or built a public library in the first decades of the twentieth century, usually near the courthouse or shopping district. By 1930 all but two of the Indiana towns with more than twenty-five hundred people had a public library, though there was still work to be done in extending library services to rural areas. The Indianapolis Public Library grew rapidly in the 1920s, nearly tripling its circulation between 1919 and 1928. With more than half a million volumes, it was by far the largest public library in the state, though the Fort Wayne, Evansville, and Gary public libraries all had more than 100,000 volumes by 1929. After World War I the Indiana State Library in Indianapolis began to serve more fully the information and education needs of the people, especially with the creation of the Library and Historical Department in 1925 and the dedication of the State Library and Historical Building in 1934.[61]

[59] For efforts to deny this loss of appeal see Corbin Patrick, "The Indiana Literary Tradition at Midcentury," in R. E. Banta (ed.), *Hoosier Caravan: A Treasury of Indiana Life and Lore* (2nd edition, Bloomington, Ind., 1975), pp. 9-11.

[60] Wilson, *Indiana*, p. 206.

[61] Indiana *Year Book*, 1930, pp. 195-229; 1941, pp. 855-860; *The Leisure of a People*, p. 314; Larry Joe Barr, The Indiana State Library 1825-1925 (Ph.D. dissertation, Indiana University, Bloomington, 1976), pp. 218-226.

§ § § § § §

Indiana's art was not unlike its literature. The paintings Hoosiers liked tended toward the romantic and sentimental, often
landscape scenes of rural Indiana. Several of Indiana's artists had
studied in Europe in the late nineteenth century and returned
home eager to proclaim the state's natural beauties in their paintings. Often called the Hoosier group, the major figures were
J. Ottis Adams, William Forsyth, Otto Stark, and Theodore C.
Steele. While they painted portraits and still lifes, their most
popular work was Hoosier landscapes that were characterized
by "hazy atmosphere, rolling hills, and winding streams."[62] The
Hoosier group did much to promote art and appreciation of
nature, aided by local art associations founded in many cities in
the late nineteenth and early twentieth centuries. The Art Association of Indianapolis with the bequest of John Herron
founded the John Herron Art Museum and Institute in the first
decade of the twentieth century. Here many Indiana artists taught,
studied, and exhibited their work. The director of the Herron Art
Museum after 1928 was Wilbur D. Peat, who played an important
role in promoting art in the state, as did Donald Mattison, head of
the Herron Art School from 1933 to 1970. The Hoosier Salon of
Chicago, which had its initial opening in March, 1925, provided
annual opportunities for Indiana artists to exhibit their work
beyond the state.[63]

Outside Indianapolis the most important locale for Indiana artists after World War I was Brown County, where the rustic
beauty and sense of isolation from the modern world appealed to
many artists. Steele moved there in 1907, followed by Adolph

[62] Work Projects Administration, *Indiana: A Guide*, p. 130.

[63] Phillips, *Indiana in Transition*, pp. 546-550; Peckham, *Indiana: A Bicentennial History*, pp. 168-173; *The Leisure of a People*, pp. 429-435; *Art Guide to
Indiana* (Indiana University Extension Division *Bulletin*, XVI, April, 1931), pp.
7, 24. This guide includes a listing of artists active in Indiana in 1928-1929, with
some biographical and professional data. For other listings see Mary Q. Burnet,
Art and Artists of Indiana (New York, 1921), pp. 353-405; *Biographical Directory
of Indiana Artists 1937* (n.p., 1937); Flora Lauter, *Indiana Artists (Active): 1940*
(n.p., 1941).

Robert Shulz and some other friends in 1908. By the 1920s there often were as many as fifty or sixty painters working in Brown County, about fifteen of whom maintained studios or residences there. The organization of the Brown County Art Galleries Association in 1926 enabled them to display their work to the thousands of visitors who thronged to Nashville in the spring and fall. The Brown County art colony in the interwar years included Ada Walters Shulz, Will Vawter, Marie Goth, and Curry Bohm, each of whom achieved a respectable reputation.[64] Its most influential member until his death in 1926 was Steele, who lived not in Nashville but on the western edge of the county. With their rural landscapes Steele and his Brown County colleagues provided, in the view of one of them, "a great force in the maintenance of sanity in art in this part of our country during the confusion of late years."[65] A similar judgment from a different perspective, expressed in the WPA guide to Indiana published in 1941, was that much Indiana art had "become conservative and provincial, pleasant in its mood, and reassuring in its optimistic point of view."[66] In these characteristics Indiana's art was much like its literature, except that none of the Hoosier painters achieved the national distinction of Tarkington and his literary colleagues.

Nor did there emerge among Indiana artists a figure comparable to Dreiser to provide a strong counterpoint to the central tendencies. But even while the romantic rural landscapes continued to enjoy great popularity, there were signs of change in the 1930s, as some artists expanded the scope of their subject matter and began to paint bolder and more socially involved works. A few of the examples included in the 1940 directory of Indiana artists

[64] Frank M. Hohenberger might also be added to this list, even though he worked with a camera rather than brush and canvass. See Lorna Lutes Sylvester, " 'Down in the Hills o' Brown County': Photographs by Frank M. Hohenberger," *Indiana Magazine of History*, LXXI (1975), 205-244, LXXII (1976), 21-62.

[65] Adolph Shulz, "The Story of the Brown County Art Colony," *Indiana Magazine of History*, XXXI (1935), 285. See also Josephine A. Graf, "The Brown County Art Colony," *Indiana Magazine of History*, XXXV (1939), 365-370; Selma N. Steele, Theodore L. Steele, and Wilbur D. Peat, *The House of the Singing Winds: The Life and Work of T. C. Steele* (Indianapolis, 1966).

[66] Work Projects Administration, *Indiana: A Guide*, p. 130.

and the federally sponsored murals and panels done in public buildings in the 1930s reflected some of these more modern tendencies, though there was great variety. And the murals done by the non-Hoosier Thomas Hart Benton for Indiana's contribution to the Century of Progress Exposition at Chicago in 1933 presented a variety of Indiana scenes that ranged from lime-stone quarries, to basketball, to a burning cross of the Ku Klux Klan. But neither the dark realism nor the abstract modernism that developed in New York and elsewhere by World War II had significant expression or popularity in Indiana.[67]

Other art forms did not receive the attention in Indiana that painting did. Sculpture was largely neglected by Hoosiers. Most of the state's memorials and monuments were done by artists from out of state, although the contributions of highly skilled limestone carvers in Monroe and Lawrence counties were widely evident. In pottery, the Overbeck sisters of Cambridge City achieved a local reputation and some recognition outside Indiana. And a variety of folk art and crafts survived, though threatened by modern manufacturing and production methods.[68]

§ § § § § § §

Music changed, too, after World War I—more than did art or literature. There was evidence of greater interest in traditional forms of music in the variety of musical clubs and societies in cities; in the Indiana Federation of Music Clubs organized in 1916; in church choirs and church music; in summer band concerts; and in continuation of folk music. The formation of the Indiana State Symphony Society in 1931 was an important beginning toward a permanent symphony orchestra in the capital city. In 1936 Fabien Sevitzky was appointed conductor of the Indianapolis Symphony which began the transition to a major orchestra. In the next five years the Indianapolis Symphony gave 239 concerts in the capital

[67] Ibid., pp. 130-132; Lauter, Indiana Artists: 1940; David Lawrence Chambers, A Hoosier History Based on the Mural Paintings of Thomas Hart Benton (Indianapolis, 1933).

[68] Work Projects Administration, Indiana: A Guide, p. 129; Kathleen R. Postle, The Chronicle of the Overbeck Pottery (Indianapolis, 1978).

city and in 69 other towns, most in Indiana. Sevitzky was a highly professional musician and a builder, but his headstrong ways and his occasional programming of modern music caused controversy.[69]

The most controversial music came not from the Indianapolis Symphony but from the pianos, saxophones, and other instruments of jazz musicians. Combining elements from various sources and especially from the black South and Midwest, jazz in its "hot" and "sweet" modes swept black nightclubs, college campuses, and eventually white hotels, restaurants, and clubs after World War I. Many black musicians and groups in Indiana played important roles in creating and fostering the new music, especially Noble Sissle. Born in Indianapolis in 1889, Sissle teamed with Eubie Blake to perform across the country, and they did a "record business" in their Indianapolis appearance in 1925.[70] Black clubs and theaters on Indiana Avenue in Indianapolis became a major scene of the new music and often attracted large numbers of whites. But increasingly, white musicians and bands took over jazz and offered it in a watered-down form for wider appeal. Bands such as the Syncopating Five and Hoagy Carmichael's several groups represented this trend. Many, including Carmichael, made records with Gennett Studios, a subsidiary of the Starr Piano Company of Richmond. These groups prompted a growing interest in dancing, and in the 1920s dance halls, outdoor pavilions, and hotel ballrooms were constructed across the state for young couples to listen to music their elders did not always understand and to dance in ways they did not always approve. The Depression was detrimental to this form of leisure, despite the marathon dance craze, but by the late 1930s, with the emergence of the so-called swing bands, music and dancing again became a major part of popular entertainment.[71]

[69] Martha F. Bellinger, "Music in Indianapolis, 1900-1944," *Indiana Magazine of History,* XLII (1946), 47-65; Samuel Wasson Siurua, History of the Indianapolis Symphony Orchestra (Doctor of Music Education dissertation, Indiana University, Bloomington, 1961), pp. 31-217.

[70] Indianapolis *News,* January 15, 1925.

[71] Duncan Schiedt, *The Jazz State of Indiana* (Pittsboro, Ind., 1977); *The Leisure of a People,* pp. 498-500. For continued opposition to jazz music see *Indiana Catholic and Record,* September 7, 1945.

Indiana State Library

Workers going to Charlestown Ordnance Works, June, 1941

Indiana Historical Society

Defense workers, Continental Optical Company, Indianapolis

Lebanon High School war bond rally

Two Hoosier soldiers with their parents, December, 1944:
the Weatherfords, Ruby Mae, Harvey, David, and Ira, at the Anderson railroad station

§ § § § § § § §

The culture, information, and entertainment available to Indianans after World War I changed significantly as the result of two new technologies—radio and movies. Both offered the possibilities of widening the scope of leisure-time activity, of "raising" the level of culture and entertainment, of appealing to larger numbers of listeners and viewers, and of bringing cultural homogeneity to Indiana and the nation.

Radio was the wonder of the modern world in the early 1920s. In 1922 citizens of Shelbyville organized a radio club and gathered around the few sets in the town, and the Elks Club created a stir when it bought its own radio. In 1922 Hoosier newspapers began carrying information on radio technology and programs, and Senator Harry New became one of the first candidates for political office to use the new marvel when he transmitted a speech from Washington to Indianapolis. By the mid-1920s the living rooms and parlors of many homes contained radios, and by the end of the decade the instrument was a commonplace household fixture.[72]

Both because radio sets could receive distant signals at night and because by the late 1920s the two national radio networks, the Columbia Broadcasting System and the National Broadcasting Company, had reached Indiana, Hoosiers listened to the same information and entertainment heard elsewhere in the nation. Musical programs, ranging from country and western music to the Metropolitan Opera and by the late 1930s the NBC Symphony, the radio comedy of Fred Allen and Jack Benny, the radio plays of Orson Wells, broadcasts of the World Series, children's shows such as Gang Busters and the Lone Ranger—all were heard in Indiana as in New York and Oregon. But Indianans listened not only to the network programs but also the local programs from Chicago and Cincinnati, as powerful stations in these two cities

[72] McFadden, Shelbyville, pp. 302-303; Indianapolis News, March 29, April 8, 1922. Democrats were especially thankful for the radio because it provided an entry into the many communities served by Republican newspapers and because of the effective use of the radio made by Franklin D. Roosevelt. Margaret S. Hilterman to May Thompson Evans, November 29, 1939, Box 210, Women's Division, Democratic National Committee Papers; Lynd and Lynd, Middletown in Transition, p. 361.

366 INDIANA THROUGH TRADITION AND CHANGE

attracted large audiences in Indiana and probably helped to retard station growth in the state. Although by the eve of World War II thirteen cities in the state had one or more radio stations, most were only 1,000 watts or less, the major exception being Fort Wayne's WOWO with 10,000 watts. These small stations helped counter the trend toward radio homogeneity as they devoted major attention to programs of local interest. Farm market reports, high school basketball broadcasts, and chatty talks with local citizens made the town radio station an important part of the community as well as a conduit to the outside world. And one local program—the Indiana Farm and Home Hour, originating from WIRE in Indianapolis—was broadcast coast-to-coast by one of the major networks. Radio was modern but never revolutionary, and it was seldom even controversial, a consequence in part of advertisers' sensitivity to the need to sell soap, hair oil, and razor blades.[73] Traditional observers concerned about the decline of morals and family life, such as the editor of the *Indiana Catholic and Record*, were grateful that radio, unlike automobiles and motion pictures, "has cultivated a taste for better entertainment in the great mass of people . . ." and provided "the means of uniting the family once again in the home circle."[74]

More than radio, motion pictures seemed to be a direct assault on traditional values and ways in Indiana. The new technology could be used for a variety of purposes, as exemplified in the showing of educational films by state and local tuberculosis societies and widespread use of the film "Lest We Forget" by the Indiana Anti-Saloon League.[75] But the products of California

[73] Hartman, Brookston, p. 116; Work Projects Administration, *Indiana: A Guide*, p. 115; Lynd and Lynd, *Middletown in Transition*, pp. 263-264; Charles C. Alexander, *Nationalism in American Thought, 1930-1945* (Chicago, 1969), pp. 93-99. One local controversy erupted in 1935 in Muncie when Francis Dillon, president of the United Auto Workers, came to town to organize workers. The local radio station at first agreed to and then canceled a sale of air time to Dillon, who then broadcast his speech to Muncie listeners from a nearby Anderson radio station. Lynd and Lynd, *Middletown in Transition*, pp. 37-38; Indiana State Federation of Labor, *Proceedings*, 1936, p. 37.

[74] *Indiana Catholic and Record*, October 26, 1928. See also *The Leisure of a People*, p. 85.

[75] Indiana Anti-Saloon League, *Annual Report, January 19, 1926* (Indianapolis, 1926), p. 12.

studios were of a different order. Often sex was a major ingredient —prominent in movie titles and promotional materials. Playing at a theater in Crawfordsville in 1924 was the movie "Single Wives," advertised in the local newspaper as "the wives that husbands neglect! The wives who are hungry for romance! The wives who sometimes listen when forbidden love calls."[76] Attempts at state censorship of movies in the early 1920s failed, though some local communities exerted pressures on movie operators. And the motion picture industry began to censor itself with the appointment in 1923 of Hoosier Will H. Hays as "movie czar," responsible for enforcing a national moral code. Complaints continued, however, including arguments that declining morality and rising crime were the consequences of suggestive movies that romanticized criminals and were "overweighted in sex stuff."[77] More restrained critics such as George Ade asserted that most films were "addressed to the intelligence and the cheaper emotions of the immature gigglers and gum-chewers."[78] Such objections had limited effect. Hoosiers flocked to movie theaters, especially as talking pictures arrived in the late 1920s and as audiences sought in the 1930s entertainment and perhaps escape from the Depression. In Muncie by the mid-1920s nine motion picture theaters operated seven days a week, while in Indianapolis in 1929 there were more than fifty. A survey of 1,654 children from "representative" sections of the capital city that year disclosed that more than half attended a movie at least once a week, with Saturday matinees most popular. Cowboy actor Tom Mix was the most popular movie star in Indianapolis, followed closely by the "it" girl, Clara Bow.[79]

Movies were a threat not only to traditional morality but to live theater also. Indianapolis's major legitimate theaters struggled to compete with motion pictures, and many closed in the postwar

[76] Crawfordsville *Journal*, October 14, 1924.

[77] *The Leisure of a People*, p. 487. See also Indianapolis *News*, March 5, 1921; Indiana Committee on Observance and Enforcement of Law, *Report*, pp. 10, 27; Nash, *The Nervous Generation*, p. 146.

[78] Ade to Francis Sonday, September 3, 1933, in Tobin (ed.), *Letters of George Ade*, p. 172.

[79] Lynd and Lynd, *Middletown*, p. 263; Lynd and Lynd, *Middletown in Transition*, pp. 261-262; *The Leisure of a People*, pp. 267-269, 484.

decade. The English Theater, though closed temporarily in 1930, continued to provide excellent stage productions with some of the world's greatest performers until its demise in 1948. Live drama was also available in the productions of the Civic Theater of Indianapolis, organized in 1926, and in the New Deal Federal Theater Project during its brief existence in Indiana under Lee Norvell in 1936 and 1937.[80]

Serious live drama, as well as traditional vaudeville, chautauqua lectures, and summer band concerts, lost ground to movies, radio, and other new forms of entertainment and culture, such as professional sports and popular magazines. Here, as much as anywhere, Hoosiers became a part of a standard American culture, for what they heard, watched, and read often reflected the nation's tastes rather than those distinctly of Indiana. The national culture was hardly revolutionary: much of the nation's art, literature, music, sports, and popular entertainment reinforced traditional values and bound together Hoosiers and other Americans of different social, economic, and political circumstances. Yet sometimes there appeared in cultural and leisure-time activities the divisions and conflicts that also marked other aspects of life. Some new cultural forms, such as jazz music, shocked traditionalists and appealed more to the young than the old. Many organized sports and other leisure activities were closed to women and blacks or were available only on a segregated basis, and some forms of leisure were less readily enjoyed by rural than urban Hoosiers. Economic barriers existed also, so that lower-class Hoosiers often participated less fully than middle-class citizens. Golf provides a good example of a new sport played largely by urban middle-class men, joined by a few women. Poorer urban Hoosiers had less free time generally, the women especially, while men often found entertainment in pool halls and cigar stores rather than in state parks, athletic clubs, golf courses, or the resort spas

[80] Indianapolis News, June 4, 1930; Work Projects Administration, Indiana: A Guide, pp. 139-141; William George Sullivan, English's Opera House (Indiana Historical Society Publications, XX, No. 3, Indianapolis, 1960), pp. 377-378; Lee Norvell, The Road Taken (Bloomington, Ind., 1980), pp. 247-249.

and hotels at French Lick, West Baden, and the northern lakes.[81] Despite the differences, however, the lives of nearly all Hoosiers were affected by the changes in leisure, sports, and culture in the decades after World War I.

[81] Thornbrough, *Since Emancipation*, p. 88; *The Leisure of a People*, p. 95. In 1929 there were 280 pool rooms in Indianapolis. The city's chief of police described them as "cesspools of evil," while the Marion County probation officer thought them "the rendezvous of the unadjusted . . . ." *Ibid.*, pp. 491, 493. For Booth Tarkington's view see *Alice Adams* (Garden City, N.Y., 1921), pp. 240-244.

CHAPTER XII
WORLD WAR II AT HOME

THE WAR changed everything. Politics, social relations, culture, and above all, the economy were bent to the overarching need to defeat the Axis powers. Often the changes that occurred were an intensification or exaggeration of tendencies that had begun decades before, but there was also discontinuity with the past. Some of the wartime changes proved to be temporary, quickly abandoned after the defeat of Germany and Japan. Others were more permanent—becoming part of the postwar society. The Indiana of 1945 was not radically different from the Indiana of 1939, despite the major disruptions of war. And yet it was not the same either, as the war generally pushed the state and its people in the direction of a more modern, urban, and industrial society farther and farther removed from the rural, agrarian traditions of the nineteenth century. Hoosiers never fully abandoned their traditions, however, clinging to old and familiar ways, to the beliefs and patterns of behavior inherited from their parents and grandparents, as the world around them seemed more than ever before to have been set loose from its traditional moorings.

Hoosiers did not favor a rush into war. The state was generally among the most isolationist in the nation in the 1930s, as many Indianans and their spokesmen preferred to let the rest of the world go its own way. The disillusionment with World War I and its aftermath was especially strong, as a resolution approved at the annual session of the Indiana Conference of the Methodist Church in 1934 indicated: "A few years ago we mixed religion and war. We became drunken upon the potion. But we have learned our lesson. 'Never again' is the cry now."[1] Such antiwar and isolationist sentiments were translated into political action by

[1] Indiana Annual Conference of the Methodist Episcopal Church, *Minutes*, 1934, p. 390.

Louis Ludlow, a prominent newspaper correspondent who was first elected to the United States Congress from Marion County in 1928 and served until 1949. A strong spokesman for democracy and peace, Ludlow emerged in the 1930s as the national leader of the war referendum movement. From 1935 to 1941 he proposed a Constitutional amendment requiring a popular referendum to declare war, except in case of attack. Such a plan, Ludlow argued, would prevent military and business leaders (especially munitions makers) from maneuvering America into war and would keep ambitious presidents and diplomats from intervening unwisely in the affairs of others.[2]

Congress never approved the Ludlow amendment, and the nation gradually drifted into more involvement in European affairs, as Poland fell to German armies in 1939 and France in 1940, while England seemed on the brink of defeat. Some Hoosiers responded to these distant events by arguing for American aid to England and for military preparedness at home. The Indiana Committee for National Defense began to make this case after the fall of Poland. By early 1941 Governor Schricker co-operated fully with President Franklin D. Roosevelt's cautious moves to aid England, but noninterventionist sentiment remained strong in Indiana. Even as late as May, 1941, a Gallup poll reported that only 15 percent of Hoosiers favored entry into the European war, making the state among the most noninterventionist of the forty-eight.[3]

Pearl Harbor ended the doubt and debate. After December 7, 1941, Hoosiers lined up to support the war effort as strongly as Americans did generally. Indiana sent its share of men and women into the armed forces: approximately three hundred thousand Hoosiers served during the war, and more than ten thousand died.

[2] Ernest C. Bolt, Jr., *Ballots before Bullets: The War Referendum Approach to Peace in America, 1914-1941* (Charlottesville, Va., 1977), pp. 152-185; Walter R. Griffin, "Louis Ludlow and the War Referendum Crusade, 1935-1941," *Indiana Magazine of History*, LXIV (1968), 267-288; Louis Ludlow to Franklin D. Roosevelt, January 21, 1935, PPF 2007, Roosevelt Papers.

[3] Calvin C. Berlin, Indiana's Civilian Soldiers (Ph.D. dissertation, Indiana University, Bloomington, 1956), pp. 3-4; George M. Blackburn, The Hoosier Arsenal (Ph.D. dissertation, Indiana University, Bloomington, 1956), p. 124; Wayne Simpson to Roosevelt, January 17, 1941, PPF 2895, Roosevelt Papers; Wayne Coy to Grace Tully, November 6, 1941, PPF 7809, *ibid.*

Men and women from the state served in all theaters of the war and in all branches of the service, generally without separate recognition as Hoosiers. The major exception was the Indiana National Guard, which with some additional members from Kentucky and West Virginia was mobilized in January, 1941, as the 38th Infantry Division. The 38th did not experience combat until late 1944, but it played an important role at Leyte Gulf and on Luzon in the Philippine Islands, where the division achieved distinction as the "avengers of Bataan."[4]

Although those in uniform were most drastically affected by war, Hoosiers who remained at home also found their lives rapidly changing, in part because of the absence and sometimes death of husbands, fathers, sons, and daughters. Nearly all Indianans had close relatives and friends in uniform and spent anxious days and weeks waiting for letters and reading about the war in newspapers, particularly the reports from Hoosier correspondent Ernie Pyle.[5] But lives at home changed also because of the reorganization of the American homefront necessary to win the war. As those who stayed at home were constantly reminded, Germany and Japan would be defeated not only by men in foxholes, fighter planes, tanks, and battleships, but by hard work and sacrifice at home. Above all, the war on the homefront was an economic war, a battle of production in which America's capacity to produce would decide the victor. The necessities of war production were the primary determinants of change in Indiana.

§ §

The most striking reminders in Indiana of the European war were the military installations that began to appear in 1940 and 1941, often where cornfields had existed the previous year. More

[4] Indiana *House Journal*, 1945, p. 15; *Indiana in World War II*. Volume I: *Gold Star Honor Role: Adams County*, compiled by Indiana Historical Bureau (Bloomington, Ind., 1949), p. 3; William J. Watt and James R. H. Spears (eds.), *Indiana's Citizen Soldiers: The Militia and National Guard in Indiana History* (Indianapolis, 1980), pp. 158-179.

[5] Howard H. Peckham and Shirley A. Snyder (eds.), *Letters from Fighting Hoosiers* (Bloomington, Ind., 1948); Ernie Pyle, *Here is Your War* (New York, 1943); Ernie Pyle, *Brave Men* (New York, 1944).

than two dozen army and navy training centers, camps, depots, and other military installations were located in the state during the war.[6] Among the most important were Camp Atterbury in Bartholomew, Johnson, and Brown counties, which served as a combat training center and prisoner-of-war camp; the Jefferson Proving Ground, which covered parts of Jefferson, Ripley, and Jennings counties in southeastern Indiana and was used to test ammunition and military components; and the Crane Naval Ammunition Depot in Martin County, where ammunition was produced and stored. These three large military installations were among the most important in Indiana and shared common features. All sprawled over large tracts of land in southern Indiana—generally in areas that had been marginal or submarginal in farm production since World War I and had been hit especially hard by the Depression. The new military installations thus removed some of the least productive land from agriculture and provided jobs for large numbers of unemployed or marginally employed Hoosiers, considerations that were significant in the choice of location. Camp Atterbury covered more than forty thousand acres and employed several hundred civilians from nearby farms and villages. Jefferson Proving Ground sprawled over fifty-six thousand acres and reached a peak of twelve hundred civilian employees, 22 percent of whom were women. Crane spread over more than forty-four thousand acres, more than one fourth of Martin County, and at its peak in 1944 employed nearly ten thousand workers, more than a third of whom were women. While the new payrolls were usually welcomed in southern Indiana, these gigantic military installations were not without social costs. Above all, many families were forced to sell their homes and farms, sometimes at prices they regarded as unfair, and to seek new jobs and new homes in a highly competitive and expensive housing market. Schools, churches, and stores were closed, and cemeteries moved, uprooting families and communities that had

[6] For a list of military installations with dates of commissioning see Dorothy Riker (comp.), *The Hoosier Training Ground: A History of Army and Navy Training Centers, Camps, Forts, Depots, and Other Military Installations within the State Boundaries during World War II* (Bloomington, Ind., 1952), p. xiv.

spent generations on these southern Indiana farms. Many of the displaced families found work in the military installations, but some had difficulty adjusting to the demands of modern production, particularly at Crane, where the navy supervisors encountered resentment and some unwillingness to suffer military and industrial regimentation. Not only were these Hoosiers among the Americans most disrupted by the war, they were among the first to be affected, for much of this uprooting began before Pearl Harbor.[7]

Perhaps the most impressive evidence of the disruption of war prior to Pearl Harbor was the construction of the Indiana Ordnance Works at Charlestown in Clark County, which became a model of the virtues and trials of a war boomtown. In 1939 Charlestown was a sleepy village of some nine hundred people, bounded by marginal and abandoned farms and the Ohio River. The town had two paid officials: the town marshal, who also collected the garbage, and the superintendent of the water plant, who also read the meters. In January, 1940, the War Department and the DuPont Chemical Company agreed to construct at Charlestown the world's largest powder plant, to be operated by DuPont and owned by the government. By the end of 1940 there were 13,400 workers engaged in constructing the plant, and the quiet river town was no more. As one resident complained:

We were doing all right . . . . All of a sudden real estate agents came down on us like buzzards round a dead horse and tried to force us to sell land our grandfathers had owned . . . . We're over run with riff raff coming and with these promoters out to turn us out and profit on us.[8]

The influx of promoters and workers created unprecedented problems of sanitation, housing, police and fire protection, recreation, and education. The state government sent a community co-ordinator to advise local leaders, and the federal government provided some financial help, including a step-up of the WPA sewer construction, but community services lagged far behind demands. Housing was the most pressing need and was met by converting chicken coops and barns into homes and by bringing

[7] *Ibid.*, pp. 6-79, 261-294, 305-322; Cavnes, *The Hoosier Community at War*, pp. 55-79.

[8] Cavnes, *The Hoosier Community at War*, p. 18.

in hundreds of trailers and putting up prefabricated houses. The town's first roller skating rink and bowling alley were built in 1941, and the one movie theater remained open every night in the week rather than the customary four. But new opportunities for leisure did not prove sufficient to keep young and old out of trouble. Public intoxication and theft strained the capacities of the expanded police force, while delinquent boys and girls created problems for parents and the county welfare department. Problems of child neglect grew because many mothers worked in the plants. And the six teachers in Charlestown Township schools quickly became insufficient for the growing population. A grant of $600,000 from the PWA in 1941 allowed the community to plan a modern school, complete with gymnasium (though not as large as the town wanted), but material shortages and conflict with the township trustee scuttled the project. Two temporary structures had to serve instead. These personal and community problems were costly for the people of Charlestown, but they were judged necessary to provide the materials of war. Production at the Indiana Ordnance Works began in April, 1941. By September, six thousand employees were at work on six production lines and were producing smokeless powder.[9]

Charlestown was the first and largest war boomtown in Indiana, but there were others. The Wabash River Ordnance Works near Clinton in Vermillion County offered some new employment opportunities for the hard-pressed mining communities in western Indiana but never attained the levels of employment or production of Charlestown. The Kingsbury Ordnance Works near La Porte was received less well locally than the southern Indiana facilities, as people in the area had not experienced the degree of economic deprivation that southern Indiana farmers and miners had. But neither did the Kingsbury area suffer as many community problems as other war boomtowns. Even though employment rose as high as twenty thousand workers in 1942, most were commuters from cities of the Calumet region and South Bend.[10]

[9] *Ibid.*, pp. 15-55; Blackburn, The Hoosier Arsenal, pp. 56-60, 91-92; Stoner and Field, *Public Health Services in an Indiana Defense Community.*
[10] Cavnes, *The Hoosier Community at War*, pp. 79-107; Blackburn, The Hoosier Arsenal, pp. 60-68, 94-99.

§ § §

Prior to Pearl Harbor, government-built ordnance plants and military installations stood as the most prominent evidences of the European war and as the prophets of the changes that war would bring elsewhere in Indiana. For most communities and for most businesses, the European war prior to December, 1941, was less disruptive. By 1940 the nation's defense buildup had begun to bring economic recovery to Indiana. Manufacturers eagerly began to fill consumer demand for cars, refrigerators, washing machines, and other durable goods. Only slowly did they turn to defense contracts, because they were reluctant to assume the risks involved as long as the United States was not a belligerent. The Allison Division of General Motors in Indianapolis was a major exception among Indiana manufacturers. In 1937 the army had approved Allison's airplane engine for exclusive use in its pursuit planes. With Allison's head start, defense contracts poured in during 1940 and 1941, causing major challenges in switching from a small machine shop to assembly line mass production. Some other companies also sought defense work prior to Pearl Harbor, aided by the promotional efforts of chambers of commerce and Indiana politicians. But prior to December, 1941, many manufacturers, especially in the automobile industry, were eager to concentrate on consumer rather than war production.[11]

Pearl Harbor changed that. By early 1942 a massive conversion of industry to war production was underway. Not all manufacturers were equally affected by war conversion, however. Generally, the most important war production was in the larger and more modern industries and companies—notably automobile, steel, oil, chemical, and electronics plants. The Calumet region's

[11] Blackburn, The Hoosier Arsenal, pp. 29-32, 39-40, 45-52, 142-143; Goldthwaite interview, March 9, 13, 1979, pp. 36-39, 56-57, Oral History Research Project Mss.; "City's Industry Expanding for 'All Out' Defense Effort," Indianapolis Chamber of Commerce, Activities, LVII (June, 1941), 3. For the auto industry generally see Alan Clive, State of War: Michigan in World War II (Ann Arbor, Mich., 1979), pp. 18-36. Clive's book and John W. Jeffries, Testing the Roosevelt Coalition: Connecticut Society and Politics in the Era of World War II (Knoxville, Tenn., 1979) provide very good monographic accounts of state issues elsewhere during the war.

steel and petroleum companies were critical to the war effort, and the mills and refineries operated at full capacity and often beyond their rated capacity in order to provide basic materials for war. The automobile industry was also critical, though war needs required more changes in the nature of production and product than in steel and oil. Indiana's auto plants produced trucks and other military vehicles—especially the Studebaker and International Harvester factories. But many auto-related factories were converted to the production of materials more removed from the prewar passenger car or truck. GM's Guide Lamp plant in Anderson and Chrysler's plant in Evansville made shell cases and cartridges, while Delco-Remy in Anderson produced aluminum engine castings and electrical equipment for tanks, planes, and ships. Many auto-related plants produced for the rapidly growing aircraft industry, which became the largest war industry in the state. Other than the engine work at Allison, there was practically no aircraft production in Indiana prior to 1940. With the war, Studebaker and Bendix in South Bend and several of the GM plants across the state began production of aircraft parts. Studebaker turned out a peak of twenty-three hundred airplane engines a month and by late 1943 was the sole supplier of B-17 engines. Other aircraft plants appeared after 1940, including Curtiss-Wright in Indianapolis, the nation's largest propeller manufacturer; Republic Aviation in Evansville, which made fuselages; its neighbor, Servel, a peacetime appliance manufacturer that became a wartime producer of airplane wings; and the Fort Wayne General Electric plant, which made supercharger fans for planes. Although nearly all of these major plants were experienced in mass production of metal products, for many the war required conversions and speedups that presented major challenges to the skills and patience of management and labor.[12]

The aircraft industry was Indiana's largest and perhaps most glamorous war industry, but other manufacturers made important contributions to the war effort. Major shipbuilding yards boomed in Jeffersonville and Evansville. Like Servel, other home appliance

---

[12] Blackburn, The Hoosier Arsenal, pp. 224-227, 270-280, 303-305, 333-336.

manufacturers stopped production of consumer products in 1942. Bendix Home Appliances of South Bend converted from washing machines to parachute flares, and Sunbeam in Evansville from refrigerators to tools that could be mass produced and used by unskilled men and women for mass production work. Other companies made radical conversions, as, for example, the Starr Piano Company of Richmond, which manufactured screws for Allison engines and armor-piercing bullets, while the C. G. Conn Company of Elkhart converted from musical instruments to precision aircraft instruments, such as altimeters and compasses. Bloomington's RCA plant opened in 1940 and soon switched to proximity fuses, while Fort Wayne's Magnavox factory changed from radios and phonographs to solenoids for firing mechanisms. Magnavox led all Indiana plants in the number of army-navy "E" awards received for production.[13]

Other industries were less directly relevant to war production. Some furniture and woodworking companies made office and classroom equipment for the military, but the war did not provide as large an economic boost for them as it did for other manufacturers. The Indiana limestone industry was among those which benefited least from war production and did not reverse its post-1929 decline.[14]

The critical industries in war production were steel, petroleum, metalworking—especially the converted auto plants—electronics, and chemicals. These were the same industries that had risen to prominence in Indiana in the post-World War I era. They included the largest and most modern companies—the big businesses that stood at the center of the state and national economies by 1940. War dramatically increased the demand for their technological, labor, and managerial skills. Indeed, military and government officials much preferred to contract with big business suppliers rather than deal with smaller companies, placing greater

[13] *Ibid.,* pp. 205-207, 215-235, 280-284, 363.

[14] *Ibid.,* pp. 194, 200-202, 219-223; Batchelor, *An Economic History of the Indiana Oolitic Limestone Industry,* pp. 311-312. See also R. T. King, "From Kitchen Cabinets to TV Sets: A Select Historical Perspective on Industrial Transition in Bloomington, Indiana, 1920-1980," videotape, Indiana University Oral History Research Project, 1980.

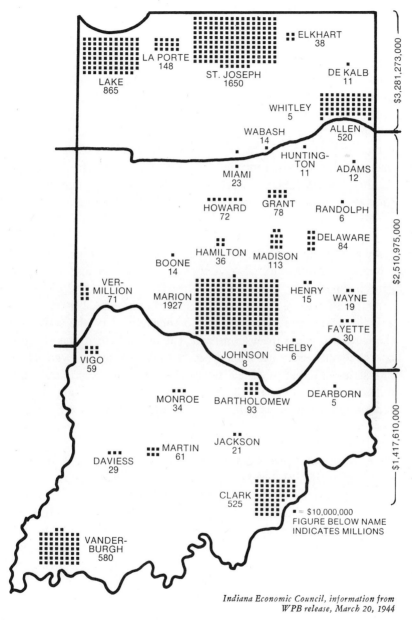

ELKHART
38

LA PORTE
148

DE KALB
11

LAKE
865

ST. JOSEPH
1650

WHITLEY
5

ALLEN
520

WABASH
14

HUNTING-
TON
11

ADAMS
12

MIAMI
23

HOWARD
72

GRANT
78

RANDOLPH
6

DELAWARE
84

BOONE
14

HAMILTON
36

MADISON
113

VER-
MILLION
71

MARION
1927

HENRY
15

WAYNE
19

FAYETTE
30

VIGO
59

JOHNSON
8

SHELBY
6

MONROE
34

BARTHOLOMEW
93

DEARBORN
5

MARTIN
61

JACKSON
21

DAVIESS
29

CLARK
525

■ = $10,000,000
FIGURE BELOW NAME
INDICATES MILLIONS

VANDER-
BURGH
580

$3,281,273,000

$2,510,975,000

$1,417,610,000

*Indiana Economic Council, information from
WPB release, March 20, 1944*

War supply contracts in Indiana, by county

faith in the big companies' ability to adapt technology, meet schedules, and provide the large-volume, efficient production necessary to win the war. Although the federal government made some attempts to direct work to small manufacturers and although many contributed to the war, often as subcontractors, the war of production was led by big business. And because many of these businesses operated under cost-plus-fixed-fee contracts and received government loans and large tax incentives, they avoided many of the usual economic risks while enjoying large profits. At the same time, however, they wrestled with labor and material shortages, government red tape, and externally imposed production controls.[15]

The industries and companies that contributed most to the war were at the center of the Indiana economy even before the war. There was continuity also in their geographical location. The growing industrial cities received nearly all the war supply contracts: Indianapolis, South Bend, Gary, Hammond, Fort Wayne, and Evansville led the list. The northern third of the state was the leader in war supply contracts, the central third was second, and the southern third trailed far behind. Although Evansville's industries did very well, elsewhere in southern Indiana only the military installations and a handful of companies brought large federal contracts or payrolls. Terre Haute was perhaps the Hoosier city with the least successful record in attracting war-related production contracts, and it continued its prewar economic decline. Richmond manufacturers also failed to convince the government of their ability to make large contributions to the war.[16]

The economic effects of war thus differed among sections and cities and among industries and companies, but they largely reinforced prewar trends. The overall consequences of the war for the state's economy were momentous. Indiana received a much larger-than-average share of war contracts, hence its manufacturing industry grew more rapidly than that of most states. In major war

---

[15] Cochran, *American Business in the Twentieth Century*, pp. 139-152; Blackburn, The Hoosier Arsenal, pp. 147-153, 372-374; Bernard Friedman, *The Financial Role of Indiana in World War II* (Bloomington, Ind., 1965), pp. 26-38.

[16] Blackburn, The Hoosier Arsenal, pp. 154-156, 242-244.

combat equipment supply contracts Indiana ranked eighth among the states—receiving $7,657,863,000 in contracts, 5.6 percent of the nation's total combat supply contracts. In major war industrial facilities projects, the federal government spent $961,425,000 in Indiana, mostly helping businesses build and expand aircraft and other metalworking plants. These Indiana industrial facilities projects were 5.7 percent of the national total, which ranked the state eighth here also.[17]

Other data show the effect of these contracts and the war generally on Indiana's industry. Manufacturing employment increased by 49 percent in the period 1939-1942. Among its east-north-central neighbors (Wisconsin, Michigan, Illinois, and Ohio) only Ohio showed a larger percentage increase. In 1944 payrolls of war industries accounted for nearly one third of all Indiana income payments, ranking the state fourth nationally (behind Michigan, Connecticut, and Ohio) in impact of war industry payrolls. Important also was the rapid rise in per capita personal income, not only in absolute terms but also in comparison to regional and national averages. Indiana jumped from 93.4 percent of the nation's average per capita income in 1939 to 101.0 percent in 1941, peaking at 102.7 percent in 1943. Thereafter Indiana's per capita income remained about the same as that of the national average through the 1940s. The state's per capita income also grew more rapidly than its east-north-central neighbors, as the state narrowed but did not fully close the gap that had separated Hoosiers from residents of Illinois, Michigan, and Ohio since the nineteenth century.[18] The 1947 manufacturing census demonstrated the general economic progress of the war years and also indicated that the end of the war in 1945 had not seriously slowed the Indiana economy. The state's manufacturing work force in 1947 had increased 66.2 percent over the 1939

[17] United States Bureau of the Census, *County Data Book, 1947* (Washington, D.C., 1947), p. 7.

[18] Indiana Economic Council, *Hoosiers at Work: What They Do—What They Make—What of the Future?* (n.p., 1944), p. 25; Hanna, *State Income Differentials*, pp. 29, 40; Indiana Economic Council, *Indiana's Economy: Pt. II: Indiana's Economy as Revealed by Income Payments to Individuals . . .* (Indianapolis, 1950), pp. 3-21.

figure—a percentage increase above the east-north-central average of 63.4. The 1947 census also showed a continuing and increasing trend toward concentration in heavy durable goods, reflecting the state's strength in production of heavy metals, automobiles, machinery, and electrical appliances. There was only a limited growth in light consumer goods. And manufacturing in 1947 remained largely concentrated in the cities of the Calumet, Indianapolis, South Bend, Fort Wayne, and Evansville, which accounted for over half of the state's total value added by manufacturing in 1947.[19]

§ § § §

The war of production in Indiana presented many economic challenges, but probably the most difficult was the shortage of labor—a radically different situation from the high unemployment levels of the 1930s. By mid-1942 labor shortages were widespread, as war factories demanded more and more workers and as the military put more and more of the most able-bodied citizens into uniform. Business, government, and labor began to seek ways to maximize the productivity of the nation's dwindling labor supply. State government through the Employment Security Division played some role in recruiting workers, but increasingly this and related tasks were assumed by the federal government. The federal government played an expanding role in encouraging and sometimes requiring people to work where they were most needed and in attempting to reduce turnover. The federal War Manpower Commission, established in 1942 and headed by former Indiana Governor Paul V. McNutt, attempted with limited success to control and allocate labor resources efficiently. Government also began to train unskilled workers—notably through the Training-Within-Industry program—and to encourage and later require essential businesses to increase the workweek to forty-eight or more hours. Beginning in 1943 some German and Italian

[19] United States Bureau of the Census, *Manufactures: 1947*, III, 199-216; Indiana Economic Council, *Indiana's Economy:* Pt. I: *Status and Trends in Indiana Manufactures: An Analysis of the First Post-War Census* (Indianapolis, 1949).

prisoners of war were used to supplement labor supplies—mostly in agricultural harvesting and tomato canning.[20]

Government and business also joined with organized labor to prevent production losses due to labor disputes and strikes. With the return of prosperity in 1940 and 1941, labor unions began more aggressive campaigns to organize workers and raise wages. In 1940 there were 67 work stoppages in the state; in 1941 there were 161, including a major strike at International Harvester that brought intense conflict and some violence to the company's Richmond plant. After Pearl Harbor, labor and business joined in a no-strike pledge, and strikes and labor disputes declined greatly. There were only 92 stoppages in 1942, most of very limited duration and impact. Labor grew restive under wartime inflation and wage controls but generally held to the no-strike pledge, except for the coal strike of 1943.[21]

During the war unions made great strides in organizing workers and strengthening their position economically and politically—continuing the process begun in the mid-1930s. The Congress of Industrial Organizations (CIO), with its strength in the auto and steel industries, became especially powerful, not only in plants and mills but also in politics. The state and national CIO took very liberal political positions, including strong opposition to discrimination against black workers and support for continuation and expansion of New Deal social reform programs. In August, 1943, the Indiana State Industrial Union Council—representing CIO unions in the state—joined the national leadership in forming the CIO Political Action Committee (CIO-PAC) to support lib-

[20] Work Projects Administration, "Indiana Industrial Activity and the Need for WPA Employment," April, 1941, State Administration Reports, Indiana, Records of the Work Projects Administration, RG 69; Hugh M. Ayer, Hoosier Labor in the Second World War (Ph.D. dissertation, Indiana University, Bloomington, 1957), pp. 180-201, 247-252; Hugh M. Ayer, "Hoosier Labor in the Second World War," Indiana Magazine of History, LIX (1963), 95-104. Subsequent citations to Ayer's study of labor are to the more detailed doctoral dissertation. See also Flynn, The Mess in Washington.

[21] Ayer, Hoosier Labor, pp. 129-173, 254-263; Witney, Indiana Labor Relations Law, p. 51.

eral and prolabor candidates and programs. The Indiana CIO-PAC was very active in the 1944 elections and generally supported Democratic party candidates. The CIO's political activity and its growing power inspired considerable resentment and some counterattacks from businessmen, politicians (especially Republicans), and also at times from the Indiana State Federation of Labor. Opponents charged that the CIO was infested with communists and was becoming a powerful threat to the individual freedoms of workers, owners, and all other citizens. These antagonisms were only overtures to struggles that would become more important in the postwar years; during the war they were generally muted, because business and labor joined to produce the materials of victory—to their mutual benefit.[22]

But even total harmony between labor and management could not alone have met the demands of war production. As the labor shortage grew more serious, it became necessary to employ workers who had been represented only in small numbers in manufacturing prior to 1941. The most important new recruits in the war of production were blacks and women.

As earlier chapters have noted, racial prejudice was broad and deep in Indiana, and blacks faced discrimination in all areas of life. Many factories and nearly all skilled jobs were closed to blacks prior to 1941. The war changed this in large measure. Some whites doubtless saw the gross incongruity of blacks fighting for freedom against Nazi Germany while they were largely segregated from whites in the military forces and denied full rights at home. Many whites responded to the more pragmatic dictates of devastating labor shortages and stifled their antipathy to hiring or working alongside blacks in order to meet production schedules and to win the war. And many whites also responded to a rising intensity of black resentment against discrimination, evidenced nationally in A. Philip Randolph's March on Washington Movement and in the race riots that occurred in Detroit and New York.

[22] Ayer, Hoosier Labor, pp. 121-128, 379-395, 467-507; Synopsis of the Sixth Annual Convention of the Indiana State Industrial Union Council . . . 1943 (n.p., n.d.), pp. 9, 12, 19-21; Indiana State Chamber of Commerce, "Jesse James In His Heyday . . . Had More Principles" (Indianapolis, 1943).

Indiana experienced no serious racial violence, but there was considerable evidence that blacks would not continue to tolerate traditional patterns of racial discrimination.[23]

The issue of discrimination in employment was first raised seriously in the 1941 General Assembly, when J. Chester Allen, a black representative and lawyer from South Bend, introduced a fair employment practices bill. House Bill 445 prohibited discrimination in defense employment and quickly passed the house by a unanimous vote. In the Indiana senate it encountered strong criticism, as groups, apparently taken by surprise earlier, now rallied opposition. American Federation of Labor lobbyists argued that the bill would weaken collective bargaining, and the Indiana State Chamber of Commerce vehemently criticized the proposal as government interference with employer freedom, the kind of interference advocated by communists. The Chamber's position was clear: it was "unalterably opposed to any legislation, either state or federal, on the subject of anti-discrimination between races . . . ."[24] Faced with this opposition, the antidiscrimination bill failed in the senate—"a stinging slap in the face" to blacks, the Indianapolis *Recorder* stated.[25]

But the issue was not dead. Clarence A. Jackson, executive vice-president of the Indiana State Chamber of Commerce and a former member of McNutt's administration, pushed for action on the issue of racial discrimination, warning that "governmental intervention harmful to both employees and employers [is] certain to result from failure to act now."[26] Indeed, in June, 1941, President Roosevelt signed an executive order creating the Fair Employment Practices Committee, which was charged to end discrimination in businesses that accepted federal defense contracts—the beginning of the kind of civil rights action Jackson hoped to avoid. Jackson and the Chamber moved quickly—pre-

[23] Richard Polenberg, *War and Society: The United States 1941-1945* (Philadelphia, 1972), pp. 99-130; Indiana *Year Book,* 1945, p. 789.

[24] Indiana State Defense Council, *The Problem in May, 1941: The Action Toward a Solution* (n.p., 1941). See also Thornbrough, *Since Emancipation,* p. 40; Cavnes, *The Hoosier Community at War,* pp. 112-115.

[25] Indianapolis *Recorder,* March 15, 1941.

[26] Indiana State Defense Council, *The Problem in May, 1941.*

paring several publications on the question in 1941 and co-operating with the Indiana State Defense Council (of which Jackson also served as director) to gain the appointment in June of Representative Allen to the new position of Coordinator of Negro Activities for the Defense Council. Also in June, 1941, the Chamber and the defense council sponsored the first meeting of the committee that created the Indiana Plan of Bi-Racial Cooperation. With Allen and Jackson providing the leadership and with very strong support from Governor Schricker, the state's business, black, and labor leaders agreed to work together to improve job opportunities for blacks and to win the war. In twenty-three Indiana communities Allen helped form committees representing local blacks, businessmen, and union members pledged to carry out these twin objectives.[27]

The Indiana Plan of Bi-Racial Cooperation was an important milestone in the evolution of race relations. It signaled a recognition by the most important political and economic groups in the state of the existence of a civil rights problem and helped to publicize that problem, and it represented a tentative step toward solution. But the Indiana plan and the pamphlets and committees that resulted were far from revolutionary in intent or impact. In his preface to the general description of the Indiana plan, published in April, 1942, Jackson provided the context: "The grim fact that idle hands cannot be tolerated with the nation committed to 'all-out war' has been stressed rather than the emotional appeal of fair play . . . ."[28] A year later the Chamber of Commerce head reiterated the boundaries: the Indiana Plan of Bi-Racial Cooperation was "not concerned with questions of 'social equality' which are generally conceded to be personal matters . . . ." And, Jackson warned, "Negroes who use the present emergency to apply pressure for unwarranted advancement will find their new status im-

[27] *Ibid.*; Indiana State Defense Council, *Job Opportunities for Negroes* (n.p., 1943), p. 11; Cavnes, *The Hoosier Community at War*, pp. 115-119; Lynn W. Turner and Heber P. Walker (comps.), *Indiana at War: A Directory of Hoosier Civilians Who Held Positions of Responsibility in Official, Volunteer and Co-operating War-Time Organizations* (Bloomington, Ind., 1951), pp. 500-507.

[28] Indiana State Defense Council, *The Indiana Plan of Bi-Racial Cooperation* (Indianapolis, 1942), p. 1.

periled when the emergency which supports it has passed." Allen
adopted a similar tone, urging fairness in employment for blacks
but counseling moderation and limited expectations.[29] Through
the war, the Chamber of Commerce successfully forestalled any
but voluntary state efforts to respond to discrimination. The 1945
General Assembly did pass a state fair employment practices act,
but compliance was voluntary and the act proved of little concrete
effect, though it represented an important precedent of government recognition of the problem.[30]

While the full and exact consequences of the Indiana Plan for
Bi-Racial Cooperation are impossible to assess, there is little doubt
that by 1943 the war itself had created a manpower shortage that
absolutely required the use of black workers. Thus blacks were
hired in plants and industries where before only whites had
worked. There was considerable variation in local response, however. Some factories, such as RCA in Indianapolis and Chrysler
in Evansville, hired large numbers of blacks. Others, such as
Hoosier Lamp and Stamping in Evansville and the Fairfield Manufacturing Company in Lafayette, hired none or very few. Some
made sincere efforts to upgrade blacks—moving them into semiskilled positions as machine operators. Others, such as Guide
Lamp and Delco-Remy in Anderson and Studebaker's Fort
Wayne plant, continued the tradition of employing blacks only
as janitors and common laborers. At times, white workers objected to the hiring or upgrading of black workers, and on a few
occasions they went on strike in protest, as at Allison in Indianapolis in 1943, when blacks were first placed on machines. State
and national union leaders generally supported black employment
rights. The CIO was especially vigorous in defending black workers, but some CIO locals did not always follow this policy, as,
for example, the United Auto Workers in Anderson, which in
1944 voted to bar blacks from the union hall. And industries in

[29] Indiana State Defense Council, *Job Opportunities for Negroes.* The quotations are on pages 1 and 2. See also Clarence A. Jackson to Local Defense Directors, August 18, 1942, Box 251, Indiana War History Commission Records,
Archives Division, Indiana Commission on Public Records, Indiana State Library
and Historical Building.
[30] Thornbrough, *Since Emancipation,* p. 41.

some towns were generally reluctant to hire blacks. As late as 1944 Muncie's largest plants—Ball Brothers, Warner Gear, and Durham Manufacturing Company—employed a total of only 215 blacks. Rather than hire blacks, Muncie manufacturers, like some others elsewhere, helped meet their labor shortages by recruiting and hiring large numbers of southern whites, to the great resentment of local blacks.[31] The new workers from Kentucky, Tennessee, and other states often brought with them traditional racial prejudices toward blacks, while they themselves were only slightly more welcomed than blacks by older white residents. As one Muncie citizen complained, "there are only forty-five states left in the Union. Kentucky and Tennessee have gone to Indiana, and Indiana has gone to hell."[32]

There is no doubt that the war greatly enlarged economic opportunities for blacks. And because blacks were needed as workers and soldiers, there was increased attention to issues of discrimination and segregation generally. The war effected no social revolution, to be sure. Throughout the war years blacks encountered discrimination in housing, education, entertainment, recreation, and in the daily routines of their lives. Taxicabs in Indianapolis and Evansville often refused to carry black passengers, the best restaurants in many cities and towns did not serve them, some hospitals would not treat them, and USO clubs often failed to provide adequate recreation for black servicemen. The social problems of race relations remained, but, as the war years

[31] Cavnes provides an excellent discussion of the variety of black employment. Cavnes, *The Hoosier Community at War*, pp. 120-137. See also Thornbrough, *Since Emancipation*, pp. 77-79.

[32] John Bartlow Martin, "Is Muncie Still Middletown?" *Harper's Magazine*, CLXXXIX (July, 1944), 98. The same joke, substituting Michigan for Indiana, circulated in Detroit during the war. See Clive, *State of War*, p. 179. Racial tension in Muncie was very high and in May, 1944, almost produced the lynching of a black man by an angry white mob. Blacks blamed the tension on local manufacturers and unions, the press, the mayor, and police—all of whom, they charged, condoned or exacerbated racial prejudice and discrimination. See J. Chester Allen, Report on Racial Situation at Muncie, typescript, May, 1944, Box B, Drawer 150, Henry F. Schricker Papers, Archives Division, Indiana Commission on Public Records, Indiana State Library and Historical Building; Cavnes, *The Hoosier Community at War*, pp. 157-159.

enlarged economic opportunities and encouraged blacks to be less content with their status as second-class citizens, the way was prepared for greater change in the postwar decades.[33]

Women also were recruited for war production, with significant effects on their lives. Like blacks, few women worked in manufacturing prior to 1940, reflecting considerable prejudice against women in industry—especially married women.[34] Of the 250,148 women in Indiana working outside the home in 1940, most were in clerical and service occupations. With the war, the number of women in the work force increased dramatically, to 390,000 by 1943. Equally important, women worked not only in traditional occupations but also in war industries, particularly by 1943, when war production was at its peak and the male labor force fully employed. From January to October, 1943, the number of women employed in Indiana manufacturing increased by nearly 22 percent, while the number of men in manufacturing dropped slightly. By the end of 1943 more than one third of Indiana factory workers were women. The largest increases occurred in the central war industries, those that shaped and fitted metal to produce the instruments of war. In some plants women constituted the majority of workers, such as the tank armor plant in Gary, the RCA factory in Bloomington, and most of the ordnance plants. Women workers, like the stereotypical "Rosie the Riveter" of World War II, were actively recruited by industry and encouraged by government and other agencies to regard jobs as patriotic obligations. Many were also influenced by the need and opportunity to provide income for themselves and their families.[35]

The flood of women into wartime employment was the most critical factor alleviating the shortage of labor and had an impor-

[33] Cavnes, The Hoosier Community at War, pp. 137-179; Thornbrough, Since Emancipation, pp. 89-96.

[34] Manning and Phillips, Wage-Earning Women and the Industrial Conditions of 1930: A Survey of South Bend, p. 9; Lynd and Lynd, Middletown, pp. 26-27; Indiana State Federation of Labor, Proceedings, 1934, pp. 58-60.

[35] United States Bureau of the Census, Seventeenth Census (1950), II, Population, Pt. 14, pp. 48-49; Indiana Economic Council, Hoosiers at Work, p. 22; Ayer, Hoosier Labor, pp. 357-362, 586-590.

tant effect on the achievements of war production. But, predictably, there were also difficulties and costs. Women, like blacks, often were relegated to the least desirable and lowest paying jobs, as some companies were reluctant to train them for skilled work. Unions and male workers also showed some tendencies to treat women as second-class employees—sometimes agreeing to different wage scales for men and women and not always pushing for upgrading of women. Black women had special difficulties in finding industrial employment and in receiving equal treatment inside the plant.[36]

Many women faced increased challenges not only in employment but also as a consequence of being working mothers. Often with husbands away in uniform or in war work, women assumed sole responsibility for rearing their children. A major difficulty for working women was child care, much of which was provided as in the past by neighbors, friends, and relatives. But the demands of war work strained these informal arrangements so that organized child-care programs were needed. In October, 1942, Governor Schricker appointed a Committee on Care of Children in Wartime. Its primary responsibility was to co-ordinate efforts to establish nursery schools and day-care centers for children of working mothers. The state committee assisted in the formation of local child-care committees, numbering forty-two by mid-1943. The local and state committees worked with schools, churches, businesses, and public and private welfare agencies and groups to establish child-care facilities, the number of which was increased from twelve in Indiana in 1940 to seventy-six by June, 1944. Two thirds of the child-care centers received federal financial support under the Lanham Act of 1940, designed to aid community services in wartime. Though many Hoosiers believed that the development of organized child care was a necessary response to war, not all agreed that this break with tradition was wise or necessary. Some argued that the war effort did not require the services of women with small children and asserted that children left in day-care centers were being deprived of essential

[36] Lane, "*City of the Century,*" p. 211; Cavnes, *The Hoosier Community at War,* pp. 121-123.

maternal love and attention. Some mothers were reluctant to leave their children with strangers in a new environment, and some could not afford the fees charged. And the day-care services were almost entirely an urban phenomenon, as rural and small-town Indiana continued to rely on traditional methods of child care.[37]

§ § § § §

The war changed the lives and relationships of mothers, fathers, and children, of husbands and wives. The social disarray of war—most evident in the absence from home of fathers and husbands and working wives and mothers—created new tensions for families. The war prompted couples to rush into marriage, often just before the new groom was shipped overseas. And separation and stress sometimes led to divorce, despite efforts by the government and others to encourage marital stability.[38] But perhaps the family problems that evoked most comment were those of troubled and troublesome youths, who were affected just as profoundly as their elders by the dislocations of war. Young people had always caused anguish for their parents. The 1920s marked perhaps the beginning of a more intense anguish, as some youths asserted a new freedom that sometimes included drinking, smoking, premarital sex, and coarse language—all producing cries of shock and dismay from their elders. Commentators blamed youthful transgressions on movies, automobiles, materialism, and overly indulgent parents. After their second visit to Muncie, in the mid-1930s, the Lynds concluded "that no two generations of Americans have ever faced each other across as wide a gap in the customary attitudes and behavior as have American parents and children since the World War."[39] In one of modern America's many ironies, as parents limited family size through increased practice of birth

[37] Cavnes, *The Hoosier Community at War*, pp. 228-245; Turner and Walker, *Indiana at War*, pp. 1056-1057; Indiana State Defense Council, *Feeding Children in Group Care* (Indianapolis, 1943).

[38] *Indiana Catholic and Record*, August 24, 1945. As early as 1925 one church group deplored the perceived increase in the number of divorces. Northwest Indiana Conference of the Methodist Episcopal Church, *Minutes*, 1925, p. 187.

[39] Lynd and Lynd, *Middletown in Transition*, p. 168. See also Indianapolis *News*, October 5, 1926; *Indiana Catholic and Record*, May 16, 1930.

control[40] and devoted more attention to child rearing, children seemed to cause more parental despair and anguish.

The gap between the generations increased remarkably during World War II, as young people encountered both new frustrations and opportunities. Young men eighteen and older volunteered or were drafted into military service. Youths who stayed at home became recruits in the war economy. Many older students dropped out of school—attracted to war jobs—as Indiana high school enrollment in school year 1943-1944 was nearly 12 percent below enrollment in 1941-1942. Others took part-time jobs, finding work on weekends and evenings and in the summer as a consequence of labor shortages. The money they earned gave them new freedoms. And during the war many adolescents developed an intense feeling of distinctiveness, of being teenagers—different from adults and from younger brothers and sisters. With clothing, music, and a slang of their own, teenagers emerged during the war as a more separate and distinct segment of society.[41]

Nowhere was this more apparent than in the problem of increased juvenile delinquency. Adolescents misbehaved long before Pearl Harbor, but the war brought an increase or at least the perception of an increase in juvenile crime. Vandalism, intoxication, shoplifting, youth gangs, and general disrespect for elders seemed to signify a new lawlessness and a decline of community and family authority—providing the topics for club and

---

[40] By the 1920s use of contraceptive methods was very common among the middle class, less so among the working class. The 1930s produced a large interest in family planning, wide publicity for birth control, and extensive support from the medical profession. Lynd and Lynd, *Middletown*, pp. 125, 131; Lynd and Lynd, *Middletown in Transition*, pp. 164-167; "Birth Control," *Journal of the Indiana State Medical Association*, XXVIII (1935), 386; "That Birth Control Program," *ibid.*, XXX (1937), 396. The Roman Catholic Church remained staunchly opposed to birth control. *Indiana Catholic and Record*, September 3, 1926, November 11, 1932.

[41] United States Office of Education, *Biennial Survey of Education in the United States, 1944-46*, p. 17; Richard M. Ugland, The Adolescent Experience during World War II: Indianapolis as Case Study (Ph.D. dissertation, Indiana University, Bloomington, 1977), pp. 100-123, 151-210, 346-400; Richard M. Ugland, "Viewpoints and Morale of Urban High School Students during World War II— Indianapolis as a Case Study," *Indiana Magazine of History*, LXXVII (1981), 150-178.

church meetings and newspaper and magazine features. Probably the most shocking form of youthful excess was the perceived increase in sexual activity, with most concern focusing on young girls. A misplaced sense of patriotic duty and other social disruptions, it was believed, led young girls into premature and sometimes promiscuous sexual relationships, often with servicemen. The "uniform chasers" and "victory girls" aided unwittingly in the wartime crackdown on prostitution but set back the campaign against venereal diseases and caused great anguish for parents, social workers, and legal authorities. By 1943 the extent and variety of juvenile delinquency led to concerted action at the state and local levels. Representatives of several public and private welfare groups met in the fall of 1943 to plan a statewide campaign against juvenile delinquency, and the Indiana Committee on the Care of Children in Wartime formed a subcommittee on the problem. Local committees representing social welfare organizations and civilian defense agencies appeared in most Indiana cities. They urged more attention to law enforcement and lobbied, usually successfully, for a curfew ordinance. Most important, they organized efforts to extend recreational opportunities for young people, especially through formation of teen clubs or canteens, which provided a dance floor, juke box, and snack bar. Michigan City's Jive Jar, South Bend's Hi-Spot, Anderson's Club Tom Tom, Clinton's Wildcat Den, and dozens of other teen canteens in most cities were responses by young people and adults to the disruptions of the war and a recognition of the emergence of teenagers.[42]

The war also altered everyday routines of life, sometimes making a luxury of what had seemed commonplace. Sacrifices required by wartime inflation, shortages, and rationing of food, tires, and gasoline caused frustration. Housing shortages developed in industrial and military areas, and rents skyrocketed,

[42] Cavnes, The Hoosier Community at War, pp. 246-271; Ugland, The Adolescent Experience during World War II, pp. 219-276, 313-337; Ronald D. Cohen, World War II and the Travail of Progressive Schooling: Gary, Indiana, 1940-1946 (unpublished typescript, in author's possession), pp. 11-15; Indiana State Board of Health, Indiana's Wartime Program against Venereal Disease (Indianapolis, 1942); Indiana State Defense Council, Teen-Canteen (n.p., 1944).

leading to experiments with government rent control. Medical care became more difficult to obtain, as 1,275 Indiana physicians, more than one third of the total number in practice in 1940, served in the armed forces. Opportunities for leisure declined. The war closed the Indianapolis 500 race and the Indiana State Fair, and by 1943 attendance at state parks dropped to only about one third the attendance in 1941.[43]

Education also bent to the war effort. Under the guidance of the Department of Public Instruction's Education War Policy Program, high schools increased attention to vocational training to prepare students for defense jobs and placed more emphasis on physical education, health, and mathematics, all considered more relevant to the war effort than the rest of the curriculum. Schools attempted to explain the war and boost morale, often through support of scrap drives and war bond and stamp sales. Many schools struggled with rapidly rising costs and a shortage of teachers, and some small township schools were forced to close. Schools in communities with defense industries were flooded with new students. On college campuses, many students and faculty departed for war jobs and military service and were replaced by military personnel and military training programs. All Indiana colleges participated in the war effort—ranging from pilot-training programs on several campuses to a program at Earlham College to train conscientious objectors for overseas relief duty. College faculty members contributed many talents to the war— extending from service in Washington bureaucracies, to research on powdered eggs, to work on development of the atomic bomb.[44]

Farmers and other rural Hoosiers were also affected by the war. The changes in agriculture since World War I had produced an

[43] Friedman, *The Financial Role of Indiana in World War II*, pp. 39-66; Turner and Walker, *Indiana at War*, pp. 200, 557; Indiana *Year Book*, 1946, p. 668.

[44] Turner and Walker, *Indiana at War*, pp. 213, 222-299; Indiana *Year Book*, 1945, p. 724; John E. Stoner and Oliver P. Field, *Public Schools in an Indiana Defense Community* (Bloomington, Ind., 1946); H. B. Knoll (ed.), *1941-1945: A Record of a University in the War Years (Archives of Purdue No. 4,* [West Lafayette, Ind.], 1947); Clark, *Indiana University*, III, 119-121; Charles B. Hirsch, "Conscientious Objectors in Indiana During World War II," *Indiana Magazine of History,* XLVI (1950), 61-72.

abundance of farmers and farm production, which the war quickly depleted. Rural out-migration, which had halted during the Depression, resumed as Hoosiers abandoned marginal land and smaller farms for higher paying war jobs and military uniforms. From October, 1940, to October, 1941, approximately 12,600 persons moved to Indianapolis: 53 percent were from elsewhere in Indiana, almost all from rural areas and small towns. Indiana's total population declined 1.2 percent between April, 1940, and November, 1943, but in twenty-six counties the percentage decline exceeded 10 percent. All of these counties were largely rural and most were in southern Indiana. In the longer period 1940-1947 the population of the state increased 10.7 percent, but in the thirty-seven southernmost counties it grew by only 3.8 percent overall. In sixteen of these counties, population declined. The federal Farm Security Administration contributed to this population shift away from southern Indiana when it began in 1942 a program of recruiting and transporting surplus farm labor from southern Indiana to the central and northern sections of the state.[45]

The depletion of farm and rural population caused by war placed a heavy burden on those who remained. Although plagued by material and labor shortages, Indiana farmers during the war exceeded the high levels of output achieved during the late 1930s. Corn maintained its place as the most important crop, while soybeans continued their rise to prominence, with more than 25 million bushels harvested in 1945 compared to nearly 14 million in 1940. And hogs remained the most important livestock, with 3.2 million hogs reported on Indiana farms in 1945, compared to 2.4 million in 1940. This increased agricultural production was achieved as farms declined in number but grew in size—a general trend through the twentieth century. The number of farms

[45] Work Projects Administration, Recent Migration into Indianapolis, Indiana, mimeograph, December 4, 1941, File 55, Box 84, Indiana War History Commission Records; United States Bureau of the Census, County Data Book, 1947, pp. 134-146; John V. Van Sickle, Indiana's Outlook: Some Basic Facts About the Hoosier Economy (Indianapolis, 1948), p. 32; Ernest H. Shideler, Farm Security Administration: History Material for Indiana War History Commission, typescript, August, 1945, Box 66, Indiana War History Commission Records.

dropped from 184,549 in 1940 to 175,970 in 1945, and the average size of farms increased from 107.3 acres in 1940 to 113.8 acres in 1945—notably as the number of farms over 175 acres increased. Farm mechanization also continued during the war, which greatly helped to alleviate the labor shortage. Tractors increased in number from 73,221 in 1940 to 105,263 in 1945, and the number of corn pickers rose from 11,900 in 1942 to 15,700 in 1945. And, with continued encouragement from Purdue experts, the Agricultural Extension Service, and the federal government, Indiana farmers increased their production by greater use of fertilizer, hybrid corn seed, and a variety of other techniques and materials developed and disseminated from West Lafayette. As a consequence of wartime changes, many Indiana farmers paid off debts they had owed for years and entered the postwar era better off economically than at any period since World War I.[46]

§ § § § § §

Government also had to change in order to direct the war effort. State government agencies suffered loss of staff members, and those who remained were assigned new responsibilities. Recognizing early both the likely effect of war on state government and the potential of government to respond positively to the war effort, Governor Schricker and the General Assembly established in 1941 the Indiana State Defense Council. The council's initial emphasis was on civil defense—particularly preparation for air raids. Local citizen defense corps planned and practiced air-raid blackouts and warning systems. As the probability of German and Japanese planes appearing in Indiana skies declined, the State Defense Council and local groups shifted their attention to aiding war production and boosting civilian morale. The State Defense Council sponsored the Committee on Care of Children in Wartime

[46] *United States Census of Agriculture: 1945*, Vol. I, Pt. 4, *Indiana* (2 volumes, Washington, D.C., 1946), pp. 2-8; Robertson and Butz, *Indiana's Agriculture*, p. 40; Schoeft and Robertson, *Agricultural Changes from 1910 to 1945. . .* , pp. 18, 21; Knoll (ed.), *1941-1945: A Record of a University*, pp. 136-163; Hassil E. Schenck, Indiana Farm Bureau, Inc., typescript, June, 1945, Box 66, Indiana War History Commission Records; Friedman, *The Financial Role of Indiana in World War II*, p. 202.

and the Indiana Plan of Bi-Racial Cooperation, already mentioned. The council helped co-ordinate the early rationing program, beginning with tires in January, 1942, but the federal government soon assumed authority for rationing. And the council planned various scrap drives, asking Hoosiers to collect metal, rubber, paper, and kitchen fat. In the major scrap drive conducted in the fall of 1942, the Defense Council proudly reported that Indiana ranked fourth in the nation in per capita pounds of scrap collected. The council also co-ordinated various programs to encourage women to aid the war effort through Red Cross and other volunteer work.[47]

While state government played a large role—especially through the Indiana State Defense Council—major government responsibility for the war at home quickly lodged in Washington. To a greater extent than in fighting the Depression of the 1930s, federal programs and agencies, while they often had state or regional offices, were co-ordinated and controlled in the nation's capital. The War Production Board, War Labor Board, War Manpower Commission, Office of Price Administration, and other federal agencies directed the nation's homefront, often allowing little authority to state and local agencies. The Office of Price Administration (OPA) began in early 1942 delegating significant responsibility to states, but by May prices were under full federal control. In addition to a district office in Indianapolis, OPA opened a second office in South Bend, thereby dividing the state, and then detached Lake County from the Indiana district, placing its jurisdiction within the Chicago district—a violation of state lines and usurpation of Indianapolis's authority that dismayed some defenders of states' rights. World War II thus brought to Indiana a new and higher level of federal government intervention and regulation with less state and local intermediation.[48]

[47] Berlin, Indiana's Civilian Soldiers, pp. 129-149, 187-234; Indiana *Year Book*, 1942, pp. 850-853; 1944, pp. 587-591; Indiana State Defense Council, *Civilian Defense in Indiana Manual* (5th revision, Indianapolis, 1943); Indiana State Defense Council, *Annual Report of Public Health Functions, 1941-1942* (n.p., n.d.); Indiana State Defense Council, *Indiana Women in Defense* (n.p., n.d.).
[48] Friedman, *The Financial Role of Indiana in World War II*, pp. 153-161.

The war also affected partisan politics, although less so than many other aspects of life. The major partisan battle of the early 1940s was fought in the 1941 General Assembly, which met early in the year and thus before Pearl Harbor. As a result of the 1940 elections, Republicans dominated the legislature for the first time since 1929, holding 64 of 100 seats in the house and 31 of 50 in the senate.[49] And they controlled all elected state offices except the most important one. Governor Schricker was the lone Democrat. Schricker offered compromise and co-operation to the Republican majority, not only because of his political vulnerability but also because he had never been closely tied to the McNutt or Townsend wings of the Democratic party and philosophically was lukewarm at best to the New Deal. In his first message to the Republican-dominated legislature, Schricker appealed to their sense of patriotism and harmony and promised that he did "not crave dictatorial power." In direct repudiation of his Democratic predecessors, he called for repeal of McNutt's reorganization act of 1933—arguing that the measure gave too much power to the governor. And, demonstrating his break with McNutt and Townsend, he made major changes in appointive offices, removing many McNutt Democrats who had been in Indianapolis since 1933.[50]

Schricker might protest that he was not a McNutt Democrat, but Democrat he was, and Republicans were in no mood for compromise. In one of the most thoroughly partisan ventures in Indiana history, they set about to dismantle the gubernatorial power McNutt had created and to reduce Schricker to a figurehead. The Republican majority passed some two dozen bills that were chiefly designed to deprive Schricker of his power to make executive appointments to departments and agencies of state government. The State Administration Act of 1941 repealed the 1933 reorganization act and, combined with a series of "little ripper

---

Local rationing boards continued to play a role but under federal direction. For general trends in these national programs see Polenberg, *War and Society.*

[49] Indiana Legislative Bureau, Indiana General Assembly, p. 56.

[50] Indiana *House Journal,* 1941, pp. 131-145. The quotation is on page 145. See also Indianapolis *Times,* January 14, 1941.

bills," as the Democrats labeled them, abolished, recreated, and restructured boards, commissions, and departments of state government. In each case the new structure made the governor a minority board member. The new board directing the Department of Public Works, for example, was composed of the governor, lieutenant governor, and treasurer, each having one vote in appointment of members to the state highway commission and other agencies in the department. Under this scheme, Schricker would always be outvoted by the two elected Republican officers, and the executive branch of government would fall from his influence and control. Such a condition was only right, Republicans argued, for the new structure would decentralize authority that had been overly centralized under McNutt and would return government to closer popular control. Moreover, they argued, the people had shown their overwhelming support of the Republican party in the 1940 elections: the aberration of a Democratic governor, they felt, ought not stand in the way of the need to undo the evils of eight years of Democratic rule.[51]

Schricker might have seemed to some to be the type of person who would surrender to this mountainous opposition. The governor was thin and short and wore a white hat and pince-nez glasses on a black ribbon. But Schricker was shrewd and popular, perhaps better able than any other twentieth-century Indiana politician to behave without affectation like the typical small-town Hoosier, the friendly, honest neighbor. At church suppers and county fairs he talked with people rather than giving speeches, and he chewed tobacco and smoked cigars while wearing or waving his white hat.[52] Kind and folksy but not easily pushed around, Schricker came out fighting in March, 1941. He had warned the General Assembly that, although eager to compromise, he did not intend to have only "errand boy authority."[53] When the legislature reduced him to just that, he first responded by vetoing more

[51] Indiana *Year Book*, 1941, p. 846; *Laws of Indiana*, 1941, pp. 31-48; Charles Francis Fleming, *The White Hat: Henry Frederick Schricker: A Political Biography* (n.p., 1966), pp. 67-79; Indianapolis *News*, March 11, 1941.

[52] Fleming, *The White Hat: Henry Frederick Schricker*; Peat, Lazarus, and Ruegamer, *Portraits and Painters of the Governors of Indiana 1800-1978*, p. 84.

[53] Indiana *House Journal*, 1941, p. 145.

than two dozen bills. Republicans overrode all but one. Schricker then moved to the courts, successfully seeking a temporary injunction against the Republican reorganization, which was to take effect on April Fool's Day, 1941. In the case of *Tucker* v. *State* the issue went to the state supreme court, which held in June, 1941, that the legislative reorganization of the executive branch deprived the governor of his legitimate constitutional authority and violated the state constitution's principles of separation of powers and checks and balances.[54] With this decision, the Republican effort at enfeeblement of the governorship collapsed. It is likely that Hoosier Republicans in 1941 did little to help their party or state. Schricker charged, in an uncharacteristically bitter statement, that "no cheaper brand of politics ever was played in Indiana,"[55] and the Indianapolis *Times* concluded that the Republican legislature had spent "three-quarters of its time setting up a system of government to give Republicans as many jobs as possible . . . ."[56] Democratic party leaders were even less charitable, hurling such epithets as "booty-mad partisans" and "gang of Republican racketeers."[57] Republicans responded that they were undoing eight years of Democratic patronage and McNutt power. And they did succeed in passing bills in 1941 that slightly extended the merit system for some state employees and reduced some of the most patronage-oriented features of the Alcoholic Beverage Commission.[58] But Republicans had been too eager and reached too far in their attempts to repudiate McNutt and to even the partisan score. Their hunger for patronage and power would continue after the failed effort of 1941, but they proceeded more slowly and achieved more success.

[54] Indiana *Year Book*, 1941, pp. 846-847; Indianapolis *News*, June 27, 1941; Indianapolis *Times*, June 27, 1941; Fleming, *The White Hat: Henry Frederick Schricker*, pp. 79-103. The Indiana Supreme Court in 1941 consisted of four Democrats and one Republican.

[55] Indianapolis *Times*, June 27, 1941.

[56] *Ibid.*, March 11, 1941.

[57] Fred F. Bays, *An Episode in Petty Politics: The Account of an Amazing Session of an Indiana General Assembly* (n.p., 1941), pp. 6, 3.

[58] Indianapolis *News*, March 11, 1941; Greenough, *A History of the League of Women Voters of Indiana, 1920-1952*, pp. 55-58; Indiana *Year Book*, 1941, pp. 886-887.

After 1941, partisan politics was less visibly intense in Indiana but always present. Elections assured the health of politics even in wartime. In the off-year elections of 1942, Republicans continued their revival with landslide victories—winning nine of eleven congressional seats[59] and increasing their seats in the state senate to thirty-eight and in the house to eighty-two. Democrats clearly failed in 1942 in their efforts to brand Republicans as prewar isolationists and to convince voters that the war effort required a united Democratic front.[60] Governor Schricker's message to the Republican-dominated 1943 General Assembly was moderate and undemanding. He did not ask for extraordinary war powers, as some governors elsewhere were doing, nor did he call for social change at home. The Republican legislators responded in kind and adjourned two months later, with their leaders stressing their record "of not having passed crackpot or disturbing bills."[61]

Though Republicans were beset with factional struggles throughout the war years, they knew that the 1944 elections presented the opportunity for a clean sweep. Their 1944 convention produced a very strong ticket, headed by Ralph F. Gates, a Columbia City lawyer who had served as Indiana head of the American Legion in 1931-1932 and as Republican state chairman since 1941. The two Republican candidates for United States Senate seats were Homer E. Capehart, a pioneer manufacturer of automatic phonographs, who had entered Republican politics with his "cornfield conference" in 1938, and William E. Jenner, a Paoli lawyer, who entered the state legislature in 1935, where he

[59] Democrat Louis Ludlow barely held his seat in the eleventh district (Marion County), and Democrat Ray Madden was elected in the first district (Lake County), the beginning of a long career in Congress for Madden. Francis and Doerner (comps.), *Indiana Votes: Election Returns for United States Representative, Election Returns for State General Assembly, 1922-1958,* pp. 52-53.

[60] Ray E. Smith to Oscar Ewing, March 7, 1942, Box 1125, OF 300, Democratic National Committee Papers; Indianapolis *Times,* November 4, 1942; Indiana Legislative Bureau, Indiana General Assembly, p. 56.

[61] Indianapolis *News,* March 1, 1943. See also *ibid.,* March 9, 1943; Indianapolis *Times,* January 9, 1943; Berlin, Indiana's Civilian Soldiers, pp. 153-158; Indiana *House Journal,* 1943, pp. 31-44.

made a lively record attacking McNutt.[62] These men were very effective campaigners: each was able to draw on rural and small-town origins, and each was able to spellbind a crowd with little obvious effort. Talented, young, aggressive, they were the leaders of the new Republican party in Indiana, and the Democrats were hard-pressed to match them. The state constitution prohibited Schricker from a second consecutive term, so the party nominated him for United States Senator against Capehart. For the short term, to run against Jenner, Democrats nominated Cornelius O'Brien, a businessman and banker from Lawrenceburg. And for the governor's race they selected Samuel D. Jackson, a Fort Wayne lawyer who held Van Nuys's Senate seat from January 28, 1944, until replaced by Jenner after the November, 1944, election.[63]

The Republican candidates in 1944 campaigned against the New Deal in nation and state, lumping Schricker with Townsend, McNutt, and Roosevelt as power-hungry radical reformers; charging the undemocratic use of political influence by organized labor, especially the Political Action Committee of the CIO; raising the specter of communism at home; challenging the audacity of Roosevelt in seeking a fourth term; and insisting that only Republicans in Indianapolis and Washington could provide prosperity and protect free enterprise and home rule in the postwar era. Democrats responded defensively in a campaign that showed signs of mediocre organization and limited enthusiasm. Voters showed their sentiments in the November elections by giving Republicans a nearly clean sweep, electing, in addition to Gates, Capehart, and Jenner, nine of eleven congressmen, sixty-nine state representatives, and thirty-seven senators. And Hoosiers, as they

[62] Because of the death of Senator Frederick Van Nuys on January 25, 1944, two senatorial elections were held in November, 1944—one for the short term, to fill the seat until January, 1945, and the other for the long term, to serve from January, 1945, until 1951. Jenner won the short term seat and after filling it returned to Indiana as the Republican state chairman until his election to a regular term in 1946, replacing Republican Senator Raymond E. Willis.

[63] Indianapolis *Times*, March 10, 1941; McCarty (ed.), *Indiana Today*, pp. 312, 172; *Who's Who in Indiana* (Chicago, 1947), p. 45; *Biographical Directory of the American Congress, 1774-1971* (Washington, D.C., 1971), pp. 1179, 1187.

had done in 1940, also refused to cast a majority vote for Roosevelt. Republicans ran very well in rural and small-town Indiana, with Democrats winning some southern counties and large majorities only in the industrial centers of Lake, St. Joseph, and Vanderburgh counties.[64]

January, 1945, thus returned a large Republican majority to the General Assembly and brought a Republican to the governor's office for the first time in twelve years. Republicans may have remembered the consequences of similar party dominance in 1933, but 1945 produced no such dramatic change. Governor Gates promised his Republican colleagues that he would not use strong-arm tactics to force legislation and that he would respect the prerogatives of the legislative branch. It is unlikely that Gates could have been a Republican McNutt even if he had wished. Though he had an estimated five thousand patronage jobs to fill, the wartime labor scarcity and relatively low pay of government employees meant that there were no hordes of office seekers waiting in line as they had been in 1933.[65] Nor did Gates propose a long list of changes. He and his Republican colleagues had talked at great length about the necessity of repealing the "little" New Deal of McNutt and Townsend.[66] But many of those programs were firmly in place, were too popular to risk tampering with, or were beyond state control, especially as long as the war continued. The legislature of 1945 did expand and improve the operation of the State Board of Health but made few significant changes

[64] William B. Pickett, Homer E. Capehart: The Making of a Hoosier Senator (Ph.D. dissertation, Indiana University, Bloomington, 1974), pp. 226-238; Indianapolis News, November 6, 1944; Republican state platform, 1944, in Indiana State Platforms, II; Indianapolis Star, November 10, 1944; Pitchell (comp.), Indiana Votes: Election Returns for Governor, 1852-1956, and Senator, 1914-1958, pp. 90-93.

[65] Indianapolis Star, November 9, 1944; Indianapolis News, November 10, 1944; Indiana House Journal, 1945, p. 88.

[66] This sentiment was expressed in the Republican-sponsored investigation of the Indiana Department of Public Welfare, which in its report was especially critical of the large role played by the federal government and professional social workers in welfare. See A Statement by the State Board of Public Welfare Regarding the Official Report of the Indiana Welfare Investigation Commission (n.p., 1944), pp. 3, 5-7.

elsewhere. It adjourned, the sympathetic Indianapolis *News* reported, receiving "more credit for what it refused to do than what it did in a positive way."[67]

The war ended with the Republicans effecting no dramatic changes in Indiana. But they had clearly turned back the threat of dominance by a New Deal-liberal coalition of urban, labor, and black voters and had developed a level of voter support and power by 1945 that boded well for the party in the postwar years. The average Republican share of the two-party vote for the three elections of 1940, 1942, and 1944 was 52.5 percent, close to the average of 54.9 percent in the 1920, 1922, and 1924 elections and far above the 45.2 percent average of 1932, 1934, and 1936. Republican strength had increased considerably in rural and small-town Indiana, where the party generally revived more strongly after the Depression of the 1930s. And, while many voters in urban and industrial areas held on to their Depression-formed ties to the Democratic party, Republicans continued to have strength in cities—particularly Indianapolis and Fort Wayne.[68] Their primary objective of repealing the New Deal would prove harder than they imagined, but Republicans would achieve considerable success in preventing its extension in Indiana and would provide evidence of the continuing importance and distinctiveness of state and local politics and government in modern America.

§ § § § § §

Republicans had talked about more than the New Deal in 1944 and 1945. They and Democrats, too, had given considerable attention to shaping the postwar world and particularly to the immediate issues of reconversion to peace. Determined to avoid the economic and social disruptions that followed World War I and fearful that the end of the war might mean the resumption of depression, Hoosiers began to prepare for peace and reconversion long before Germany and Japan surrendered. In February, 1943,

[67] Indianapolis *News*, March 7, 1945. See also Indiana *Year Book*, 1946, pp. 259-263; Plan for the Future Development of the Indiana State Board of Health, mimeograph, May, 1944, Box B, Drawer 150, Schricker Papers.
[68] Hyneman, Hofstetter, and O'Connor, *Voting in Indiana*, pp. 112-119.

the Indiana State Chamber of Commerce took the lead in forming the Indiana Committee for Economic Development, headed by Louis Ruthenburg, president of Evansville's Servel Company. Emphasizing the importance of averting factory closings and mass unemployment at the end of the war, the committee sponsored programs and meetings, including a major reconversion conference in Indianapolis in 1944. Also formed in early 1943 was the Indiana Economic Council, a state government agency responsible for co-ordinating postwar planning by state and local officials. The Indiana Economic Council encouraged communities to form planning commissions, suggested public works projects to improve community services and alleviate unemployment, and discussed responses to the housing shortage that was sure to intensify as the veterans returned.[69]

Various agencies began also to prepare directly for the return of the veterans. The federal government played the largest role through the Veterans Administration and the administration of the GI Bill of Rights. Passed in 1944, the GI Bill provided federal aid to help veterans obtain education and buy houses. The bill represented an unprecedented level of government response and greatly affected postwar society. The 1945 General Assmbly established the Indiana Department of Veterans' Affairs, which soon employed officials in most communities to assist returning veterans, especially in obtaining federal benefits for education and housing.[70] The surge of GI Bill veterans onto Indiana college campuses—approximately 13,000 by 1946—required major changes in nearly every aspect of higher education, from college housing to curriculum to athletics.[71]

Business and labor also began to plan for a world of peace and consumer buying. The D-day landing in France in June, 1944, stimulated some reconversion of war plants, but the German

[69] Turner and Walker, *Indiana at War*, pp. 1277-1282; Indiana *Year Book*, 1946, pp. 221-226; Indiana Economic Council, *Indiana Postwar Planning Conference Program, May 8-9, 1944* (n.p., n.d.).

[70] Indiana *Year Book*, 1946, pp. 427-430.

[71] *Ibid.*, p. 428; David Roland Warriner, The Veterans of World War II at Indiana University, 1944-1951 (Ph.D. dissertation, Indiana University, Bloomington, 1978).

resurgence at the Battle of the Bulge in late 1944 dampened the trend. By spring, 1945, however, many Indiana companies were seriously planning for production of peacetime goods. By the fall, after Japan's surrender in August, the products of peace were rolling off the lines: the first radio from RCA in Bloomington in September, 1945; the first refrigerator from Servel in Evansville in October; the first Studebaker in South Bend in January, 1946. Through the reconversion period, business faced major challenges of shortages of materials, continued government regulation, and turnover of labor as workers sought jobs that would promise the most security and highest pay in a postwar economy.[72] Organized labor refused to return to prewar conditions, especially of lower pay. In order to preserve wartime pay levels unions called major strikes in Indiana in late 1945 and early 1946 in oil, auto, steel, and coal industries. Although these labor strikes sparked a conservative reaction that had significant political consequences in the postwar years, by late 1946 industry and labor had settled down to steady employment and production, preparing the way for a period of unprecedented material prosperity in Indiana and throughout the nation.[73]

§ § § § § § § §

No bombs dropped on Indiana; no enemy soldier set foot on Hoosier soil except as prisoner of war. Yet World War II was a total war—one that affected the economic, social, and political life of everyone—sometimes temporarily, sometimes permanently. The war at home was, above all, a war of production that speeded economic changes that had begun years earlier with the growth of big business and big labor in the most important industries. Business and labor prospered during the war, and the Indiana economy grew rapidly—expanding the base for a new era of postwar prosperity rather than the return of depression as many had feared. Many farmers, too, enjoyed prosperity, as they continued the adoption of modern methods of agricultural production. Wartime labor shortages pulled more blacks and women into jobs,

[72] Blackburn, The Hoosier Arsenal, pp. 465-478.
[73] Ayer, Hoosier Labor, pp. 535-564.

including industrial production. Problems of racial discrimination remained unsolved, but the war years brought an important new recognition of these problems and marked a significant break with past traditions of ignoring the consequences of racial prejudice. Women went to work outside the home in unprecedented numbers. Many abandoned or lost their jobs after 1945 and returned to full-time work in the home, but the war left some increased awareness of more diverse roles for women. The war also affected young people, calling new attention to teenagers and to juvenile delinquency. And the war expanded the power of the federal government in many economic and social areas. During the war Indiana politics featured the continued revival of the Republican party, begun in the late 1930s, thereby assuring strong two-party rivalry and significantly reducing the possibilities of liberal reform that had appeared in the early and mid-1930s.

None of these changes was unique to Indiana. Indeed, the war helped make the state more like the rest of modern America—more urban and industrial, perhaps also more cosmopolitan and more outward-looking. Those who served in uniform returned with friendships and experiences drawn from the whole nation and often from other continents as well. Those who remained at home saw their lives connected more fully to national and international changes in government, the economy, and society. They were all Americans—more alike than ever before perhaps, but they were Hoosiers, too, and citizens of Muncie, Shelbyville, Gary, or Crawfordsville. Their attachments to state and community continued to constitute an important part of their efforts to retain and modify their traditions and to resist, encourage, or adjust to change in twentieth-century America.

BIBLIOGRAPHICAL ESSAY

This essay is not all-inclusive. Rather, it attempts to indicate the most significant materials for the study of Indiana for the period 1920 to 1945. Since not all items cited in the footnotes are included in the bibliography, readers with specific interests are advised to use the index to locate a topic and relevant citations. The bibliography also contains some items not cited in the notes in the hope that they will be useful to persons pursuing more intensive research than was possible for the present volume.

Readers familiar generally with scholarship in Indiana history know that for the period after 1920 there is a significant decline in the quantity and quality of scholarly, analytical accounts of the state's past. Most major subjects have not yet received the scholarly attention they deserve. The dearth of good secondary accounts is balanced by an abundance of source materials, as the volume—especially of government documents, reports, and data—increased greatly in the twentieth century. For the persistent and imaginative researcher nearly every major subject or historical question offers opportunities to contribute to an understanding of Indiana's past.

This bibliography is organized initially by type of material and then by subject, generally following the order and format of the book chapters. The categories are the following: unpublished materials, general works, politics, transportation, agriculture, business and economics, labor, race and ethnicity, education, religion, public health and public safety, cultural and social issues, and World War II.

UNPUBLISHED MATERIALS

MANUSCRIPTS

The most extensive collections of manuscripts are located in the Indiana Division of the Indiana State Library, Indianapolis; the Lilly Library, Indiana University, Bloomington; and the Indiana Historical Society Library, Indianapolis. The collections of these institutions are generally richer for the nineteenth century than for the twentieth, but each contains important materials for the period after 1920, as noted in the subject sections of this essay. The Archives Division of the Indiana Commission on Public Records, Indiana State Library and Historical Building, contains a large quantity of state government records, only a small portion of which has been catalogued. Several of these collections are discussed below. Indiana materials gathered for the Federal Writers' Project in the 1930s are housed at Indiana State University, Terre Haute, and described in Robert K. O'Neill, "The Federal Writers' Project Files for Indiana," *Indiana Magazine of History*, LXXVI (1980), 85-96. There are many important manuscript collections located outside the state, especially, as noted below, at the National Archives, Washington, D.C., and the Franklin D. Roosevelt Library, Hyde Park.

ORAL HISTORY

Oral history projects have proliferated in many Indiana communities and institutions. One major collection of oral history transcripts is located at the Indiana State Library and consists largely of interviews with political figures. Another major collection is the work of the Indiana University Oral History Research Project, which covers a variety of subjects but is especially strong for aspects of the state's economic history. Transcripts for the latter project are located in the Lilly Library. Developments in oral history are noted in *The Recorder*, a newsletter published by the Indiana Oral History Roundtable.

UNPUBLISHED THESES

Masters' and doctoral theses provide important information about Indiana's past and often contain useful leads for source materials. They vary greatly in quality. The most useful are noted under appropriate subject sections below. A very good bibliography is Betty Jarboe and Kathryn Rumsey, *Studies on Indiana: A Bibliography of Theses and Dissertations Submitted to Indiana Institutions of Higher Education for Advanced Degrees, 1902-1977* (Indianapolis, 1980).

PUBLISHED MATERIALS

GOVERNMENT DOCUMENTS—UNITED STATES

The published United States censuses for the period covered by this volume were most valuable, especially those dealing with population, agriculture, manufacturing, and religion. The United States Bureau of the Census also prepared a variety of special volumes, some of which are noted below. The two major government documents libraries in Indiana are the Indiana State Library, Indianapolis, and the Indiana University Library, Bloomington.

GOVERNMENT DOCUMENTS—INDIANA

The major published state government documents are found in the Indiana *Year Book*, issued annually throughout the years 1920-1945. Each volume contains reports of the bureaus, departments, and offices of state government, often with extensive statistical data. The Indiana *House Journal* and *Senate Journal* report only in vague outline the proceedings of the General Assembly. Legislation passed is printed in *Laws of Indiana*, often referred to as *Acts*. Special state government studies proliferated after 1920, the most detailed and useful of which is the Indiana State Committee on Governmental Economy, *Report* (Indianapolis, 1935).

NEWSPAPERS

Major collections of Indiana newspapers are located at the Indiana State Library, Indianapolis, and the Indiana University Library, Bloomington. Newspapers are essential sources for many aspects of the state's history. The Indianapolis newspapers are especially valuable as they often reported on issues of statewide interest. They provided fullest coverage of state politics, with the Indianapolis *Star* and Indianapolis *News* generally taking more conservative and Republican editorial positions and the Indianapolis *Times* adopting a more liberal and independent or Democratic position.

GENERAL WORKS

There are many general histories of Indiana, but they are usually less thorough in their treatment of the period after 1920. The best account is John D. Barnhart and Donald F. Carmony, *Indiana: From Frontier to Industrial Commonwealth* (4 vols. [III and IV are biographical], New York, 1954). Other general histories include Logan Esarey, *History of Indiana from Its Exploration to 1922* (2 vols., Fort Wayne, Ind., 1924); William E. Wilson, *Indiana: A History* (Bloomington, Ind., 1966); and Howard H. Peckham, *Indiana: A Bicentennial History* (New York, 1978). Ralph D. Gray (ed.), *The Hoosier State: Readings in Indiana History* (2 vols., Grand Rapids, Mich., 1980) is a good collection of primary and secondary materials. John Bartlow Martin, *Indiana: An Interpretation* (New York, 1947), is an excellent effort to provide an interpretative framework for the state in the first half of the twentieth century, but the argument for the "decline" of Indiana is exaggerated, especially in its assumptions of a golden age prior to World War I. Less substantial contemporary characterizations of the state include Heath Bowman, *Hoosier* (Indianapolis, 1941), and Irvin S. Cobb, *Indiana* (New York, 1924). The Work Projects Administration's *Indiana: A Guide to the Hoosier State* (New York, 1941) includes a narrative history and general accounts of aspects of life in the state in the 1930s.

The best treatments of Indiana for the period prior to 1920 are Emma Lou Thornbrough, *Indiana in the Civil War Era, 1850-1880* (Indianapolis, 1965), and Clifton J. Phillips, *Indiana in Transition: The Emergence of an Industrial Commonwealth, 1880-1920* (Indianapolis, 1968), which are volumes III and IV in *The History of Indiana.* These two books provide essential background for many of the issues treated in the present volume.

The *Indiana Historical Collections,* published by the Indiana Historical Bureau, and the Indiana Historical Society *Publications* include a number of scholarly works. The *Indiana Magazine of History,* published quarterly by the Department of History, Indiana University, in co-operation with the Indiana Historical Society, is the most important journal for the publication of scholarly articles in Indiana history. Many of the articles in the *Magazine* have been helpful in writing this volume and are cited in notes and bibliography. Representative selections from the *Magazine*'s first seventy-five years are reprinted in Lorna Lutes Sylvester (comp.), *"No Cheap Padding": Seventy-five Years of the Indiana Magazine of History, 1904-1979* (Indianapolis, 1980). There are general indexes covering volumes 1-25 and 26-50, with a third general index covering volumes 51-75 scheduled for publication in 1982. Annual indexes are located in each December issue of the *Magazine.* The Indiana Historical Society publishes several special interest journals: *Indiana Military History Journal, Indiana Medical History Quarterly, Hoosier Genealogist,* and *Genealogy.* The *Indiana History Bulletin,* published by the Indiana Historical Bureau, also contains items of interest.

City, County, and Regional Histories

County histories are neither as rich nor as abundant for the twentieth century as the nineteenth. The nation's bicentennial celebration sparked the preparation of some new county histories, but the results generally pale in comparison to the outpouring that followed the centennial celebration of 1876. Among regional studies Powell A. Moore, *The Calumet Region: Indiana's Last Frontier* (Indianapolis, 1959), continues to be very useful. The 1977 reprint edition includes an afterword by Lance Trusty summarizing events from 1933 to 1977.

City and community histories are more abundant: indeed, the 1970s witnessed the renewal of interest in local history. Nonetheless, most of Indiana's major cities, including Indianapolis, lack a good history that adequately covers the twentieth century. James B. Lane, *"City of the Century": A History of Gary, Indiana* (Bloomington, Ind., 1978), is an example of one way of making a community's history accessible to its residents and interesting to outsiders as well. Robert S. Lynd's and Helen Merrell Lynd's sociological studies of Muncie still offer critical insights into the way an Indiana community functioned and into the values and attitudes of its residents. Their initial work, *Middletown: A Study in Contemporary American Culture* (New York, 1929), was followed by *Middletown in Transition: A Study in Cultural Conflicts* (New York, 1937). Interest in Muncie and *Middletown* continues, as exemplified in the articles by Richard Jensen, Carrolyle Frank, and Theodore Caplow in the special issue of the *Indiana Magazine of History*, December, 1979. Very good studies of smaller communities include Grover L. Hartman, *Brookston: A Study of the Cultural Evolution of an Indiana Agricultural Community 1829-1940* (Ph.D. dissertation, American University, 1946); and Marian McFadden, *Biography of a Town: Shelbyville, Indiana, 1822-1962* (Shelbyville, Ind., 1968).

Many local historical societies publish newsletters and magazines that make contributions to history. Good examples are the *Old Fort News*, published by the Allen County—Fort Wayne Historical Society, and *Old Courthouse News*, published by the Northern Indiana Historical Society, South Bend. An example of local and family history written by college students is *Steel Shavings*, published at Indiana University Northwest, Gary. Interest in historic preservation has spurred work in local history in several communities, exemplified in Karen S. Craig and Diana M. Hawes, *Bloomington Discovered* (Bloomington, 1980). Statewide attention to preservation is provided by Historic Landmarks Foundation of Indiana and the state historic preservation office in the Indiana Department of Natural Resources. Some of the variety, challenge, and excitement of local history is found in the papers presented at workshops sponsored by the Indiana Historical Society and later published: Richard Jensen, Robert M. Sutton, Thomas D. Clark, and Thomas J. Schlereth, *Local History Today* (Indianapolis, 1979); and David J. Russo, Dorothy Weyer Creigh, Roger Fortin, John J. Newman, and Pamela J. Bennett, *Local History Today* (Indianapolis, 1980).

BIOGRAPHICAL MATERIALS

The Indiana Division of the Indiana State Library has good biographical indexes to newspaper clippings and other sources. Published biographical information for the period 1920-1945 is found in: *Who's Who in Indiana* (Chicago, 1947); C. Walter McCarty (ed.), *Indiana Today: A Work for Newspaper and Library Reference* (Indianapolis, 1942); Kin Hubbard (ed.), *A Book of Indiana: The Story of What Has Been Described as the Most Typically American State . . . Told in Terms of Biography* (n.p., 1929); volumes III and IV of John D. Barnhart and Donald F. Carmony, *Indiana: From Frontier to Industrial Commonwealth* (4 vols., New York, 1954); R. E. Banta (comp.), *Indiana Authors and Their Books, 1816-1916* (Crawfordsville, Ind., 1949); Donald E. Thompson (comp.), *Indiana Authors and Their Books, 1917-1966* (Crawfordsville, Ind., 1974); and Donald E. Thompson (comp.), *Indiana Authors and their Books, 1967-1980* (Crawfordsville, Ind., 1981).

POLITICAL HISTORY

Manuscript collections at Lilly Library, Indiana University, that relate to important political activities during the period 1920-1945 include the papers of the following persons: Claude Bowers, newspaperman and author; Warren Fairbanks, publisher of the Indianapolis *News*; Powers Hapgood, socialist and CIO organizer; Charles Halleck, congressman; Richard Lieber, conservationist; Louis Ludlow, newspaperman and congressman; Paul V. McNutt, lawyer, educator, governor, federal administrator, and diplomat (the collection is for the periods prior to and after his governorship); Samuel M. Ralston, Democratic party leader and senator; Boyd M. Ralston, Indianapolis Democrat and realtor; George W. Rauch, congressman; Walter E. Treanor, Indiana Supreme Court judge; and Wendell L. Willkie, presidential candidate.

The Indiana Division of the Indiana State Library has papers of Republicans Harry S. New, Will H. Hays, Warren T. McCray, Raymond E. Willis, and Homer Capehart. Democrats represented include Virginia Jenckes and Thomas Taggart. Other important collections in the Indiana Division are those for the Ku Klux Klan and the Indiana League of Women Voters.

The most valuable political collections in the Archives Division, Indiana Commission on Public Records, Indiana State Library and Historical Building, are the governors' papers, although they vary greatly in volume and content and are primarily composed of routine correspondence. The collections for the governors of the 1920s are generally disappointing, with Harry Leslie's papers the most useful. Thereafter the collections are voluminous and, regrettably, not well organized.

The Indiana Historical Society Library has a few manuscript collections relevant to politics after 1920. Especially good are the papers of Carleton B. McCulloch, Indianapolis Democrat. There is also a good collection of materials relating to the Ku Klux Klan.

Published reference materials for politics and government include Harold C. Feightner, *Our State Government* (Indianapolis, 1930); Pressly S. Sikes, *Indiana State and Local Government* (Bloomington, Ind., 1940); Indiana League of Women Voters, *Indiana Voters' Handbook* (Indianapolis, 1930); and Office of Government Reports, *Indiana: Directory of Federal and State Agencies* (Indianapolis, 1941). Very useful also is Charles Kettleborough (ed.), *Constitution Making in Indiana: A Source Book of Constitutional Documents with Historical Introduction and Critical Notes*, Volume III, *1916-1930* (Indianapolis, 1930, reprint edition, 1977); and John A. Bremer (ed.), *Constitution Making in Indiana: A Source Book of Constitutional Documents with Historical Introduction and Critical Notes*, Volume IV, *1930-1960* (Indianapolis, 1978). Voting returns are printed in the Indiana *Year Book* and compiled in Robert J. Pitchell (comp.), *Indiana Votes: Election Returns for Governor, 1852-1956, and Senator, 1914-1958* (Bloomington, Ind., 1960); and Wayne L. Francis and Sharron E. Doerner (comps.), *Indiana Votes: Election Returns for United States Representa-*

tive, Election Returns for State General Assembly, 1922-1958 (Bloomington, Ind., 1962).

A good study of politics, emphasizing turnout and voting differences in the electorate, is Charles S. Hyneman, C. Richard Hofstetter, and Patrick F. O'Connor, *Voting in Indiana: A Century of Persistence and Change* (Bloomington, Ind., 1979). For a critical assessment of this important book see Paul Kleppner, "Searching for the Indiana Voter: A Review Essay," *Indiana Magazine of History*, LXXVI (1980), 346-366. A very good general study of twentieth-century politics is Frank James Munger, Two-Party Politics in the State of Indiana (Ph.D. dissertation, Harvard University, 1955). Studies of aspects of the General Assembly include William E. Bicker, The Assembly Party: Change and Consistency in Legislative Voting Behavior in the Indiana House, 1923-1963 (Ph.D. dissertation, Indiana University, 1969), and Charles S. Hyneman, "Tenure and Turnover of the Indiana General Assembly," *American Political Science Review*, XXXII (1939), 51-67, 311-331. The papers of Claude R. Wickard at the Franklin D. Roosevelt Library, Hyde Park, New York, contain a large and excellent collection of constituents' correspondence during the important 1933 General Assembly. General party positions are found in Indiana State Platforms (2 vols., Indiana Division, Indiana State Library). The Indiana Division also has a large number of state party pamphlets and other publications.

There are very few good biographies of political leaders and office-holders of the interwar years. John Braeman, *Albert J. Beveridge: American Nationalist* (Chicago, 1971), is helpful for the early 1920s. Taggart, Ralston, New, Watson, Hays, and many others deserve additional serious study, if not necessarily full-scale biographies. Paul McNutt towers over the 1930s, yet there exists no satisfactory biography. I. George Blake, *Paul V. McNutt: Portrait of a Hoosier Statesman* (Indianapolis, 1966), is brief and unanalytical. Robert R. Neff, The Early Career and Governorship of Paul V. McNutt (Ph.D. dissertation, Indiana University, 1963), is the best introduction to McNutt but is marred by the author's strong sympathy with McNutt and aversion to the New Deal. McNutt's career with the War Manpower Commission is treated in George Q. Flynn, *The Mess in Washington: Manpower Mobilization in World War II* (Westport, Conn., 1979). James E. Watson, *As I Knew Them: Memoirs of James E. Watson* (Indianapolis, 1936), is anecdotal and disappointing. Wendell Willkie has been the subject of several studies, though his connections to Indiana politics were few. See, for example, Donald Bruce Johnson, *The Republican Party and Wendell Willkie* (Urbana, Ill., 1960), and Warren Moscow, *Roosevelt and Willkie* (Englewood Cliffs, N.J., 1968). An autobiography, in fictional form, of an anti-McNutt Democrat is Walter Myers, *The Guv: A Tale of Midwest Law and Politics* (New York, 1947).

One of the most important political movements of the interwar years was the Ku Klux Klan. Despite the abundant literature relating to it, basic questions about the Klan's origins, motives, and influences remain unanswered. There is important manuscript and printed material relating to the Indiana Klan in the Indiana Division, Indiana State Library, the Indiana Historical Society Library, and the Lilly Library, Indiana University. Useful testimony and other materials are found in *State of Indiana* v. *The Knights of the Ku Klux Klan*, Marion Circuit Court, Attorney General, Ku Klux Klan, microfilm (Archives Division, Indiana Commission on Public Records). The Indianapolis *Fiery Cross* provides examples of the Klan's public appeals. The best secondary accounts are unpublished: John Augustus Davis, The Ku Klux Klan in Indiana, 1920-1930: An Historical Study (Ph.D. dissertation, Northwestern University, 1966), and Norman Frederic Weaver, The Knights of the Ku Klux Klan in Wisconsin, Indiana, Ohio and Michigan (Ph.D. dissertation, University of Wisconsin, 1954). The relationship of newspapers to the Klan is treated in Bradford W. Scharlott, The Hoosier Newsman and the Hooded Order: Indiana Press Reaction to the Ku Klux Klan in the 1920s (M.A. thesis, Indiana University, 1978). Among the most useful studies at the local level are Kenneth T. Jackson, *The Ku Klux Klan in the City, 1915-1930* (New York, 1967), which has a chapter on Indianapolis; William E. Wilson, "Long, Hot Summer in Indiana," *American Heritage*, XVI (1965), 57-64, which concerns Evansville; Neil Betten and James B. Lane, "Nativism and the Klan in Town and City: Valparaiso and Gary, Indiana," *Studies in History and Society*, IV (1973), 3-16; Jill Suzanne Nevel, Fiery Crosses and Tempers: The Ku Klux Klan in South Bend, Indiana, 1923-1926 (Senior thesis, Princeton University, 1977); and Robert Coughlan, "Konklave in Kokomo," in Isabel Leighton (ed.), *The Aspirin Age, 1919-1941* (New York, 1949), pp. 105-129. Other studies are listed in William H. Fisher, *The Invisible Empire: A Bibliography of the Ku Klux Klan* (Metuchen, N.J., 1980).

Studies of other groups that played an important role in politics include Richard Morris Clutter, The Indiana American Legion, 1919-1960 (Ph.D. dissertation, Indiana University, 1974), and Katherine Croan Greenough, *A History of the League of Women Voters of Indiana, 1920-1952* (n.p., n.d). A large collection of materials relating to the League is in the Indiana Division, Indiana State Library. There is no serious study of the important work of the Indiana Anti-Saloon League, but the organization's annual report provides some information. Also useful is Frances Hendrickson, *Hoosier Heritage, 1874-1974: Woman's Christian Temperance Union* (n.p., 1974).

The politics of the 1930s were dominated by questions of depression-era relief. The records of WPA, FERA, and other federal relief agencies in the National Archives (Record Group 69) are essential to understanding the problems, as are McNutt's gubernatorial papers and the Records of the Governor's Commission on Unemployment Relief, both in the Archives Division, Indiana Commission on Public Records. Published statistical data and reports are found in the *Year Book* of the Governor's Commission on Unemployment Relief and the *Quarterly Statistical Survey* of the Indiana Department of Public Welfare. Contemporary accounts include Alice Shaffer, Mary Wyson Keefer, and Sophonisba P. Breckinridge, *The Indiana Poor Law* (Chicago, 1936); R. Clyde White, "Recent Public Welfare and Social Legislation in Indiana," *Social Service Review*, X (1936), 206-226; and Indiana Department of Public Welfare, *Four Years of Public Welfare in Indiana* . . . (Indianapolis, 1940). The changes in state government's role in relief and other areas are reflected in Indiana State Planning Board, *Preliminary Report on a State Plan for Indiana* (2nd ed., n.p., [1935]); Indiana Committee on Governmental Economy, *Report* (Indianapolis, 1935); E. B. McPheron, *A Summary of Indiana Centralization* (Bloomington, Ind., 1938); and Indiana Inter-Organization Council, *Eleven-Year Trend in Indiana State Government Payments and Receipts, 1928-1938* (Indianapolis, 1938). Opposition to the growth of state government is best reflected in the pages of the *Indiana County and Township Officer*, published by the Indiana County Commissioners' Association and the Indiana State Association of Township Trustees.

Essential to study of the partisan politics of the 1930s are the McNutt papers in Indianapolis and Bloomington and several collections in the Franklin D. Roosevelt Library, Hyde Park, New York, including the papers of the Democratic National Committee and of Franklin D. Roosevelt, Wayne Coy, and Claude R. Wickard. The Republican comeback in the late 1930s is treated expertly in William B. Pickett, "The Capehart Cornfield Conference and the Election of 1938: Homer E. Capehart's Entry into Politics," *Indiana Magazine of History*, LXXIII (1977), 252-275. Also useful is Harold C. Feightner, 150 Years of Brewing in Indiana: The Story of Politics, Prohibition, and Patronage (typescript, Indiana Division, Indiana State Library, n.d.).

TRANSPORTATION

Data on highway transportation are found in United States Public Roads Administration, *Highway Statistics: Summary to 1945* (Washington, D.C., 1947) and in the Indiana *Year Book*. Highway construction and maintenance are treated in Lawrence H. Wendrich, *The State Highway Commission of Indiana: A Study of Organization and Functions* (Bloomington, Ind., 1942); and John E. Stoner, *Comparative County Highway Administration: A Study of Steuben County, Indiana, Branch County, Michigan, Williams County, Ohio* (Lafayette, Ind., 1955).

Data on steam railroads and electric interurbans are found in the annual reports of the Indiana Public Service Commission, published in the Indiana *Year Book*. Secondary studies include George W. Hilton, *Monon Route* (Berkeley, Calif., 1978); Leland S. Van Scoyoc, The History and Economic Significance of the Chicago, Indianapolis and Louisville Railway Company (Ph.D. dissertation, Indiana University, 1953); Elmer G. Sulzer, *Ghost Railroads of Indiana* (Indianapolis, 1970); George W. Hilton and John R. Due, *The Electric Interurban Railways in America* (2nd ed., Stanford, Calif., 1964); Jerry Marlette, *Electric Railroads of Indiana* (2nd ed., Indianapolis, 1980); Glen A. Blackburn, "Interurban Railroads of Indiana," *Indiana Magazine of History*, XX (1924), 221-279, 426-436; and William D. Middleton, *South Shore: The Last Interurban* (San Marino, Calif., 1970).

AGRICULTURE

There is no good general history of Indiana agriculture. W. C. Latta, *Outline History of Indiana Agriculture* (Lafayette, Ind., 1938) does not deal significantly with the post-World War I era. Basic statistical data are available in the federal census reports, notably the United States Bureau of the Census, *Agriculture: Indiana*, 1940. The most useful materials are the many reports and studies prepared at Purdue University. Most appeared in the Purdue University Agricultural Experiment Station *Bulletin*: among the best are Lynn S. Robertson and Earl L. Butz, *Indiana's Agriculture: Its Output, Costs and Trends*, No. 523 (1947); Robert W. Schoeff and Lynn S. Robertson, *Agricultural Changes from 1910 to 1945 in a Central Indiana Township*, No. 524 (1947); *Indiana: The Land and the People*, No. 496 (1944); E. C. Young and F. F. Elliott, *Types of Farming in Indiana*, No. 342 (1930); G. E. Young, *Marginal Farm Land in Southern Indiana*, No. 376 (1933); and Paul L. Farris and R. S. Euler, *Prices of Indiana Farm Products, 1841-1955, No. 644* (1957). Also very useful are the annual reports of the Purdue University Department of Agricultural Extension. On extension work generally see Dave O. Thompson, *A History: Fifty Years of Cooperative Extension Service in Indiana* (n.p., 1962), and Gladys Baker, *The County Agent* (Chicago, 1939). An excellent case study of the challenges of farming in the interwar years is contained in Dean Albertson, *Roosevelt's Farmer: Claude R. Wickard in the New Deal* (New York, 1961). Albertson's interview with Wickard, a copy of which is in the Franklin D. Roosevelt Library, Hyde Park, New York, is also very illuminating.

Good examples of approaches to problems of rural life include Kathryne McMahon, *The Farm Home Kitchen* (Purdue University Agricultural Extension *Bulletin, No. 141*, Lafayette, Ind., 1926); Lynn S. Robertson and Keith Amstutz, *Telephone Problems in Rural Indiana* (Purdue University Agricultural Experiment Station *Bulletin, No. 548*, Lafayette, Ind., 1949); Gail M. Redfield and Truman E. Hienton, *Electricity Serves the Farm Household* (Purdue University Agricultural Experiment Station *Circular, No. 214*, Lafayette, Ind., 1936); E. H. Shideler, "Rural Rehabilitation Services for Indiana Farmers," *Hoosier Farmer*, July, 1937, pp. 11, 24; H. E. Moore and O. G. Lloyd, *The Back-to-the-Land Movement in Southern Indiana* (Purdue University Agricultural Experiment Station *Bulletin, No. 409*, Lafayette, Ind., 1936). Some understanding of the important work of the Indiana Farm Bureau is reflected in Edna Moore Colby, *Hoosier Farmers in a New Day* (Indianapolis, 1968), and in the periodical *Hoosier Farmer*. The co-operative movement is studied in Paul Turner, *They Did It in Indiana: The Story of the Indiana Farm Bureau Co-operatives* (New York, 1947); French M. Hyre, *Farm Co-ops in Indiana* (Louisville, 1940); and I. Harvey Hull, *Built of Men: The Story of Indiana Cooperatives* (New York, 1952).

BUSINESS AND ECONOMIC HISTORY

Indiana business and economic history has received very little attention. There are only a few good company histories, and most general business and economic problems have not yet been studied in depth. Source materials have been increased significantly by the work of the Indiana University Oral History Research Project. In 1979 and 1980 project historian R. T. King interviewed dozens of individuals who worked in key Indiana industries. Most helpful for the period prior to 1945 are his interviews with John Goldthwaite, Carl R. Dortch, Carl M. Gray, and Warren W. Parke. The Oral History Project at the Cummins Engine Company, Columbus, has produced interviews under the direction of John W. Rowell, some of which have been published in the company's magazine *Power Team* in 1979.

Statistical data on manufacturing are available in federal census reports, notably United States Bureau of the Census, *Sixteenth Census* (1940), *Manufactures, 1939* (3 vols., Washington, D.C., 1942), and *Census of Manufactures, 1947* (3 vols., Washington, D.C., 1950). For individual firms see the annual listings in *Polk's Indiana State Gazetteer and Business Directory;* Indiana State Chamber of Commerce, *Directory of Indiana Manufacturers;* and *Moody's Manual of Investments.*

For iron and steel see Gertrude G. Schroeder, *The Growth of Major Steel Companies, 1900-1950* (Baltimore, 1953), and John B. Appleton, *The Iron and Steel Industry of the Calumet District: A Study in Economic Geography* (Urbana, Ill., 1927). The best study of an Indiana auto manufacturer is Ralph D. Gray, *Alloys and Automobiles: The Life of Elwood Haynes* (Indianapolis, 1979). Also useful are Wallace S. Huffman, "Indiana's Place in Automobile History," *Indiana History Bulletin*, XLIV (1967), 11-44, and Wallace S. Huffman, "The Apperson Brothers and Their Automobiles," *ibid.*, XLI (1964), 195-202; Joseph A. Batchelor, A

Statistical Analysis of the 1930 Passenger Car Registrations (M.A. thesis, Indiana University, 1931); Kathleen Ann Smallzried and Dorothy James Roberts, *More Than You Promise: A Business at Work in Society* (New York, 1942), an incomplete history of Studebaker; and Howard R. Delancy, The History of the Cole Motor Car Company (D.B.A. dissertation, Indiana University, 1954). The best study of petroleum in Indiana is Paul H. Giddens, *Standard Oil Company (Indiana): Oil Pioneer of the Middle West* (New York, 1955). There are no satisfactory studies of the glass or chemical industries in Indiana, though Frank Clayton Ball, *Memoirs of Frank Clayton Ball* (Muncie, Ind., 1937), Frederic A. Birmingham, *Ball Corporation: The First Century* (Indianapolis, 1980), and Fred C. Kelley, *One Thing Leads to Another: The Growth of an Industry* (Boston, 1936), dealing with Commercial Solvents, are useful. There are two studies of Eli Lilly and Company, neither of which is scholarly: E. J. Kahn, Jr., *All in a Century: the First 100 Years of Eli Lilly and Company* [Indianapolis, 1975], and Roscoe Collins Clark, *Threescore Years and Ten: A Narrative of the First Seventy Years of Eli Lilly and Company 1876-1946* (Indianapolis, 1946). Food processing is studied in Lotys Benning, *The Vegetable Canning Industry* (Indianapolis, 1938), and Bernard Franklin Trimpe, The Stokely-Van Camp Company, 1898-1950: A Business History (D.C.S. dissertation, Indiana University, 1950). The limestone industry is treated very well in Joseph A. Batchelor, *An Economic History of the Indiana Oolitic Limestone Industry* (Bloomington, Ind., 1944). Good studies of the coal industry are Osmond LaVar Harline, Economics of the Indiana Coal Mining Industry (Ph.D. dissertation, Indiana University, 1958); Reed Moyer, *Competition in the Midwestern Coal Industry* (Cambridge, Mass., 1964); and C. L. Christenson, *Economic Redevelopment in Bituminous Coal: The Special Case of Technological Advance in United States Coal Mines, 1930-1960* (Cambridge, Mass., 1962).

Good local manufacturing studies include Robert N. Gold, *Manufacturing Structure and Pattern of the South Bend-Mishawaka Area* (Chicago, 1954); Alden Cutshall, "Terre Haute Iron and Steel: A Declining Industry," *Indiana Magazine of History*, XXXVII (1941), 237-244; Robert Roland Drummond, Terre Haute, Indiana: A City of Non-Growth (Ph.D. dissertation, Northwestern University, 1953); and Louis H. Orzack, Employment and Social Structure: A Study of Social Change in Indiana (Ph.D. dissertation, Indiana University, 1953). The last study deals expertly with Bloomington's work force and economy.

Data on retail trade are available in the census reports, especially United States Bureau of the Census, *Sixteenth Census* (1940), *Census of Business*, I, *Retail Trade*, 1939 (Washington, D.C., 1941), and in G. W. Starr and G. A. Steiner, "The Births and Deaths of Retail Stores in Indiana, 1929-1937," *Dun's Review*, January, 1940, pp. 23-24. Trade and commerce in Indianapolis are considered in Benjamin Moulton, Indianapolis: Its Evolving Functions and Functional Areas (Ph.D. dissertation, Indiana University, 1950). A similar topic for small towns is Miriam Joy Meloy, The Newspaper Editor as a Community Builder (M.A. thesis, Indiana University, 1940).

Banking is treated in Study Commission for Indiana Financial Institutions, *Report* (Indianapolis, 1932); Joseph Aloysius Kehoe, *Some Financial Trends of National and State Commercial Banks in Indiana, 1915-1954* (Washington, D.C., 1956); chapters four and five of Herman B Wells, *Being Lucky: Reminiscences and Reflections* (Bloomington, Ind., 1980); and Richard H. Gemmecke, W. G. Irwin and Hugh Thomas Miller: A Study in Free Enterprise in Indiana (Ph.D. dissertation, Indiana University, 1955).

The relationship of business to the local community is considered in Lawrence H. Wendrich, Municipal Policy Determination in Kokomo, Indiana (Ph.D. dissertation, Indiana University, 1947); John Paul Duncan, Control of the City Government in Indianapolis Evidenced by the Forces Determining Its Ordinances, 1925-1941 (Ph.D. dissertation, Indiana University, 1943); Carrolyle M. Frank, "Who Governed Middletown? Community Power in Muncie, Indiana, in the 1930s," *Indiana Magazine of History*, LXXV (1979), 322-343; the Lynds' two *Middletown* books; and Garland August Haas, The Legal Background to the Preparation and Administration of Zoning Ordinances in Indiana (M.A. thesis, Indiana University, 1948).

Labor History

Labor is among the least studied of major subfields in Indiana history. There are a few good treatments of union activity, but very little exists concerning the labor force, conditions of work, or the workers' broader world. The federal census provides basic statistical data, illuminated by a few government reports, notably Caroline Manning and Arcadia N. Phillips, *Wage-Earning Women and the Industrial Conditions of 1930: A Survey of South Bend* (Washington, D.C., 1932). A good account of legal problems is Fred Witney, *Indiana Labor Relations Law* (Bloomington, Ind., 1960). Union activity may be followed in the published annual *Proceedings* of the Indiana State Federation of Labor and of the Indiana State Industrial Union Council. Individual unions important in Indiana have not yet received serious scholarly analysis. The best work deals with the United Auto Workers and especially the sit-down strike of 1937: Sidney Fine, *Sit-Down: The General Motors Strike of 1936-1937* (Ann Arbor, Mich., 1969); Victor Reuther, *The Brothers Reuther and the Story of the UAW* (Boston, 1976); and Claude E. Hoffman, *Sit-Down in Anderson: UAW Local 663, Anderson, Indiana* (Detroit, 1968). There are good interviews with auto workers in the Indiana University Oral History Research Project and the Michiana Oral Labor History Project, the latter based at Indiana University, South Bend. Also useful for the auto industry is Frederick H. Harbison and Robert Dubin, *Patterns of Union-Management Relations: United Automobile Workers (CIO)—General Motors—Studebaker* (Chicago, 1947). For steel workers see Robert L. Tyler, "The Little Steel Strike of 1937 in Indiana: An Episode in the Continuing Conflict over a Philosophy of Labor Relations," Indiana Academy of the Social Sciences, *Proceedings*, II (1957), 113-123. Estimates of union membership are found in Leo Troy, *Distribution of Union Membership among the States: 1939 and 1953* (New York, 1957). More radical response to labor problems is represented in Kim McQuaid, "Industry and the Co-operative Commonwealth: William P. Hapgood and the Columbia Conserve Company, 1917-1943," *Labor History*, XVII (1976), 510-529, and Michael D. Marcaccio, *The Hapgoods: Three Earnest Brothers* (Charlottesville, Va., 1977). The papers of a younger member of the family, Powers Hapgood, are in the Lilly Library and deal with socialism, labor organizing, and the CIO in the 1930s and 1940s. Questions of social and economic mobility for labor and the population generally have received little analysis. An important exception is Natalie Rogoff, *Recent Trends in Occupational Mobility* (Glencoe, Ill., 1953), based on Indianapolis data and revised in Otis Dudley Duncan, "Methodological Issues in the Analysis of Social Mobility," in Neil J. Smelser and Seymour Martin Lipset (eds.), *Social Structure and Mobility in Economic Development* (Chicago, 1966).

RACE AND ETHNICITY

The published federal census reports provide basic data, especially the volumes on population. A useful special study is United States Bureau of the Census, *Negroes in the United States, 1920-1932* (Washington, D.C., 1935). Black newspapers are very important sources and include the Indianapolis *Recorder*, Indianapolis *Freeman*, and Gary *Colored American*.

The best work on the history of blacks and race relations is Emma Lou Thornbrough, *Since Emancipation: A Short History of Indiana Negroes, 1863-1963* (Indianapolis, 1963), and Emma Lou Thornbrough, "Segregation in Indiana during the Klan Era of the 1920's," *Mississippi Valley Historical Review*, XLVII (1961), 594-618. In addition to Thornbrough's work the Indianapolis black community is studied in Judy Jolley Mohraz, *The Separate Problem: Case Studies of Black Education in the North, 1900-1930* (Westport, Conn., 1979). The best account of blacks in Gary is Elizabeth Balanoff, A History of the Black Community of Gary, Indiana, 1906-1940 (Ph.D. dissertation, University of Chicago, 1974). See also Neil Betten and Raymond A. Mohl, "The Evolution of Racism in an Industrial City, 1906-1940: A Case Study of Gary, Indiana," *Journal of Negro History*, LIX (1974), 51-64. Less scholarly but useful for Muncie is Hurley Goodall and J. Paul Mitchell, *A History of Negroes in Muncie* (Muncie,

Ind., 1976). Max Parvin Cavnes, *The Hoosier Community at War* (Bloomington, Ind., 1961), has an excellent chapter on race relations.

Indiana's ethnic groups have been little studied. Especially noteworthy is the lack of serious published work on the many important German-American communities in the state. A brief introduction is provided in Darrel E. Bigham, *Reflections on a Heritage: The German Americans in Southwestern Indiana* (Evansville, Ind., 1980). Among the most useful ethnic studies are: Evangelos C. Vlachos, The Assimilation of Greeks in the United States with Special Reference to the Greek Community in Anderson, Indiana (Ph.D. dissertation, Indiana University, 1964); Myra Auerbach, A Study of the Jewish Settlement in Indianapolis (M.A. thesis, Indiana University, 1933); Francisco A. Rosales, Mexican Immigration to the Urban Midwest during the 1920s (Ph.D. dissertation, Indiana University, 1979), focusing on East Chicago; and Edward Andrew Zivich, From *Zadruga* to Oil Refinery: Croatian Immigrants and Croatian-Americans in Whiting, Indiana, 1890-1950 (Ph.D. dissertation, State University of New York, Binghamton, 1977). For Gary's ethnic population see Raymond A. Mohl and Neil Betten, "Paternalism and Pluralism: Immigrants and Social Welfare in Gary, Indiana, 1906-1940," *American Studies*, XV (1974), 5-30, and Raymond A. Mohl and Neil Betten, "Ethnic Adjustment in the Industrial City: The International Institute of Gary, 1919-1940," *International Migration Review*, VI (1972), 361-376.

EDUCATION

Statistical data on public schools are found in United States Office of Education, *Biennial Survey of Education in the United States, 1944-46* (Washington, D.C., 1949), and in the annual report of the Department of Public Instruction, published in the Indiana *Year Book*. Several reports were prepared on public education, the most thorough of which is Indiana Education Survey Commission, *Public Education in Indiana: Report . . .* (New York, 1923). Other published reports include Indiana Rural Education Survey Committee, *Report*, March, 1926 (Indianapolis, 1926); Joint and Consolidated School Survey Commission, *Report* (Indianapolis, 1931); Commission for a Survey of the Problem of State Aid for Public Schools, *Report* (Indianapolis, 1931); portions of Indiana State Committee on Governmental Economy, *Report* (Indianapolis, 1935); and Edwin B. McPheron and Pressly S. Sikes, *Indiana's Program of Relief of Common School Units* (Bloomington, Ind., 1943). Also useful is Roland E. Young, The History of School District Reorganization in the State of Indiana (Ed.D. dissertation, Indiana University, 1968). Some important and much routine information is found in the minutes of the Indiana State Board of Education and in the papers of the Indiana Department of Public Instruction, in the Archives Division, Indiana Commission on Public Records.

Evansville schools are treated in Harold Spears, *The Emerging High-School Curriculum and Its Direction* (New York, 1940), and *Your Schools: A Report of a Survey of the Public Schools of Evansville, Indiana, 1936* (n.p., 1936). The best study of Gary's schools is Ronald D. Cohen and Raymond A. Mohl, *The Paradox of Progressive Education: The Gary Plan and Urban Schooling* (Port Washington, N.Y., 1979). On youth generally see Lynn Robertson *et al., Rural Youth in Indiana* (Purdue University Agricultural Experiment Station *Bulletin, No. 467*, Lafayette, Ind., 1942); Otis E. Young, Migratory Trends of Graduates of Indiana High Schools, 1900-1930 (Ph.D. dissertation, Indiana University, 1930); and Charles E. Gibbons, *School or Work in Indiana?* (New York, 1927).

Statistics for higher education are found in the annual report of the Department of Public Instruction in the Indiana *Year Book.* Two contemporary reports are very good: *Financial and Statistical Studies of Indiana University, Purdue University, and Indiana State Normal: A Preliminary Report to the Indiana Education Survey Commission* (New York, 1922), and Charles H. Judd *et al.,* Survey of the State Institutions of Higher Learning in Indiana, *Report* (Indianapolis, 1926). Private normal schools are studied in Eber W. Jeffery, History of Private Normal Schools in Indiana (Ph.D. dissertation, New York University, 1932), and Kent D. Beeler and Philip C. Chamberlain, " 'Give a Buck to Save a College': The Demise of Central Normal College," *Indiana Magazine of History*, LXVII (1971), 117-128. The best history of an institution is Thomas D. Clark, *Indiana University, Midwestern Pioneer* (3 vols., Bloomington, Ind., 1970-1977), which should be supplemented by Herman B Wells, *Being Lucky: Reminiscences and Reflections* (Bloomington, Ind., 1980). Other institutions are treated in Glenn White, *The Ball State Story: From Normal Institute to University* (Muncie, Ind., 1967); William O. Lynch, *A History of Indiana State Teachers College* (Terre Haute, Ind., 1946); Frank K. Burrin, *Edward Charles Elliott, Educator* (Lafayette, Ind., 1970); Thomas J. Schlereth, *The University of Notre Dame: A Portrait of Its History and Campus* (Notre Dame, Ind., 1976); George B. Manhart, *DePauw through the Years* (2 vols., Greencastle, Ind., 1962); William C. Ringenberg, *Taylor University: The First 125 Years* (Grand Rapids, Mich., 1973); William C. Ringenberg, "A Brief History of Fort Wayne Bible College," *Mennonite Quarterly Review*, LIV (1980), 135-155; John L. Bloxsome, *Rose: The First One Hundred Years* (Terre Haute, Ind., 1973); Marvin L. Henricks, *From Parochialism to Community: A Socio-historical Interpretation of Indiana Central University, 1902-1975* (n.p., [1977]); Opal Thornburg, *Earlham: The Story of the College, 1847-1962* (Richmond, Ind., 1963); William Alfred Millis, *The History of Hanover College from 1827 to 1927* (Hanover, Ind., 1927); and James I. Osborne and Theodore G. Gronert,

Wabash College, the First Hundred Years 1832-1932 (Crawfordsville, 1932).

Religion

Church membership data are in the United States Bureau of the Census, *Religious Bodies, 1926* (2 vols., Washington, D.C., 1930); and United States Bureau of the Census, *Religious Bodies, 1936* (2 vols., Washington, D.C., 1941). Two studies with important implications appeared in the 1920s: Benson Y. Landis, *Rural Church Life in the Middle West as Illustrated by Clay County, Iowa and Jennings County, Indiana, with Comparative Data from Studies of Thirty-five Middle Western Counties* (New York, 1922), and Walter S. Athearn *et al., The Indiana Survey of Religious Education* (3 vols., New York, 1923-1924). A very good study of Sunday schools is Grover L. Hartman, *A School for God's People: A History of the Sunday School Movement in Indiana* (Indianapolis, 1980).

Most of the secondary studies of religion are in the form of church or denominational histories. A good example of the history of a congregation is Eli Lilly, *History of the Little Church on the Circle: Christ Church Parish Indianapolis 1837-1955* (Indianapolis, 1957). Denominational histories include Henry G. Waltmann (ed.), *History of the Indiana-Kentucky Synod of the Lutheran Church in America: Its Development, Congregations, and Institutions* (Indianapolis, 1971); John F. Cady, *The Origin and Development of the Missionary Baptist Church in Indiana* (Berne, Ind., 1942); Henry K. Shaw, *Hoosier Disciples: A Comprehensive History of the Christian Churches (Disciples of Christ) in Indiana* (St. Louis, 1966); Clarence E. Flynn (ed.), *The Indianapolis Area of the Methodist Episcopal Church 1924-1928: A Record and History* (Indianapolis, n.d.); Jack J. Detzler, *The History of the Northwest Indiana Conference of the Methodist Church 1852-1951* (Nashville, Tenn., 1953); Frederick A. Norwood, *History of the North Indiana Conference 1917-1956: North Indiana Methodism in the Twentieth Century* (Winona Lake, Ind., 1957); and Humbert P. Pagani, *200 Years of Catholicism in Indiana* (Indianapolis, 1934). Published denominational proceedings and minutes are also very useful, including those of Methodist and Baptist gatherings. Two important religious publications are the *Indiana Catholic and Record* and the *Indiana Jewish Chronicle.* One of the few studies to relate religious change to broader contexts is Anton T. Boisen, "Divided Protestantism in a Midwest County," *Journal of Religion,* XX (1940), 359-381, focusing on Monroe County.

Public Health and Public Safety

Mortality and morbidity statistics are found in United States Bureau of the Census, *Vital Statistics Rates in the United States, 1900-1940* (Washington, D.C., 1943), and in the annual reports of the Department of Public

Health, published in the Indiana *Year Book.* Incomplete but helpful as introductions to health issues are Dorothy Ritter Russo (ed.), *One Hundred Years of Indiana Medicine, 1849-1949* (n.p., 1949), and Burton D. Myers, *The History of Medical Education in Indiana* (Bloomington, Ind., 1956). *Journal of the Indiana State Medical Association* contains many good articles and also editorials on medical and health issues. Thurman B. Rice, *The Hoosier Health Officer: A Biography of Dr. John N. Hurty* (n.p., 1946), is a very good study of an important pioneer. An excellent study of one community's medical facilities is Allon Peebles, *A Survey of the Medical Facilities of Shelby County, Indiana: 1929* (Chicago, 1930).

Of the many diseases and health problems tuberculosis has been most studied. See Harriet Salinger Iglauer, *The Program for the Control and Prevention of Tuberculosis in Indiana* (Indianapolis, 1943), and Indiana Tuberculosis Commission, *Report,* 1930 (n.p., 1930).

Studies of sanitation and water pollution include John E. Stoner and Pressly S. Sikes, *Water and Sewerage Systems in Indiana: The Planning of Future Construction Now* (Bloomington, Ind., 1944); B. A. Poole, "Progress in the Control of Stream Pollution in Indiana," Purdue University Engineering *Bulletin,* XXIV (July, 1940), 142-145; Indiana State Planning Board, *Preliminary Report on a State Plan for Indiana* (Indianapolis, 1934); Carrolyle M. Frank, "Who Governed Middletown? Community Power in Muncie, Indiana, in the 1930s," *Indiana Magazine of History,* LXXV (1979), 332-343.

Data on crime and police work are in the annual reports of the state police bureau in the Indiana *Year Book.* State studies include Indiana Committee on Observance and Enforcement of Law, *Report* (n.p., 1931), and sections of the Indiana State Committee on Governmental Economy, *Report* (Indianapolis, 1935). John Dillinger's life is chronicled in John Toland, *The Dillinger Days* (New York, 1963). Evidence of increasing sophistication in approaches to crime and criminals is found in John H. Klinger and Thomas G. Hutton, *Indiana and the Adult Offender: A Study of the Crime Problem* (n.p., [1939]); Helen Wilson, *The Treatment of the Misdemeanant in Indiana, 1816-1936* (Chicago, 1938); United States Prison Industries Reorganization Administration, *The Prison Problem in Indiana* (Washington, D.C., 1938); John H. Klinger, *Indiana's Convicted Criminals: A Discussion of Prison and Parole Problems as They Appear in 1938* [Indianapolis, 1938]; and R. Clyde White, "The Relation of Felonies to Environmental Factors in Indianapolis," *Social Forces,* X (1932), 498-509.

CULTURAL AND SOCIAL ISSUES

LEISURE AND SPORTS. *The Leisure of a People: Report of a Recreation Survey of Indianapolis* (n.p., 1929) is an excellent, detailed study. Despite the popularity and importance of sports and increased leisure time, they have received very little attention from historians. Even basketball has not yet received the scholarly history it deserves, one that sets the game in its full context. Herbert Frederic Schwomeyer, A History of Indiana High School Basketball (D.P.Ed. thesis, Indiana University, 1970), is largely a compilation of game scores and team records. G. Dale Glenn, The History of the Indiana High School Athletic Association (Ed.D. dissertation, Indiana University, 1975) is of some value in understanding the role of this important body, as is the IHSAA Annual Handbook. An introduction to the 500-mile race is Al Bloemker, 500 Miles to Go: The Story of the Indianapolis Speedway (New York, 1961). Jane Fisher, Fabulous Hoosier: A Story of American Achievement (New York, 1947), is a biography of Carl Fisher, one of the founders of the race, by his wife. Indiana's state parks are the subject of a good unpublished study: Robert Allen Frederick, Colonel Richard Lieber, Conservationist and Park Builder: The Indiana Years (Ph.D. dissertation, Indiana University, 1960). Also helpful is David M. Silver (ed.), "Richard Lieber and Indiana's Forest Heritage," Indiana Magazine of History, LXVII (1971), 45-55, and Charles B. Hosmer, Jr., Preservation Comes of Age: From Williamsburg to the National Trust, 1926-1949 (2 vols., Charlottesville, Va., 1981), which contains an excellent account of Lieber's preservation work at Spring Mill State Park.

There has been little analysis of the important roles played by social organizations and clubs, especially women's organizations. Some basic information is provided in Grace Gates Courtney (comp.), History: Indiana Federation of Clubs (Fort Wayne, 1939); the yearbook of the Indiana Federation of Clubs; and The Indianapolis Local Council of Women, 1892-1924 (n.p., n.d.).

JOURNALISM. A starting point is Ronald Beathard, Cyndi Lach, and Mark Popovich, Indiana Newspaper History: An Annotated Bibliography (Muncie, Ind., 1974). There are several reminiscences of newspapermen: Hilton U. Brown, A Book of Memories (Indianapolis, 1951); John Lewis Niblack, The Life and Times of a Hoosier Judge (n.p., [1973]); and Louis Ludlow, From Cornfield to Press Gallery (Washington, D.C., 1924). Helpful studies include Guido H. Stempel, III, A Study of Content, Make-Up, and Bias of Editorial Pages of Small and Medium Indiana Daily Newspapers for the Period of 1912 to 1948 (M.A. thesis, Indiana University, 1951); Norma Jean Thiele, A History of the Fort Wayne News-Sentinel (M.A. thesis, Indiana University, 1958); Hartence Harlin, The Indianapolis Recorder: A History of a Negro Weekly Newspaper (M.A. thesis, Indiana University, 1951). Scheduled for publication by the Indiana Historical Society in the spring of 1982 is Indiana Newspaper Bibliography, by John W. Miller, which includes brief histories of all newspapers published in Indiana since 1804 and the locations of original and microfilm copies.

LITERATURE. The best and most comprehensive study is Arthur W. Shumaker, *A History of Indiana Literature with Emphasis on the Authors of Imaginative Works Who Commenced Writing prior to World War II* (Indianapolis, 1962). Basic biographical and literary information is found in R. E. Banta (comp.), *Indiana Authors and Their Books, 1816-1916* (Crawfordsville, Ind., 1949); Donald E. Thompson (comp.), *Indiana Authors and their Books, 1917-1966* (Crawfordsville, Ind., 1974); and Donald E. Thompson (comp.), *Indiana Authors and their Books, 1967-1980* (Crawfordsville, Ind., 1981). Other works helpful for general views are John H. Moriorty, "Hoosiers Sell Best," *Indiana Quarterly for Bookmen*, III (1947), 7-14; Richard A. Cordell, "Limetsone, Corn, and Literature: The Indiana Scene and Its Interpreters," *Saturday Review of Literature*, December 17, 1938, pp. 3-5; R. E. Banta (ed.), *Hoosier Caravan: A Treasury of Indiana Life and Lore* (2nd ed., Bloomington, Ind., 1975); A. L. Lazarus (comp. and ed.), *The Indiana Experience: An Anthology* (Bloomington, Ind., 1977). Good studies of individual authors include James Woodress, *Booth Tarkington: Gentleman from Indiana* (Philadelphia, 1954); Lee Coyle, *George Ade* (New York, 1964); and Terence Tobin (ed.), *Letters of George Ade* (West Lafayette, Ind., 1973). Theodore Dreiser's autobiography, *Dawn* (New York, 1931), is especially interesting. For one of the most important publishing houses see Jack O'Bar, *A History of the Bobbs-Merrill Company, 1850-1940: With a Postlude through the Early 1960s* (Ph.D. dissertation, Indiana University, 1975), based on the collection in Lilly Library, Bloomington.

ART. Data on Indiana artists are found in *Art Guide to Indiana*, Indiana University Extension Division, *Bulletin*, XVI (1931); Mary Q. Burnet, *Art and Artists of Indiana* (New York, 1921); *Biographical Directory of Indiana Artists 1937* (n.p., 1937); and Flora Lauter, *Indiana Artists: 1940* (n.p., 1941). The Brown County group is treated in Josephine A. Graf, "The Brown County Art Colony," *Indiana Magazine of History*, XXXV (1939), 365-370; Selma Steele, Theodore L. Steele, and Wilbur D. Peat, *The House of the Singing Winds: The Life and Work of T. C. Steele* (Indianapolis, 1966); and Lorna Lutes Sylvester, "Down in the Hills o' Brown County: Photographs by Frank M. Hohenberger," *Indiana Magazine of History*, LXXI (1975), 205-244, LXXII (1976), 21-26. Historical interest in architecture has focused largely on the nineteenth century. Only recently has the important historic preservation movement drawn attention to post-World War I buildings. The program to collect architectural records at the Indiana Historical Society Library provides an important beginning for future work. A good study of important Indiana potters is Kathleen R. Postle, *The Chronicle of the Overbeck Pottery* (Indianapolis, 1978).

MUSIC AND THEATER. Introductions to music are provided in Martha F.

Bellinger, "Music in Indianapolis, 1900-1944," *Indiana Magazine of History*, XLII (1946), 47-65; Samuel Wasson Siurua, History of the Indianapolis Symphony Orchestra (D. Music Ed. dissertation, Indiana University, 1961). An excellent treatment of popular music is Duncan Schiedt, *The Jazz State of Indiana* (Pittsboro, Ind., 1977). For Indianapolis's most important theater see William George Sullivan, *English's Opera House* (Indianapolis, 1960).

WORLD WAR II

No major aspect of Indiana's history since 1920 has been studied so thoroughly as World War II on the Hoosier homefront. The Indiana War History Commission, based at Indiana University, Bloomington, did excellent work in gathering materials, now located in the Archives Division, Indiana Commission on Public Records, and in sponsoring studies, published and unpublished. There are some important gaps in the commission's work, including the roles of women and farmers and of partisan politics, but the overall accomplishment is most impressive and stands as testimony to the positive results that can be achieved when historians and public officials co-operate in a task relevant to society's needs and interests.

The most important studies of the war at home, most sponsored by the Indiana War History Commission, include: Howard H. Peckham and Shirley A. Snyder (eds.), *Letters from Fighting Hoosiers* (Bloomington, Ind., 1948); Dorothy Riker (comp.), *The Hoosier Training Ground: A History of Army and Navy Training Centers, Camps, Forts, Depots, and Other Military Installations within the State Boundaries during World War II* (Bloomington, Ind., 1952); Lynn W. Turner and Heber P. Walker (comps.), *Indiana at War: A Directory of Hoosier Civilians Who Held Positions of Responsibility in Official, Volunteer and Cooperating War-Time Organizations* (Bloomington, Ind., 1951); Calvin C. Berlin, Indiana's Civilian Soldiers (Ph.D. dissertation, Indiana University, 1956); Charles B. Hirsch, "Conscientious Objectors in Indiana during World War II," *Indiana Magazine of History*, XLVI (1950), 61-72; George M. Blackburn, The Hoosier Arsenal (Ph.D. dissertation, Indiana University, 1956); Bernard Friedman, *The Financial Role of Indiana in World War II* (Bloomington, Ind., 1965); Hugh M. Ayer, Hoosier Labor in the Second World War (Ph.D. dissertation, Indiana University, 1957); Hugh M. Ayer, "Hoosier Labor in the Second World War," *Indiana Magazine of History*, LIX (1963), 95-120; and Max Parvin Cavnes, *The Hoosier Community at War* (Bloomington, Ind., 1961). The book by Cavnes focuses on social issues and remains the single most important study of the war years—an excellent piece of scholarship.

Several reports of the Indiana Economic Council are important sources, notably *Hoosiers at Work: What They Do—What They Make—What of the Future?* (n.p., 1944). Also the Indiana State Defense Council published many pamphlets and reports. Especially interesting are those on the race question, such as *Job Opportunities for Negroes* (n.p., 1943) and *The Indiana Plan of Bi-Racial Cooperation* (Indianapolis, 1942). These reports and many others important to the war years are readily available in the Indiana War History Commission Records, Archives Division, Indiana Commission on Public Records. This collection also includes various manuscript reports and correspondence and is essential to nearly any aspect of the history of the war years.

Politics in the 1940s has received almost no scholarly analysis. Charles Francis Fleming, *The White Hat: Henry Frederick Schricker: A Political Biography* (n.p., 1966), contains some useful information but is flawed by incomplete research and the author's political biases. A highly partisan account of the 1941 legislature is Fred F. Bays, *An Episode in Petty Politics: The Account of an Amazing Session of an Indiana General Assembly* (n.p., 1941). William B. Pickett, Homer E. Capehart: The Making of a Hoosier Senator (Ph.D. dissertation, Indiana University, 1974), is one of the few efforts to approach the period's politics in a scholarly manner. Two other recent unpublished studies are also important: David Roland Warriner, The Veterans of World War II at Indiana University, 1944-1951 (Ph.D. dissertation, Indiana University, 1978); and Richard M. Ugland, The Adolescent Experience during World War II: Indianapolis as a Case Study (Ph.D. dissertation, Indiana University, 1977). The state's military contribution is treated in William J. Watt and James R. H. Spears (eds.), *Indiana's Citizen Soldiers: The Militia and National Guard in Indiana History* (Indianapolis, 1980).

INDEX

Adams, J. Ottis, 361.
Adams, Thomas H., 69, 70.
Ade, George, 352, 355-356; quoted, 1, 350n, 367.
Adolescents, and World War II, 391-393.
African Methodist Episcopal Church, 295.
Agricultural Adjustment Act (AAA), 178-179.
Agriculture, value of products in 1939, p. 153; corn and hogs economic mainstay of, 153-154; mechanization of, 155-157, 159; high cost of mechanization, 164; and the car and motortruck, 157; effects of scientific developments on, 157-161; and Purdue University, Experiment Station and extension service, 159-163, 178; and county agricultural agents, 160-163; vocational courses in, 163; modernization increases differences between large and small farms, 164-165; contrasts in farmland in Indiana, 166; decline in acreage devoted to harvested crops, 166; modernization of, successes and failures of, 169-170; farm prices, 170; lack of prosperity in, compared with other economic sectors, 170-171; and Indiana Farm Bureau, 173-174, 176; and co-operatives, 174-175; and federal aid, 175, 176, 178; formation of first formal farm bloc in General Assembly, 175-176; and New Deal programs, 178-180; declining number of workers in, 245, 246; and World War II, 372, 373-374, 395, 406. See also Farmers; Farm-

land; Farms; Purdue University; and under individual crop names.
Airplanes, 199; aircraft industry, 377-378.
Air pollution, 310n.
Alcoholic Beverage Commission, 400.
Alcoholic beverages, legislation regulating manufacture and sale of, 97-99; patronage in control of, 97-99.
Alexandria (Ind.), 231.
Allen, J. Chester, 385, 386.
Allen County, number of families on poor relief, 105; manufacturing center, 230.
Allen County Public Library, 126n.
Allison, James A., 184, 213n, 344.
Allison Engineering Company, 184, 212. See also General Motors Corporation, *Allison Division*.
American Association of Women in Public Health, 322.
American Farm Bureau, 173.
American Federation of Labor (AFL), 252, 385.
American Federation of Teachers, 283.
American Legion, 344; and Americanization movement, 17; national headquarters located in Indianapolis, 38; as political force, 38-39; violation of prohibition by posts of, 41; and Ku Klux Klan, 54; Paul V. McNutt's participation in, 77; "school" for McNutt's political staff, 77-78; and Democratic party, 140.
American Medical Association, 309, 323.
American Protective Association, 61.
American Unity League, 51.

Bobbs-Merrill Company, 358.

Bohm, Curry, 362.

Book, William H., Jr., 109, 113, 115, 117.

Boone County, 172.

Borg-Warner Corporation, 212.

Bosse, Benjamin, 57n.

Bossert, Walter, 59-60, 68.

Bowers, C'aude, 75, 358.

Bowman, Heath, 4.

Bowman, Lewis S., 66.

Branch, Emmett F., 50.

Brazil (Ind.), 231.

Brethren, see Church of the Brethren (Conservative Dunkers).

Breweries, see Distilleries and breweries.

Brophy, John, 259.

Brown, Hilton U., 59.

Brown County, number of farms with telephones, 172; artists' colony, 361-362.

Brown County State Park, 166.

Brubeck, Frank, of Terre Haute, quoted on McNutt, 140.

Bryan, William Jennings, 304.

Bryan, William Lowe, 286, 287.

Burnham, D. H. and Co., of Chicago, 195.

Burris, Benjamin J., 271.

Buses, compete with railroads, 198; regulation of, 200, 201.

Business, see Chain stores; Retail stores; Banks; Industry and manufacturing.

Butler University, 288, 290.

Cady, John, 304.

Cahoon, Sam, 332.

Calumet region, lax enforcement of prohibition, 41; iron and steel production, 206, 208; petroleum refining, 213; concentration of industry in, 229, 231, 382; Negro Baptists in, 295; and defense production, 376-377. See also Lake County and under names of various cities.

Camp Atterbury, 373.

Campaigns and elections, upsurge in voting, 24, 82, 135-137; mayoralty (1921), 33n; (1929), 73; vote for secretary of state (1920, 1924, 1928), 82; voter turnout for presidential elections (1920-1948), 136; state and national offices (1920), 27; (1922), 31-35; (1924), 57-66; (1928), 72-73, 178; (1930), 78; (1932), 44, 81-83; (1934), 132-134, 141; (1936), 134-135, 143; (1938), 147-148; (1940), 149-150, 398; (1942), 401; (1944), 401-403. See also Democratic party; Republican party.

Canning industry, 219-221.

Capehart, Homer E., organizes Cornfield Conference, 147; U.S. senator, 401, 402.

Capper-Ketcham Act (1928), 162-163.

Carmichael, Hoagy, 364.

Carnegie, Andrew, 360.

Carroll County, farms with telephones, 172.

Carroll County Farm Bureau Cooperative, 181.

Case, Everett, 340.

Catholic Information Bureau, 51.

Catholics, see Roman Catholic Church.

Cattle, dairy, value of (1939), 153; increase of, 154.

Central Normal College, Danville, 284, 285.

Chain stores, tax imposed on, 236, 237.

Charities, private, 105.

Charities and Corrections, State Board of, 119n.

Charlestown (Ind.), and Indiana Ordnance Works, 374-375.

Chemical manufacture, 216-217.

Chicago, Indianapolis and Louisville Railroad, see Monon.

Child care, number of centers grows during World War II, 390.

Child labor law, 276.

Children, see Indiana Committee on the Care of Children in Wartime.

Children and infants, health of, 320-322.

Indiana Council of Churches, 298.
Indiana Council of Religious Education, 297-298.
Indiana County and Township Officer, 112, 124.
Indiana County Commissioners' Association, 112.
Indiana County Superintendents Association, 271.
Indiana Department of Conservation, 96, 337, 338-339.
Indiana Department of Financial Institutions, creation of, 240.
Indiana Department of Public Instruction, 265-266, 273-274, 276-277, 394, 403n.
Indiana Division of Labor, 257.
Indiana Economic Council, 405.
Indiana Education Survey Commission, report, 266-271; members of, 266n.
Indiana Farm Bureau, a political force, 39, 176-178; supports McNutt's tax program, 88, 176; supports Executive Reorganization Act, 92; organization and membership, 173; strength of, 173-174; and farm co-operatives, 174-175; works for federal aid for agriculture, 177-178; supports AAA, 178; produces and refines crude oil, 214; lobbies for strip mining law, 238; opposes reorganization of schools along county lines, 272; supports vocational school courses, 277n.
Indiana Farm Bureau Cooperative Association, 174-175.
Indiana Federation of Clubs, 346.
Indiana Federation of Farmers, *see* Indiana Farm Bureau.
Indiana Federation of Labor, supports Executive Reorganization Act, 92; attacks Governor McNutt, 257.
Indiana Federation of Music Clubs, 363.
Indiana Harbor (Ind.), 198, 208.
Indiana High School Athletic Association, 341, 342.
Indiana Historical Bureau, 358-359.
Indiana Historical Society, 126n, 358.

Indiana Jewish Chronicle, 52, 65, 351.
Indiana League of Women Voters, 346; interests of, 37-38; supports merit system, 100, 101, 145; and public health, 321, 322.
Indiana Library Association, 97.
Indiana Limestone Company, 224.
Indiana Ordnance Works, 374, 375.
Indiana Parent-Teacher Association, 271.
Indiana Plan of Bi-Racial Cooperation, 386-387, 396-397.
Indiana Prohibition party, 41.
Indiana Public Service Commission, 199-200, 200-201, 238-239.
Indiana Railroad Company, 197.
Indiana Republican Editorial Association, 69.
Indiana Society of Chicago, 4.
Indiana Star League, 348.
Indiana State Association of Township Trustees, 112.
Indiana State Athletic Commission, 344.
Indiana State Board of Education, 18, 271, 275.
Indiana State Board of Health, founding, 309; develops regional, multicounty units, 111n, 325-326; ranked nationally, 309; combats water pollution, 309-310, 312, 315; gathers morbidity and mortality statistics, 315; programs to control and prevent tuberculosis, 317; campaigns against venereal disease, 319, 320; Division of Infant and Child Hygiene, formed, 321, 322, 324; becomes Division of Public Health, 324; federal and state appropriations received (1939), 327n; criticizes state's health services, 328; changes made in, 403.
Indiana State Chamber of Commerce, works against racial discrimination, 385-387; and formation of Indiana Committee for Economic Development, 405.
Indiana State Committee on Governmental Economy, 93, 99-100, 110-111, 118, 119.

investigations of, 70; moves black vote to Democratic party, 138; not responsible for segregation in Indianapolis schools, 281n; tries to acquire Valparaiso University, 284.

Labor, Indiana Advisory Committee for Relief of the Unemployed, 106-107; state division of, established, 145; number of workers employed (1920-1940), and occupational distribution, 245-246; ratio of female to male workers, 246; effect of new technology on, 246-247; increase in younger workers, 247; improvement of working conditions, 248; and Great Depression, 249-250; child labor law, 276;
and racial segregation and discrimination: 9-10; and Ku Klux Klan, 54; during World War II, 384, 386-387, 388;
and World War II: increase in pay, 381-382; shortages of, 382-383; and Indiana Plan of Bi-Racial Cooperation, 386-387; blacks and women recruited into work force, 384; recruitment of southern whites, 388;
organized: opposition to McNutt tax program, 88; supports Executive Reorganization Act, 92; pushes for an old-age pension, 120; strikes and violence in post-World War I period, 247; and antiunion sentiment, 247, 248; and Indianapolis (1919) antipicketing ordinance, 247-248; declining power (1920s), 248, 249; and anti-injunction law, 250-251; and National Industrial Recovery Act, 251; and National Labor Relations Act, 251; and American Federation of Labor and Indiana State Federation of Labor, 252; and Congress of Industrial Organizations, 252; unionization of automobile industry (UAW), 252-255; resistance to, in Indiana, 253,

254, 256-257, 258; unionization in the steel industry (SWOC), 255-256; union membership in Indiana, 256; recognized as political force, 257-258; lack of radicalism in Indiana, 258; and Columbia Conserve Company, 258-259; and strikes during World War II, 383; no strike pledge, 383; increase in union power, 383-384; strikes called at end of World War II, 406.
See also Strikes; Unemployment.

Lake County, bill to permit secession from Indiana, 23n; public relief in, 106; repatriation of Mexican immigrants, 106; voter realignment, 137; election of blacks to General Assembly, 138; industry and manufacturing, 208, 213-214, 229, 230; Catholic population, 294; Negro Baptists in, 295; John Dillinger escapes from jail in, 331; detached from the Indiana district by the Office of Price Administration, 397.

Lake Michigan, pollution of, 311.
Landis, Frederick, 133n.
Lanham Act, 390.
LaPorte County, 230.
Law enforcement, influenced by partisan politics, 329, 333; inadequacy of, and efforts to improve, 330-331, 332-333. *See also* Crime; Prisons.
Lawrence, Benjamin F., 347-348.
Lawrence County, 223-225.
Lawrenceburg (Ind.), 219.
Leach, Matt, 332.
League of Nations, 26.
League of Women Voters, *see* Indiana League of Women Voters.
Leisure, increase in, and use of, 336-337, 368-369. *See also* Clubs; Literature; Motion pictures; Music; Radio; Sports; State parks and memorials; Theater.
Leslie, Harry G., governor, 12, 72, 90; reluctant to recognize need for government action in Great Depression,

DATE DUE

10/25/85			

C. 1